Yours truly in the Lord,

Andrew A. Bonar

ANDREW A. BONAR

Diary and Life

ANDREW A. BONAR

Diary and Life

Edited by
MARJORY BONAR

THE BANNER OF TRUTH TRUST

THE BANNER OF TRUTH TRUST
3 Murrayfield Road, Edinburgh EH12 6EL
PO Box 621, Carlisle, Pennsylvania 17013, USA

*

First published 1893
First Banner of Truth edition 1960
Reprinted 1984
ISBN 0 85151 432 4

*

Printed and bound in Great Britain at
The Camelot Press Ltd, Southampton

Contents

		PAGE
INTRODUCTION	. . . . . .	vii
PREFACE	. . . .	xvii

DIARY

CHAPTER I

CONVERSION AND COLLEGE LIFE, 1828-1834 . 3

CHAPTER II

WORK IN JEDBURGH AND EDINBURGH, 1835-1838 25

CHAPTER III

COLLACE, 1838-1856 67

CHAPTER IV

EARLY YEARS IN FINNIESTON, 1857-1864 . 181

CHAPTER V

MINISTRY IN GLASGOW, 1864-1875 . . . 223

CHAPTER VI

LABOURS MORE ABUNDANT, 1876-1888 . . 305

CHAPTER VII

CLOSING YEARS, 1889-1892 363

LIST OF DR. BONAR'S WORKS REFERRED TO IN
HIS DIARY 388

REMINISCENCES OF HIS LIFE

CHAPTER VIII   PAGE

A Minister of Christ 391

CHAPTER IX

The Good Pastor 409

CHAPTER X

In the City 419

CHAPTER XI

Echoes of Spoken Words 431

CHAPTER XII

A Basket of Fragments 445

CHAPTER XIII

Among His People 453

CHAPTER XIV

Manse Memories 467

CHAPTER XV

Nearing the Goal 485

CHAPTER XVI

Faith and Doctrine 505

APPENDIX

Andrew Bonar's Introduction to *Nettleton and His Labours* 529

Introduction

DR. ANDREW A. BONAR is widely known as the author of the *Life of Robert Murray M'Cheyne*, a book which has brought blessing to thousands.[1] Although he was responsible for a number of other works, foremost among them being *A Commentary on the Book of Leviticus* and *Christ and His Church in the Book of Psalms*, he never allowed literary work to take the chief place in his life. He considered his one great work was the ministry of the Gospel and nothing was allowed to interfere with this object. Valuable as his writings are, it was chiefly his life that bore testimony to the grace and power of God, and happily that testimony was preserved for the generations following in two works edited by his daughter, Marjory Bonar. These were published a few years after his death; the first to appear was his *Diary and Letters* in 1893, followed two years later by the *Reminiscences* of his life.

With the exception of the non-biographical material which made up the second half of the *Reminiscences*, these two works are here reprinted together in one volume. Marjory Bonar had already given a fair amount of biographical information with the *Diary and Letters* and consequently did not write the *Reminiscences* as a Life of her father; nevertheless when taken with the former work they do in fact provide a Life, hence the sub-title of this present volume. As the Reminiscences of his life presume an acquaintance with the information contained in the Diary the order of their original appearance has been retained in this reprint.

[1] An unabridged paperback edition of this spiritual classic has now been reprinted by *The Banner of Truth Trust*, at 2s. 6d.

The age in which Andrew Bonar grew up was one of Moderatism on the one hand, and yet one of great quickening and reviving on the other. About the time of his birth, on May 29th, 1810, there was much prevailing spiritual darkness in Scotland, but in the years following there appeared in various places stirrings which foreshadowed the beginning of a new era. Indeed the year 1810 is regarded by many as the turning point, for it was in that year that an event took place which was destined to have far-reaching effects. It was the spiritual birth of Thomas Chalmers. The year in which Bonar first saw the light of day was the same year in which the parish minister of Kilmany first saw the light of life. This meant that the ablest Moderate minister of the day joined the ranks of the Evangelical Party. At the same time as God was preparing Thomas Chalmers for great usefulness in the Church, He was also raising up a band of young men who were destined to be His instruments in the times of awakening. These included Andrew Bonar, his brothers, Horatius and John, Robert M'Cheyne, William Burns, Alexander Somerville, John Milne and Moody-Stuart.

Andrew Alexander Bonar, the seventh son of James and Marjory Bonar was born in an old-fashioned house in Paterson's Court, Broughton, Edinburgh. Three of the children did not survive infancy and Andrew was only eleven when his father died, but cared for by their godly mother and elder brother, James, the family of five sons and three daughters grew up happily together. Andrew entered Edinburgh High School in 1821 and it is reported that the Rector spoke of him as 'the best Latin scholar who had ever passed through his hands.'

For many generations the family of the Bonars had been closely connected with the evangelical witness in Scotland. From 1693 until 1747 John Bonar had kept the light of Gospel truth burning in West Lothian; his eldest son, of the same name, had likewise ministered for a number of years before he died prematurely and left his widow, who removed to Edinburgh, to struggle with the burdens of poverty and a large family. Andrew Bonar's father was the seventh son in this family. He was evidently a man of many gifts and became a Solicitor of Excise and an elder in Lady Glenorchy's Chapel—a church which enjoyed the powerful ministry of Dr. Jones, a Welshman, trained at the Countess of Huntingdon's college at Trevecca.

Such was the spiritual heritage into which Andrew Bonar was born, yet though greatly impressed by the Gospel at an early age it was not until he was twenty that the great change came. 'It was in the year 1830,' he wrote on his eighty-second birthday, 'that I found the Saviour, or rather, that He found me and laid me on His shoulders rejoicing, and I have never parted company with Him all these sixty-two years.' Thus prepared, in both mind and heart, Bonar entered the Divinity Hall and began his theological studies.

The influence which Thomas Chalmers was exercising at that time in the theological chair of the University was shaping the future religious life of Scotland and no one entered more deeply into that influence than Andrew Bonar. If Bonar and his fellow students loved the Gospel before they entered the Divinity Hall it is certain that that love was greatly increased by sitting at the feet of Chalmers. By the year 1838 each of that band of young men had found a sphere of labour. In that year Andrew Bonar was settled at Collace, a country parish in Perthshire, having served a probationary period first at Jedburgh and then at St. George's Church, Edinburgh.

Scotland was at this time in the grip of the 'Non-Intrusion controversy.' The burning issue, which had brought Evangelicals and Moderates into a final collision, was whether or not ministers could be intruded on congregations at the wish of patrons even

when such a settlement was contrary to the will of the
people. The upholders of patronage appealed to the
civil courts, while Chalmers led those who, honouring
the Headship of Christ over the affairs of His Church,
maintained that the civil courts had no jurisdiction in
the spiritual realm. In this conflict the re-affirmation
of the Lord Jesus Christ as King and Head of the
Church was indeed owned of God, and there followed a
series of religious awakenings such as had not been
witnessed in Scotland since the middle of the previous
century.

Although the revival movement of 1839–40 is
associated especially with the names of William Burns
and Robert M'Cheyne, there were others at that time
remarkably owned of God. Among them was Andrew
Bonar.[1] He reported that his weekly prayer-meeting
was attended by five hundred persons and added that
a marked change had taken place on the whole aspect
of his locality. Another year of blessing was experienced
in Collace in 1843, the year in which the Disruption
took place when over 400 ministers who were opposed
to the pretensions of the civil courts separated from the

[1] It is noticeable how the Bonar family was always deeply
conscious of the Church's continual need of such outpourings
of the Holy Spirit. Andrew's great-grandfather, when a frail
old man, had ridden for three days to be present at the
revivals of 1742 in Kilsyth and Cambuslang and we are told that
on arriving 'his heart was so full that after being helped into
the tent he preached three times with great vigour. On
returning home, full of joy at what he had seen and heard,
the aged patriarch lifted up his hands as he crossed the
threshold of his house and exclaimed, "Lord, now lettest
Thou Thy servant depart in peace, for mine eyes have seen
Thy salvation".'
There is little doubt that under the ministry of Dr. Jones of
Trevecca Andrew Bonar and his brothers learned much of
former revivals in England and Wales and this subject
became their lifelong interest. Horatius Bonar (1808–1889)
edited a new edition of John Gillies' *Historical Collections* in
1845, a book which is, as far as it goes, probably the most
complete history of revivals ever published.

Established Church. The times of quickening at Collace, as at other places, passed, and during the later years of Bonar's ministry there the work of God was not so visibly apparent. Nevertheless, they turned out to be years of prayer and preparation for greater work.

As the years passed Bonar's mind turned more and more to mission work as he thought of the multitudes in the large cities who were never reached with the Gospel. In 1856 he consented to be called to a newly erected church in Finnieston, a dark district close by the docks of Glasgow. The beginning of the work there was difficult and progress at first seemed slow. For a year his average congregation did not amount to two hundred persons, but it was not long before the power of the Gospel was being felt in Finnieston. Times of revival were again experienced, the most notable being in 1859 and 1873. By the time of his death in 1892, he had a church membership of nearly eleven hundred and few exemplified more than he, the wisdom of which the Scripture speaks, 'He than winneth souls is wise.'

Having traced the outward life of the man we must now turn to the inward. If it were not for the record of his spiritual experiences left us in his Diary we would not have much knowledge of his inner life. His own generation witnessed how brightly his life shone; his Diary reveals how it was sustained. It has been said that Dr. Bonar's Diary takes us behind the wall in the Interpreter's House, to see the man with the vessel of oil in his hand, continually casting it upon the fire, so that it burned always higher and hotter.

In reading through the Diary one cannot but be struck by the constant references to prayer. Entering within the veil through the blood of Christ was to him the chief exercise of the Christian life. It was for that reason that 'Christ and Him crucified' was at the very centre of his thoughts and of his preaching.[1] As

[1] 'For fifty years,' he wrote in his latter days, 'the Lord has kept me within sight of the cross.'

clearly as he knew there was no way to the Father but through the death of Christ, so surely did he believe that the strength to live and work for God was only obtained as Christians made use of this great privilege purchased for them by Christ. He did not believe in any short-cut to holiness and usefulness in the work of God. He knew that the one and only way to grow in grace and in the knowledge of the Lord Jesus Christ was daily and hourly communion with the Father and the Son.

If the cultivation of the inner life is the secret of consistent Christian living, it is surely time that we in the Church today paid more attention to it. For it is apparent to all right-thinking people that there is a lack of depth and reality about the lives of Christians today. We are in too frequent fellowship with outward things. There is little about our lives which lifts men's thoughts to God and make them take 'knowledge of us that we have been with Jesus.' Our lives are not God-centred; they are not Christ-centred. We allow other things to usurp that place and so we miss the real blessing.

The main lesson we learn from the life of Andrew Bonar, as indeed from all the great saints of God, is that what is real in the life of man has more affinity with the solitude of the closet than with the stir of outward things. If reality in religion is to be reached again by the present generation of Christians, then the outward must occupy less of our time and the inward more. There must be more privacy than Christians seem now to think needful; there must be more waiting upon God in the secret place; there must be more unbroken fellowship with the Father and the Son.

What is important in the lives of the generality of Christians is even more important in the lives of those called to office in the Church. If ordinary Christians are called to a life of prayer and holiness how much more so God's chosen servants. This is illustrated in

the life of Andrew Bonar, as indeed in the lives of those
others used in the revival of 1839–40. Above all else
they were men 'of peculiar grace, mighty in the
Scriptures, full of the Holy Ghost and of faith.'
'God works most by holy instruments,' writes
Bonar in one place, and again, 'I am more than
ever convinced that unholiness lies at the root of our
little success.' As early as 1842 we find him saying
that he had learned by experience that it is not
'much labour' but 'much prayer' that is the
only means to success. He was aware that multiplying
words was not the way to win souls. 'Felt after
speaking today how much may be effected by a very
few words when the person is filled with the Holy
Ghost.' In his latter years, when asked to tell a
gathering of young ministers the secret of a consecrated
life, his simple answer was, 'I can only say to my
young brethren that for forty years there has not been
a day that I have not had access to the Mercy-Seat.'

At the present time there is no want of speaking and
writing and preaching and teaching, but there is little
abiding fruit from it all. There is too much time taken
up with active work for the kingdom of God and too
little time given to prayer for the kingdom. Surely if
God's servants are to speak and preach in the power of
the Holy Spirit they must again give themselves
'continually to prayer, and to the ministry of the
word.'

In view of the fact that a Christian's life is moulded
by the doctrine believed, it is important to remember
the doctrines which Bonar held to as the Truth of God.
Someone is said to have remarked in his hearing that
she did not like doctrine; it was not practical. At once
he replied, 'Doctrine is practical, for it is that that
stirs up the heart.' What were the doctrines which
stirred the heart of Andrew Bonar, and which he used
to stir the hearts of his hearers? They were the
doctrines of God's free grace to sinners—doctrines

which reveal man's salvation to be entirely in the
hands of God and which have as their aim and end the
glory of the Triune God.[1] While the person and work
of the Lord Jesus Christ occupied Andrew Bonar at all
times, he never fell into the error of forgetting that all
three Persons of the Godhead are equally united in
man's salvation. As well as proclaiming the Lamb of
God he upheld the Divine sovereignty and the honour
of the Holy Spirit, for he realized that to omit the work
of One of the Persons was to destroy the true glory of
the plan of salvation. He saw clearly that the Scriptural order is *the glory of God* in the salvation of man.
His preaching as well as his life was God-centred and
when we say God we mean Father, Son and Holy
Spirit. Now we fear that among preachers today there
is a tendency not only to dishonour the Father by
denying His absolute sovereignty but also to grieve
the Holy Spirit by failing to acknowledge that a
believer in Christ is born, not by his own fleshly will,
'but of God' (John i. 13). Surely if we ever hope to
see days of the outpourings of the Spirit as was witnessed during Bonar's life-time, we must first of all
return to a full-orbed Gospel in which the predominant
theme is the glory of the Triune God.

But if Andrew Bonar's Life reminds us of the
necessity of a pure Gospel, it also serves as a warning
against thinking of any doctrines as an end in themselves. The example of Bonar's inner experience constantly speaks to our consciences of the worthlessness
of clarity in the mind, without love, humility and
prayer in the heart. The doctrines of grace are the
foundation of Christian experience, but if we truly
realize this it should lead us, as it did Bonar, to live an
overflowing life characterized by an ever deepening
knowledge of God and Christ.

Perhaps this lesson is particularly needed in these

[1] Dr. Bonar's views on the importance of these doctrines
will be found in the appendix at the end of this volume.

days when there is a revived concern that the doctrines of grace should be restored in the Church to that pre-eminent position which they occupy in the Word of God. Not only did Bonar have a firm belief in these profound truths of Scripture, but united with them was his joyous and triumphant hope. Not only did his consciousness of sin make humiliation and self-abasement his everyday spiritual exercise, but at the same time we find him pressing on in a life of rejoicing. It would be well for all who are concerned for the cause of Christ to remember that these are things which must never be separated. One who knew Bonar well wrote of him: ' Calvinism and the evangelical creed were never so fairly (their critics might say insidiously) recommended, as by this man who stood by every doctrine, even the most severe and difficult to believe, while he seemed to live in a perpetual sunshine, and to spread not gloom but brightness and good nature wherever he appeared.'

In conclusion, we can do no better than take up the words with which Andrew Bonar closed his sketch of Samuel Rutherford, a man whom he so closely resembled: ' He is now gone to the " mountain of myrrh and the hill of frankincense "; and there no doubt still wonders at the unopened, unsearchable treasures of Christ. But O for his insatiable desires Christward ! O for ten such men in Scotland to stand in the gap !—men who all day long find nothing but Christ to rest in, whose very sleep is pursuing after Christ in dreams, who intensely desire to "awake with His likeness".'

John J. Murray

78B Chiltern Street,
 London, W.1.
July 1960

Preface

THE Diary is the revelation of the life of one who prayed always, who prayed everywhere, who, the nearer he came to the other world, was every day more constantly enjoying closer intercourse with it. As he led his congregation in prayer at a Sabbath-day service, or an evening prayer-meeting, often it seemed as if he had forgotten the presence of any other, and were speaking with his unseen God and Saviour 'face to face, as a man speaketh unto his friend.' His Diary does not reveal much of the bright, joyous, happy spirit which was so characteristic of him, but his letters are pervaded by it, as was his whole life and conversation. We think of him now as having entered into the joy of his Lord, in whom on earth he rejoiced 'with joy unspeakable and full of glory.'

The Diary is published at the earnest request of many of Dr. Bonar's congregation and personal friends, by whom it will be read reverently, as the expression of his deepest and most sacred spiritual experiences. Only one consideration has led to its publication, and that is the belief that the voice now silent on earth will still be heard in these pages calling on us as from the other world to be 'followers of them who through faith and patience are inheriting the promises.'

Marjory Bonar.

Glasgow, 1893.

' 'Tis only for a season;
   How long we cannot tell,—
A quickly passing season,
   And all will then be well.

We parted at the river,
   They hasted on before;
And we behind them tarried
   On this tempestuous shore.

They went to be with Jesus;
   We could not stay their flight:
They rose above the darkness;
   We still remain in night.

They sweetly sleep in Jesus
   Beyond the fear of ill;
Theirs is the blessed resting;
   Ours is the watching still.'

Horatius Bonar.

ANDREW ALEXANDER BONAR, D.D.

DIARY AND LIFE

'It keeps the threads of the past disentangled, and has been useful to me on some memorable occasions when I was called on to speak about times past and brethren gone.'

(Written on a fly-leaf of the Diary.)

CHAPTER I

Conversion and College Life

1828-1834

21st August 1828.—About this time I thought of marking occasionally my thoughts and God's dealings. It was this week that I resolved to enter upon the study of divinity. My chief motive was the indistinct hope and belief that thereby I should be more likely to find salvation, being much taken up, as I thought I must be, with the pursuit of divine things. For I felt myself unsaved, and felt a secret expectation that in the course of my studies in divinity I might be brought to the truth. My inclination for Biblical Criticism, too, and fondness for languages, had much weight, I suspect, in the determination, rather than higher motives.

Sunday, 24th.—Never able to keep the impression of one Sabbath till another comes round. I resolve to do such and such things, but the desire fades away, and before next Sabbath I give up the attempt.

Tuesday, Oct. 14th.—Heard some lectures on Biblical Criticism. I was led after to think I got 'tastes of the good Word of God;' because I enjoyed the light cast upon the passages of Scripture. Not that they convinced me of sin, or showed me more of Christ, but the light I got was light upon the Word of God, and so it seemed light upon divine things.

Sunday, 26*th*.—Heard Mr. Carey, missionary, nephew of the famous Carey, preach in the evening, and thought, 'O what if the Lord send me to the heathen yet?' Indeed, I have often had feelings of this kind.

Sunday, Nov. 2*nd.*—A most impressive sermon in the evening from Mr. Purves, upon John ix. 4: 'I must work the works,' etc.   I came home in deep anxiety to be saved, and I was, I trust, enabled to choose Christ Jesus for my Saviour, depending upon the Holy Spirit's assistance to keep me.   But still I fear and tremble lest all be not well.

Tuesday, 4*th.*—Began Moral Philosophy class.   I soon grow cold.   I grieve that I do not sorrow more for sin.

Sunday, 9*th.*—Had a view of my guilt that I never had before, and a view of my need of Christ.   May God cause it to last and to deepen.

Tuesday, 11*th.*—Hearing Dr. Chalmers' second lecture in the Divinity Hall.   He prayed, 'that we might study the Scripture till the Day-Star rose in our hearts.'

1*st January* 1829.—God is helping me to feel more love to Jesus.

Tuesday, 6*th.*—I strive to keep the feeling of eternity before me always.   The Lord perfect that which concerneth me.   It is labour, indeed, to resist temptation, or to be satisfied with the present.

Tuesday, March 31*st.*—To-day —— —— took me into his study, and after a short conversation asked me to be his sons' teacher during summer, at his summer residence, to teach them Latin and Greek.   I declined instantly, thinking what would my soul do in such company.

Tuesday, April 14*th.*—Hearing Mr. Buchanan of Leith, who showed me I was resting my hope *upon my belief,* not upon the object of that belief, and not drawing joy from that object.

Saturday, 18*th*.—The vastness of the word '*eternity*' impressed upon me.

Sunday, 26*th*.—Have had my desires much excited by seeing many of my friends, and those I respect most, already in Christ.

Sunday, *May* 3*rd*.—Great sorrow because I am still out of Christ.

Thursday, 7*th*, *Fast-Day*.—It has been much impressed upon me that, if convinced of sin at all, I must be so by the view of it in Christ's love.

Sunday, 10*th*.—I thought that I received my first real impression of the Saviour's love this day, when Mr. Purves preached upon 1 John iv. 10 : 'Herein is love.'

Monday, 11*th*.—The clearest impression I ever felt of what it would be to have eternal separation from God.

Tuesday, 12*th*.—I sometimes think God is thus dealing with me that I may afterwards be better fitted to teach others.

Sunday, 24*th*.—Have been hearing Mr. Irving's lectures all the week, and am persuaded now that his views of the Coming of Christ are truth. The views of the glory of Christ opened up in his lectures have been very impressive to me.

Sunday, 31*st*.—My birthday is past, and I am not born again. It often comes to my mind, 'my friends will be for ever lost to me,' for they shall be taken and I shall be left. Reading Guthrie's *Trial of Interest in Christ*. Mr. Irving's lectures go on with great power.

Sunday, *June* 7*th*.—My brother John preached on 1 Pet. ii. 7 : 'To you who believe He is precious.' I

sometimes think I may be believing ; but yet I do not
see the forgiveness of sin to be above all other things
desirable. I rest much upon my prayers, and feel
anxiety rather about being holy, set free from the
power of sin, as if that were the way of salvation.

Sunday, 28*th*.—I long to know Jesus as the Beloved
One, but my love of praise and fondness for some friends
are my snare. Felt more than usual pleasure in singing the Psalms to-day. I have had many remarkable
answers to prayer, in regard to temporal things upon
which my heart was set, which I have thought may be
a token that God is leading me.

Sunday, July 5*th*.—God has let me seek salvation by
trying to perform duties that would please Him, and are
a satisfaction to my own mind ; and, especially this last
year, I have been trying to do this by keeping before me
motives drawn from thoughts of heaven and hell. But
now He seems leading me away to the *love of Christ* as
what is to do this. I was struck with the Moravians
having no success till they preached Christ's love.
Boston's Life has been very interesting to me. I think
I may be like him if ever I am brought to the truth.
There is something in his mind that I can enter
into.

Thursday, 10*th* [1] [9*th*].—Dr. Gordon on John vi. 68.[2]
He remarked that some wait, and think they must wait,
till they are better prepared, if not by themselves, yet by
the Spirit, before they will take the promise and believe.
This is my case, I suspect.

Sunday, 12*th*.—Sacrament in Lady Glenorchy's. I
have not received Christ into my heart. My feeling
vanishes when I come into contact with any spirit but
my own. I felt the deepest grief. I wept when I got

---

[1] These dates are given as they are in the manuscript.

[2] Dr. Robert Gordon of Edinburgh.

home, just from feeling the misery of not being in Christ.

Sunday, August 2nd.—Dr. Gordon upon 'To whom shall we go?' Impressed with the truth that I am seeking, *before* coming to Christ, what I cannot get till I *do* come. He can deliver me from worldly thoughts, earthly desires, darkness, temptations, rebellious will, etc.

Sunday, 16th.—A wish to be approved by man is my besetting sin at present.

Sunday, 23rd.—Have been some time in Leven.[1] It is a help to me even to think that once in Christ I can never fall away. I have lived nineteen years without this knowledge of Him. Sometimes I am tempted to wonder if there be any real pleasure in Christ. I would not think this if I knew what it is to be free from con-demnation. I am much tempted to impute worldly motives to the saints I see around me.

Tuesday, September 1st. — I feel, somehow, almost sure from the state of mind I have been in, and from which God so often has delivered me, and from continual preservation in me of these earnest desires, that God has a purpose with me, and is seeking me for salvation. I have got the answer to some more prayers, namely, about thinking of God in the midst of common things and rising early in the morning.

Sunday, 13th.—Still longing to be a partaker of divine grace. How difficult seems to me the 'narrow way' that leads to life !

Saturday, Oct. 17th.—Visited the Jews' Synagogue. Interesting, and instructive too, to us who look upon their delusion with a better knowledge.

Thursday, 29th.—For the first time in my life I visited, last Monday, a sick person, a lad John Macarthur, in order to try and say a little about his soul. I read to

---

[1] Where his brother John was at that time assistant to Mr. Brewster.

him about the earnest seeking of the people in the time of the Plague, and about the three persons converted at the Kirk of Shotts.[1]   It was a duty, but little else.

Saturday, 31*st.*—My brother John, going to Leven to be assistant, asked me if I would take part with Horace in evening worship.   I could give no answer.   He left it entirely to myself.

Sunday, Nov. 1*st.*—I feel again my sad state.   I have missed *three* opportunities of doing or getting good, viz., the Lord's Supper, taking a Sabbath School, and taking part in family worship.   I noticed and felt James's prayer in the evening, for those who had not joined in the Lord's Supper.

Sunday, 8*th.*—James told us to-day that he did not think it necessary now to take us in at night [for instruction] as formerly, so that another bond of family union to each other is loosened.   For nearly twenty years I have had the privilege of Sabbath evening instruction, and yet still am not in Christ.

Friday, Dec. 4*th.*—Thoughts of delaying my going to the Divinity Hall for another year, because I feel still so far from Christ.

Sunday, 6*th.*—I still see that my besetting sin is to draw the love and attention of others toward me, not God's glory.   Reading Thomas à Kempis showed me this yet more.

Sunday, 13*th.*—I get many temporal blessings and answers to prayer about temporal things.   These seem tokens of good.   Perhaps God has in view others whom, in future years, He may use me to benefit by all this darkness and perplexity.   But I see, at the same time, that it is just in Him to deal so with me.

---

[1] There were said to have been 500, but there may have been three cases which had specially interested him.

1st January 1830.—I have thought reputation much, but I see that, to one who believes the Word of God regarding the last days, such a desire is folly. My father often laments in his diary the want of religious companions, but I am much better in this respect than he, although my companions do not speak very much about the state of their souls to each other.

Sunday, *3rd.*—Much grieved on hearing that Horace was going to the Lord's Table; my mother told me this. It grieved me, because it makes me feel myself left, while others seem pressing into the kingdom.

Sunday, *10th.* — Last week discovered accidentally, from a letter Horace had written to John, what was the state of his soul; how deeply he is lamenting his inability to profit by public ordinances, etc. O that I were saved!

Sunday, *17th.*—Reading Mrs. Judson's Life, I felt as if I could willingly labour as a missionary, or do anything to save one soul.

Friday, *Feb. 26th.*—I see some of Christ's love in all He did to men; but am not able to love Him because He came into the world to save sinners; nor do I really see the evil of sin. But, because I have got some sight of His love in His dealing with men while on earth, I feel as if this little attainment (if it be one) makes me not expect more for a while.

Sunday, *March 7th.*—The Theological Association is of use to me. It vexes me to see so many of my friends beyond me. Some conversation with friends has led me to think much of being a missionary, and my aptitude to learn languages has struck me as a qualification. But then I have not the love of Christ, and so am unfit for anything.

Saturday, *13th.*—Again feel deep sorrow, so that I let myself sleep for an hour in the evening, just to pass it away. I see that all this is not godly sorrow. It is rather vexation at not being able to do as others, and to have their esteem and fellowship. And there is often a feeling of concern as if I were an afflicted man without cause. Saturday night and the Sabbath are often to me the season of the deepest sorrow ; and yet I can never but wish they were come.

Sunday, May 30*th.*—Yesterday was my birthday. I am not born again.

Tuesday, June 29*th.*—At a meeting of the Classical Society.[1] The young men, many of them very thoughtless, presented me with a copy of Pindar, accompanied with expressions of regard. What will these young men think if, in after days, I become a missionary ?

Sunday, Aug. 8*th.*—At Leven. All appearance of grace in me is only desire after Christ, and no more. I am still without Christ and without hope. I have no hatred of sin ; I seek Christ with little ardour, rather because not happy in the world than because of anything else.

Sunday, Sept. 5*th.*—I mean to delay entering the Divinity Hall this year, because I am not yet brought to the knowledge of God.

Wednesday, 8*th.*—Still at Leven. Horace came over. He told me a saying of Augustine's : ' If we who are only seeking Thee have such delight, what shall they have who find Thee ? '

Saturday, Oct. 2*nd.*—Came home from Leven yesterday. I am to delay entering the Hall, chiefly because I am not yet in a state of grace, though I put it also on the ground of wishing to study more ; which I also *do* wish, but which would not have prevented me going on,

[1] Mr. Bonar was secretary of this society, and among other members were James (afterwards Lord) Moncreiff, Warren, who wrote the *Diary of a Physician,* and William Edmondstoune Aytoun, the poet.

had I felt true conversion. I should labour first to be taught of the Spirit myself, before I learn how to teach other men. In regard to my studies, I feel in all my compositions a labour and anxiety to succeed, and in almost all my studies there is the wish to be high and eminent ; and yet I fear that I shall never be so at all.

Sunday, 17*th*.[1]—In reading Guthrie's *Saving Interest* I have been led to hope that I may be in Christ though I have never yet known it. All the marks of faith in a man which he gives are to be found in me, I think, although very feeble. This is the first beam of joy, perhaps, that I have yet found in regard to my state, and yet it is scarcely more than a hope.

November 3*rd*.—A few days ago bought a Hebrew Bible, with the Rabbis' notes, etc. It may be important to my studies hereafter. I have thought that I may yet be able to read Hebrew with as much ease as ever I can read Latin or Greek.[2]

To-morrow is the Fast-Day. I have much more light and expectation. It will be right in me, and would be so in all students, to devote these few days to entire prayer and seeking after God, as a preparation for the winter session.

Sunday, 7*th*.—For about two weeks past, ever since I read a passage in Guthrie's *Saving Interest*, I have had a secret joyful hope that I really have believed on the Lord Jesus. I heard with much feeling, and I think understanding, Mr. Purves's sermon to-day, ' He that spared not His own Son,' etc., and I think that next Communion I may go forward to the Lord's Table as one that has received Him. If now at length

[1] On the margin here is written, ' assurance begun.'

[2] The volume mentioned has been presented to the Free Church College Library, Edinburgh, in accordance with the written wish (found with the Will) of Dr. Bonar.

I have reached a place of safety, it is solely through divine grace. I did nothing but receive. Nearly twenty years of my life have been spent in the world without Christ, and even yet I am not free from fear and sorrow.

Tuesday, Dec. 14th.—Some days ago I wrote to John at Leven, stating my feelings, asking if I should go to the Lord's Table. To-day he wrote me a very affectionate answer, strongly advising me to go ; he thinks my state warrants it.

The following is the letter referred to :—

' Monday, Nov. 29, 1830.

' MY DEAR JOHN,—I am not writing this letter to give you any news further than to tell you that John Purves gave us a farewell sermon, on Sabbath afternoon, on the words, " Now then we are ambassadors of Christ, as though God did beseech you by us." It was an excellent and very solemn sermon, showing the responsibility of ministers and people, addressing in conclusion the various classes of the congregation with great earnestness and affection, desiring their prayers to follow him. The last prayer also was very particular and solemn.

' What I wish to write to you of is on a question that has been much in my thoughts, but on which I never have spoken to any one ; yet I have no fear of being unwelcome in writing to you, if only I can explain distinctly all my feelings. You know that I have never yet been a communicant, yet for some time past I have been seriously thinking more than hitherto of this duty, and of the privilege of those who can join in that ordinance worthily. And now I hope that I may come, for I feel habitual dissatisfaction with the world, desire after God, and love to our Lord Jesus Christ, although all are feeble. But there are some things which shake my hopes—and will you faithfully tell me if, in such circumstances, I dare to partake of the Lord's Supper, and direct me to the remedy. One thing is this : Sometimes for days together I cannot see the hatefulness of sin in any degree, I am unhappy, and know that it arises from sin separating me from the favour and from any encouraging views of God, yet I feel no power to abhor it, and as little power to look to Jesus except in the way of cold belief. At other times, especially on Sabbath days, in the midst of prayer in the congregation, the temptation of wandering worldly thoughts, completely overpowers and distracts me, and so also I often come away unprofited by the preaching of the Word. And this also troubles me,—that while I can be glad to feel my heart kindled at hearing the love and promises of Christ, the *threatenings* of God never much affect me, so that the fear of His wrath would not so move me to avoid a sin, as would the fear of a present punishment in the world. Now I know that the saints have still within them the remains of sin and corruption, and that therefore *those* may expect to feel sin stirring in them and leading often to what causes great spiritual loss to those who are just beginning to contend against their affections and lusts, even aided as they are by the Holy Spirit ; yet it is to me exceedingly difficult to know whether or not I may be hoping with a false hope and deceiving myself, in supposing that my convictions are more than the natural unrenewed conscience can feel.

'I have tried to tell you faithfully what my state is, just as I would do in prayer before God—I mean, as seriously as I would then do. I hesitated long before writing thus freely, but resolved to do so because, in whatever way you see it right to direct me, I hoped it would be for my good, and certainly not the less that it comes from my brother.—I am, my dear John, your affectionate brother,   ANDREW A. BONAR.'

Sunday, 19th.—I have been reviewing my life to see the steps of my change. In my boyhood I was selfish in a very apparent manner, although never boisterous in seeking gratification. Fear and shame often restrained me. I quieted conscience by repeating prayers, and forgot God in truth. Three years ago Dr. Gordon preached in the Chapel[1] upon, 'Thou shalt love the Lord thy God,' etc. The sermon I quite forget, but the text was what remained long in my mind, and often came to me as the standard by which I was to be tried. I often tried to bring up my mind to some feeling by thinking upon eternity. I used to think it no wonder that Christians sometimes engaged in the world's pleasures, because I thought it must be a wearisome time to

[1] Lady Glenorchy's, Edinburgh.

them till they were in heaven.   Then at other times, I exceedingly wondered at the indulgence which Christians seemed to allow themselves in mirth and thoughtlessness.   In reading Doddridge's *Rise and Progress*, I wished much to be such a Christian as is there spoken of, but tried in vain to work any feeling.   Next winter Mr. Irving's lectures used to give me great ideas of the world to come, and his 'parable of the Sower' cast in some of the first beams of light into my soul as to spiritual truth.   From that time I kept away from the world, and could not bear its pleasures.   But it was seeing many friends whom I loved *in Christ* that led me most of all to be always anxious for a change. My confessions of sin itself were very slight, nor are they very deep even now.   Reading Guthrie's *Trial of a Saving Interest* was very much the means of giving me any hope that I had undergone a change.   The marks laid down there apply to me.   This has filled me with great joy.   Is this really passing from death to life?   I was always scrupulous in the letter about doing anything against conscience.   I never learned a lesson on Sabbath but once, when I learned six words of the Latin vocabulary when at the High School for the second year, and it gave me great regret.   I used to practise self-denial, but somewhat in the spirit of penance and mortification.

Sunday, *26th.*—Last Monday Dr. Jones examined me in his own house, and admitted me a communicant. He explained the ordinance, taking for granted that I understood it clearly.   Asked some doctrinal and some experimental questions.   I see that when I dwell any time upon myself, and think upon my attainments, my heart is not profited ; but, whenever I get a sight of Christ's love, it is full of life then.   I must rise earlier, for, though I seldom am longer in bed than half-past

six, yet I go to bed at half-past eleven.   Perhaps I can
do with an hour less sleep.

Friday, 31*st.*—Among many other blessings this
year, these I see : that I have been brought to the
Lord's Table ; have been much helped in study ; we
have had little deep affliction in our family.

1*st January*, 1831.—Wars and rumours of wars prepare us for things coming upon the earth.   It may be,
also, the sudden appearing of the Lord Jesus Christ.
The nations are waking., I am to begin to-day the
practice of learning a little of the Bible by heart every
morning before breakfast.

Saturday, 8*th.*—Thinking upon baptism, I am not
clear upon it, but I see this, that it is in a manner the
occasion where a promise is given under seal to be
opened afterwards and used ; while the Lord's Supper
is the occasion where, in presence of that promise, we
receive the stores laid up.

Sunday, 9*th*, *Communion.*—I sought beforehand that
at this season I might get more love to the souls of men,
more understanding of the Word of God, and more
power to keep my thoughts from wandering.   I felt
little excitement, but much calmness at the Table.   I
believe I have got increase of power to look at God.
I have sometimes fears, though not very distressing.

Sunday, 23*rd.*—Went with John Burne to his Sabbath
School.   I hope God may yet make me useful in this way.
I wonder so few children are sanctified from the womb.

Wednesday Evening, *Feb.* 9*th.*—Indeed a most awful
and solemn event has come upon the city.   Dr. Andrew
Thomson [1] has suddenly dropped down dead at his own
door.   It is a time when we all thought the Church
required every support.

---

[1] Minister of St. George's Church, Edinburgh, and one of the leaders
of the Evangelical party in the Church of Scotland.

Saturday, 12*th.*—Never anything remembered like the great and universal grief. In reading the Book of Ecclesiastes I have felt something of Christ's sympathy. I see by that book how well God has understood human feelings and misery.

Tuesday, 15*th.* — To-day attended Dr. Thomson's funeral with a vast crowd of ministers of all denominations and the students of divinity.

March 14*th.*—Much vexed by being obliged to-day in the Classical Society to insist upon examination into the report of a duel between two of our members. God gave me courage and strength, though naturally I shrank from any such thing.

Monday, 28*th.*—Earthly affections and desires sometimes assail me. But God by giving me joy in divine things, in the absence of all I wished from the earth, has shown me that there is better happiness. Saturday evenings are often times of peculiar wandering and unhappy longings in my soul.

Sabbath, May 29*th.*—This time last year, I could not say that I was in Christ, now I believe that I can ; and if the Lord has shown me much kindness this last year, though I have been so short time within His fold, what may I not expect in days to come ?

Sabbath, June 19*th.*—I believe Satan is working upon my imagination in order to withdraw me from heavenly meditation. Great sorrow at not getting any opportunity of intercourse with some friends. Also, Satan suggested to-day that I could never have a high place in heaven : and this proud imagination vexed me, till the Lord showed me reason to be contented, if I got to heaven at all.

Saturday, July 9*th.*—I have been devoting an hour on Saturday morning after breakfast to prayer and meditation. I hate sin very feebly ; I do not know it.

Friday, 22nd.—Last meeting of the Classical Society. Excellent farewell by George M'Crie in verse. I was helped to pray for all my companions there, both before and after coming home. O that the ministers of these companions of mine may be successful in bringing them all to the truth !

Sabbath, 24th.—Awful struggle in my soul. In reading Henry Martyn, saw that I must give up all earthly friends, the most loved even, if I should be called by God to such work as he in other lands.

Monday, August 1st.—Came over to Leven ; happier far this year than last, because now I know that Christ loves me.

September 7th.—Have not been much tempted with the love of friends of late : nor have I had that great sorrow that I once had. I feel sometimes quite willing to give up all things and go to the heathen, if the Lord call me. I think this state of mind is in answer to a time of special prayer which I observed, asking the Lord to enable me when here to spend my time profitably. An old Christian—Peter Ramsay—who sits and prays or meditates all day long, asked me what I was to be, that he might pray the more intelligently for me.

October 1st.—Yesterday morning kept a season of thanksgiving, and this morning a time of confession of sin ; especially in reference to the time we have been here. We returned from Leven on Monday.

Monday, 3rd.—More and more convinced that the time of Christ's Coming is before the thousand years; often grieved by hearing opposition to this.

Sabbath, 9th.—Taught again by God's providence to put no trust in man, and yet I ever slide back to try that broken cistern. Augustine's confession, x. 36, is true of me : ' Instat adversarius veræ beatitudinis nostræ, ubique spargens in laqueis, *Euge, euge,* ut incaute capiamur ; et a veritate tuâ gaudium nostrum deponamus, atque in hominum fallaciâ ponamus ; libeatque nos amari et timeri non propter te, sed pro te.' I was this week sometimes led to long to die.

Sabbath, 23*rd.*—Thanksgiving for the harvest, I felt more than usually able to join in thanks. Glad to know that Eliza is about to sit down at the Lord's Table; so that now all our family seem to be in Christ.

Saturday, 29*th.*—Last Wednesday I passed easily and comfortably through the examination before the Presbytery, previous to entering the [Divinity] Hall. It led me to review the steps of my life. I always kept back till I was in Christ, before I could think of entering the Hall; and this made me choose to remain behind two years, when I might have pressed forward. Last Friday set myself to pray for the nation, especially in prospect of the cholera.

Sabbath, Nov. 6*th.*—I fear that my delight in the Scriptures is very much because of the joy of the understanding.

Sabbath, 20*th.*—First session in the Hall begun. On Saturday morning we began a society, the ' Exegetical,' at 6.30 A.M.[1] It is to meet for the purpose of Biblical Criticism, begun and concluded with prayer ; in some sort a prayer-meeting over our studies in the Bible.

Sabbath, Dec. 18*th.*—I never get any one to whom I can unbosom myself. God alone has been my Counsellor and Teacher ; but I should never complain. I sometimes think myself neglected by friends and others. But God is opening up ways of usefulness to me ; I have some

---

[1] The members of this Society included, besides Horatius and Andrew Bonar, William Laughton, Thomas Brown, Henry Moncreiff, William Wilson, John Thomson, Walter Wood, John Millar, Robert Hamilton, John Burne, Patrick Borrowman, Alex. Somerville, and Robert M'Cheyne.

influence among my fellow-students, and am beginning to visit among the poor this week.

Sabbath, 25th.—Along with Robert Hamilton, went up to the Castle Hill to visit some of the poor ; much pleased with his way of dealing with them—easy and kind.

3rd January 1832.—Mercies during last year were very many in answer to prayer. The pestilence is in other places of Europe and in Ireland.

Sunday, 22nd.—Find the difficulty of visiting the poor to be less than I thought. Much helped yesterday in an essay upon the *First Resurrection,* defending the doctrine of Christ's reign, in the Exegetical Society. Disappointed still in my worldly desires, and often think that God may wish me not to care for these at all. He has some great intention in regard to all this way by which I am now led. I desire more zeal, more love, more faith, more hope of things to come ; more sorrow over things coming upon the land, more sensibility to my own and other people's sins.

Sunday, 29th.—Cholera has come among us. My visiting goes on. I generally begin with reading a chapter, then say a few words, and pray. Many are attentive and thankful, especially at this present time when they are under some alarm. We have begun a meeting in our district on Friday evening for reading Scripture and prayer.

Sunday, Feb. 19th.—Often I have to drag myself to visit the poor. This shows me the great corruption in my heart, how very little love and zeal, how little I dwell in heavenly places. We have been much helped in our Friday evening meetings, which are uninterrupted as yet. We do not cease visiting on account of the appearing of the cholera. It is the very time for visiting more.

Thursday, March 22nd.—The National Fast, the first for these sixteen years. Much impressed still with the duty of going to the heathen. My little anxiety about Christ's Second Coming makes me often mourn. It is only when I am sorrowful that I feel much desire for it.

May 5th.—A remark of my brother Horace went far to satisfy me about missionary labour. He spoke about the need of labourers and ministers at home, and the witness for Christ's Second Coming borne by few in this land. That may be part of our work.

June 9th.—I never almost felt a more lonely sorrow than settled down upon me this evening. Indeed hitherto in my life, especially since I became alive to eternal things, all delight in earthly things of whatever kind seems to come only in order to depart.

Sunday, July 29th.—Yesterday concluded our Exegetical Society for the season. Mr. Hamilton proposed singing two verses of thanksgiving before parting. All joined with deepest fervour.

Tuesday, Aug. 14th.—Pestilence in all the land, yet no man seems repenting.

Saturday, Sept. 1st.—Leven. Since coming here have devoted Saturday morning to prayer and meditation, the time we used to spend in our morning society. Very sweet season to my soul.

Saturday, Nov. 17th.—Began our Exegetical Society for Biblical Criticism, at half-past six in the morning. Some of the presence of God among us. Nothing is more disheartening to me than the coldness of ministers towards students, the little interest they show in them ; and also the coldness of students toward one another in spiritual things. But this drives us more upon God Himself.

1st January 1833.—I began last year the custom of private fasts, and never have I found more answers to direct petitions than since then. The pestilence this year has been a call to prayer, and its removal now a call to praise. A thanksgiving has been ordered by the Presbytery.

Saturday, 12*th.*—We should, if we would be thankful, notice God's mercies at the moment we get them, and not wait till afterwards until we thank Him.

Friday, 25*th.*—Delivered a discourse at the Hall upon 2 Tim. iv. 6-8—a lecture. Passed the morning in asking that it might be blessed, even to the students who heard it ; a token of future days. Having got a reading of one of Dr. Gordon's MSS., was much struck at the great plainness and commonplace remarks even of a sermon that struck very many. It is God's blessing that makes it powerful.

Saturday, *April* 27*th.* — This time six years ago John was licensed, and to-day Horace was licensed at an adjourned meeting of the Presbytery.

Sabbath, *May* 12*th.*—Believing in the speedy coming of Christ, I thought it comforting to look upon diseases such as this influenza that is cutting off many, as one of the last diseases of this world.

Friday, 24*th.*—Removed to our house in York Place. Oh how many mercies in our last habitation, since our father's and sister's death !

July 28*th.*—Concluded our morning society for the season. Felt more joy in singing our parting psalm than I ever remember in my life while praising.

August 9*th.*—I thought to-day, had all the world been willing to be saved, and had God been unwilling that any should, oh what a scene of groans and cries and agonies !

October 3*rd.*—Spent some time in praying for the spread of the study of prophecy ; then wrote a reply to an article in the *Christian Instructor* against the

Pre-millennial Coming of Christ. Writing upon this subject makes me long much for that glorious day.

November 17th.—Began school at Leith on Sabbath evening ; much prayer, some hope.

Saturday, 23rd. — John came from Leven. Mr. Brewster does not need him any more ; he expects to go to Greenock.

3rd January 1834.—My cousin, John Bonar of Kimmerghame, is dying.

Sunday, March 2nd.—Several things encourage me in my Sabbath School at Leith, especially the good order and quietness in comparison with some others. Since last Communion I have seen more than before of Christ's substitution in our room ; His righteousness the only ground of our acceptance.

Monday, 24th.—Being the first free day since the classes broke up, spent it till four o'clock in reading Scripture, devotional books, and prayer. In some measure joined thanksgiving and confession.

April 13th.—John Bonar of Kimmerghame died last Sabbath evening. Much solemnized.

Sunday, June 22nd.—A week ago we had two accidental visits from Dr. Jones ; and now he has met with a paralytic stroke, and will probably never again be with us. He believes himself to be near death. I begin more than ever to think of missionary duty—I am left free to take my own path without consulting any earthly friend, and I used to think that, whenever I saw that no tie of duty bound me to home, I would then give myself up to foreign labour. I must think of it more.

Wednesday, July 9th.—Sorrow this day came in like an oozing tide. Perhaps this sorrow will prepare for the ministry, in the good providence of God.

Nov. 1st.—Last night one of the few dreams that I ever took notice of impressed me. I thought myself under sentence of death, to which I had become subject for the sake of some other.   I remember nothing of the cause, but just that I was dying as a servant of Christ. I felt resolved to suffer without drawing back, yet within I trembled ; and, as it was the early part of the day, I thought I went to engage in something that would delay the death for some hours.   But the time came, and I went back to die.   I somehow felt still as if I were a substitute for others, and dying thus ; but suddenly the thought of *Christ's* love to me, and His work for me, rushed into my mind, and I was filled with the joy of complete salvation, which took away all my fear.   I awoke, and rejoiced as I lay reflecting upon this source of gladness.

' The kingdom that I seek
Is Thine ; so let the way
That leads to it be Thine,
Else I must surely stray.'
                    —*Horatius Bonar.*

CHAPTER II

Work in Jedburgh and Edinburgh

1835-1838

1st January 1835.—Yesterday I was proposed in the Presbytery to be taken on trials.

This evening, conversing with my fellow-student, Robert M'Cheyne, who is already threatened with dangerous symptoms about his lungs, I was impressed with noticing how deeply impressed *he* seems with the necessity of doing all he can for God's glory immediately, and his anxiety to keep that ever before him.

February 15*th.*—A strange flood of sorrow and vexation, from earthly cisterns being dry to me, often comes upon me on Saturday and Sabbath. It is plain that I have not learned yet to place Christ in the room of all things, but I think it shows that the Lord loves me, and is calling me away from all other things to Himself.

Friday, March 27*th.*—This day have finished my study at the Hall and at College altogether.

May 25*th.*—Having prayed this morning for the General Assembly and my own future usefulness in the Church, went up to hear Mr. Duff address the Assembly upon the India Mission. I have returned, entreating God to direct my path in life as He will, through whatever clouds and darkness.

Saturday, 30*th.*—In a walk round Duddingston Loch with Robert M'Cheyne and Alexander Somerville this afternoon, we had much conversation upon the leading of Providence and future days. We sang together, sitting upon a fallen oak-tree, one of the Psalms. There is some prospect of Robert M'Cheyne going to be a missionary at Dunipace very soon.

Monday, June 1st.—John Purves spoke to me to-night about getting licence and coming to him this summer as missionary. I have committed the case to the Lord, by prayer, and also have sought the prayers of Alexander Somerville, from whom I had a note just after, telling of the death of a sister.

Wednesday, 24th.—Much encouraged by finding in my district that a Roman Catholic woman gives evidence of a real change, and ascribes her conversion to me as the instrument. She spoke with the deepest feeling of gratitude I ever remember any such one expressing.

Friday, 26th.—To-night closed my meeting with the people on the Castle Hill. William Laughton addressed them.[1] I opened and concluded with prayer. At the conclusion many came up and expressed themselves most affectionately, among others the Roman Catholic woman. Oh what a joy, that even that one soul has been brought to Christ. I shall see her in eternity, and behold her blessedness when she praises the Lamb for His love and providence and grace. I shall hear her thank God for me, and I shall in turn take up the song and praise the Lord alone. I hope there may be more fruit than this one ; yet, considering the four years, how very much more I might have done, had there been more devotion and prayer. But often I was weary, often languid, often hurried away to the meeting in an earthly frame ; often formal and glad to be done. I feel to-night more than usual the *love of the Spirit*, for the conversion of a soul is His own work, His new creation. Oh may He be with me where I go, and send a revival

[1] Rev. Dr. Laughton, afterwards of St. Thomas' Free Church, Greenock.

in the parish where I am now to preach and work, showing the truth of a Saviour crucified to the heart of every one. The Lord has led me gently and wonderfully until now.

Monday, 29th.—Yesterday I took leave of my Sabbath scholars ; felt it very sad. Prayed earnestly for them. To-day the death of John B. Patterson, so unexpectedly, has deeply affected us all. I go to-morrow to the beginning of my trial examination. That death sends me forth with this lesson, that I should seek for nothing but the true, immediate, direct glory of Christ and salvation of souls.

Mr. Bonar's first experience of pastoral work was in Jedburgh, and it was always memorable to him as the place where he preached his first sermon. He went there as missionary to Mr. Purves in 1835, and delighted to recall in after days the happy intercourse he had with him while living in his house.[1] Mr. Purves said to him, after some of their long discussions on Scriptural subjects, 'I think, Andrew, you belong to the old dispensation ! ' In a letter to a friend some years later, Mr. Bonar writes : ' Mr. Purves gathers in souls as the farmer does under a lowering sky in autumn, believing that the storm may next day rush down upon his fields.' His affectionate regard for Mr. Purves began during the latter's ministry in Lady Glenorchy's Chapel, and continued till his death in 1877.

Wednesday, July 1st.—Arrived yesterday at Jedburgh. Went to the Presbytery with Mr. Purves. Some discussion whether they should hear me all in one day. They at length heard three discourses at the beginning and the remainder at the end, and licensed me, and now I am sent forth to preach the Gospel of Christ. This verse was upon my mind through the day, ' Faithful is

[1] Mrs. Purves was Mr. Bonar's cousin, being a daughter of the Rev. Archibald Bonar of Cramond.

He that called you, who also will do it,' so that I had no
anxiety almost as to the issue of the discussion concerning licensing me that day. I knew that if it were delayed
God had some intention in that delay. May the Holy
Spirit fill my soul with the awe of Himself! I felt the
same fears in looking forward to-night to my preaching
for the first time on Sunday next. Mr. Purves in the
family, both night and morning, prayed earnestly
for me.

Thursday, 2nd.—I am now seated in the study of the
manse to write out my first discourse. I wrote the
substance some Sabbaths ago, but am putting it into
more correct form. Isaiah lv. 1-3 is the subject. I have
endeavoured to prepare myself, first of all, by reading
Acts xx. 18, and in reading, the clause which struck me
much was '*From the first day until now,*' 'serving the
Lord with all humility of mind, and with many tears
and temptations.'   And then verse 24 appeared also
much to be noticed : ' That I might finish my course
with joy, and the ministry which I received.'   Then,
too, the command to 'feed the church of God which is
among you,' is to be my direction in selecting subjects ;
I must desire only to be useful.

Friday, 3rd.—Felt in the afternoon as if I could
speak without fear, being taken up with the subject
itself. The Lord has also so often assisted me. I consider it too as a token for good that this night I had the
spirit of prayer in some degree, and a longing desire that
souls might be saved upon Sabbath next. Perhaps this
spirit of prayer was given me in answer to the prayers
of my former little flock on the Castle Hill, who would
be meeting at that very time.

Saturday, 4th.—Found encouragement in Psalm xi. :
' In Thee do I put my trust. Why say ye to my
soul, Flee as a bird to your mountain ? '   Also in Psalm

xiii: 5 : ' I have trusted in Thy mercy.'   And I hope to
be able to use the next clause to-morrow evening, ' I will
sing unto the Lord, because He hath dealt bountifully
with me.'   I read to-day in Cotton Mather's Life that in
preparing for preaching he used to go over every para-
graph of his sermon that he had written, applying it to
his own soul ; and this he found an excellent means of
exciting him to warmth in delivering it to his people.   I
have tried this method.   In the afternoon I walked three
hours about the Dunion Hill, committing my sermon
and praying to my God.   I found Psalm cxix. 116 very
strengthening : ' Uphold me that I may live, and not be
ashamed of my hope.   Hold Thou me up, and I shall be
safe : I shall have respect unto Thy statutes continually ; ' and many other things came with power.   I
thought upon the privilege of speaking to-morrow to
nine hundred souls, speaking joyful tidings ; and of being
perhaps blessed to save one, and to make many glad.
Should I not reckon this a great honour ?   Now I feel
good hope that I shall preach not only without anxiety,
as one getting through a first sermon, but with real
desire for souls.   The evening prayer of John Purves has
greatly refreshed me.

Sabbath, 5th.—Anxious when I rose, yet drawn out
in prayer.   Psalm cxv. read in the family was encouraging, for not only the house of Israel, but especially the house of Aaron has a blessing of its own.   I
thought of my father's house being the house of Aaron,
and I have risen up to become one of them.   Was able
to pray in secret for others, companions and friends.
Were I not to succeed this day, it would be for the
glory of God and my good, after I have thus committed
my way to Him.   But it is not His way so to encourage
and then disappoint : it would contradict the providence
that brought me here, hindering my usefulness.

Afternoon.—I have indeed found God to be my helper in a time of need, and praise and bless His name. I felt uncertain of my own voice and action while reading the first psalm (lxiii. 1-5), but, after that, was composed, and was able to speak with great desire to do good by my words. It is a solemn thought, suggested by Mr. Purves's prayer in the afternoon, that this is the day on which John Patterson is lamented at Falkirk. Let me be stirred up to work while it is day ; and may I have grace to sustain me, while I see, also, the solemnity of a charge when it shall be sent. He used in his delirium to talk of his charge, and once was heard resigning it into the hands of the Moderator of the General Assembly. I feel this night happy, and in a frame to pray for others, and to praise the Lord. Specially to pray also for those who, I suppose, have this day prayed for me.

Thursday, 9th.—After a visit of two days to Edinburgh, I have now come to begin my labours in Jedburgh. I resolve in the strength of the Lord to rise at six o'clock at least,[1] and to read morning and evening, not only my Bible carefully, but also some biographical notices and some practical works, and O may the spirit of prayer be given me every day, and the gifts of the Spirit. And every day may the Lord look down upon my mother and sisters at home who will not forget me, and upon my brothers where they are ; and 'as a father pitieth his children' may He pity us. Robert M'Cheyne was licensed and preached on the same day as I.

Saturday, 11th.—Last night, perhaps in answer to the prayers of my people on the Castle Hill, for it was at that hour, John Purves and I had an interesting

---

[1] On the margin is written here : Οὐαί ! ἡμιτέλεστον ⎫
                                    ——ἕως ἄρτι. ⎬ 1844.

and profitable conversation on the Second Advent, and the exaltation of Christ.

Sabbath, 12*th.*—Preached twice to-day in Jedburgh. Jail to about thirty people, from Acts ii. 23. Showed them Jesus the only way of reconciliation to God, and what He had done. Next, in the afternoon, showed them Jesus the only way of stilling the conscience and taking away the pangs of guilt ; they were very attentive. I prayed much to-night as well as in the morning for them ; and was more excited by John Purves remarking in the evening ' that now we must go to the yet greater part of our day's work, namely, prayer.'

Thursday, 23*rd.*—Fast-Day of the Church of Scotland. Spent the morning in prayer, and in the forenoon went and spoke to the prisoners in the Jail upon the subject of 1st Peter iv. 17 and 18. Between sermons meditated upon the evils of sin. In afternoon found myself much drawn out in prayer and while singing verse 18 of Psalm li. In the evening preached at Fendyhall upon Amos vii. 2-4, and found comfort. To-day Alexander Somerville arrived to be tutor at Edgerston, and I noticed the providence that led to this. Also the providence that led me yesterday to see a man in the prison who would have been away next day, and whom I was just passing by.

Sunday, August 2*nd.*—Being a little troubled to find that my youthful appearance seems to diminish the respect of some people, I was brought to feel the blessedness of being willing to wait God's time, and meanwhile to seek in submission the honour of being to the glory of God, servant of all, even as my Lord was.

Friday, 7*th.*—This morning had an interesting and very useful conversation with John Purves (in whose house God has made me as happy as at home) regarding the importance of looking for all comfort and joy entirely and alone to Christ's work, and not to ourselves or our frames. I first gathered the importance of this from reading a tract, *The Lord our Righteousness*, and Willcox's *Drop of Honey from the Rock Christ.*

Monday, 10*th.*—Dr. M'Crie's death[1] on Wednesday last seems a providence which will affect the Church of Scotland much.

Friday, 14*th.*—Being now left alone for some weeks with the charge of the parish, I resolved to spend two hours this morning in prayer for direction and success in preaching, and for pardon of my ingratitude for mercy and help hitherto, which has been wonderful. I see that my felt remissness in family prayer and in asking blessing at meal-times might be accounted for in part as a punishment for my inattention and thought-lessness at these seasons. My tendency to neglect or shorten prayer and reading of Scripture, in order to hurry on to study, is another subject of humiliation. Prayer also that I may preach not myself but Christ Jesus alone in the Spirit.

Saturday, 15*th.*—I could not find much of the spirit of prayer till at family worship alone with the servants ; I felt then my soul drawn out to pray much and earnestly for to-morrow, and the salvation of souls here on that day.

Wednesday, 19*th.*—Greatly grieved by a letter from John, expressing deep disappointment at my not coming to his ordination [at Greenock] with all the rest, but I feel still satisfied that it is my line of duty to be here; though it would have been my exceeding pleasure to be with him. The letter saddened me much, but to-night it set me the more to pray for him being anointed

---

[1] The biographer of Knox, deeply interested in the Anti-Patronage Movement, though not himself a member of the Church of Scotland.

to-morrow with the Spirit, that he may be a John the
Baptist in preaching repentance and conversion, and
John the Apostle in speaking glorious and comforting
things of Christ.   My soul was drawn out to pray, and
this encouraged me to hope that I was right in being
here.   Also I have been preparing a sermon on the
Holy Spirit, which I felt not likely to be interesting ;
but I was anxious to give it next Sabbath on account
of the importance of the subject.   After much thought
and anxiety I got it finished and was enabled to pray
over it, so that perhaps the Lord will bless me abundantly on Sabbath, as both my prayers and the prayers
of my brother at Greenock will be offered more than
usual this week.   And the Spirit will bless His own
Word, and may He help me to set forth His glory all
the day without care about my reputation, if He will
convince sinners and edify saints.

Saturday, 22nd. — In prayer this forenoon found
access and help in viewing Jesus Christ the Mediator
as the great proof of God's being satisfied.   After
this season I felt gradually as if I had done now sufficiently for the morrow's success, and I indulged myself in a sort of leisure without much thought of God
for some hours.   I afterwards detected this sin, and saw
it was what my friend M'Cheyne spoke to me of in his
last letter, where he says he is inclined on the Monday
to say, ' I gave yesterday to God ; I may take this day
to myself.'

Sabbath, 23rd.—I never before felt the extreme difficulty of being absorbed in the desire of saving souls as
my sole object, and of taking the glory of God as my
simple aim.   I think it is a rule of Scripture (Jer. i.)
that, going with God's message and in His strength, we
are sure to be sustained.   I would never be disturbed
by inattentive looks if I always remembered that each

truth was the Lord's. It was a sort of self-denial that engaged me to preach the forenoon discourse upon Acts vii. 51. I did it because I was anxious to set the subject before them, and it had been useful to my own mind. I seldom prayed so much about any discourses as about these two, and yet the forenoon's, which I once preached at Kirkton also, both times has been listened to inattentively. This shows me a lesson, that I must pray as much as if I were nothing, and labour as much as if I were to do all ; but I have hopes that by this very sermon the Lord may work more because it was despised, than by any of my others.

Monday, 24th.—I feel this a consolation, that if I have done no other good, I may have given 'a cup of cold water' to some disciple yesterday, and that shall not lose its reward in heaven.

Sabbath, 30th.—As a remedy against idleness on the Monday, or against carelessness in private prayer, I observe (Mark i. 35) Christ, after the work of Sabbath, rose early to pray.

Wednesday, September 16th.—Found much joy and encouragement this morning in devoting a season for prayer, and I now pursue the plan of praying chiefly about what has come to my notice lately. I read the 'Retrospect,' which greatly refreshed me, and I have here been at least useful in stirring up some to the desire of wider acquaintance with Scripture. I mean to-day to begin visiting in a place here where are many gipsies. The prisoners are very attentive, and, from conversation with them, I perceive that they do feel in their conscience very much occasionally, especially in the night. I have the prospect, too, of beginning a class of young people, for all which objects I shall pray to-day, and I have read Ecclesiastes xi. Of late, especially after two sermons of John Purves on the subject, have felt more truly than before the desirableness of the Coming of our Lord.

Monday, *21st*.—Having spent a good while in the forenoon reading light things, and some things that were not right being contained in them, I felt on going out to visit some sick people a most complete languor or slowness, a sort of restraint of heart. Whereas, when my mind has been occupied beforehand with right thoughts, generally my conversation with the people flows freely and happily.

Monday, *October* 19*th*.—Yesterday I was again disappointed in regard to something in my preaching. I had chosen a subject suited to the case of the two prisoners who were soon to be removed and reprieved, but on coming up I found they had been sent up-stairs on account of a quarrel between them and some others ; and so they missed this opportunity : however, it may strike them the more, for last time I saw them I had read our Lord's words : ' If thou hadst known, at least in this thy day,' etc.

Tuesday, *20th*.—In visiting the prisoners I found that Providence, by removing the two convicts to separate cells, had provided a way for my seeing them more to advantage and speaking to each individually what I meant to say on Sabbath.

A few extracts from a letter to his youngest sister, telling of his work and occupations at this time, may be interesting :

TO HIS SISTER ELIZA.

'Jedburgh, Oct. 7, 1835.

' MY DEAR ELIZA,—I have little to tell you, though there is some variety in my occupations, and the Circuit Court and Registrations have caused a bustle among the townspeople these two last weeks. Two of my *parishioners* were condemned by the "Lords" to fourteen years' transportation, one of them long an inhabitant of

Larbert, and knew John Bonar. John visited him to-day with me and spoke a long while to him.

'I have been reading an excellent book lately, Goodwin's *Christ Set Forth*, also the *Marrow of Modern Divinity*, which contains excellent things. I daresay you remember that John Purves was accused often in Edinburgh of *Rowism*, but I am sure he is altogether right in his views. The point is chiefly as to how a person *may get assurance*, which he maintains (as do Luther, etc.) is not by a long experience and by our feelings, but may be got at once, and can be got certainly only, by directly looking out of ourselves to the fulness of Christ. When you have read the little tract send it back to me, and give me your opinion. It is a tract that explains the whole of what people call *Rowism* as to assurance. When you have told me what you think of that I will tell you what more to read on the subject—which is nothing else than the pure, plain Gospel.—I am, my dear Eliza, yours truly,

'ANDREW A. BONAR.'

Wednesday, Nov. 4th.—All is now arranged for regular Sabbath evening sermons once a fortnight, and for other labours here; so that now I see before me a winter that may be profitably spent in the service of God.

Monday, 23rd.—I began my monthly meeting with the Sabbath-school teachers to-night. I have been occasionally refreshed at their prayer-meeting by the simplicity of their prayers and earnestness, and they never fail to remember me when I am present. Mr. Purves has been much upon prayer lately, and he has also stirred me up more than before. Alexander Somerville has been very useful to me, and, though at present he is doubtful of remaining, yet I pray God that it may yet be ordered that he shall.

Monday, Dec. 7th.—Greatly encouraged to-night, and see it an answer to Saturday's prayer. A woman came to Mr. Purves, and he brought her to me. She has long been awakened to feel that she needed something better than this world; she has been in that state that feels its need of some better portion, but knows not yet exactly what the thing is which is required. This woman had often thought of coming, but it was my sermon yesterday which kindled her desire still more, so that she came at last. I directed her to seek Christ alone, and that would bring her out of her groping after something she felt to be necessary. My sermon was upon ' All things are now ready, come to the marriage,' and I never felt more assisted than yesterday. This woman's case, as far as I as yet understand it, is just what my own once was, until gradually I was led to Jesus. And I think I can remember that my way was just a gradual groping after the truth, but that I at length came to find most comfort in whatever spoke of the sufferings of Jesus and His love ; and thus I came at last to see Him, justification and redemption.

Wednesday, 30th.—This evening the prayer-meeting was made very useful to instruct and incite me. I saw that I was not living every hour on Christ, and I got a view of the great sinfulness of my life on this account. I felt deeply grieved at the review. Then I saw the importance of God's people being edified, as bringing glory to God, even though no sinner should be converted. Also our duty to *preach* in faith, as well as *prepare* for preaching in faith. And then that in prayer the speaker ought to try to move the heart of God and not the feelings of man, and that I should be much more fervent in private prayer. I was struck with the truth that our Christian undertakings generally flourish most at first, just because there is more simple faith while the thing is beginning, and resting on God for a blessing. A letter from Robert M'Cheyne has made me resolve to pray for a revival at Larbert and Dunipace.

1st January 1836.—Spent this morning in meditation

and prayer. Saw most strange providence leading me here, and bringing Alexander Somerville too, and so strengthening the hands of John Purves in this dark spot. To-day no less were we reminded of this, by hearing of Robert M'Cheyne's illness, he being threatened with consumption, and obliged to return home. God gives me no small blessing in permitting me to labour for Him in health, with scarcely one single pain in my body all these past years ; and He has given me, too, a field of labour and usefulness seldom bestowed on any so early, and given me gifts which many have not. Oh, may this year be more spent in drawing continually out of the Fountain of life.

Friday, 15*th.*—I have been struck at reflecting upon God laying aside M'Cheyne, who seems far more completely devoted to the work than I ; and it has taught me that free grace and special goodness must be the only reasons why I have been sent here with health and strength. It cannot be because of my gifts of grace in the least degree. I see also that in preaching I have hindered the effect by trusting to my prayers as the reason of success, which is just another form of self-confidence. I have prayed regarding my journey to Edinburgh on Monday. An old man, whom I have been visiting, encouraged me by simply saying, 'that he had experienced great blessing by the words that came from my mouth.' My going to him has been in a manner accidental, but I hope the Lord had a purpose in it.

Feb. 3*rd.*—Came home to Jedburgh yesterday. I have met with much of the kindness of the Lord. I was called to preach the Gospel in Lady Glenorchy's, St. George's, the College Church, and St. James', Leith.[1]

---

[1] Mr. Horatius Bonar was then assistant to the Rev. James Lewis of St. John's, Leith.

I had opportunity of preaching, too, to my former people on the Castle Hill, and also of preaching in the Broad Wynd, and speaking to my Sabbath scholars. Horace's people are attentive and strongly attached to him. Robert M'Cheyne remarked to me in conversation, that, perhaps, one reason why we are not favoured with a revival is, that we are not ready for it ; the ministers would not be able to direct the people in their alarms. Was humbled by finding that Robert M'Cheyne had already been honoured more than I have been to the eternal salvation of some souls. Spoke of *Jesus alone* to several of my poor people. On the Castle Hill, an old woman whom I had often seen, actually, as I came along the close, took hold of my hand and kissed it in her fervour.

Monday, *22nd.*—This evening Mr. Purves, along with Alexander Somerville and myself, met together for prayer, for ourselves and the parish.

Monday, April 18th.—Since last time, the Lord has often given me much comfort in my work. Yesterday was the Communion Sabbath here. I got up in the morning, after having desired especially to realise the Saviour as *God* speaking to us as man would do to one he loved ; I wished to lay before Him my case, especially in regard to my often having days wherein His Word is little thought of for my own profit, and seasons wherein I go forth to speak to others when very dull myself. I never before understood the ordinance so well as since I came here, through John Purves preaching upon it. I felt and prayed for a revival to my own soul, for really I seemed as thirsty ground. I remembered, too, at the Table, how that the last time I sat there was in Edinburgh, in Lady Glenorchy's, and that since that time God had sent me to this place to be a preacher of the Gospel among the people with whom

I sat. I have been meditating and writing a sermon upon the promise of the Spirit given when Christ went away, and this led me to pray for Him especially at the Lord's Table. Yet after rising from it, when I went to the Jail, I was much burdened, and much so in the evening when preaching. I was also depressed a good deal, but I have just afresh gone to the Fountain of pardon and life.

Saturday, 23rd.—On Monday evening I walked up with Alexander Somerville to Edgerston. We sang and repeated psalms by the way, and in our room we had a season of prayer together such as I seldom have enjoyed more.

Thursday, May 12th.—Expecting my brother William on a visit, and he having at last come, I have been for three days much distracted. I have now got to Selkirk, and God has this night graciously visited my soul with a feeling of joy in Himself, and with the spirit of prayer, especially for the place. The thought of some good people in it of whom I had heard, led me first to pray specially, and God drew me gradually on. I was much struck, too, by reading in the Epistle to the Colossians, how Paul 'laboured fervently in prayers ;' also, with his prayer that 'a door of utterance may be opened ;' and also with his continual thanksgiving for having been made partaker of the Gospel ; 'rooted and grounded in the faith . . . with thanksgiving.'

Friday, 13th.—Unexpectedly met at Moffat a friend and companion, Robert Johnstone, and in the evening agreed with him to have a prayer-meeting to-morrow.

Saturday 14th.—Met [him] in the evening, along with a Mr. Todd, who is going to be missionary in Greenock in [my brother] John's chapel. We three in turn offered up our supplications, and immediately after, it appeared strange to me, that those two went to the minister and brought back to me an invitation to preach to-morrow evening.

Sunday, 15*th.*—Preached on 'Behold the Lamb of God.' This was the day of the eclipse, and we had had short sermons in the forenoon. It was providential that I had that sermon ready in my memory, having preached it at Jedburgh Jail the Sabbath before. I remembered how my attention had been directed to the 'opening of a door of utterance.'

Sunday, 29*th.*—This is my birthday. At this season last year I was beginning to feel my entrance upon public duty as a preacher of the Gospel, and how wonderfully I have been led. Especially blessed be God for bringing me to Jedburgh, where my views of truth have been greatly quickened, and the necessity of preaching Christ in every sermon impressed upon me by example and by experience. If already God has so wrought, I sometimes cherish the hope that, when He has ordained me, and actually put me into the ministry, I shall be a thousandfold more useful. Since last year at this time my times of strong sorrow and vexation have been few ; I find that the constant service of Christ is the true remedy.

Wednesday, *June* 29*th.*—This is the day when last year I came out here. I spent it in thanksgiving and prayer, except when engaged in public duties. I was the more stirred up also to gratitude from hearing a full account of the happy settlement of everything concerning John's church, which is crowded, and his elders busy in the parish. I had finished too, some days ago, my father's diary, observing the way Providence led him. I may expect now some change ; for Alexander Somerville leaves us at the end of this month. I have reason to say, as in the day when I was licensed, 'Faithful is He that called me,' and again, 'I will sing unto the Lord, because He hath dealt bountifully with me.' And now this evening a new providence may be arising, for I have got a letter telling me that I am one of those nominated for Dundee, and am to preach there soon, along with Somerville and M'Cheyne.

Sunday, July 3rd.—What fears had I this time last year. Now the Lord has most graciously led me. I perceive that while seeking a revival I have been expecting and seeking it little within my own soul.

August 1st.—Preached yesterday at Dundee as candidate for St. Peter's Chapel. I think the result may be nothing at all, as all the six candidates may be set aside by the people because not chosen by them. Yet I have had opportunity of preaching Christ to them.

Saturday, 27th.—Some days since Dundee Chapel was settled ; Robert M'Cheyne chosen. I am now rejoiced at this, and think that perhaps it is a mark of God's kindness to this parish as well as to myself in giving me more leisure and more preparation. For now there is hope of a chapel at Edgerston, to which Alexander Somerville may be brought.

Sunday, Sept. 4th.—After preaching all day I felt very downcast. I think the causes were two : I had spoken rashly before sermon to a gentleman I met, and that remained in me all forenoon. But especially, I have not of late been thankful enough, nor have I prayed on behalf of God's truth regarding Christ's Coming, which John Purves has been preaching, and which is here greatly opposed by an old saint with whom I had just met.

Edinburgh, November 3rd.—In deep perplexity. Mr. Candlish [1] has offered me the situation of assistant and parochial missionary among his people, and I am much urged on every side, so that this season

[1] St. George's Church, Edinburgh.

seems to be turned into sorrow and anxiety instead of rest.

Sunday, 6th.—Had to preach for Mr. Lewis at Leith all day. Have written to John Purves telling him how I feel moved by circumstances.

Tuesday, 8th.—Got a letter from John Purves which moved me exceedingly, wherein he beyond measure dreads my going away, and I think does so very much upon the ground of the work that will be left incomplete.

Saturday, 12th.—Preached at Greenock for my brother John. The story of my subject, ' Joseph unexpectedly coming to the Cross,' led me to see how easily God could raise up instruments for Jedburgh if I left it. I feel every way drawn to come to St. George's, yet on account of John Purves, I can decide nothing till I have seen him. Acts xx. 22 was upon my mind, and the context led me to see that it may be right to leave a people, even though much trouble was coming in afterward, and the work appeared to be stopped and broken off.

Wednesday, 16th.—I have come again to Jedburgh, and am now in the very depths of perplexity. As to leaving things undone here, I believe that God sent me only to commence, and that other instruments will be raised up whenever the people are come to trust only in God. I perceive that many deep impressions may be left by my departure upon the very people from among whom I have gone. Then I am moved to come to Edinburgh by the providential aspect which things seem to me to bear. The district is most needy and destitute. The place is my native town, and full of irreligion, full of lukewarmness also, which thing, it seems to me, God might make me useful in testifying against. Also, my intercourse with Mr. Candlish would be perhaps useful in many things ; and my preaching to his people gives such large opportunity of usefulness among the intellectual classes, and among many of my old school-fellows, who are anxious for my coming.   I feel that I might help in the study of prophecy, especially if Horace goes away.   I feel that if John Purves were to advise my going, I would be quite satisfied, and believe it the leading of Providence.

Friday, 18th.—I have now written to Edinburgh accepting the invitation to come there, and I have been somewhat confirmed that I am right by coming upon Jer. xxxiii. 3 : 'Call unto me,' etc.   And being led to much prayer in the evening of yesterday, the chapter read in family worship was John xiv. 1 : 'Let not your heart be troubled.'   And further still, while in Edinburgh I had got a book, *Elijah the Tishbite*,[1] which James accidentally mentioned in the letter in which he told me of this new situation, and which John praised very much.   In this book I find two chapters most exactly suited to me, respecting the state of perplexity in which God sometimes leaves His servants, in order to make them feel better at other times the blessedness of God taking His own will and way with them.

Wednesday, 23rd.—Resolved this forenoon to spend my time in prayer and thanksgiving and reviewing all my life in this place.   My last Sabbath is fixed to be the 18th of December.   I lament the sins of coldness and earthliness ; wandering in prayer ; seeking to benefit others without being benefited myself ; something of discontent at little annoyances ; chagrin and envy ; opportunities lost ; sick persons ill-advised ; my class of young people too little taught Christ ; and in all my preaching very inadequate setting forth of Christ and the Spirit I have reason to give thanks especially for wonderful

[1] By F. W. Krummacher, D.D.   London, 1836.

ease in committing and preaching my sermons ; the great opening for usefulness here ; the favour in sight of man given me ; the hope of having done good to a few immortal souls, though I do not know even one that I can say I have altogether awakened. The Lord has been teaching me to be glad at the opportunity of ministering to the refreshment of saints, and this has been my chief joy here, along with hopes of setting the truth forth before some others, so as to have excited their desires for salvation. I have hope also of some that were in prison. I have been taught also to be content with sharing in the work of saving souls with others, and not to seek the whole honour to myself. And this very great lesson I have so far learned, that God alone, in the absence of friends, with none to sympathize, can be the joy and portion of my soul. Another experience I have found is this, joy beyond all others and beyond all other times in meeting for prayer and thanksgiving.

Saturday, 26th.—I have been much comforted by a letter from my mother yesterday. She says in it : 'That day I got your letter informing me of your resolution to come in [to Edinburgh] I have been earnest in prayer for you, that, if it were the Lord's will that you should leave your present situation, He would show you the path of duty and take you by the hand and lead you in the way He designed for you. Indeed from the time your removal was spoken of I never left a throne of grace without seeking this for you, nor durst I ask in any one way, but only that the Lord would lead and guide.'

Sunday, 27th.—Heard of the death of [my cousin] John Bonar of Ratho, after a few days' illness. It has made a great sensation in the town among his acquaintances.

Thursday, Dec. 8th.—Last night had a very encouraging letter from Horace, who among other things tells me that since their Wednesday evening prayer-meeting began Mr. Moody [1] has had some persons under conviction every week. I got an invitation to preach at Dundee as candidate for an assistantship, but have refused.

Wednesday, 14*th.*—Last night, in concluding my weekly class, I felt real trembling lest I should not speak as I ought to their souls. Many have been greatly affected, and I think I see the answer to the special prayer which I so frequently beforehand offered for them, asking the power of the Spirit. That morning I had received a ring from the families attending the class, accompanied by a kind letter. I really felt that night penetrated with deep concern for their souls. Heard several proofs of the concern, and anxiety, and love of the young people.

Friday, 16*th.*—Meet everywhere with strange kindness from the people.

Saturday, 17*th.*—Taking leave of the sick persons. Have great hope of the gipsy family, Douglas. Spent a while among them speaking of Jesus, and they stood round in great attention.

Sunday, 18*th.*—Rose early and engaged in prayer till breakfast. Felt a sensible assistance of the Spirit in the prison while preaching. Preached in the evening upon Song ii. 16, 17 with great ease to a very numerous congregation, and afterwards, by the particular invitation of the Sunday-school teachers and a few others, held a prayer-meeting for the purpose of commending me to God and the word of His grace. Each prayed in turn, very happy; and in concluding I asked them to pray that I might have the disposition to ' pray always for them.' I left them with deep regret ; some scarce refrained from

[1] Rev. Alex. Moody-Stuart, D.D., of Free St. Luke's, Edinburgh.

tears. It is strange how God is giving me proofs of
their love ; and, though to-morrow I have to attend a
meeting held in express purpose to present me with a
Bible and to bid me farewell, yet God has taken away
my fears, giving me very deep interest in the eternal
salvation of all. The greater my love to their souls
becomes, the less I fear anything.

Monday, 19*th*.—Felt last night and this morning many
fears lest in Edinburgh I should grow weak and cold, or
be led by reputation. The prayers of last night will be
a witness against me if I yield to self-gratification, or
seek my own advantage, or become cold. John Purves
alluded to me in family prayer this morning, asking
communion for us in heaven all together. After I got
time for thanksgiving I was helped to pray several times
through the day for the people with much earnestness.
I was much surprised to find some of the people of
whom I had thought little moved even to tears as I took
farewell. In the evening meeting as appointed, Mr.
Elliott presented the Bible in a very feeling speech,
declaring their respect and love. I was enabled to
speak without faltering in a very subdued voice. The
boys of my class presented me with a small Bible and
pencil. They too have shown great interest and concern.
And now I feel deeper sorrow than ever because I am
about to leave them.

Tuesday, 20*th*.—Learned to-day that not only in our
meeting upon Sabbath night, but also through the week,
my departure has been a subject about which they have
prayed. Hence, no doubt, my great help in all I have
undertaken through these last weeks. And a special
object of their prayers has been that the seed sown may
spring up into fruit ere long. The attention and concern of the people is very encouraging, because though
it be not itself conversion, yet it is a token for good. I

have felt this day far more intense sorrow than ever before. The Provost and Magistrates presented me with a purse of sovereigns, and the Provost gave me thanks most cordially.

Edinburgh, Friday, 23rd.—Visited the District School which I am to be connected with. Proposed a plan of having sermon upon Sabbath evening. Have begun regular visiting upon Tuesday. Altogether I have felt of late somewhat as I suppose *death* would make me feel in parting from friends ; and often have I rejoiced in hope of our gathering together in Christ for ever.

Monday, 26th.—For some days it seemed as if I had passed through a sort of death in coming away. To-day I began to visit in Rose Street. If the Lord has brought me here He must have some work for me to do. I feel loosened from the earth, and longing for Christ's appearing.

Wednesday, 28th.— I had been praying that God would be pleased in this place also, as in Jedburgh, to open up usefulness to me, and not throw me aside as one in whom He had no pleasure, when, just as I was still thinking over the matter, a message came to me asking me to preach that evening. I considered this an intimation from the Lord to wait patiently, and He would find me enough to do.

Thursday, 29th.—Being still in some measure very depressed, was cheered by conversing with Horace about his people, and hearing how an opening there had come most unexpectedly. I remembered, too, how gradually the Lord dealt with me at Jedburgh. Also by finding some of the young people at William Street quite willing to come to me when I spoke of catechising them before sermon every evening I could be there. Still more to be noticed, that I have had as yet unceasing desire after the people of Jedburgh, and a spirit of prayerfulness for them, so that once or twice I could do nothing but go alone and weep over them and pray. Now that seems an answer to that part of our prayer-meeting on the last Sabbath, whereon I asked them to request this spirit to be given to me. And, if God has answered me thus far, He will answer the rest of their prayers for me, regarding opening up usefulness. Meanwhile, it is perhaps His design to keep me specially praying for the seed sown in Jedburgh, and to wait with patience here as a trial of faith.

Saturday, 31*st*.—Certainly I have reason to bless and wonder at the Lord's goodness this past year, for He gave me favour in sight of the people of Jedburgh to an extent unusual, and gave me what is far better, usefulness there too, to a great extent. He has brought me to care far less than ever in my life about temporal enjoyments, if only I may be an instrument of saving souls. And He has promoted the cause of Christ's Coming by my means, and made me long for it myself; and now He has, by a strange providence, called me home to Edinburgh, where I know not what is to be done. I am leaving myself entirely in His hand at His will and pleasure, believing that He is leading me to some new view of Himself and His ways of providence.

Wednesday, 4*th Jan.* 1837.—Have glanced now and then at what God may have sent me to do, but as yet no opening. There are two great lessons to me at present: willing to be nothing, if God so please, and prayer for the past opportunities being blessed. I feel as if God had put me now for a time in a lower place of His vineyard, [with] less work.

Thursday, 5*th*.—Hope of seeing some Jews in the town. Began prayer-meeting in the evening with John Thomson [1] and Laughton.

---

[1] His class-fellow at the High School, and afterwards minister of Mariners' Church, Leith.

Saturday, 7th. — No prospect yet of any regular preaching on Sabbath, but this new situation just calls the more for faith. Alexander Somerville is now in a very busy and useful situation, and Robert M'Cheyne also, and Horace too, and John Thomson. Will the Lord not remember me yet? I am permitted to enjoy the Communion season at Lady Glenorchy's to-morrow.

Sunday, 8th.—This morning, after much prayer, I was led to see that my present unhappiness rose from my unwillingness to be humbled and be nothing. I desire now just to enjoy Christ as my Lord and my Friend, and let Him send me among men, or keep me unknown and unoccupied, as He pleases. What I imagined to be openings at a distance are now all closed up; but it may be darkness to make the light more precious. It is my delight at present to read Rutherford's *Letters*, where they speak of his being laid aside from preaching.

Thursday, 12th.—Led to reflect much upon the fact that our place in Christ's kingdom will be determined by our progress in holiness personally, as much as by the efforts we have used for converting men to Jesus. I was considering, too, that my having little preaching was equivalent to God restraining me from work by sickness, or any cause like that. Now I would have been satisfied had the cause seemed inevitable; why not also now?

Tuesday, 24th.—Spent a happy and prayerful season at Larbert with Alexander Somerville. We talked over all God's dealings with us, and prayed much for our former people and present situations. I feel resolved, in the strength of God, just to look at each day's work and seek to do it in God's might, whether it be small or great. This day I have been, more than ever yet, received with kindness in my visiting, and have seen a door of usefulness opened in this part of the district.

Also to-day the proposal came for Horace to go as candidate to Dunnichen. All this is in answer to our prayers, and because going forth in simple faith.

Monday, 30th.—God has at last opened two preachings for me, one on Saturday night, another on Sabbath night, in the Tontine. God is surely bidding me go forward and wait patiently.

Saturday, Feb. 18th.—Ever since I was led to rest in God's will I have been happy, and things have gone on more hopefully, and now Horace is to-day gone to Kelso to preach, and I am asked to go to Cardross. The Lord has most remarkably kept me from wearying of waiting upon Himself in regard to this matter, for I cannot tell what joy I had, even at the thought of hearing by Horace, who is to visit Jedburgh, about all that is there. I mean this day to pray much regarding Cardross, to be directed as to it. I have been led to complete satisfaction as to my present opportunities here, by the thought of God perhaps intending to bless more abundantly a few than a great many. If at any meeting, where only twelve were present, God in true grace were to send His Spirit upon all, this surely is giving greater usefulness than merely letting us preach to hundreds. And at night a letter from Robert M'Cheyne came in, wherein this is excellently stated, and deeply impressed me, and set me upon prayer far more for the parish, and Mr. Candlish, and my opportunities through the week.

Friday, March 3rd.—Dr. Jones died this morning. All we can suffer here will soon be so ended too, and the bosom of Christ is rest.

Saturday, 18th.—This day is just three months since I left Jedburgh, and I have been reading something more of *Elijah the Tishbite* sent from Horeb. While reading this I was struck with the thought suggested that God is honoured by our believing in Him amidst darkness. I had really a happy forenoon to-day in meditating upon the things of eternity and God's grace. And lately I have seen several Jedburgh people, and had a visit of one to-day.

Monday, 27th.—Last Monday, after spending the morning in thanksgiving and prayer for Jedburgh and Mr. Purves, and Alexander Somerville, and others, I enjoyed uncommon help and comfort through the day. On Saturday last I read an essay to the Missionary Association [1] regarding the duty of giving the first place in missionary labours to the Jews, which was received with great attention, and seemed to convince all present, so that they wished it to be printed. I think that God has brought me here, among other, things, for the sake of drawing attention to the Jews, and being able to do something for them.

April 3rd.—Much more peace and serenity of life. I feel that God can make a man useful in any circumstances when he least thinks it. I remember one day lately when under very deep despondency and unwillingness to go forth, the text '*all souls are mine*' came powerfully to my soul, and instantly Satan's snare seemed to break. I was quite happy.

Tuesday, 11th.—The Committee of the Jewish Society have made me acting secretary to them. God may be thus using me for some of His purposes as to His beloved people.

Tuesday, 18th—I had read yesterday that God,

---

[1] This Association was connected with the University and met every Saturday for prayer. From twelve to twenty students were members, and they used to go out to visit by twos. Mr. Robert Johnstone, missionary in India, traced his conversion to this society. He read a notice of its meetings, went to them, and there heard men whom he had known as students only, praying and taking part. He was greatly impressed, and soon after led to decision for Christ.

in the case of Israel, had shown that we must think
nothing comes from self. I have been taught this by
the extraordinary difference in the manner in which the
people here receive me from what was the case in the
country. Also, I learned to-day that there is something
in my manner, both in private and public, which does
not commend itself, but rather gives the idea of feebleness. And then Cardross vexes me, for I am asked to
go again. And in the daily work of the parish I see
indifference everywhere. I heard that my sermon to
the hostlers last Sabbath upon the conversion of Paul
has been felt very much by some.

Wednesday, 19th.—Have been with Mr. C., at whose
house twelve of us were present to see how the Passover is kept by the Jews. Very illustrative of the
Scripture. I felt something of the reality of the twelve
disciples sitting down with Christ. Prayed and rejoiced
in hope that something was doing here for the Jews. I
think the cause of the Jews is one reason of my having
been brought from Jedburgh here.

Sunday, 30th.—Felt a strange and sad joy in reading
of Philip sent to the desert to preach there to one man,
though he had been in a populous town before.

Thursday, May 4th, Fast-Day.—Have seen of late
my very obscure way of stating grand truths ; my want
of holiness of heart ; my restraining of prayer. Holiness
is the great secret of a full way of preaching. God has
been teaching me to be contented with His will, and
patient under it ; but I have not yet come to live in
the continual dependence for joy on the light of His
countenance.

Sabbath, 7th.—I go this day to St. George's to
receive Christ, not to speak of Him or do anything for
Him. And I find that simply to receive Him and wait
upon Him is as difficult a matter as to speak of Him

aright. I was greatly impressed with thinking that I have spiritual *weariness*, but not spiritual *hunger*. I do not feel a constant craving after Christ, nor am I so hungry that the same simple fare will always satisfy me.

Friday, 12*th.*—I have this week felt more of communion with Christ than at any time I remember during common days.

Saturday, 27*th.*—I have come out on a visit to Jedburgh again. I seem to feel this evening, in the quiet of the country and beautiful verdure of all things, how refreshing the day of removal into the peace of heaven. Coming on old friends is just suited to remind me of our meeting together at Christ's Coming again, just as at my departure I remember how much I was reminded of death.

Sunday, 28*th.*—Felt strange and rather confused at first. Preached on ' David's last words,' as full of Christ. Then in the evening in the Castle. Never felt less weariness on a Sabbath day.

Edinburgh, Saturday, June 17*th.*—Since I came home my visiting has been every day more encouraging and more pleasant. I am better acquainted with all the people.

Saturday, 24*th.*—Horace heard last night more about Kelso, and it seems now settled that he will go.

Saturday, July 1*st.*—Conversation with a Jew, Joseph Leo.

Sunday, 2*nd.*—This day two years [ago] began to preach at Jedburgh. Horace's millenarian views are likely to keep him from Kelso.

Friday, 7*th.*—Began this evening to instruct the Jew, who seems really anxious to know.

Sunday, 16*th.*—Praying for Horace in regard to Kelso, that his testimony to Christ's Coming again may be honoured of God.

Thursday, 27th. — Mr. Moody's ordination. Very solemn, and especially I felt it so because of the prayer-meeting the night before, during which, in praying for him that the Spirit might come down from the opening heavens and descend to baptize him anew, I had felt the evident presence of the Holy Spirit. After it was done I returned in great depression, having been reminded by some of the remarks that personal progress in religious ways is essential to a minister, and feeling that I have made no progress lately, I felt all afternoon filled with sadness at this and at my past useless year.

Wednesday, Aug. 9th.—Letter from Robert M'Cheyne told me of some souls awakened under his ministry. Heard of efforts making for me for Baldernock, and Kelso is now likely to be settled in favour of Horace.

Saturday, Sept. 9th.—Heard yesterday about John's marriage with Isabella Watt. This may introduce a new train of events in our family circle. To-day and last night greatly cast down by the circumstance of my being kept out of several appointments on account of my millenarianism chiefly. I had prayed about the matter in the full conviction that bearing testimony to this and other truths was the way of duty.

Tuesday, 12th.—Unexpectedly led to a journey to the West and then to England.

Wednesday, 13th.—Much refreshed by thinking upon 'Who shall separate us from the love of Christ?' for no distraction in my journey will ever keep me from being an object of Christ's love and care. Even if I should grow cold He will love me so that He will revive me, and not turn away and leave me alone.

Saturday, 23rd.—Liverpool. We this morning got into the synagogue, where I got opportunity of leaving a Jewish tract.

Saturday, 30th.—Home. At York I heard by letter

that to-morrow I was to preach as candidate for Newhaven.   To-day heard that Alexander Somerville was
chosen for Anderston [Glasgow], and had some conversation with him.   God deals according to His own will.
I feel no decided wish as to Newhaven, for I do not
understand the people nor the situation, but Christ our
Captain apparently is determined to take away my pride
and leave me to be nothing but His servant.

Friday, Oct. 27th.—Felt this night deep sorrow at
being so completely bustled with outward labours.   I
think that we are to be content to labour little comparatively, if we cannot water all that with abundant
prayers.   Better do a little with prayer, and in the Spirit.
I must seek for this day to live more every hour in
communion with Christ ; never to be hasty or vain in
my conversation ; oftener be alone with God ; pray
more for conversions.

Tuesday Morning.—Got a note telling me that Mr.
Fairbairn [1] was chosen for Newhaven.   I was more discon-
solate than I expected.   I believe that Christ desires
to subdue in me the disposition of the sons of Zebedee,
for I have often greatly wished and expected to be
honoured in the Church.   Now I feel that I am not
cared for, and in St. George's I am counted heavy and
lifeless.   I think Christ is casting me more upon His
simple power and favour.

Saturday, Nov. 25th.—God has placed me a step lower
in the esteem of men by this delay.   I am now more
drawn back from the eyes of men.   I felt this much at
first, but now I am content to be meanest of all and
servant of all.   It is remarkable that this week and last
I have been better able than before to persuade the poor
and careless people in Rose Street to come out.

---

[1] Rev. James Fairbairn, D.D., minister of Newhaven from 1838 till
the Disruption, and afterwards minister of the Free Church there.

Sunday, Dec. 3rd.—Last Thursday God permitted me
to see Horace ordained at Kelso. At the moment of
laying on of hands I felt a strange thrill of solemnity
and love towards him. The prayer was most excellent;
I think the Lord was there.

Monday, 11*th.*—Meeting last night much encouraged
me ; many men and two Jews, one lately come, Louis
Königsberg. The death of Dr. Gibson, of Leith, with
whom I used to teach a Sabbath School, just the day
that Horace was ordained, and the death of Patrick
Borrowman's father so soon after Patrick was ordained,[1]
struck me much as showing God's providence ruling
as He will, and by affliction making men turn to lean
upon Himself alone.

Wednesday, 20*th.*—I have been considering these
two last days the Lord's dealings with me, for it was
exactly the 18th of this month last year that I came
into town, and upon the 19th called upon Mr. Candlish
to begin work. In looking back, I regard nothing of
my sore perplexity and trouble ; they have taught me
much and led me near to God. Now my work in Rose
Street is prospering much. A hundred and twenty
attentive souls on Sunday evening at the meeting, and
some cases wherein the Lord appears to be blessing my
labour.

Saturday, 23*rd.*—More and more convinced, by the
very want of it, that the way to be successful is to be
within the sanctuary with God, and then come out to
the people.

Saturday, 30*th.*—Have been writing for to-morrow,
' They drank of the Rock that followed them.' Christ
has followed me and brought me to deeper calmness
than I ever enjoyed before, and from Robert M'Cheyne's
conversation and preaching I observe the power God

---

[1] The Rev. Patrick Borrowman of Glencairn.

gives to strong faith. What change another year may bring I cannot tell. M'Cheyne says that he and some of the elders of Chapelshade in Dundee intend to ask me to preach quietly there. My removal to Edinburgh has taught me very much, and God has blessed me.

Monday, 1st January 1838.—Yesterday was a happy day throughout ; near to Christ and seemed to get answer from Him all the day.

Wednesday, 24th.—God has brought me back from Kelso and Jedburgh. I heard at Kelso of a work beginning ; two or three have already come to Horace in deep anxiety, chiefly people that seemed to know the truth. At Jedburgh heard of some young people who have died in the Lord. Found at home a letter from M'Cheyne wherein he tells me that had Mr. Reid removed from Chapelshade, it was astonishing how many of the people who had never heard me were desiring me to come as his successor. And yet again God has set me by. He accounts that the reason may be either to reserve me for some honourable place in His cause afterwards, or He is to remove me to praise Himself above. Horace and I had two happy evenings of prayer together for each other. At present God is sending me back to my town labour without a word of explanation as to the matter and very little success at present.

Friday, Feb. 2nd.—Had a letter from Mr. Wodrow [1] in Glasgow telling me that he was to present a memorial to the Presbytery about the Jews next Wednesday, and requesting the prayers of all the friends of Israel here for that object.

Monday, 12th.—There seems to be now really interest excited among some of the ministers for the Jews. I

---

[1] Mr. Wodrow was one of the deputation appointed to go on the mission of inquiry to the Jews a year later, but was unable to go on account of illness.

regard this as a direct and memorable answer to prayer, and all the more that I have had no direct hand in the matter.

Tuesday, 13*th.*—Visiting the girl Elizabeth Mackenzie, who has been in depression of mind arising from having fallen back after knowing the truth, I was glad to witness an instance of the power of the truth to clear the mind. She had said to me when I went in that she was better now and more able to believe that Christ would still receive her. When I began to speak of Christ directly as source of joy, she said that she thought she had been trusting too much for comfort to her evidences. I then read part of 1 John ii. 1, 2, dwelling much upon our being sinners even after coming to Christ, and that our comfort came from knowing our justification complete, not from our holiness. While conversing about this she said, ' Oh, I see now, I see it ! I have been looking much into myself.' Afterwards she again said the like, and two or three times repeated ' I see it, I see it ! I should always look to Christ.' She then remarked that she had often found great joy while hearing Christ preached, but it went away. I showed her that this was because all the time of hearing she had been thinking of *Christ*, and not of herself. Again she said, ' I see it now,' and there was great peace upon her countenance and a smile of joy. I never before really understood how fully the Gospel is ' glad tidings of great joy.'

Sunday, 25*th.*—Heard yesterday more news about what the Glasgow Society mean to do for the Jews. Now there is hope of getting our cause brought forward here and in several other places, and even expectation that the General Assembly this very year may be brought to take it up.

Monday, March 5*th.*—Resolved to pray three times every day this week for the following things :—revival in our prayer-meeting, and that my heart may be knit together with the person praying. Reading of Scripture more profitable to me. Opening and enlarging to Mr. Candlish, Moody, and John Thomson, in regard to those things they seem to me especially to need. Myself to get nearer to God in common prayer. Higher tone in family, and in family-prayer. Greater union of heart. Blessing upon reading the Scripture to others, and if God see good, that I may hear of some conversions by this means. More of the Holy Ghost to me and to my sphere of labour, and the town. That my occasional preaching may be blessed ; be nails fastening something in a sure place.

Saturday, 10*th.*—The Lord through the week has shown me much favour. Many of my special prayers begin to be answered. The Scripture has been much more profitable to me this week. In the case of all the persons I prayed for, in regard to enlarging of soul, I have seen something that seems cheering.

Sunday, 11*th.*—I have seen now that my object in asking to be means of conversion to souls has been very much to have glory to myself ; but God has been showing me that in that work *Himself* is the only true agent, so that if I desire this work I never can have glory at all, just being an instrument to give a blessing.

Monday, 19*th.*—At Dundee, for Robert M‘Cheyne, who has not been very well. Most unexpectedly. Greatly helped, three times in the day. Before each service Robert came into the study, and we prayed together, and then went forth. I learned much from him, especially and chiefly from his *recollectedness* of soul and nearness of communion with God. The attention of his people is remarkable, standing up, sometimes, in their eagerness.

Tuesday, 27*th.*—Preached in Glasgow for Mr. Duncan

and Alexander Somerville. Had a large prayer-meeting
in Mr. Wodrow's house on Monday evening for the
Jews. The kindness and respect of people towards
me struck me much as a doing of the Lord. I think
there is some work of God in Somerville's congregation.
Learned much.

Saturday, 31*st*.—Heard of a school in Bombay where,
by assistance from our societies, 200 Jewish children
were taught by Dr. Wilson.

Saturday, April 7th.—Visited to-day by Mr. Nairne
of Dunsinnane, wishing to get me as assistant and
successor to Collace, near Perth.

Bandirran, Perthshire, Saturday, 21*st*.—Staying with
Mr. Nairne. Came yesterday. This forenoon alone;
felt nearness to God. Providence seems to have led
me, for a letter inviting me to Glasgow, as well as the
one to Dundee, have both been anticipated by this
unexpected call. Unexpected leadings of Providence
are just in accordance with my past life.

Monday, 23*rd*.—Yesterday all well. Ministers have
been most cordial. Dr. Thomson from Perth and Mr.
Mellis [of Tealing] present. Preached upon Rev. xiv.
1-3; Micah vi. 8, and read the 21st chapter of John.
This forenoon the meeting of the people was held.
I remained at home, praying. God made the meeting
very harmonious.

Tuesday, 24*th*.—Returned home. Found all things
well. I must wait the result with patience. I rejoice that
Robert M'Cheyne has been an instrument in this matter.

Thursday, May 17*th*.—Had a very full meeting to-night
to pray for the Jews. Myself and Mr. Wodrow officiated
Prayed for the General Assembly in the matter.

Friday, 18*th*.—Found unexpectedly that the Jewish
cause is to be brought forward to-morrow in the
Assembly. A few of us agreed to meet in the evening

for prayer. Accordingly we met—Mr. Wodrow and his wife, Alexander Somerville, Jonathan Anderson, and some of our family. Talked over God's most wonderful ways. Agreed also specially to remember the subject in our prayers to-morrow.

Saturday. 19th.—Prayed much in the morning for Israel. Saw in God's past doings, in regard to their cause among us, a most special answer to prayer, and encouragement to go forward, and remembered the promise, ' Blessed is he that blesseth thee.' So many ministers and people seem interested all at once. Went to the Assembly. It was the last part of their business, and was carried with much unanimity that a committee be appointed. Praise, praise! I hope now it will be said of us, ' Rejoice ye with Jerusalem ; ' our Church will be blessed in the joy of Zion. I look upon this as given for encouragement to pray for anything according to His will in the name of Christ, and as another token making us hope for revival among ourselves, and more blessing upon our missions. May God help me, and the rest who prayed with us, to be as earnest in thanksgiving to-night and hereafter.

Monday, 28th.—On Saturday the Committee for the Jews was appointed. At the sermon last night was collected £61.

June 8th.—Bridget Bonar (my cousin) died this forenoon, after an illness of four days, very happy, after seeing that nothing but clear, simple faith was needful. I saw her twice in her illness, and spoke to her once upon ' accepted in the Beloved,' and then, ' My peace I give to you.' She asked for me when she felt herself so ill, her brother not being come.

Tuesday, 12th.—Have been much at a loss by hearing that my uncle's application for Glammis is likely to succeed at the very time that I have got the presenta-

tion to Collace. If I had to write my letter of acceptance
before hearing anything of the other place, I would not
hesitate a moment to bind myself up to Collace, for I
think Providence has led me to it, and the people in the
parish and around have been led to expect and wish
for me.   I feel somewhat, as in the case of coming to
Edinburgh from Jedburgh, that the fear of displeas-
ing my uncle is the only very strong argument in
favour of Glammis.   I have heard many things about
Collace which seem to make it a likely field of usefulness, and a field which the Lord will bless ; and my
impression is that there the Lord might pour out His
Spirit.   Whereas, I have not one such feeling about
the other place.   It seems to me that if I choose it, it
will be choosing earthly comforts at the loss of spiritual
blessing.

Tuesday, *19th.*—God seems so to arrange this matter
that my uncle's heart is turned thus far, that he is quite
satisfied with my resolution.

Thursday, *21st.*—Coming in this afternoon, after
being busy all day, was told that the matter was settled,
Glammis being given away.   Thus I am at perfect
liberty, and have set my face to seek the Lord more
earnestly than ever.

Saturday, *23rd.*—God has been teaching me that the
most effectual way of seeing the evil of sin is in the
face of Christ.

Wednesday, *July* *18th.*—John's marriage [yesterday].
All went on easily and calmly, very pleasant and happy.
The secret of true and complete composure is just feeling
God behind all things going on.   At the same time
God Himself must be the fulness of everything.

Sunday, *22nd.*—Led to pray yesterday very much for
the Holy Ghost, and to pray for Him to be poured
upon Collace.   In the morning was specially impressed

with the awful fact that by losing one hour of prayer every day by not rising early, I lost twenty days of prayer in the course of a year. Enabled also to pray much for my poor people in Edinburgh.

Tuesday, 24th.—Led to see how much God had blessed me through means of my firm hold of the doctrine of Christ's Second Coming. I see it in regard to the situation chosen for me ; the manner it has acted upon my studies ; the necessity of seeking only God's glory. Mr. Cunningham [1] has been taken very ill of typhus fever, which began just the day after John's marriage.

Friday, August 3rd.—Mr. Cunningham's case has excited great sympathy, much prayer. Psalm i. 3 again occurred to me, keeping up our first love. This seems to me what Robert M'Cheyne is eminent for. On Tuesday last my people in Rose Street and William Street presented me with a Bible. The meeting was held in Young Street schoolroom, and after prayer by Mr. Moody, Mr. Candlish presented the book in a speech of great kindness. After I had replied, he prayed. I feel the blessedness of thus being sent away with prayer on all sides. It is remarkable that, just as when going to Jedburgh John Patterson's death took place, so now this illness of another friend is sent to make me gird up my loins. It seems, too, so plain that God has completed some purpose with me in Edinburgh, for as at first I was discouraged, so now I feel it all full of hope, full of interest. I intend to spend this forenoon in prayer and preparation for preaching at Collace, which I do by appointment of Presbytery, next Sabbath.

Collace, Saturday, 4th.—In the evening went to see Dunsinnane, where I am to stay when settled.

---

[1] Afterwards Principal Cunningham of New College, Edinburgh.

Sunday, 5*th.*—Much helped. Thought and prayed for Joseph Leo, the Jew, who is to be baptized to-day in St. George's.

Tuesday, 14*th.*—Much helped on Sabbath. Found that God removes difficulties most wonderfully. These two occasions have taught me to give up the use even of my notes in the pulpit. I am free, then, and my manner more animated. Find also in conversation that some of us who are so much together are considered by ministers as making a new school of preaching. The call is to be moderated on Wednesday.

Friday, 17*th.*—Felt that in the sanctuary we should stand to speak with deep horror of sin in our souls, and zeal for God like Elijah. Being at Kelso for a few days, much rejoiced that Horace has proposed to pray together every evening before going to service. This was a thought that I had prayed concerning, that it might be brought about. Heard from Perth. Everything went on well at Collace.

' I ceased not to warn every one night and day with tears.'—*Acts* xx. 31.

CHAPTER III

Collace

1838-1856

Wednesday, 5th Sept. 1838.—Got through all my trial
discourses at Perth last week, and the 20th is fixed for
my ordination. I look forward to that day now as a day
whereon I shall receive both grace and apostleship.
To-day I fast and pray, and am to be present at the
ordination of Robert Johnstone for India. I feel the
exceeding love of the Spirit in praying with me, when
my thoughts change so quickly to common things, and
leave off the things of God.

Wednesday, 12th.—In the evening with Mr. Moody.
Talked over ordination. He suggested this to me, that
being ordained over that people in particular, I might
expect to be blessed chiefly to that people. I have been
thinking of the case of Moses. He trembled and resisted
before being sent, but from the moment that he was
chosen we never hear of alarm or fear arising. The hand
of God was with him. I observe that it is the ministers
who are engaged in setting one apart that are especially
to give themselves to 'fasting and prayer.' I consider
that the laying-on of hands is a sort of relic of the gifts
of the Holy Ghost in the primitive church; it does as
really convey grace as their hands laid on any one gave
the gifts of the Spirit. *Veni, Creator Spiritus!* Mr.
Moody prayed that even beforehand I might be receiving
much, that the vessel might be enlarged to take in very
much more grace than usual.

Wednesday Night, 19th.—I tremble at Christ's word
to the seven churches. May I be enabled to lean over
the well of Jacob every morning and evening to draw
water.

Collace, Thursday, 20th.—I have been a good deal
exercised in seeking and wishing to possess, but tremble
lest I have not, faith to expect that my ordination will
be so blessed that there will be a change in me such as
in the disciples after Pentecost, and in Moses, after the
call was really received. This morning, so soon as I
awoke, which was early, I read over the confession of
sins for ministers and preachers, drawn up by the
Assembly in 1661, applying it to myself. Psalm li.
seemed to me very suitable, also Psalm xxvi. 7, 8. Both
express zeal for God's glory, and also that the minister
should wash in the blood of Christ before going to
proclaim with voice of thanksgiving God's salvation
for men. I remembered too, that as Christ after His
baptism was tempted, so Satan would be watching me.
I thought over 'to me, who am less than the least of all
saints,' etc. I wished for deeper views of my sinfulness
in its length and breadth, that I might feel as Paul, and
go to present myself just as an empty vessel which the
Lord is to fill. O that I felt really disinterested zeal for
God's glory, for this seems to me even more difficult to
attain than the other, love to Christ and desire of saving
souls. May I ever feel complete victory over that shame
which is ready to come upon us when we are with the
world and the world cannot see nor know this thing.
May 'another heart be given me.' I wished much that
I had been alone instead of being at Bandirran, but,
nevertheless, I feel comparatively little distraction, and
have got good from conversing with Mr. Mellis of
Tealing on the subject, and with my brother Horace,
who is here also. I pray that I may receive the spirit

of love, affection for the people, and anxiety about the old minister's soul, and may I receive this at ordination. O that Isaiah xi. 1-9 may be fulfilled to me, that I may be like Christ, daily His witness, His Spirit of wisdom and understanding teaching me the Scriptures. I shall look back often upon this day, but always to the great Author of the blessing, the Giver of it. Walking through the wood that led to the church of Collace over the hill, I mentioned that I had been struck with the expression this morning, ' Ye shall receive power,' etc. My brother Horace called my attention to the frequency with which Whitefield mentions his *preaching in power*, as his own feeling, apart from its effects upon the people. My brother John's letter was very useful to me, in the way of strengthening and confirming. ' Ordination is not a sacrament, but the fact of being set apart contains a pledge of grace on the part of God, just as a sacrament does.'

Evening.—The ordination sermon was upon Isaiah liii. 3-5. Mr. Findlay of Perth preached, and all the while I was happy and composed. But his prayer, as he came down to lay his own hands and the brethren's upon my head, struck me as specially directed by the Holy Ghost. He asked Isaiah xi. 2-4, the very thing I had myself sought. While their hands lay upon me, and the words of prayer ascended, I felt like one for whom very strong intercession was going up to God to the very highest heavens, and in great calmness and strong desire I gave myself to God my Saviour, and expected henceforth His promised Spirit. I rejoice that many of my dear friends were present, mother and sisters and brothers ; and among the ministers present were Robert M'Cheyne, Robert Macdonald,[1]

---

[1] Minister at Blairgowrie, then at Leith, who died in Edinburgh on the 21st of August 1893.

Mr. Candlish, Frank Gillies,[1] James Lewis, as well as my own brothers. O may I have true grace and apostleship from this hour. I felt affection to my own friends and family increased when I saw them present. The people were very cordial in their welcome at the door of the church. I thought of the prayers that my people at Jedburgh, and our family, and Alexander Somerville, and John Thomson at Leith, were to offer for me this evening, and also others in other places. If I have so little grace, notwithstanding all these prayers and this ordinance, O how deep must be my corruption, and the devil's temptations how strong, and the world how deep within me! And O what should I have been this year without the benefit of these prayers of other saints! This one consideration humbles me very low.

Saturday, 22nd.—Yesterday was like a blank day, through my being unusually in company, and also busy at my house, seeing it arranged, that I may get in next week. O that my heart were filled with grace and love and clear truth! It would then overflow upon souls in common conversation. I do feel a real joy in looking forward to the rest remaining for God's people, and I think I could leap for joy if, instead of my ordination, I were receiving from God the assurance that my labours were to end in a few days, and I to be with Christ! If there really be such joy in the hope of bringing a few souls in a parish to Him, oh, what will be the joy of His appearing and His kingdom, when all things are under Him, and we are in His bosom and in His joy! I have been drawing encouragement as to after success from Exod. xxxiii. 16, since many ministers and others look upon our way of preaching and acting

---

[1] Minister at Rattray, afterwards of St. Stephen's Free Church, Edinburgh.

as rather peculiar. I may plead, 'If Thou goest not with me, then shall Thy name be dishonoured.'

Sabbath, 23rd.—Morning very stormy, but I felt great composure, and soon all cleared up. Mr. Candlish preached upon ' Knowing the terrors of the Lord, we persuade men.' I preached upon John i. 8 ; rather laboured for some time, but afterwards much helped. People very attentive, and Mr. Candlish remarked afterward that he saw many in tears, and he thought even the old minister was affected. I do think God is visiting this place ; everything has been so apparently directed of Him. My very text, I felt, was given me by Him for the occasion.

Tuesday, 25th.—Last night one of the elders said to me that ' there were many tears in the kirk on Sabbath.' The few people that I have seen have received me most cordially.

Wednesday, 26th.—I see now that once preaching on a Sabbath may work God's purpose as well as if I preached from morning to night. For, if God speaks from heaven once, and for only a minute, yet that voice should be felt in the parish all the week, yea, for months after. Horace remarked, too, that if few came, the comfort was those were the persons *sent to us* by God. I purpose (and yet I cannot effect even this unless I get help from the Lord) to go earlier to bed and rise at six ; and spend from six to eight in prayer for myself, my parish, and the cause of God through the world. Oh, if I could do this all the days of my life while I have health, for I have never yet succeeded in such resolutions, and never yet have I given much time to prayer daily. Neither cold nor darkness need hinder me. I may just rise and at once begin communion with God, and my soul's fervour will heat the body. O, Lord, grant me the power.

Sunday, *30th.*—Have been answered in my prayer, being able to rise at six, as I sought. I announced a Sunday-school.

Monday, Oct. 8th.—Yesterday my first baptism, and I felt the responsibility of administering ordinances to men whose hearts I do not know. Preached upon Bochim. Began Sabbath-school. In the evening was so drawn out in prayer for the people of this parish that it seemed as if the Lord was now about to give them to me.

Thursday, 18th.—Felt great encouragement in regard to the future in my hopes of ministerial usefulness by reading Hebrews xi., where those that rested upon God in faith are held forth. They did not see the things, but waited on God for the event, and great wonders were thereby wrought of every kind. Thus the Lord has been reviving and blessing me to-day, and as this has been just after two days' attendance at the Synod in Perth, where the case of Lethendy and some others were discussed, I look upon it as His seal to my duty of attending church courts. We were last night in the Synod till three in the morning.

Friday, 26th.—I was thinking over God's ways with me, and all at once God opened clearly to my view a feature in my character which I had not perceived before. I have been for a long time very soul-satisfied, wondering why others have been placed in more useful situations than I, *e.g.* Horace, Somerville, M'Cheyne, etc. But God let me see that I have been thinking very highly of myself. I never before felt so satisfied to be left alone. In times past I have been like the sons of Zebedee.

Thursday, Nov. 1st.—Preached in Perth in the Middle Church. I remembered that my grandfather had stayed here and preached seventy years ago.

Thursday, 8th.—Returned from Dundee, and Robert

M'Cheyne remained with me here till this morning. I have been much refreshed, but upon Sabbath at the Communion it was remarkable to myself that the blessing was given in so different a way from what I expected. 'I asked the Lord that I might grow,' etc., was suitable to me indeed, for the Lord let me feel no liveliness nor power of prayer till the evening sermon, and then in time of need, for the sake of the people to whom I was to preach, He opened my heart fully. I was made to see that I was very far backward in point of real holiness, and was led much more to plead that I was the 'least of all saints,' though that is difficult with me because of the pride of my heart. O what I wonder at in Robert M'Cheyne more than all else is his simple feeling of desire to show God's grace, and to feed upon it himself. To-day after much prayer, and with considerable fear of disappointment, I spoke to the old minister, and got his consent to a week-day [service] in Kinrossie, which I shall make a prayer-meeting. Perhaps now the Lord will visit us, when the people are sending up their cry.

Saturday, 10*th.*—A letter from Alexander Somerville showed me how I have been really murmuring against God in regard to the old minister. I felt pained at the discovery, since God had requited me with loving-kindness.

Monday, Dec. 10*th.*—I have observed how Satan tries to get me employed on Sabbath and on Saturday evenings in other things than the direct work before me, and this especially keeps me from prayer. I think now I see that prayer and fasting unto prayer should be the employment of Saturday night and Sabbath evening. These will be times when Satan will be busy to prevent the word getting root. So also Monday morning. Want of this has kept me from being useful.

Tuesday, 1st January 1839.—Rose early to pray and review the past year. I see in the past year the death of three very intimate friends; John's marriage; my removal to Collace; and baptism of Leo and Königsberg. Learn also that God this past year has been so ordering my spiritual experience as to teach me more of constant living upon Him for *myself*, if I would hope to be of use to others. As yet I can't say that I see souls converted in my parish; but I remember how God kept me as a trial of faith very long in Edinburgh. To-day I preach at Dundee with the object of seeking a pouring down of the Spirit. 'I wait for God, my soul doth wait, and in His word do I hope.' Robert M'Cheyne also is another call upon me to be girding up my loins.

Tuesday, 8th.—Much helped on Sabbath while preaching on Isaiah v. 1-7. Have been thinking much upon how God permits His people in Christ to count upon Him. Faith may reckon upon God being always near. I can do so as to mercies; answers to prayer in common things have confirmed me much in this; but I must rise up and do it in daily and hourly things, such as, state of mind while going to preach, etc.

Friday, 11th, Evening.—The families of the parish presented me to-night with a timepiece and silver candlesticks. I felt quite at a loss at receiving them, not knowing well how to express my gratitude, and wishing also to say something to them about being made to love the Lord, my Master, more than me. It was presented by some of the older people in name of the families. It shows wonderful affection, considering how short a time I have been with them, and it may be a token that God is moving their souls.

Saturday, 12th.—I observe in revival that the people were often greatly roused to attention and interest before the Spirit was poured forth ; perhaps, therefore, it is to be so with my people. Of late God has been stirring them up to very deep attention, especially on Wednesday evenings, though not exclusively then, and I have been speaking much, and preaching upon, the Spirit's work.

Wednesday, 16*th.*—Greatly grieved at discovering that many people of Collace, even many of whom I had hopes, were quite intoxicated on Monday ;[1] and I find that they scarcely thought it a sin upon that day. This led me to speak most solemnly to them at night upon the subject.

Friday, February 1*st.*—Grieved at the thought that I do not see any real spiritual movement among any of my people ! ' Lord, how long !' Attention to me is not conversion to God. Last Sabbath was at Dundee for Robert M'Cheyne. I am afraid that I am losing the spirit of prayer.

Sunday, 3*rd.*—Preached on Psalm xxii. Wondering if God will come and visit my people, I met in the evening this remark in [Jonathan] Edwards : ' It is God's way to let ministers try all their strength first, and then He Himself comes and subdues the hearts they cannot.' Perhaps God is trying me thus. I am using all means, and all my power, and it avails nothing.

Sabbath, 17*th.*—Jedburgh Communion. God seemed to be with us to refresh. I have been somewhat unsettled by the occurrence of a proposal in Edinburgh to send Robert M'Cheyne and myself for six months to inquire about the Jews throughout the Continent of Europe and even round Jerusalem. The very thought of it, however, had the effect of making me feel more called upon to speak now with earnestness while at home.

[1] ' Handsel Monday,' as it was called, was always kept as a holiday in Collace and the neighbourhood.

Jedburgh, Monday, 18*th.* — Prayer - meeting in the evening, and saw many of my old friends during to-day. Last night met with about 100 of the children of the Sabbath-schools.

Kelso, Wednesday, 20*th.*—Preached for Horace in forenoon, and then in the evening, and addressed the Sabbath-school children about the Jews, which brought to my mind much the strange proposal now going on. Much helped. I thought of 'the hand of the Lord was upon me.' I am now able to pray that if this proposed mission be one that will effect anything I may be sent. Horace's people seem very much solemnized.

Edinburgh, Thursday, 21*st.*—A meeting with my old flock at William Street; very attentive. I think God has been with me. Heard of my brother William's proposed marriage. It seems ordered by the good providence of God.

Collace, Friday, March 1*st.*—I have been praying about attention to the sick, being grieved that I never see any of the sick affected. I have been able to pray hitherto, and to-day with some solemnity and feeling of the solemn nature of the work, regarding the proposal of sending us out to seek the Jews.

Saturday, 2*nd.*—Enabled to-day and last night to feel more closeness and reality in prayer for revival among my people, and in regard to the Jews. The prospect of going away soon for six months upon that duty has quite composed my mind under the solemn feeling that I should work while I had opportunity. Next week I shall have finished the catechising of the parish; I must make this matter a constant object of prayer.

Friday, 8*th.*—Heard from home to-day that I am appointed along with M'Cheyne, Wodrow,[1] and Dr.

---

[1] Mr. Wodrow's place was taken by the Rev. Dr. Keith of St. Cyrus.

Black to go upon the expedition. I am giving this
night wholly to prayer about this matter, its success,
and my part in it. I feel very great reluctance about
leaving my people. The Lord is He that can take my
feet out of the net. I feel very much humbled at consideration of my entire want of a real missionary spirit.
I feel specially alarmed at leaving the young people of
my flock lest grievous wolves enter in among them. I
feel more anxious about my people's condition than ever.

Saturday, 9th.—Got the letter of the Committee requesting me to go to the Jews. It is a very solemn
matter to me. How strange is the doing of God sending
me here for a short time, then away to another part of
the earth! The arrangements for this parish in my
absence will be the most difficult matter ; but at family
worship we came upon Psalm cxii. 4. Spent the forenoon in prayer.

Wednesday, 13th.—I am sore vexed in spirit, the
matter is taken so deeply by my people, and they
are so alarmed at the thought of being left without a
shepherd.

Saturday, 16th.—I cannot read providences well, but
strange that hindrances so many have arisen. I cannot now draw back, yet had I known from the first
what was the feeling perhaps I would. For the old
minister has insisted upon putting in a man of his own
to succeed me ; the people are in great distress about
the whole matter, still I think I am right in going. The
issue may be entire removal. My people have no
conscience of the duty of attending to the Jews ; it is
perhaps the very way by which God will have them all
round get this, for neighbouring parishes are quite struck
with this event, as well as my own, but oh, it is trying
to set before me the prospect of leaving my people
desolate.

Sabbath, 17*th.*—Preached upon Acts viii. 39, then upon 'Went on his way rejoicing.' The first part for myself, the other for the people. Much helped all day both in church and in the class ; people much solemnized, I thought ; still it is most awful to leave them to one that does not care for their spiritual state.

Wednesday, 20*th.*—Yesterday the Presbytery gave me leave to go for six months. To-night spoke to my people for the last time for a season at least : it may be for ever. Immense number present, but I felt strengthened very much ; just when pressing upon them these words, ' *God Himself.*' I leave them to-morrow.

There are no entries in the Diary for the next few months, as a full record of the travels of the Deputation was published in the *Narrative of a Mission of Inquiry to the Jews.* A journey to Palestine in those days was an event of great interest and some concern to the Church and country, as well as to the people of Collace. An old woman in the parish, when told that Mr. Bonar was going to the Holy Land, asked how he would go. When told that he would first go to Egypt and then into Palestine, she held up her hands and exclaimed, ' Oh, then, we 'll no see him again for forty years !' During his absence Mr. Nairne of Dunsinnane had three of Mr. Bonar's Pastoral Letters printed, and the old precentor used to sit on a grassy knoll in the village and read them aloud to the people on Sabbath evenings. By the time the travellers returned in the month of November, showers of blessings were beginning to fall over many parts of the country.

Sabbath, November 24*th.*—Arrived in Edinburgh last week on Thursday afternoon, the 14th, from London, and last Friday, the 22nd, reached Collace in the evening. Preached to-day on Jethro meeting Moses, Exod. xviii. Cannot yet tell almost anything about my people. The

church was crowded to hear something about Jerusalem.
The old minister is strong and vigorous. Have heard of
revival at Blairgowrie and other places ; Jedburgh also
seems moved.

Sabbath, Dec. 1st.—I have found that the people are
much as when I left them. Some are impressed by
hearing of the revivals, but as yet I have seen no conversion among them. On coming home to-night was
much refreshed by meeting with a young woman who
was awakened at Dundee, and has not yet found Jesus—
Elizabeth Morrison. She has been there a month for
her health at sea-bathing. She is to come and speak
with me. Oh, if this were to be to me the beginning of
souls coming to ask for Christ.

Wednesday, 4th. — After being at the meeting of
Presbytery at Perth, where I was called to give a state-
ment of our mission to the Jews, in which I felt considerable freedom, came out to our usual prayer-meeting.
At the end two people came to me asking about their
souls, and entreated me to come soon and visit them ;
oh, it has made me glad! I trust that these are the first
drops of a coming shower. Mr. Cumming[1] and I had
prayer together during a short season when we met in
the town, and I felt then the nearness of God. I feel
that for the relief of anxious souls I must betake myself to
prayer; the Holy Ghost can show them the object Christ.

Friday, 6th.—The woman, Elizabeth Morrison, came
to me and found peace this evening while we were
speaking together. I see it is the work of the Holy
Spirit. I had been praying for her that she might find
it through the Spirit showing Christ to her ; and the
failure of past attempts made me feel that I could not
give it. So soon as I was convinced of its being nothing

---

[2] Minister at Dunbarney, and afterwards of Victoria Free Church,
Glasgow.

I could do, and [made] to trust to the Spirit using me as an instrument only, then it was granted.

Sabbath, 22nd.—Returned yesterday after being at Glasgow and Greenock attending meetings for the Jews, where I felt especially helped in preaching upon the subject.

Sabbath, 29th.—An anxious woman waited for me and walked along the road seeking peace. She said she was awakened some time ago, but was not able to rejoice in Christ. She cannot yet lay hold upon Him as a poor sinner.

Friday, 3rd Jan. 1840.—Coming from Dunbarney was persuaded to remain in Perth, where there has been a work of the Spirit. William Burns preached in the evening upon the Ethiopian finding peace in Jesus alone. Conversed with many people through the day in a most interesting state of mind.

Sabbath, 12th.—To-day preached upon John iii. 1-5. One woman from Sachar[1] spoke afterwards to my sister Christian under deep impression.

Monday, 13th.—This evening God has indeed shown how willing He is to answer prayer, and how willing to bless us in this parish, for our meeting was quite full, and the meeting with the class was also full. It far exceeded what at first I thought at all likely. Perhaps this is just a preparation for greater things. I ask and expect His Spirit this year to be poured out upon us.

Friday, 24th.—Last Friday preached in Dundee upon the Ethiopian with great freedom. Upon Sabbath much helped in Table Services. Robert M'Cheyne preached upon 'Father, I will that they also,' etc. Full of life and truth. Happy season. Mr. Cumming with us also. On the Monday was much helped in preaching upon Psalm cxvi. 16: 'Christ the looser of bonds.'

---

[1] One of the little villages in the parish of Collace.

It was indeed with me a day of thanksgiving, and
William Burns was excellent in the evening upon
Psalm ciii. 1 : altogether a time of refreshing. Intense
look of interest among the people, deep solemnity. I
think God has blessed me there. Delighted to hear
upon Wednesday evening the proposal of some of my
young people to form a prayer-meeting before the class
meets on Sabbath in the session-room.

Sabbath, Feb. 2nd.—To-day found T. G. in deep distress, actually trembling, awakened to see his sins under
William Burns last Friday in Perth.

Monday, 3rd.—T. G. better, though there is too much
of terror. The lesson God is teaching me is this,
that William Burns is used as the instrument where
others have been labouring in vain, because he is much
in prayer, beyond all of us. It is not the peculiar words
he uses that God blesses.

Sabbath, 16th.—Last week have been encouraged by
finding out two more that I think are under impression, and the prayer-meeting in Collace of the men,
and that of the five young people in I. Y.'s house, is
very encouraging ; also this morning much blessing
attending that which meets in the session-room. On
Thursday was at the prayer-meeting in Tealing ; on
Wednesday in Perth, where the work is going on ; and
on Friday Robert M'Cheyne's visit quickened me to
faith in prayer.

Wednesday, 26th.—Returned from Kelso, Ancrum,
and Jedburgh much refreshed. On coming out heard
of a prayer-meeting among the young Sabbath-school
children ; I think God is about to bless us. On the
Monday evening at Kelso there was a solemnity and
stillness which I almost never saw before anywhere ;
when I spoke upon John xii. 35-41, I felt unusually
solemn.

Sabbath, March 8th.—I feel afraid of myself on the ground that I am less prayerful than I used to be, although often more helped in preaching than ever, and I am less full of praise than I used to be, having very little pleasure in this yet; also tempted much to be content with very little of Scripture.[1]

Tuesday, April 7th.—Feel still a constant desire to be holy myself, and to see many others holy too.

Wednesday, 22nd.—After the close of our prayer-meeting (A. Cumming and Horace were with us) many waited behind in distress when Horace ended his address. Very great solemnity, some really very deeply awakened. It is wonderful indeed [how] God is thus answering our prayers; praise, praise, His name. I remark upon God doing this, bringing matters to this point by the hand of my brother, that it is unspeakable kindness, for thus I am kept low and humble, quite dependent upon Himself; He is sovereign, yet most glorious in free grace.

Thursday, 23rd.—I am amazed at my coolness, even callousness, though God is thus honouring me by the evidence of His Spirit among us, yet now this fore-noon I feel both fear and great joy: it is a very awful and serious time. After the evening meeting was over one girl was quite overwhelmed, and her weeping was heard through the place. I see that God, having used Horace as the instrument of bringing out the people to this open, full confession of their state, teaches me the great lesson I have needed to learn, that there are many parts of work and duty for which I am quite unfit, and God therefore wisely uses [other] instruments: it also keeps me humble.

[1] He writes to his brother Horace at this time: 'Pray for Collace. We have no more than a few drops as yet, and I believe I am to blame. I *work* more than I *pray*.'

Friday, 24th.—I feel the greatest anxiety about the relief of the distressed.   Excited to prayer and excited to study *the Gospel* much.

Saturday, 25th.—Felt a heart to pray much and earnestly ; have felt it easy to pray all day. Towards night rather troubled at the people not coming to converse with me, though I felt it a voice to me, this being the preparation for the Sabbath, and probably some of them are engaged to-night in prayer. I never felt it easier to pray for the old minister than to-night. I have great hope and great desire that he may be one of the fruits at this season ; I feel also anxiety relieved by remembering that the work is entirely in God's hands ; if it is His work, why should I be, like Uzzah, afraid of the Ark shaking and falling ?

Sabbath, 26th.—I had very great freedom all day, especially in the evening in praying and preaching upon 1 Peter ii. 24 ; in the forenoon the people were very attentive and church very full ; several were weeping, and two of the men I noticed specially, while I preached upon John xxi. 15-17. Some have got great relief from their anxiety ; with others it continues.

Friday, May 8th.—Have been away at Leith introducing John Thomson to his new church.

Sabbath, 24th.—Attended the General Assembly on Friday to give in our report. Came home last night wearied and, above all, prayerless. I wish to set apart this week for special prayer to recover from my state. Some interesting conversation with people to-day.

Friday, 29th.—While sitting in the wood among the firs I began to look back. This day last year we were in the desert within sight of the hills of El-khulil (Hebron). Oh, what strange scenes we have been brought safely through ! But I have felt not only that there has been marvellous love to me in Providence all along till now, but it fills me with regret and sorrow when I remember that I have lived thirty years and am so unholy. David began to reign at this part of life, and how much he had felt and known of Christ! Joseph was just this age when he stood before the king. How much I have lost that I might have attained; perhaps God will now use me in a different way. It was at this age that the Levites entered upon their office in the Tabernacle; it was then that the Baptist began his ministry, and our Lord Himself came into public duty. I cannot tell how much the thought has struck me of my low attainments at this part of my life, compared with what others have gained. I feel altogether sinful, worthless, something very small and insignificant.

Friday, June 26th.—There is a general anxiety throughout the whole parish at this season, and much fear.

Sabbath,28th.—Our Communion. An immense crowd; my heart grieved that there was such entertainment for so many souls: sought for myself more grace, more prayerfulness, more love, more realising of all things spiritual.

Tuesday, Sept. 8th.—Much refreshed by a letter from Mr. Milne[1] telling me of a boy converted by my sermon last Sabbath evening at his Communion; also by a letter from Edinburgh telling me of an old man who was converted by my words when visiting him. Preached at Burrelton in the evening for Robert M'Cheyne, who was to have preached and was taken ill; heard of a very interesting case of a person awakened last time he was there, or at least very deeply quickened by his visit. The doctor at Balbeggie seems in real anxiety; he is dying.

Saturday, 19th.—God has this week been impress-

[1] Minister of St. Leonard's Church, Perth.

ing much upon me the way of redeeming time for
prayer by learning to pray while walking or going from
place to place.   Also He has been showing me how to
make more direct use of Scripture to my own case in
daily reading.   To-morrow is the anniversary of my
ordination day.   I feel my unholiness, my prayerlessness, and my want of solemnity and sense of responsibility.   I seem to have done nothing at all for this
people, and I wonder much at my indifference to the
salvation of the old minister ; and my little regret at the
expressed indifference of neighbouring clergymen. I feel
also a great deal of envy at hearing of others' success.

Wednesday, 23rd.—Reminded the people that I began
my ministry this day among them two years ago; a very
solemn night, while we recounted God's benefits.

October 9th.—Upon Thursday last, on occasion of
Miss N.'s marriage, many festivities and much dancing in the parish.   I am afraid it has injured many
of my people ; I have seldom felt more grieved, for I
find so very few of those I expected most of to have
stood quite aloof, although there was little drinking.
The dancing was chiefly among the farmers.   My comfort is that thus God is calling upon me to bear a testimony at once and openly against such things ; perhaps
He is thus also awaking my people who may not have
thought of the evil.

Monday, 12th.—I feel that God is drawing me back
to see wherein I am deficient in my ministry.   I feel
now, after the appearance of revival among us, as if God
were showing me not to draw my joy from my people,
but from Himself.   Still the appearances of the revival
are not withdrawn ; it always was chiefly among the
older people, and these continue steady.   I am not much
surprised at many of the younger people, for I never
believed them true converts.

Saturday, 17*th.*—I still feel the bitter vexation and disappointment. I have met with some petty annoyances too, that make me remember Psalm cix. 4.

November 6th.—After being in Edinburgh and Perth at the Communion, went straight to Huntly. Much helped in all these places throughout the last fourteen days. There are droppings of the Spirit throughout the whole region of Strathbogie.

Tuesday, 17*th.*—Met with some of the young people to-night, and spoke most seriously to them as to the danger of deceiving themselves. I have felt very deep grief from time to time at the complete want of decision in some of whom I had better hopes. The Lord makes me feel how sore a trial it is to be thus vexed. O what is it, then, when I myself disappoint and vex Him ? I have heard, too, of the mockery and taunts of the ungodly among us. This I feel more for the cause of Christ. What must He have felt when they wagged their heads at Him on the Cross ?

Saturday, 21*st.*—I find that reading much Scripture beforehand is excellent preparation for prayer, and that the time occupied is nothing in itself. The business done in that time is the great matter. Coming home through the wood last night, I was refreshed and comforted in looking up to the stars. Ministers, like these stars, are set to give light through the night. We shine on, whether travellers will make use of our light or not.

Sabbath, 29*th.*—Preached yesterday at Rattray. In conversation with Robert Macdonald and Robert M'Cheyne we were led to notice that God blesses ministers most when they are seeking the ' travail of Christ's soul,' letting Him take His own way and time. Felt this much, and also another point they talked of, viz., that God works most by holy instruments.

This morning suddenly called to St. Martin's, the minister being taken ill, and was thus put to the test whether or not I had let the Lord take His own time and plan.

Saturday, Dec. 12th.—Had the Thanksgiving Day upon Wednesday. Very pleasant. In the morning my class much impressed. At the evening meeting many in tears while Robert M'Cheyne spoke.

Saturday, 2nd Jan. 1841.—We concluded the year on Thursday evening by a general assembling of all the prayer-meetings throughout the parish. About 100 persons came, and it was, on the whole, a profitable meeting, and, I trust, was acknowledged by God. Yesterday spent at Dundee, but never felt more bound and constrained in my spirit. God seemed to humble me in the presence of the people, both morning and evening. I felt quite useless, and I grieved exceedingly at the loss of such an opportunity of preaching to many souls. This lesson may be useful to me. Robert M'Cheyne told me how much of late he has felt of the immediate presence of Christ, as one that is near at hand to him ; His divine nature conveying to his human, full knowledge of the slightest feeling of His people.

Through the past year, God has shown me new things indeed : a revival, a shower of the Spirit in my own parish, a thing I had long prayed for, and reckoned among the highest blessings I could ever receive. Many new trials came along with it, and as it has been only a shower, not very extensive, I am left with much to desire and pray for. More vexation and more opposition, too, this year than ever before. I have been permitted to visit and preach in many more places than before, in this way experiencing the blessing of the Jewish cause.

Friday, 22nd.—God has been pleased greatly to

restrain the people at this season, so that Monday last
['Handsel Monday'] passed by in perfect quiet, and
we had a crowded attendance at night. But I have felt
unsettled, and a prey to distraction more than usual.
I find that the cause is this—I have been conversing
much with men, and been much outwardly engaged, but
I have not been closely, or for any length of time, with
God Himself. I see, too, that to be close with God
gives abundant strength, and is like light shining upon
a gloomy country in summer time; it makes things
look different indeed. I ought to preach and speak
always, as '*not alone.*' I should have the feeling that the
Father is with me, to *draw souls* while I speak. But
many, many a time have I felt that I had come to
worship quite alone, and that I was there in my own
name, and nobody helping me.

February 27th.—Last week was at Edinburgh assisting Mr. Moody, and attended a Jewish meeting. This
week have just come from assisting John at Greenock.
Enjoyed all much. But I find this new experience. I
was willing to pray, and felt much in the disposition for
it, yet prayed little, one thing interrupting after another.
Now, I find that in consequence my soul has become
low. God will not let me get the blessing without
asking. To-day I am setting my face to fast and pray
for enlightenment and refreshing. Until I can get up
to the measure of at least two hours in *pure prayer*
every day, I shall not be contented. Meditation and
reading besides.

March 12th.—The day whereon the first missionary
to Israel was ordained in Edinburgh. A memorable
day for the Church.

Wednesday, 17th.—Prayed for the gloomy state of our
Church affairs.

Sunday, 28th.— I felt uncommonly overawed in

preaching to-day, just in reading the words of my text, Isa. vi. : ' Holy, holy, holy,' and for a few minutes the same feeling seemed to prevail throughout the church. I think it was the Spirit resting upon me.

Wednesday, May 12th.—Walked out from Perth with William Burns. His conversation roused me much to seek deeper views of sin, but I think he is in error as to the place wherein he puts the preaching of freeness of the Gospel. He thinks it hurtful to speak too much and too often about ' look to Jesus.' I have heard some instances of blessing upon the neighbouring flock of Snipeton.

June 6th.—Began my class of young communicants. Two of them, whom I thought rather doubtful, seemed much impressed on my speaking to them alone.

Monzie, Wednesday, 30th. — Several people much impressed, several in tears.

Thursday, Aug. 26th.—Yesterday attended the great meeting in Edinburgh in defence of the Church. An immense assembly of ministers and elders, the numbers beyond anything known hitherto since our fathers' days. Both the Commission and the meeting in the evening very solemn. We have now looked our danger fully in the face, and it is wonderful how many are standing fast. I feel, however, too little concern, too little anxious or excited to pray.

Wednesday, Sept. 22nd. — Reminding my people to-night that it was now just this time three years ago when I first preached among them after being ordained. A most solemn evening. I felt myself as if I were speaking things too terrible, and really almost was afraid to say all I felt. There is stronger opposition and bitterness on the part of the ungodly just now than ever, but God's people are more decided and more prayerful.

Tuesday, Nov. 23rd.—Our Communion has just passed over. A most blessed time. I think it has been blessed to several, and I never saw more solemnity among the people, or more attention. Especially, too, there seems to have been impression, or, at least, solemnizing upon the old minister and some of the guardians. I have heard of one person who has been brought to light and comfort, and some others impressed. I myself have been taught a great deal : much humiliation, much defect. I have been taught, also, my want of prayerfulness and want of concern about preparing my sermons, and in this I have been immensely far behind. My brother John has been assisting me, and Mr. Manson.[1] I never heard John preach so plain, and powerful, and pure Gospel truth.

Two letters to Mr. Milne of St. Leonard's, Perth, written at this time, may be interesting, as illustrative of the simple playfulness, along with intense earnestness, which characterises so many of Mr. Bonar's letters :—

TO REV. JOHN MILNE, PERTH.

'*Dunsinnane, Dec.* 14, 1841.

'DEAR BROTHER,—In my own and my people's name I thank you for agreeing to come on Wednesday. Come with " your feet shod with the preparation of the Gospel of Peace," so that when you are seen climbing the braes of Collace, angels may be looking down and saying, " How beautiful upon the mountains are the feet of him that publisheth peace ! " But, if you will be advised (" submit yourselves one to another "), when you come out on your pony, lodge all night under the shadow of my roof, and next morning ride over to Errol, which is just about ten miles from Collace. If you do not take this advice, I undertake to prove that Errol will suffer by it. For, first, is it not clear that your body will be weary? Second, is it not clear that your mind will be

---

[1] Minister at Abernyte, afterwards of Dean Church, Edinburgh, and Boston Church, Duns.

drooping? Third, What time will you have for devotion at night if you ride in and fall asleep through weariness, and find yourself next morning too sleepy still to wrestle for a blessing? Now, the nearer shelter of Dunsinnane would avert these three evils.

' " Cast your net on the right side of the ship." I am to be that night, at the same hour, preaching in the depths of Glenshee, where many are seeking bread of life to eat, and am to remain two days. Now, farewell.—Believe me, dear brother, yours truly,
'ANDREW A. BONAR.'

TO REV. JOHN MILNE, PERTH.

'*Saturday afternoon.*

' DEAR BROTHER,—Threefold thanks : for your letter on Tuesday, your services on Wednesday, and your note to-day. My visit to Glenshee was very interesting to me. It is singular that I found the good people there exactly resembling my own "little flock" in regard to their views and their trials. They rejoice in Christ alone, "knowing whom they have believed," and cold-hearted professors stand aloof, contented with head-knowledge and uncertainty. I did feel the presence of God there. The journey was not pleasant in point of weather or roads, but Paul shuts our mouth : "in journeyings often, in *weariness*, in NAKED-NESS." Thanks for your hints as to Errol, and I take them as calmly and obediently as you take directions about your health. What's this that is said of you? A *Saturday evening* service ! ! John Bunyan and Whitefield took *five* in the morning—that would be better. O, brother, brother, *frater fratrissime*, it is not right in you to try to be first away from your post. Be patient, live a little longer, and let us go into heaven together. Perhaps we may both live till the Lord Himself come. *O præclarum diem !* I suspect you are weary of your work, and wish it were done. Or are you afraid of the cloudy and dark day that is coming on our land, and so you hasten on to get away before the storm? You are an Ignatius, you choose martyrdom, and even provoke the lions to tear you.

' Be admonished, yet at the same time pray that I may have equal zeal, and love, and singlemindedness. Farewell.—Yours truly in the Lord.   ANDREW A. BONAR.'

Monday, 3rd Jan. 1842.—Have had lately some interesting cases from the neighbourhood that have come under my notice, and hopes of Snipeton people now. A few are in a state of great anxiety. Had an interesting visit to Glenshee a few weeks ago. Yesterday was at Dundee, at their Communion, after being on the Fast-Day at Perth. On looking back I am grieved and vexed, most of all at my few hours of real prayer all this year. How little have I done for God *in the Spirit*. I feel myself a very dim-shining light ; a vessel much soiled.

Wednesday, 19*th*.—I feel that in preaching on any occasion, it is no preaching at all unless I speak with the solemnity, and earnestness, and affection that Jesus would have had had He been there. Every such opportunity is really just a time when Christ has a message to deliver to those people that are gathered there. The affairs of our Church are very dark. I often feel deep soul-compassion for poor deluded souls that will not come now to Christ while the light shines. My removal to another house in the parish is now probable, and will be a trial ; but it seems necessary, in order to testify to the people that I seek only their souls, and that neither the great nor the small have any influence in turning me away from the path of duty. Our ' Travels '[1] are now in a fair way of being finished.

Saturday Evening, April 9*th.*—Returned this week from Dundee, where I have been for four weeks, Robert M'Cheyne taking my place here. While there preached at St. Andrews, Newburgh, Foulis, and some other places. Much labour, but learned by experience that much prayer is the only means to success. Twice I had blessed hours in the church alone praying. I see so few conversions. Ah, this must be the cause, as well as my not dwelling enough upon a free Gospel.

Tuesday, 26*th.*—Had a most delightful meeting in

[1] The *Narrative of a Mission of Inquiry to the Jews.*

Sachar Green.   William Burns preached, continuing
till half-past nine.   Began, after prayer, with reading Eph.
i. 1-6, then sang Psa. lxxxv., the two last verses, upon
which he commented freely.   Mercy and truth kissing
mutually over the dead body of the Son of God after
He said 'It is finished,' and Justice setting open the
prison door.   Then prayed.   Preached upon Eph. i. :
'Made us accepted in the Beloved.'   Showed, first of
all, man's ruined state, condemnation, and death ; then
the deliverance by the payment of Christ's blood.   Sang
in closing, 'Come then to Me all ye who groan,' and
next, for the occasion of the moment, 'Hark, how
the adoring hosts above ;' then finally, 'All blessing to
the Lord of hosts let be ascribed then,' etc.   Great
solemnity, some much affected.   Parted, with the stars
shining in the blue sky, the moon not yet risen.   A
remarkable providence ; the wind quite fell just before
we began.   Only three people moved away during the
whole time.   Many of the farmers there.   I never heard
William Burns preach so free a Gospel.

June 6th.—The General Assembly, of which I have
been a member, has now passed.   Most important acts
have been resolved upon.   Patronage has been declared
a grievance that cannot be borne longer.   There was a
calmness and subdued feeling in our debates, that
showed our sense of the seriousness of the crisis.   There
seemed much interest taken in the general schemes for
promoting the cause of Christ.   The spiritual interests
of Christ's kingdom were much more felt than in
former days.   The prayer-meeting of the Assembly
upon Sabbath evening was also very refreshing.

July 16th.—Alarmed at seeing how God has been
afflicting Mr. Milne and Robert M'Cheyne, and other
useful ministers, while He leaves me well.   I feel that,
unless the soul be saturated with prayer and faith, little

good may be expected from preaching. The Communion at Abernyte has been very solemn and remarkable. One soul was awakened at the Table.

Sunday, 24th.—Exchanged with Robert M'Cheyne in Dundee on the Fast-Day. That day was very solemn in the afternoon and evening with us at Dundee, and here also it was remarkable too. I felt drawn out in prayer much on this occasion. I never felt my entire want of all good so much as now, so that never till now could I so truly cry, 'in my flesh, no good thing.' I had prayed and had spoken of, in our Wednesday meeting, the probability that God the Holy Ghost might use new plans and new measures. That same night the formation of a class of young people in my house was suggested to me.

August 4th.—Passed six hours to-day in the church in prayer and Scripture-reading, confessing sin, and seeking blessing for myself and the parish. I was led afterward to see that I should consider the Lord in regard to every visit I pay to my people. That in body and soul I should never do anything that does not bear in some way upon the glory and honour of God. I must deny myself the pleasures that have not this end.

Sept. 4th.—Jedburgh Communion. Much blessed. I see how, at the time of our awakening in Collace, I have been unfit to be used as an instrument. I was averse to the shame and inconvenience, and had no burning love to souls. I was living very grossly, namely, labouring night and day in visiting with very little prayerfulness. I did not see that prayer should be the main business of every day.

Sunday, 18th.—I think that though God honours some ministers much, who are not directly preaching the Gospel, the true explanation is this: it is the minister who is speaking in faith, or in a sense of God's presence, that is most blessed. Now, if one minister feel most of God in speaking the Word, he will be most blessed after. If another feel most of God in telling the *good news*, it is his part to speak that, and he will be blessed. All must be done in faith at the time. I think this must have been the cause of my past want of success, in some measure. *Realizing faith* is what I have not had at the time, and I have been very far from preaching the true Gospel fully.

Friday, 23rd.—My ordination day. Now four years since I came to this people. How few saved! John's youngest child, William, died on Tuesday. He feels the death terribly. It is difficult for us to enter into his feelings fully.

Monday, 26th.—I need more love to God to melt my heart. Some of my own people seem quicker in discerning the real truth than I am.

Sabbath, Nov. 13th.—Our Communion day. One of the most blessed I ever remember. Much helped in the morning, preaching upon Isa. l. 4-6, and in fencing the tables; then in the prayer before the elements were set apart. John, too, greatly helped to-day and in the evening upon Isa. vi. A great multitude from various places, besides the parish round, and Perth and Dundee. Calm, pleasant weather added to our comfort. Perhaps this is the last such day before our Church be broken up. Our servant was so affected that she could not go to the Table. Many children were present all day.

Saturday, Nov. 26th.—Returned yesterday from the Convocation in Edinburgh.[1] We met from Thursday

---

[1] Mr. Bonar took full notes of the proceedings in shorthand, which were of much use afterwards. On the fly-leaf of the note-book is written: 'Taken at the time in shorthand each day by Andrew A. Bonar, Collace, one of the ministers present—on the principle that one line on the spot is better than a page of recollections.'

last week till Thursday this week. It has been a very remarkable time ; much prayer. Very great unity among the brethren. There was a spirit, too, of brotherly love and Christian feeling that was quite unusual. Often our discussions ended with unanimity, although previously there seemed complete opposition of views. There was a solemnity, too, over all, for we felt the circumstances were imminent to the land. Of those present upon Tuesday evening, 340 resolved to leave the Church in event of no response being obtained from Government, after our remonstrance and application had been laid before them.

Saturday, 7th January 1843.—Last Sabbath at Dundee. The Communion in St. Peter's. Most precious time. I got real blessing. I have seen those few days how we should pray with the belief of receiving something as good as we seek always, if not the very thing. We thus cannot pray without being the better of it.

Sunday, February 5*th.*—Have been nearly three weeks away in the north, visiting the Presbyteries of Garioch and Strathbogie. Many interesting meetings. Almost daily held two meetings at different places. Probably this is part of that warning voice that is now going over the land, ' Come, my people, enter into thy chambers ! '

Monday, 6th.—Have been struck at noticing how often, especially no later than yesterday, in going forth to preach, I was like one seeking his own entrance into the holy place and fellowship with God; not like one coming out from enjoying communion to speak to others.

Sunday, 12th.—Felt much last night in my bed in praying for an edge to be put on all I said. To-night going through the wood, R. B., from Cairnbeddie, spoke with me, telling me that this afternoon's sermon had shed in a new light from God upon his soul, showing

him where he had been wrong all along. I felt it very
solemn and very sweet to have the presence of God
thus experienced among us, and at my very side.

Friday, March 24th.—Some very remarkable conversions of late, and I have notea the account of them elsewhere. God seems to be beginning to work by my hand.
O that I were holy! I am very unholy, very earthly.

Saturday, 25th.—This afternoon about five o'clock,
a message has just come to tell me of Robert
M'Cheyne's death.[1] Never, never yet in all my life
have I felt anything like this. It is a blow to myself,
to his people, to the Church of Christ in Scotland. O
Lord, work, for Thine own glory's sake. Arise, O Lord,
the godly ceaseth and the faithful fail. My heart is
sore. It makes me feel death near myself now. Life
has lost half its joys, were it not the hope of saving
souls. There was no friend whom I loved like him. I
have been feeling lately very much my evil neglect of
privileges and opportunities, and my very small degree
of holiness. This startles me. It is as if God were
striking myself. Perhaps He may be taking me next.
The same fever may come to me now, but the time at
any rate is short. Rode down to Dundee as requested.

Sunday, 26th.—O, what a night was Saturday! In
coming to the town about nine, the people had met
for prayer in the church, and wished me to come up. I
could scarce go, only I felt it was easy to weep with
those that lamented such a minister. During prayer,
the cries and lamentations of the people resounded
through the church, as if their hearts were bursting.
They would not go away till I had spoken a little,
which I did upon Rev. xxi. 1-6. O, it was truly solemn,
and when I gazed upon Robert's face, I cannot tell what

---

[1] A letter had been sent earlier to tell him of Mr. M'Cheyne's illness
but, being addressed to ' Collessie,' did not reach him in time.

agony it was to think he was away.   His face as he lay, was so calm, so expressive, [with] the very indentation that used to mark it when he spoke.   Oh, it is bitter!

Monday, 27th.—Yesterday was truly solemn from morning to evening.   I was able to preach composedly, but often at intervals, while the psalms were singing, and sometimes in prayer, the thought of Robert away was overwhelming.   I had too much feeling of the event, too little care for God's glory in it.   The sight of his people coming out at the door, where often we passed out so happily together, his books, and then his body laid that night out of our view for ever!   I feel as if there were less of God's presence among us.   I must myself live nearer God, and find what he found. Preached on Romans viii. 38, 39, and then upon verses 28-30 ; Patrick Miller [1] upon Rev. vii., toward the end. He spoke of him removed from us in mercy and judgment ; in *judgment* upon us for prizing the man and forgetting the Master ; and *mercy*, in order to bring us more to the Master.   His forgetfulness of all that was not found to God's glory was remarkable, and there seemed never a time when he was not himself feeling the presence of God.   I feel submission, for I see my sins so great that I wonder at nothing God does in chastising me.   How very unlike Robert am I! 2 Kings ii. much in my mind.   O that his mantle would fall upon me!   Evil days are begun.   He was so reverent toward God, so full also in desire toward Him, whether in family prayer or at common ordinary meetings.   He seemed never unprepared.   His lamp was always burning, and his loins always girt.   I never knew it otherwise, even when we were journeying in Palestine. Lord, grant me henceforth more holiness ; may I work among my people with the deepest solemnity.   Whether

---

[1] Of Wallacetown Free Church, Dundee, and afterwards in Newcastle.

they feel God present or not, may I teach them *I* feel
He is there. I have had joy also in this season through
the sight of a living Saviour with whom I shall soon be,
but especially in feeling how sweet it is to be near God,
and drawn off from earth ; the thought too of Christ
coming again, it may be very soon. This terrible blow
may be the answer to my prayers for holiness, for I
used to pray that even if very awful, it were better that
God should take the way that would make me holier,
although I should suffer.

Wednesday, 29th.—Came up to Collace to attend a
meeting of Presbytery in Perth. The people here on
Sabbath were in the deepest gloom, many powerfully
moved, many in tears. To-night we expect Mr. Somerville to come up and improve the occasion. Holy
Spirit, come Thou with him ! Evening. At Presbytery
in Perth, after discussion till eight o'clock, we carried
our motion to discontinue immediately, as under
coercion and not free. [The old minister] was in for the
first time in his life, but had to return home before the
vote. How deep the determination of these men to
overthrow the truth ! Mr. Somerville preached upon,
'Shadow of a great rock in a weary land.'

Saturday, April 1st.—Came up again from Dundee
yesterday. Such a scene as was the funeral day upon
Thursday ! Crowds of people on all sides ; but, amidst
the weepers, many were hardened too. Strange mixture of both ! The grave is at the west corner of the
church, at the flat parapet, parallel to the pulpit. It is
Mizpah ; it will watch till Christ comes between him
and his flock. In the evening I preached upon Acts
xx. 32. Mr. Burns took the prayer-meeting before ;
and Mr. Somerville addressed them on, 'Putting forth
His sheep and going before them.' Immense crowd,
solemn evening. In coming away they lingered as

unwilling to go. Some asked me to come back again soon. One person said, 'What shall we do now!' The sister of James Laing came to tell me of a woman that had been awakened some days ago by reading the tract about her brother,[1] and was brought to Jesus last Sabbath, and she added, '*So I hope He is to be with us still.*' The family very sad. Leaving their house in the evening was to me unspeakably melancholy.

But how apt we are to forget all! It must be the Spirit that writes all upon our souls. I have felt a sweet, calm rest in God; but never do I think of Robert's calm blessed countenance in death without being overpowered again. The singing of the last psalm on Thursday evening brought so much to my mind, and the look of his congregation also, that I could do nothing but weep as we stood up to sing. I was glad that Alexander Somerville was beside me in the pulpit. I pray that I may ever live as I now feel, and yet much more reverently.

Tuesday, 4th.—On Sabbath I was carried through with great solemnity. Preached upon Acts xx. 25-27, and then upon Elijah; and in the evening upon Acts viii. 2. There is sadness hanging over us, and above all a feeling of duty undone, to which this event is calling me. O Lord, teach me!

Wednesday, 12th.—Have had a sweet time at Perth Communion, along with my brother Horace. I never felt more directed and helped than on Monday evening at the prayer-meeting, when led to John xxi. 18 after great darkness and confusion. To-day I have got a request from two of the elders, managers of St. Peter's, to let myself be named for that church along with Islay Burns. The manner in which this has come, not at all meant as a direct offer, but as a mere preparation for

---

[1] *Another Lily Gathered*, by Rev. R. M. M'Cheyne.

something, greatly clears my way. Besides, I can see
no reason at present for leaving this place ; but, on the
contrary, indications that God is among us. And the
very idea of being in Robert's place seems to me painful,
for I cannot be like him.

The impression of this sorrow seems never to have left Mr.
Bonar during all the course of his ministry, and affected him
powerfully. It was characteristic of him in this, as in other
trials which touched him deeply, that he did not often refer to
it. Once or twice he went with his children to visit St. Peter's,
but always seemed glad to leave the spot, as if overcome by
recollection. For the same reason he very seldom gave out
a hymn of Mr. M'Cheyne's to be sung in church. To his lifelong friend, the Rev. James Manson, he wrote at this time,
4th April 1843 :—

TO REV. JAMES MANSON.

'MY DEAR FRIEND,—I wish you had written me at greater
length. Never did I feel more need of a word in season. There
was something awfully solemnizing in the Lord's stretched-out
hand. Such an hour causes us to try our place of refuge, and
truly Jesus is the "Shadow of a great rock *in a weary land.*" We
shall meet together again at the Lord's appearing, and He is
making haste to come.

'I cannot come to you, though I earnestly wish to do it. Some
circumstances prevent me. I trust on other occasions—if we
ought to speak of these—it may be in my power, as it will be in
my heart. We are still receiving blessing here. Some more souls
are gathered.'

A few months later he writes again :—

'I have just been thinking over that promise to Israel, "Their
soul shall be as a watered garden, and *they shall sorrow no more
at all.*" What a day ! Every plant of grace growing in the
glorious Sun, watered by the Holy Spirit ; no serpent in the
bowers of that garden ; no sorrow, because nothing to vex the
heavenly Husbandman. I am sure my soul is no more like this

than Eden was like the wilderness of Judah. I think my soul is like some of the vine terraces on the hills of Palestine—the vine-dresser needs to bring *soil*, and then to build it up lest the very rains sent to bless it should sweep it out of its place. Constant care and training is the only process to keep it a vineyard at all. "Grace" is a sweeter sound every day. How is it with you? I am urged to have my *Memoir of Robert M'Cheyne* ready by the end of the year.'

Sabbath, 16th.—Returned from Dundee, where I was upon the Fast-Day. There was a quiet sadness over all the people, very deep. Some of them have begun an eight days' concert for prayer, in order to humiliation before the Lord. Some of them wish me to let myself be named for the vacancy. I have refused to be nominated, and even were there a call to me, I do not see how I can leave my charge here until the Lord has given some express token that I may leave my watch-tower. But never did I feel sympathy for any people like what I feel for them. Horace and Robert Mac-donald are there to-day. We have now fewer earnest prayers for blessing, fewer entreaties to flee from wrath, fewer souls likely to be saved.

Saturday, 22nd.—I have been led to feel that where we see grace decline in a preacher it is a time when we may expect less for ourselves; for his prayers will be feeble, and less of the presence of God will be among us. Began this week to get the plan of our new church fixed.

Wednesday, May 3rd.—Rose a little earlier than usual to fast and pray. I see that fasting and retirement, along with prayer, should go together. The effect upon the body and soul is somewhat like affliction. It brings down the tone of the spirit, subdues the flesh, draws off the soul from self-complacence, and makes the flesh un-satisfying. It discovers much to me that is humbling, it helps to remove my lightness of mind. Heard that

St. Peter's is settled ; Islay Burns chosen. I have reason
to bless the Lord that my way has always been so clear
hitherto. I was afraid of being proposed, but left all to
God. Many of the electors could not bear my views of
Christ's Advent. Many other reasons.

Thursday, 4th.—I feel as if calamity may be near ; I
feel great want of strength of faith ; my hand seems to
hold Jesus with a feeble grasp.

Saturday, 6th.—Our servant seems to have got a sight
of the truth, and it was on the Fast-Day. This seems a
token of the Lord among us.

Wednesday, 17th.—Edinburgh. Attended meeting
before the General Assembly. There has been remarkable unanimity, also great calmness, and a vein of deep
solemnity. The Protest was signed to-night. I think
our great duty at present is to attend and care for
public matters.

Thursday, 18th.—We have passed a day which will be
memorable in the world till the Lord come. [St. Andrew's
Church] was crowded two or three hours before the time.
At length the time arrived. The Moderator prayed very
suitably and solemnly. Immediately thereafter he stated
the peculiar circumstances under which we met, and
that therefore this could not be considered a true
Assembly. This done, he read the Protest in his own
name and in the name of those that adhered. He then
withdrew slowly, bowing to the Commissioner, and
walked up the passage with much firmness and calmness, followed by Dr. Chalmers and Dr. Gordon and by
all on that side. Deep silence followed. In the street
occasional cheers, but all seemed solemnized also. Some
wept, none scorned. A line of people all the way to
Canonmills. Solemn meeting there. I forgot too much
at the time that the eye of Christ was upon us. He was
smiling and saying : ' I know thy works.' I was too

much occupied with thinking upon the impression this would produce upon the people. Yet I was able to pray a good deal.

Thursday, 25th.—Events pass on. Much of God's favour in our Assembly. We get accustomed to the greatest changes. I have felt far too little the deep solemnity of this crisis. Too much distracted.

Monday, 29th.—Returned to Collace, where I preached yesterday in the open air to about five hundred people at the end of the village of Kinrossie. Spoke upon the Church of Philadelphia, then upon Heb. xii. : 'See that ye refuse not Him that speaketh.'

Saturday, June 3rd.—Making up for past duty after all the duties of the Assembly. Feel the want of prayer these several days. I was struck with the remark of one that visited me : 'O sir, get much for yourself ; remember what you said about the rain coming first upon the mountain-tops.' To-morrow we are to preach in a tent of canvas.[1] The Lord seems still among us.

Saturday, 10th.—I have got a call to Huntly from elders, managers, and people. It is a wide sphere, but the Lord has work for me here.

Sunday, 11th.—To-day my preaching is to be the doing of His will. I am just a staff in His hand to do His work in the meantime. *His work* is the main thing.

Saturday, 17th.—Late this evening two girls came from Dundee, members of St. Peter's, of dear Robert M'Cheyne's flock. This is not the first visit I have had on Sabbaths of a similar kind from his flock. It brings back their shepherd to my mind most strikingly whenever I meet them. I dreamed two nights ago that I was at the side of his coffin again, and woke in tears.

---

[1] This tent was presented by Mr. Edward Caird of Dundee, who, along with his brother-in-law, Mr. Mudie of Montrose, was present at many of the Communion gatherings at Collace.

Sunday, 25th.—A most blessed day. Very great numbers from Dundee and from Perth, as well as from all parishes round. The tent not only filled, but the sides crowded all on the outside. Deep attention ; calm quiet feeling. Satan struck a blow at me in the middle of the day through the sight of a man at the Table whom I had wished to keep away, but the Lord delivered me from the harassment. Several things occurred about this time which showed Satan's watchfulness against us. Preached upon ' Having loved His own,' etc. My brother John preached upon ' We all with open face,' etc. At the Table, when giving thanks, I felt as if I could have stood there for ever to praise the Lord for His grace ; I realized the blessedness of eternal praise in heaven.

July 11th.—Found an interesting case, Elizabeth Morrison, who on the Communion Sabbath got such views of Jesus as she never had before while receiving the bread and wine. The Saturday before I had urged the communicants to seek and to expect the blessing to come in this way, and not through the addresses of the ministers.

Sunday, 16th.—After preaching at home with much freedom upon ' Nathanael,' rode down to Dundee, and was in time to serve the last table in St. Peter's, upon ' drawing water from the wells of salvation,' and then preached with extraordinary freedom in the evening upon ' the pearl of great price.' When the people were gone, walked round with Islay Burns to Robert M'Cheyne's tomb, and when I saw the grass growing over it waving in the shade, while darkness was nearly hiding it from view, I felt most solemnly. It seemed to bid me go and do nothing else but live for God a little while longer, and the text came powerfully to mind, ' His banner over *him* was love,' for that was Robert's experience surely all his days! More nearness to God is what we need, more retirement, more prayer, more fellowship.

Friday, 21st. — I see plainly that *fellowship with God is not means to an end*, but is to be *the end itself*. I am not to use it as a preparation for study or for Sabbath labour ; but as my chiefest end, the likest thing to heaven.

Friday, 28th. — More and more led into the feeling of the need of divine fellowship. Our strength lies there. Also, more holy, solemn work, and the daily taking up of the cross.

August 4th. — Yesterday preached with very great freedom and ease at Tealing twice, then in the evening at Newtyle. In riding home at night I had a sweet season of prayer and praise as I rode. To-morrow I go to Glenshee to preside at the Communion in that glen in the open air. To-night I give myself to prayer and waiting on the Lord. I have not been much in the spirit of prayer, but I see several things more clearly this night. I see that prayerlessness is one of my great sins of omission. I am too short, ask too little, ask with too much want of forethought. Then, *too little meditation upon Scripture*. I must also resist the temptation of doing or reading anything before having found God in private and wrestled with Him. Also, some time must be found for this *before family worship*. The reason of my prayerlessness when from home is that my heart is not fixed upon God alone. I fear too that I have been praying little for my people here, and not realizing my responsibility to them nearly so much as before the Disruption. Why is this?

Tuesday, 8th. — On Sabbath we met at Cray, just at the foot of Mount Blair, and had the Table in the open ier [along with Mr. Gillies]. Some felt it like a heaven upon earth, and I was much strengthened till the close. There had been some melting upon the Thursday among the people, and there was a little also upon Monday. Some came from Glenisla, Strathardle, and even from Moulin, as well as from Blairgowrie, Alyth, etc.

Friday, 18*th.*—Returned from Dumfriesshire, where I was at Horace's marriage. The unknown future makes it solemn amid all the joy.

September 5*th.*—I returned from the north, being sent along with Mr. Cumming to preach and visit in the Presbytery of Brechin and Fordoun. I have seen more marks of impression this journey than in any former that I have undertaken, at Montrose and in some other places. But still the people in general are but dry bones. Sometimes had much communion with God. Was able to pray most fervently while walking from Benholm at night. Then at the place in Fordoun where I was staying (Cushnie), when in a retired spot among the furze and broom, felt a most intense desire for the salvation of men, not at home only, but throughout the whole earth. Last Sabbath felt my soul solemnized exceedingly while preaching at Arbuthnot in a barn to about a hundred people. And last night had uncommon freedom in the close of my discourse in preaching at Luthermuir upon 2 Sam. xxiv. 16. Felt the need of power attending the word, so that when I go to preach anywhere, I am sent to preach not by my sermon only, not by the service, but by my frame of mind and by my very countenance. Lord, glorify Thyself in me, make me holy. When passing by places where holy men lived, such as Dun and Pitarrow and Baldovie, my soul was stirred to long for all the grace that was in the men of God then.

Collace, Wednesday, 6*th.*—Found that since I left, God has led a young man to Christ by means of my words in taking leave of them. Also a girl led to rest who long has been anxious. Another also about the same time enabled to take peace by the words, ' Come unto Me.'

Thursday, 14*th*.—One great part of the ministry is among believers. We are blessed if we make their life flow on in a full stream. This glorifies God, it brings Him into His own world, it subdues some of the parts of His dominion to Him again.

Saturday, 23*rd*.—The anniversary of my first sermon after ordination. It is now five years since. Now I see myself more fully than I used to do ; much of shameful sin in my thoughts and desires ; much selfishness, little of real disinterested seeking of God's glory I am now persuaded that one grand reason for the unholy bitterness among some of the people towards each other, and the harshness of temper in some Christians among us, is greatly to be attributed to my failure in prayer for them, and my not dealing with God about them. O for much of His Spirit among us ! The Disruption has this year set me free from the old minister, and placed us in new circumstances altogether. Robert M'Cheyne's death has been another event most powerfully affecting me. My brother John being here, I go to-morrow to Blairgowrie.

Monday.—In walking home from Blairgowrie and Meikleour, had great freedom in praying over the last five years of ministry. 'Cleanse me from blood-guiltiness' was my cry.

Saturday, 30*th*.—I feel sometimes an awful persuasion that there are few ministers anywhere who preach Christ fully and truly. Few of us like to be told our faults, few of us correct them when we are told, few of us pray over discovered sins, few of us have grieved at the want of success in others, few of us pray for one another, and for the Holy Ghost coming down upon every minister every time he goes forth to preach. It is exceedingly difficult for the most faithful to preach Christ aright, to show the freeness of salvation without any conditions, and to do this in the way that lays the guilt upon the sinner, and to do it in a way that glorifies every attribute of God at the same time, not casting into the shade one feature of His plan of redemption. I notice how David was called at the age of thirty. What grace had he received by that time! Many a psalm had he sung! Many a sweet hour of communion with God! Now, how little of this in me! Robert M‘Cheyne got his grace before he was thirty, and his crown of glory too. Beginning to write *Robert M‘Cheyne's Memoir*. This fills up all my leisure time. We are to choose four deacons to-morrow. I pray the Lord may make this a time like that of Acts vi. 7 : ‘Many added.’

Sabbath, October 1st.—I wish to pray from this date every Sabbath morning before going out to preach, and every time I go to preach, to stand still a little and praise the Lord for sending to sinners His glorious Gospel, good tidings!

Sabbath, Nov. 5th.—In my usual reading in the church, accidentally noticed that like Solomon's Temple, which began in the month Zif and was finished in the month Bul, our church was begun in the month of May, and is now, in November, ready, so that next Sabbath all will be completed : seven months. O to have the same glory filling the house!

Friday, 10th.—Last night four elders were chosen. One of them is not a proper man, yet the people have resolved to have him. In his case it was a struggle between the godly and the careless, and the latter gained it. What will the Lord now do? I have earnestly prayed about this matter. Stand still and see

Monday, 13*th*.—Yesterday our church was opened.[1]
I preached upon the verse that is written over our gate-
way, 'The Lamb shall overcome them,' etc.   Robert
Macdonald preached in the afternoon, 'Mine eyes and
mine heart shall be there perpetually,' and I preached
for him at the opening of his church in Blairgowrie.

Sabbath, 19*th*.—A most precious time to my own
soul, and at the close the people were so still that it was
like the Holy Place.   Surely God was in the place.   I
feel more hope that He is coming to bless us than I
have had for a long time.

Saturday, 25*th*.—Have had trouble about the elders,
but it is over.   Spoke to [one] about his besetting sin ;
he was very angry.   May it be blessed to lead him to
the fountain of pardon and the fountain of holiness.

Sabbath, 26*th*.—Before ordaining the elders, while
telling the people what steps had been taken, [one] in
the midst of the congregation spoke aloud, and said
that he was not yet satisfied as to [one who was elected].
This was altogether out of order.   It spread a very
painful feeling through the church, but I declared the
state of the case and proceeded.

Saturday, *Dec.* 23*rd*.—Finished my *Memoir of Robert
M'Cheyne* yesterday morning.   Praise, praise to the
Lord.   I have been praying, 'Guide me with Thine eye.'
I may soon be gone ; but I am glad that the Lord has
permitted me to finish this record of His beloved servant.
Yet it humbles me.   My heart often sinks in me.   Just
to-night I saw my soul full of nothing but *self*, and all
that comes forth seems a black stream of selfishness.

Near the close of this year he writes to his brother
Horatius :—

'I put you in mind of us by this note, that you may remember

---

[1] The New Free Church of Collace was built in the village of Kinrossie,
on a site given by Mr. Nairne of Dunsinnane.

us during the week of prayer. I preached lately on " The love of the Father"—one of the sweetest days I ever had in my life. The *common truth* seemed so fresh and so pleasant to the taste.

'I find that I must not think of sending you my MS. of the *Memoir*. I need to have it by me. Pray for this, " Lord, guide him with Thine eye." Tell your people we have among us " a rumbling," not " a sleeping, devil." We need brotherly love.

'Answer soon. I am often startled now at the thought of a *near* eternity. It is like a man looking over the brink of a precipice—though quite safe, yet he cannot gaze unmoved. We will soon be for ever with the Lord.'

Saturday, 6th January 1844.—Have been thinking to-day over the past year. I see three alarming things in me : (1) My feeble prayers. (2) The many prayers offered for me by others. This taken in connection with the fruit makes me feel that it may be almost wholly for the sake of others that I get such blessings as do come to me. (3) My sermons have not been much blessed as sermons. No year in my memory has been more remarkable for awakening of souls here, but very few of these were awakened by my sermons, most of them were awakened in a way that quite proved the Lord's hand without my words. Perhaps I have never yet begun to preach. I have not improved Robert M'Cheyne's death, nor the writing of his *Memoir*, at all in the manner I ought, only I never was so humbled under the conviction of my want of holiness and my real inefficiency as a minister in every department. I am ashamed of myself often before men now. Yet in several cases God has blessed me this past year, and very much indeed has there been to wonder at and adore. It will be a marked year in eternity. I often feel that Christ's Coming is nearer and nearer. I am reading passages upon this subject to my people every afternoon before preaching.

Saturday, 13*th*.—At the ministerial prayer-meeting at

Dundee on Monday. Remarkable enlargement and solemnization in prayer when together. Have been the better of that meeting ever since.

Monday, 15*th.*—It was this night last year that I last saw Robert M'Cheyne. Is there not something in this that should combine with other circumstances to make me get my lamp ready?

Friday, 26*th.*—I see that all departure from the living God is a species of unbelief, and proceeds directly from unbelief. I feel that did I live in direct faith I would live also in perpetual fellowship with God. I see also that to live a life of grace, it is needful that we feel daily that love on the side of God is the only reason why gracious feelings are ever experienced by us. Why is the fire kindled after going out every morning in my room? Just because I like to have its heat. So the Lord daily kindles love to Himself in me just because He never ceases to desire that I should be His. This is the reason of my perseverance in the narrow way. Wondrous, wondrous, wondrous! I hang upon His arm.

Monday, March 4*th.*—The *Memoir of Robert M'Cheyne* is now just about to appear. O that it may be blessed! This month last year we lost him till we go to where he is.

Saturday, 23*rd.*—It was on this day of the week last year, about sunset, that a messenger came and told me of Robert M'Cheyne's illness. It makes the day very solemn. I have grown little indeed by that providence, though it seemed sent to us for that intention. Several of us are to observe Monday as a season of special prayer and fasting to ask blessing on the *Memoir,* and the raising up of many holy men.

Thursday, April 11*th.*—Perth Fast-Day. Much helped. Never almost in my life felt more nearness to God in prayer than in the afternoon, so that it was noticed by Mr. Walker, and others in the congregation felt the same. I really longed to depart and be for ever holy and without sin.

Wednesday, 17th.—I have this some time especially felt that there is something as yet unknown to me that makes my ministry less awakening than that of almost any minister, at least among my friends that have been blessed. Indeed, I have been coming to the conclusion for some time past that I have been of far less use in any manner than I used formerly to hope. I see now that there is nothing which another cannot carry on exactly as I have done, and probably with much more success, for there is something in my ministry that is wanting. I feel willing now at once to depart and be with Christ that I may serve Him in His presence in any capacity with a perfect heart and without any secret sin, and no blight upon what I do. Or if He keeps me here, I feel that there must surely come from Himself to me some new communications of grace, some new endowment of His Spirit. I once thought myself somewhat, and I suspect that the sorrow of want of success is in my case very much the mortification of self being thrown aside as not needed by God. Indeed there is much of self in all our hours of sorrow, at least in mine.

Tuesday, May 21st.—Felt in sorrow this morning in reviewing my ministry. So little fruit, and of late so much preaching and no fruit at all to my knowledge. This is the day in the Assembly when all the ministers and elders are to be humiliating themselves for these things before God. Lord, Lord, break my hard heart. Lord, show why thou hidest Thy face from me. Wilt Thou not from this day make me wise to win souls. Found throughout the day much more than usual tenderness among the people I visited. This seemed to me to be the effect of the prayers in Edinburgh.

June 21st.—Our Communion.   The sweetest day I
have enjoyed for years ; remarkably assisted in preaching.   Great help in prayer and in the concluding
address, as well as in setting before the people the
nature of the enjoyment to be expected in the elements
themselves.   There had been much prayer beforehand
among some of the Lord's people here, and by some who
came up to the feast.   Bless the Lord, O my soul !   My
brother Horace was the only assistant, and the people
scarcely ever turned off their eye.   Sometimes deep
solemnity—' Jehovah-Shammah !'

Monday, Sept. 9th.—Preached yesterday upon baptism.
I had asked that it might be a memorable day, as was
the day when I first preached here about the Lord's
Supper.   In the interval I rode into Perth and preached
for Mr. Walker ; in coming out was thrown off my pony
by a side start and twisted my foot, so that I could
scarcely stand.   This made the people remark the day
all the more, exciting great concern.   In the evening I
had such freedom at the close that I almost never felt
more, while the people sat in breathless attention.   This
accident lays me aside for some days.   It gives me time
to read ; opportunity to learn a little of affliction ; and
is a call to more dependence upon God in going out
and in.

Friday, 13th.—Much better.   I am led to see God's
way with me.   In respect to pain and sickness, I have
scarcely known trouble, but He has not left me without
other trials.   Perhaps few have been so gently dealt
with, and yet so continually kept from seeking the
world's pleasures and drinking at its cisterns.

Thursday, Dec. 5th.—Our Fast-Day.   Ten cases of
persons who for different sins must be kept back, and
no young communicants at all have come forward.   This
state of things we must plead before the Lord.

Saturday, 7th.—Our Sabbath-school teachers' prayer-meeting this week was remarkably solemn. Two days after I heard of a man under real conviction.

Thursday, 12th.—Found two interesting cases to-day in Burrelton, and the case of a young person whom I lately married, impressed considerably by what was said, and the whole manner of the ceremony. Let us speak for God in season, out of season.

Saturday, Dec. 28th.—This night is the last Saturday of the year. How it should stir me up to review the Lord's way in the wilderness. ' The Lord alone did lead Him.' I see of late some few drops upon the pastures here.

Saturday, 4th January 1845.—Looking back on last year I feel how awfully little has been done for God. My soul has grown very little. My ministry this year has been little blessed. The *Memoir of Robert M'Cheyne* and my *Tract on Baptism* seem to me the chief way in which the Lord has been using me this year to any extent. Also this year is the first wherein I have had personal affliction. I feel that I should part with anything in order to enjoy fully every day the Lord's presence as completely felt as I feel the presence of other things around me. I never saw till now the full meaning of ' sanctifying you, body, soul, and spirit.' The tone in which we speak should be a sanctified one, the manner of our appearance, the intellectual cast of our spirit, etc. When shall this be?

Tuesday, March 25th.—I have been praying this morning in remembrance of what took place two years ago on this day—Robert M'Cheyne's death. It was also the same day of the month wherein so long since I lost my father. I feel my days gliding away. A little more grace, but very little.

Saturday, April 12th.—Have seen more than ever yet my real backsliding. I am a backslider both as a man

and as a minister. Close walking with God ; daily, if not
hourly, taste of the sweetness of Christ ; self-denial in
setting aside temptation ; all these must now be sought
by me. O God of grace, return to me from this day !
O to win Christ ! O to be as Enoch till I die !

May 23rd.—Time for prayer on Dunsinnane Hill ;
prayed for myself, the ministry, the Assembly, this place.

Sabbath, June 1st.—My quietness and retirement here
have been making me somewhat alarmed, I see so much
responsibility thereby laid upon me for growing in
holiness. The intense suffering of the girl Elizabeth
Morrison for nearly a year, though she be a true child of
God, looks to me most solemn. None can tell why the
Lord deals differently with her from what He does with
others. Such difference as this may be meant to prepare
me for future trouble and to make me say ' Thy gentleness hath made me great.'

Thursday, 5th.—To-day J. L. coming to declare to me
his determination to leave us, holding as he does strong
views, cast up to me my want of success of late. I felt
this, but knew that the cause he ascribed was not the true
one. It drove me to the Lord in some measure.

Monday, August 11th.— Now in London assisting
Mr. Hamilton (Regent Square) for four weeks.[1]

Friday, 15th.—Jewish synagogue ; it moves my compassion deeply.

Tuesday, 19th.—At Bristol ; preached amongst the
Plymouth Brethren in Bethesda Chapel. Henry Craik
invited me, and I was received with great cordiality.

Tuesday, 26th.—A meeting in a private house in
Westminster for the Jews. In the forenoon visited
Hampton Court, where I saw the vine which has

---

[1] Dr. James Hamilton was formerly at Abernyte, not far from Collace,
and there was much kindly intercourse between the two friends. He used
to say of Mr. Bonar's preaching, ' Andrew Bonar is *provokingly* natural.'

1400 clusters. It did excite desire that I might be a bringer forth of much fruit. When will there be as many graces in me? The word is sweet in these days to me; but prayer is too brief.

Oxford, Friday, 29th.—The whole city seems to concentrate its energies on study and learning. Lord, open their understanding.

Monday, Sept. 1st.—Last night Mr. Hamilton commended me to his people's prayers. Much kindness on all hands. Some good results. Often feel as if possibly the Lord might bring me here to labour.

Collace, Saturday, 20th.—To-day is the anniversary of my ordination over this people. I have been now seven years [here]. This is a Scriptural time of completeness. There is something that looks like a moving of the cloud, and perhaps my testimony here may be done.

Thursday, Oct. 2nd.—Finished to-day my notes upon the Book of Leviticus, making it ready for the press. Praise to the Lord, who alone can bless it. In the afternoon heard the rumour of a call to be given [to me] to London, which has greatly weighed upon my mind. Lord, is thy work here over? There is little doing. There is a selfish spirit creeping over the congregation. While thinking of these things to-night that passage in Augustine meets me, where he says of his mother's prayer that he might go to Rome: 'Sed tu alte consulens, et exaudiens cardinem desiderii ejus, non curasti quod tunc petebat, ut in me faceres quod semper petebat.'

Saturday, Nov. 15th.—Some light upon my path. Conversation with the brethren and with my people shows me their decided mind. To-morrow Mr. Milne summons the people to appear at the Presbytery to plead their own cause in retaining me. I do not see any strong reasons whatever for removing, and many for remaining.

Saturday, 22nd.—Preparing my *Commentary upon Leviticus* for the press, and getting to the conclusion of my corrections, I have been over-hasty in giving up to it too much time. Especially this morning, when I thought all this was over, the subject of the 'Urim and Thummim' led me away for two hours. I fear my people will suffer for this neglect of their souls. It is a wasting of my zeal upon things not immediately required.

Wednesday, Dec. 3rd. — An important day — new matter of praise. The Presbytery unanimously agreed not to remove me to London. If now the Lord has sent me back here, He must have some work [for me].

2nd January 1846.—Some thoughts upon the past ; some thoughts too upon our drawing near the Great Day of the Lord. 'In the midst of the years, Lord, make known.' For some weeks I have been considerably drawn out with longing for the power of the Holy Spirit. Reading *Gillies's Collections* has often had the effect of making me very sad, or rather full of longing with much sadness at the thought of there being no such Revival, yet with considerable hope that it might yet be in all this region.

Saturday, 10th.—Have had some times of prayer for the Spirit. *Desire* appeared to me very much to be prayer all day smoking as incense in the heart.

Tuesday, Feb. 17th.—Struck with the duty of self-denial more than ever, from i Cor. v., and especially with a minister's duty to deny himself the comforts of home and study when occasion calls him forth, from that word used by the Apostle.

Sabbath, 22nd.—Preached with little freedom. Weariness of body is against me ; but still more want of much prayer through the previous week. God will not let me preach with power when I am not much with Him. More than ever do I feel that I should be as much an intercessor as a preacher of the word. Also I have been taught that joy in the Spirit is the frame in which God blesses us to others. Joy arises from fellowship with Him—I find that whatever sorrow or humiliation of spirit presses on us, that should give way in some measure to a fresh taste of God's love when going forth to preach.

Saturday, 28th.—A remark of John Livingstone's is my prayer to-day. 'The Lord make me as humble as if I had been deserted, and yet as thankful as if it had been twice as good a day.'

From the marriage in Cana I have learned that we should look out for the Lord's most impressive teachings in common everyday concerns. They emerge from common providences.

Thursday, March 12th.—I often cannot give praise or thanks in any words but those of such songs as, 'Holy, Holy, Holy, Lord God Almighty.' These adorations serve me instead of singing.

Sabbath, 15th.—A time of much of God's presence. At the thanksgiving prayer before distributing the elements I felt more of rapturous joy than I almost ever felt. It was sweet to thank the Father for the plan of salvation revealed to us. It was sweet to thank the Son for becoming 'the Nazarite who was not known in the streets, blacker than the coal,' and gazed at as a spectacle of misery. It was sweet to thank the Spirit for revealing the Saviour, and to pray for His breath of life over the assembly, while we dropped our buckets into this well full of grace and holy love. I have more than once found that thanksgiving prayer the time of more than common freedom and gladness of spirit to me. Mr. Manson much helped too. I think that surely the Lord

was here, and that there was a token of His returning
to bless us. It might be well in the evening of the
Communion Sabbath always to read John xvii. in the
church before the sermon.

Friday, March 27th.—Received a letter to-day telling
me of the blessed effects of *Robert M'Cheyne's Memoir*
on one in London, in which he refers to the anniversary of his death—the 25th, a day I did not forget.
Many tokens have I received of the Lord's blessing
that book. It roused me to thanksgiving, and I began to
think that, if I oftener thanked God at the moment, I
might oftener hear of His blessing upon my labours.
He lets us know in order that we may give praise.

Edinburgh, Saturday, May 23rd.—Spent a little while
in meditation upon a solemn proposal made to me since
I came to Edinburgh to attend the Assembly. They
wish me to go abroad to Constantinople for three years
to the Jews there. Lord, show me Thy will. My flock,
can I leave it?

Wednesday, 27th.—Proposal was solemnly made in
the Assembly on Monday evening. I have taken it
into consideration. That evening Dr. Cappadoce addressed the Assembly very powerfully. I do not yet see
my call. I have not yet felt much of the Lord's presence
in regard to it. Only to-day, Isa. xxxii. 1, 2, has been
exceedingly sweet at all hours.

Saturday, 30th.—Yesterday was my birthday. Too
much bustled to get time for quiet thought. The Lord
spares me for His own work, I believe. I see that in
past times I have been thrust into my work, I have
not gone willingly, He has chosen my way. It is
remarkable that I should have just finished the *Commentary on Leviticus* and got it published. Is this proposal
a new way of serving the Lord? Isa. xxxvii. 3 struck
me. It is a case of perplexity difficult to decide. Lord,

this is my case at present.   Meanwhile let me spread
my case, as Hezekiah did his letter, before the Lord.
Make my way quite clear.

June 8th.—I now remember some of my prayers
have been, 'Sanctify us even if it should cost us much
suffering.'

Tuesday, 9th.—Got comfort in prayer about this matter.
Pled Isa. xlviii. 12 : 'I am the First and the Last,' seeing
the end from the beginning.   To this God I went.   In
His presence, as He allowed me, I stood and pleaded for
wisdom and light, verse 17 : 'Thy God who leadeth
thee in the way that thou shouldest go,' and verse 21
assured me that, at all events, I should not want His
presence or His blessing.   Our session last night prayed
much for direction.

Wednesday, 24th.—Very unexpectedly to-day at the
meeting of our Presbytery my case was for the present
settled.   I stated my willingness to go, for to this the
Lord had brought me ; but my remaining difficulty lay
in regard to providing for my people, as to which the
Committee offered no help.   Unless this were arranged
the object in view was not likely to be gained.   The
Presbytery was unanimously of the same opinion.   The
Lord's ways are remarkable.   I now rejoice that I was
brought to be quite willing.   I think I have not at all
opposed the leading of the Lord.   O my God, never let
me walk, even in the green pastures, without Thee !   I feel
glad to live as a 'pilgrim and stranger,' and more, far
more than before, to seek by prayer and strong crying
in secret, to see God glorified in the salvation of souls.

Friday, 26th.—Felt yesterday (our Fast-Day), after
Mr. Baxter[1] had preached upon 'the exceeding riches
of His grace,' a very deep pain of soul at the thought
that any should be leaving the place unsaved, when

[1] Of Hilltown Church, Dundee, afterwards of Free Church, Blairgowrie.

salvation was so near and so free. It was a moment
of 'travailing in birth.'

Sabbath, 28th.—A remarkable day to my soul in
regard to close enjoyment, and more especially in anti-
cipation of the rest remaining for us. Christ in His
person and God in His love shone forth all day clearly.
Much hope and expectation that souls are to be gathered
in, as well as saints built up.

Saturday, July 18*th.*—With some fear and trembling,
lest my unsanctified heart may have misled me, I have
this day written my decided answer to the Jewish Committee, declining the call to Constantinople. I am led
to apply Acts xvi. 7, for Constantinople is just opposite
the coast of Bithynia. 'I have assayed to go to the
coast opposite Bithynia, and the Spirit suffered me not.'
That is, I do not feel the Holy Spirit has stirred me
up to that work, or qualified me for it ; while yet, did
I know it as His will, I would go to-morrow.

Saturday, Aug. 8th.—Some light upon my way. The
Committee have given up as hopeless in the meantime
the attempt to supply my people for three years, and
now call me to go for life. This I have no light at all
to do. It seems contrary to God's way of training me
hitherto. Other circumstances in the matter have led
me to think the Lord is not opening up this way for
me. My brethren are now all against my going. And,
last of all, my own soul has never felt *called*. But,
O Lord, use me here. O to see souls 'growing as
among the grass, and as willows by the water-courses.'
קֹדֶשׁ לַיהוָה.

Sabbath, 16th.—It might be right in me after every
Saturday preparation to give thanks for special help.
That passage of the psalm has appeared to me very
suitable, xviii. 32 : 'It is God that girdeth me with
strength, and perfect makes my way,' etc.

Saturday, Oct. 31*st.*—Returned from the Edinburgh Communion. A time of some enjoyment, and of some remarkable experience in Providence. Heard of one case where the eyes of a person long in darkness were opened. Some things regarding my meeting with William Dickson [1] have been very pleasant, and seem to open up some prospects to me. To-night found a letter from Edinburgh from a soul that got blessing under the sermon in preaching which I had lost freedom. Thus kind and sovereign is God.

Friday, November 6th. — Still praying that the most pleasant gifts and creatures of God may be to me only helps to carry me on to rest—not themselves a rest.

Friday, 20*th.*—' Beatus qui amat te, et amicum in te, et inimicum propter te.' I seek thus to feel towards friends just now.

Being last Sabbath at Ferryden, where there is much of God's work to be seen, I have thus been led to notice how often I have helped the sick brethren, guided by God's providence. In Robert M'Cheyne's time I offered thanksgiving in his church, on a day of thanksgiving for his recovery. When Mr. Milne was ill last year I preached the Action Sermon for him. Before that I preached for Moody-Stuart, and prayed for him before his departure to seek health in Madeira. This year I preached the Action Sermon for Mr. Manson at Aber-nyte. Besides this, when abroad, my three friends were all in turn ill; I alone spared in perfect health. At present John Milne has been dangerously ill. Last Sabbath have been assisting Dr. Brewster [of Craig], and administering the Communion in his congregation, he being only able to serve one table. How singularly has the Lord dealt with me! I should remember James

---

[1] Afterwards his brother-in-law.

Hamilton too.   Last summer I preached there while
he was long ill.

Ferryden is still very interesting.   Some souls have
found rest, though most are still tossed with tempests.
It is a solemn privilege I enjoyed.

Sabbath, Dec. 6th.—Our Communion Day.   In preparation got some great help, but lost a good deal by
too little prayer last night, and by wearying myself
physically through late sitting.   Delightful message by
Mr. Hewitson [1] on Thursday, and by John to-night.

Friday, 18th.—I see that the prayers of so many
friends who pray for me are, no doubt, the cause of my
getting peculiar help in writing the *Memoir*, and then,
the [*Commentary on*] *Leviticus*.   I have often felt things
in study so plainly *given* me, not at all like the products
of my own skill, that this is the way in which I account
for them.   The Lord sends them because of people
praying for me.

Sabbath, 3rd Jan. 1847.—Last night, in reviewing
the past time, nothing shamed me more than the sin of
praying little, when we might ask in Christ's name so
much, and receive so much.   We have stood at the well
all day, and scarce drawn up a few drops.   Only this I
feel, that if I have not drunk much of the Fountain of
living waters, I have not, on the other hand, filled the
place by broken cisterns ; for hours without God have
been to me hours of no delight, no strength.

The Prayer Union has begun this morning.   We met
last night to seek grace to pray, ' abiding in Christ ' all
the time.   I seek for myself to spend this week much
as if it were a season set apart for seven days, the main
work being prayer.

Friday, 15th.—To-day I have been laying upon the
golden altar a small work upon the Second Coming,

[1] Rev. W. H. Hewitson of Dirleton.

which I have been enabled to finish to-day. I have
sought that the sins committed during its writing, and
all its imperfection, may be hid in the Saviour's fragrant
incense, and that He will present it to the Father.

London, Feb. 9th.—Called up to help Mr. Hamilton [in
Regent Square], and took the whole of his Communion
season.   There is deep responsibility laid upon me when
the Lord uses me so often in such circumstances.

Thursday, March 11th.—Conscious of backsliding I
sought last night the Lord's return, and got a sweet,
sweet sense of complete forgiveness for the past.   That
glance gave me great strength.

During this visit to London Mr. Bonar writes to Mr. Milne,
telling of his work in Regent Square, and his experiences in
the great city, closing his letter with his usual earnest appeal
for more prayer :

'Oh, brother, pray ; in spite of Satan, pray ; spend hours in
prayer, rather neglect friends than not pray, rather fast, and lose
breakfast, dinner, tea, and supper—and sleep too—than not pray.
Let even Mrs. Milne be forgotten that you may find your way into
Peniel.   And we must not *talk about* prayer—we must pray in
right earnest.   The Lord is near.   He comes softly while the
virgins slumber.   You may almost hear the breathing of the
slumberers, and the tread of Him who comes into the camp as
David did to Saul's, ere ever we are aware.'

To his Sabbath morning class for young men and women at
Collace, he wrote a letter each week while absent from them
at this time.   They show the constant and untiring interest he
took in all his people at all times.   Besides this class he had
another during the week for old women, many of whom were
unable to attend church, and were much in need of religious
instruction.   They read the Bible together, and Mr. Bonar
asked them questions.   It was one of these old women who,
when he asked her why she had passed over the long names
in Chronicles, replied, 'Well, sir, was it no' better to do that
than to *misca'* the gentlemen ?'

Saturday, 13*th*.—Living in the outer court and living not before *God*, but before 'the saints,' to please them, are both sad ways of declining. Noticed that 'the power of Christ *resting* upon us' (2 Cor. xii. 9) is ἐπισκηνώσῃ, like the curtains of a tent over a man.

Collace, Sabbath, 21*st*.—These two days have been emptied again of earthly satisfaction, and led to the Fountain of living water. There is an intense joy in God which I have not yet drawn out of Him. To-day felt much hope and expectation of souls being awakened among us.

Wednesday, 24*th*.—The National Fast for the state or famine in the land. Preached upon Isa. lxv. Personal and public sin felt and pardoned.

Monday, 29*th*.—I should love the creature as far as I see God's kindness in giving it ; in this way it will be safe. I see that we must make *efforts* if we are to be blessed. I see that I should get my texts directly from the Lord, and never preach without having got something that shows me His counsel in this matter. I should keep my eye much upon His daily providences ; they are full of wisdom and full of kindness. And these providences are like walking along the bank of a perpetually flowing stream in which we see the reflection of the glorious heavens, the works of God's hands.

April 3*rd*. — Have been instructed much by the accounts of the illness and death of William Dickson's mother. Great peace and beautiful faith brought to light in a dying hour. Many things in the whole matter remarkable. 'The Lord reigneth.' Preparing for our Communion to-morrow. Thinking of the Lord as a 'giving God.'

Saturday, 24*th*.—Tried yesterday and the night before to pray much. Often found Satan and the world striking in. Saw that, in Eph. vi. 12, our position is said to be that of fighting our daily way through armies of devils who line the road. Also, from ver. 18, saw that our praying for all saints must be very important, probably because it is our seeking the place we desire for all alike, and so asking what may be very widely useful. Sought earnestly grace to live near God, more in His love and for His glory.

May 6th.—Found the Lord putting a death upon all my plans, but found to-day, John vi. 1-20, that in *two* cases the Lord came when He had first brought them to an extremity. My way began to open. Most wonderful to see how small disappointments in providence often lead to the very best results.

Friday, 14th.—' I am not worthy of the very least of His mercies.' May the Lord keep all things henceforth in their place ; earthly affection forming but an undercurrent to the divine.

It was on this day, 14th May 1847, that Mr. Bonar was engaged to Isabella, younger daughter of Mr. James Dickson of Edinburgh. The happiness that flowed from their union was only equalled by the sorrow and desolation caused by her death seventeen years after.

Wednesday, 19th.—I wonder at my ungrateful heart. The Lord has so answered my prayers and so blessed me in His own way.

Saturday, 29th.—Spent much of the evening in meditation upon the past and in prayer. I feel deeply the sadness of living so many years to so little purpose. My selfishness is not at all cured. Every day it seems to return and fight for victory. Probably this year of my life will form an era. He has been teaching me since a good deal more of myself, and the need of striking deep roots into His own love and grace. I have

been seeking the Holy Spirit to be again to me this
night 'a well springing up.' Used Psalm xc., always
putting in '*me*,' and thus finding myself more than
usual near God as a sinner and as a believer.

June 1st.—Heard this morning that Dr. Chalmers was
gone, just when expected that day in the Assembly.
The Lord, our Head, has sent instead His message that
the God of Elijah lives, but not Elijah. It makes the
Church, as well as the world, less pleasant far. How
often he prayed that providences might be blessed, and
sent in order to be blessed. Is this one for the whole
Church sent in great mercy?

July 2nd.—Went away on Tuesday to Mr. Manson's
marriage. Had sweet prayer on Dumyat Hill alone
with Mr. Stephenson [of Pulteneytown].

Monday, 5th.—I have been much impressed with the
sin of choosing my text without special direction from
the Lord. This is like running without being sent, no
message being given me. I ought to feel, 'This I am
sent to tell you, my people.' I have begun to write out
my desires on paper like a letter, and so to pray, when I
feel my heart and thoughts wander. What is real prayer
but a letter to the Lord Jesus, reminding Him of His
words and of our needs?

Saturday, 10th.—Able for some time to-day to get
above all wish for having some pleasure here, and content with God Himself, in His fulness of grace, holiness,
and all perfections.

Wednesday, August 18th.—At times I find myself
completely free from the temptation to which Isabella's
strong attachment exposes me, so that I really long
simply for holiness and greater future usefulness. I
have felt so this day especially, in prospect of meeting
with her next week. Nothing satisfies the whole soul
but the Lord Himself.

Tuesday, 24th.—Pleasant meeting alone with Isabella ; but ' *he that drinketh of this water shall thirst again.*'

Sabbath, 29th.—Greenock Communion. Many desires after greater insight into Christ. O to have the taste of this wine ever in my mouth !

Tuesday, 31st.—Last night called to see the death of my brother's little boy Andrew, two years of age. It is the first death I ever saw. Solemn indeed to look on and see the soul leaving. It is like a flight on wings above our reach. I am thus stayed here a few days. The grief of both parents at that moment was extreme.

September 1st.—Found that John was deeply exercised by this affliction. ' All night long I was [contemplating] my boy in his temple service above,' said he. He has been praying to be kept within the ' shadow of this calamity.' Bengel says of such a time : ' When the gates of heaven open to let in a saint, delicious breezes come forth that may revive us without.'

Collace, Sabbath, 26th.—Spoke to my people much to-day about the anniversary of my ordination among them this time nine years ago. Took Matt. xvi. 20 as subject. Drawn out greatly in public prayer. Wish much to yearn toward God as God yearns towards us. This past year of my ministry has been attended with almost no power at home, and hence, perhaps, the Lord led me more away than usual this year both to England and Ireland. I never had so many letters telling of God's work as during this last year. I have been enabled to publish *Redemption Drawing Nigh* this season. One woman spoke to me between sermons in apparent awakening of soul lately begun. Lord, wilt Thou now arise ?

Wednesday, Nov. 17th.—Time of prayer alone and in expectation of meeting some of the brethren at mid-day. I feel exceedingly how little I really *converse with*

God. My prayer is like a calling to one distant, not unbosoming myself to one beside me.

Sabbath, Dec. 5th.—Much, much unsettled last week. Felt ' thou restrainedst prayer before God.' Saw ' gray hairs' here and there. No sweet delight in the Lord. It was an effort to catch something from His Word that might cause momentary refreshment. But to-day greatly revived. Much freedom in prayer, covering myself with Christ's righteousness over and over, and fully accepted therein. Some delightful moments. This was after engaging in the most painful duty of public rebuke.

Sabbath, 2nd January 1848.—Being unexpectedly enabled to be at home to-night, I have had more time for prayer and meditation. I purpose, through the Lord's grace, to mark once a week what things seem most remarkable to be thankful for. Thus to-day, bad as the weather was, I know there were three anxious souls present, evidently under the awakening of the Spirit for some time past. And yesterday, I got my tract for children printed, *Ransom for many, free to all.* Also this morning, saw some scholars in the Sabbath-school very attentive, whom I had not often been able to interest. My intended marriage may soon become a time of temptation to me. Lord, carry me this year over this danger, and make it a great blessing to my soul. Yea, make it even a time when souls shall be converted to Thee! Make me more than conqueror. I sin against the Lord by labouring more than I pray. Is not this ' serving tables'?

Sabbath, February 20th.—Remarkable. My brother John, Greenock, laid aside. I had to take the whole Communion Service for him, except one table. Saw a person in tears the whole time of the service. Felt I could long to be with Christ, even with Isabella beside me (Ps. lxxiii. 25).

Friday, 25th.—Death of Mr. Nairne of Dunsinnane this morning. I believe he has entered into rest. It may affect us here considerably, but the Lord does not wish us to lean upon instruments.

Saturday, April 1st.—Heavy through the day, but able this evening to pray with considerable fervour both for my ministry and my temporal prospects. It is all the more precious to feel great sorrow for want of success, and yearning over souls at a time like this, because I feared much that I might not get above my carnal desires and affection. But He gave me victory.

Sabbath Evening, 2nd.—A day of real desire for souls and real enjoyment of the truth itself, and a going out after souls. All this, so near my marriage, makes me hope that God has use for me, and will work here yet. Psalm cxxxviii. was our song to-night, myself and Isabella ; a review of the Lord's ways to us hitherto.

On the morning of his wedding-day, he wrote to his friend Mr. Milne :

TO REV. JOHN MILNE, PERTH.

'*Tuesday Morning,*
15 *York Place, Edinburgh.* ›

'MY DEAR BROTHER,—Your very kind note found me here this morning. You are very mindful, dear brother, you no doubt were trying to fulfil "Rejoice with them that do rejoice." At family worship this morning it was my turn (among the brothers) to conduct, and Deut. x. was the chapter in course. I found great refreshment (1) in the view of the fulfilled law—the law put into the ark ; (2) at ver. 6, the hint of all other priests passing away to give place at last to one who abideth ever ; then (3) at ver. 7, in noticing how, amid the truths, the Lord mingles temporal blessings. They come to "Jotbath," a land of rivers of waters, a very Eden compared with the sandy waste. Well, brother, I thought, is not the Lord to-day bringing me this temporal blessing? My marriage-day is my "Jotbath." And, if so, what next? Ver. 8 shows Levi *ministering nearer the ark than before* !

Ought not I so to do? Yes, but better still, it is the Lord that effects this without waiting for our advancing. He Himself puts Levi nearer the ark. And lastly, brother, notice ver. 12 to the end. What a kind, gracious, urgent exhortation to future holiness and fellowship with God ! This has been my word from the Lord to-day, and I take it as a token for good. Thanks, thanks, for your prayers and Mrs. Milne's. I trust you shall soon know my "Apphia" face to face. If ever I had true affection for any, it is for her, and yet I still feel "Christ is chief among ten thousand." I think I could, *to-day* even, welcome the cry, "Behold, the Bridegroom cometh !"

'Your kind note illustrated to me John iii. 29 : "the friend of the bridegroom."—Yours ever affectionately,

'ANDREW A. BONAR.'

Tuesday, 4th.—In the morning felt great encouragement in meditating upon Deut. x., and prayer over it at family worship, the passage occurring in our ordinary reading; the necessity for an ever-living priest ; the 'rivers of water' in the wilderness ; greater nearness to God ; holiness. Through the day many thoughts of the past, and occasionally a sort of thrill of gladness. I thought in my case 'the course of true love had run smooth,' because we had tried to acknowledge the Lord, and keep each other in our place. At mid-day, prayer with William Dickson. Mr. Charles Brown[1] at the marriage prayed for Christ's personal presence, which made me realize Him as one of the company. Everything pleasantly arranged. Got to Castlecary about half-past ten.

Wednesday, April 5th.—Felt something of the incompleteness of earthly gladness. Whatever be our gladness, this is not our heaven. I trust the Lord is making us beware of seeking a heaven out of each other. In the forenoon set off for Callander. In the evening walked out to Loch Lubnaig.

[1] The Rev. Charles J. Brown, D.D., of Free New North Church, Edinburgh.

Monday, 10th.—Preached twice unexpectedly at Callander yesterday. My experience has now led me to
great thankfulness. Distraction is over, and we can
now be calmly happy in each other's fellowship without
excitement. I feel greater desire than ever, I think, to
be the Lord's, and with the Lord.

Friday, 14th.—Collace in the evening. Not a single
disjointed arrangement. How remarkably gracious is
the Lord to us!

Thursday, May 18th.—Have just heard of Mr. Cormick's illness.[1] Last time he was here I thought him
living very near God, and wished to be often with him
and have some of his full spirit. Is he to be removed?
I feel broken at the prospect of such a stroke. In some
such way I shall probably some day be taken away
from my people ere ever I am aware. Were it not for
Isabella, I feel at times now no tie to earth ; and, since
the Lord's blessing seems withheld from the work of
our hands, I am tempted to wish I were at rest. But
the Lord's providence to me in regard to my dear wife
has been such that, I think, He has yet something for
me to learn, though it may be these kindnesses have
been fitting me for bidding farewell to earth's broken
cisterns. He may have been putting to my lips, through
Isabella, some of its sweetest comforts, and then saying,
'Come and receive the best.'

Thursday, 25th.—Death of Mr. Cormick. Oh that
it may affect me aright! Why am I spared?

Monday, 29th.—Spared to my thirty-eighth year,
while others are taken. I long to live more for God
alone. I hope for Bethel visits often yet in my pilgrimage that may quicken me. Lord, Lord, grant me this year
to live very holily, very prayerfully, very joyfully in Thee.

Saturday, June 3rd.—Have come to Kirriemuir to

[1] The Rev. Daniel Cormick of Kirriemuir.

preach on occasion of my dear brother's death [Mr. Cormick's].

Sabbath, 4th.—An impressive day to myself, and felt by many too. Saw to-day the blessed effects of preaching Christ distinctly, fully, fervently, and that it is praying much that makes preaching felt. Next to Robert M'Cheyne, this death has come closest to me; we were of late feeling more and more drawn together in spirit. I see I am favoured exceedingly by the Lord, even in regard to having such friends, and then such opportunities of usefulness. I should do things that other believers might not think necessary, since I am so favoured. Thus I should pray at times others might not. I should meditate more than others, pray more after sermons, and more for people by the wayside.

Saturday, July 22nd.—I have felt repeatedly throughout the week that nothing so strengthens the soul as a touch of the hyssop of our Priest, wet with His own blood. The moment the soul feels again the precious blessing, that leaves no darkness on the conscience, there is a power to act which nothing imparts but this.

Saturday, Aug. 12th.—Have heard of sad scenes at Collace about the market. That very morning when I heard, I came to Jer. xv. 15-21.

Saturday, Sept. 9th.—I think I see it to be somewhat as glorifying to God to keep our temper and happy frame of soul in the midst of common care, or in the midst of a rush of earthly vexations and annoyances, as it would be under the blast of persecution and dread of the sword and death. All the more glorifying, too, in the sight of God, because none else may be witness, and no motive of vainglory can creep in. The arrangements attending upon removal to the new manse[1] bring this before

[1] Until his removal to the new Free Church Manse, Mr. Bonar's home had been the Kirkton, Collace, close to the old church.

me, as also some other circumstances. I notice that, in the first chapter of Joshua, courage is four times spoken of as necessary to his discharge of duty. How often would difficulties be moved out of the way did we but go forward!

Thursday, 14th.—Tried to confess the sins committed in [this] house: the lost time, temptations, wandering thoughts; then, too, the little done for God's glory. Also, mercies received there: health, comfort, society of friends. Some souls have come there seeking salvation. I have had sorrow there too, death of friends, viz., Robert M'Cheyne. I remember so well the person coming to the door of the house and telling me of his death in a low voice. The scenes of the Disruption too are associated with that house, and my sister Christian's faithful and most patient care of me. Here, besides, it was that the Lord led me to write the *Memoir*, *Leviticus*, and *Redemption Drawing Nigh*. I went up to the garden where I used often to sit, and, after every one was away and the house locked up, sat a while musing and praying; this was on Tuesday. There are prayers offered there yet to be answered, but on that spot I have at times had some sweet moments of real fellowship. My wife has been given me, and it was there that all concerning that was transacted before the Lord. May He go with us to our new dwelling, and may my Isabella as fully as myself become every day liker those that expect a new earth and new heavens.

Saturday, 16th.—We find our house most comfortable. I cannot but record that during the time it was building I took little charge just because I feared to seem occupied with care about my worldly comfort. I often prayed about it, and the Lord inclined the deacons to see to everything. Thus I have found that while attending to the Lord's work He will attend to our comfort and advantage. Of all things of a more worldly kind *my books* are the greatest temptation.

Friday, Sept. 29th—I ought to put into practice in common duties that saying : ' Seek ye *first* the kingdom of God.' By the grace of God and the strength of His Holy Spirit I desire to lay down the rule not to speak to man until I have spoken with God ; not to do anything with my hand till I have been upon my knees ; not to read letters or papers until I have read something of the Holy Scriptures. I hope also to be able at ' cool of the day ' to pray and meditate upon the name of the Lord. It may be an Eden here.

Wednesday, 3rd January 1849.—Have tried to make these several days a time of more prayer and meditation than usual. Some success, but much to humble and even discourage. Last Sabbath was a day of power in great measure ; I realized the position of the unsaved far better. O that this week's prayers may bring down blessing upon the Church in these days of alarm and danger. My slow, slow progress in holiness and fellowship with God is what alarms me oftentimes. I can sing more than ever, however, Psalm lxxiii. 25. What mercies have been mine this past year in regard to my wife ; how the Lord has cared for me in this matter. What a calm home He has given me, and one who unselfishly cares for my every comfort far beyond what she does for her own. Lord, it is ' Thou alone that leadest, and there is no strange God with Thee.'

Saturday, 6th.—Tried to keep this day with the brethren for special prayer. Prayed for my tract for young men, *Real Joy*, of which 13,000 are to be distributed in and about London.

Saturday, Feb. 3rd.—Our day of prayer among brethren. Felt much freedom lately, and at one time rejoiced in the idea of it being *God alone* that I had to do with in going into eternity. He seemed so well known and sure. His heart is open, His grace has made all known to us. This seemed indeed a blessed blessedness, if I might so speak. Continued till three P.M. in attempts to pray and wait upon God.

Greenock, Saturday, 17th [March].—John told me of a lad led to salvation through the Communion last year when I had the whole charge.

Sabbath, 25th.—Memorable anniversary of Robert M'Cheyne's death; and as it is the anniversary of my father's death also, it struck me more. Last night and this morning this has led me to much meditation. I took up Baxter's *Dying Thoughts* to-night to help me to look into the other world.

April 4th.—This morning, in remembrance of this day last year, Isabella and I prayed together over the year's remarkable kindness; and again this evening before closing the day. O for more holiness in our walk and conversation! 'When wilt Thou come unto me?' We are loaded with benefits, and yet I feel that my unholy life is a sad expression of unthankfulness for our domestic mercies.

Tuesday, June 19th.—Have often found of late that verse powerful, Psalm xxxvii. 4: 'Delight thyself.' The more I have been able to make God my chief joy the less do I feel in any way tormented with earthly desires, and I see myself surrounded with comforts.

July 8th.—Have been much struck with being called to assist at Lady Glenorchy's, presiding in the absence of Mr. Davidson at the Communion. This is the seventh time I have been so employed, within ten years, in the absence of a sick minister on the Communion Sabbath. What does God teach me by this?

Wednesday, 25th.—When I consider my time of late, our Lord's words ring in my ear, 'Have I been so long

time with thee, and yet hast thou not known Me ? ' I
have not advanced in prayerfulness, nor have I grown
to any great extent more than in former years. I live
too much upon old manna.

August 2nd.—To-day at Torphichen, where with
peculiar feelings of solemnity and interest I have been
helped to preach. In the afternoon walked down to the
brae where the people used to come at Communion
times, under the shade of trees, often singing or praying
during the night, there being no room for them in
houses. The memory of the just is still fragrant here ;
old Mr. Bonar is well known by tradition.[1] An old
woman showed me his grave in the choir. I know not
how, but there was all the time upon me a peculiar
solemnity and pleasant yet serious delight in being
there, mixed with much hope. I felt, too, as if the Lord,
who used to be here with His saints, was still there,
remembering days of old ; and when the minister
pointed to the Kilsyth Hills from which strangers used
to come, and over which Mr. Bonar went, I felt as if the
feet of these saints were still scarcely lifted up from
these scenes. What will resurrection be, which restores
us to all these companions, the already blessed ones !

Collace, 10th.—Heavy in head and heart because
of this being the market-day in Kinrossie. Spent some
time in prayer and crying to the Lord. Found peace
and calmness. In the afternoon a very great storm
of thunder and lightning came on ; it seemed to be
from the Lord to disperse the people.

Saturday, 18th.—After reading John M'Donald's[2] life,
felt as if more than ever I could see the sovereignty
of God, for there was a man of powerful mind full
of thought and understanding, prayerful ; yet success
seemed small in proportion to efforts used. Felt stirred

---

[1] See Introduction.   [2] Of Calcutta.

up to pray for the Lord's special blessing upon my
ministry, and that He might use my far inferior talents.
Sweet prayer-meeting with Patrick Miller and William
Cousin [of Melrose], who were here till this morning.

Saturday, 25th.—Led to think to-day that my way of
praying is chiefly to be by *bolts upward*, not by very
long prayers at one time.

Saturday, Sept. 8th.—Seeking the 'joy unspeakable'
at its Fountain-head. 'In whom believing.'

Tuesday, 18th.—Yesterday was our ministerial prayer-
meeting. Met at Abernyte. Several solemn thoughts
raised, and a season of near, very near prayer, when
speaking to God about our ministry. This morning early I had awakened and looked out. It was
about four o'clock. The morning star was shining
directly before our window in a bright sky. One part
of the window was misty with frost; the other clear, and
through the clear part the star shone most beautifully.
I thought of Christ's words, ὁ ἀστὴρ ὁ λαμπρὸς ὁ πρωϊνός
(Rev. xxii. 16). Christ is all this to me in this world till
the day break. I fell asleep, and when I next awoke
the sun was shining through my room. Shall it not be
thus at the Resurrection? Our shadowy views of Christ
are past, and now He is Sun of Righteousness.

Thursday, 20th.—Calling to mind my ordination
this day eleven years ago, I spent some hours in the
afternoon in the wood, reviewing the past, confessing
sin, seeking mercy through the blood of the Lamb, who
has a fold of righteousness to spread over a minister's
sins. Some brokenness of heart and some power to
cry for future blessing. I see Ezekiel got some of his
messages in his twelfth year. May the Lord God of
Ezekiel remember me! Josiah's reformation began in
the twelfth year of his reign. The cases of blessing at
one of our Communions, and that other at Greenock

Communion, were brought to my mind when wondering if I had been of any use this year. My ordination day is always my 'month Abib,' the beginning of the year to me. Satan tries to keep us from remembering these things.

Glasgow, Tuesday, Oct. 30th.—Enjoyed communion much here. I see that a minister is to give himself to prayer more than his people. Spent a day with Alexander Somerville getting illustrations of the Scriptures from his recent journey.

Saturday, Dec. 29th.—Solemn view of last year. I get slowly, slowly on in grace. I am creeping by the shore only, not thrusting out into the deep. My chief desire should be on this day to be a man of prayer, for there is no want of speaking and writing and preaching and teaching and warning; but there *is* need of the Holy Spirit to make all this effectual. The Lord help me to pray for the eyes of believers being opened to see the Lord's Coming. Help me to pray for my poor flock! Help me to cry for my wife's growth in grace as truly as she grows in kindness and attention to me! Help me to be a blessing to the whole earth next year. And if I should enter Eternity before next year, Lord, may I be found on the mountain of myrrh and the hill of frankincense, waiting for the Daybreak with those that have gone before,—Robert M'Cheyne, Daniel Cormick, my sister Marjory, and multitudes, multitudes!

Tuesday, 1st January 1850.—It is more than usually startling to be writing a new year; the idea of being in 1850 seems to carry us on so far.

Friday, February 8th.—After a week's work my study days are times of great rest and refreshment. I have been thinking that they may be emblems to me of my whole life. Let me work on and labour, and at last will come the sweet rest that remains for the people of God.

My every week should be emblematical of this, work and rest. I am sometimes alarmed, almost terrified, at my slow advance in holiness. My constant desire is that the Holy Ghost in me may be felt springing up.

Saturday, 9th.—I find it good often to stand before God and use words of adoration in His presence, looking up to Him face to face—' to Him that loved us,' etc., etc., and ' O the depth of the riches,' etc., etc.

Friday, 15th.—Made to feel to-day, while here at Greenock Communion, the sin of desiring to be great and to have a name among men. Christ did not so desire. I have long had this sin to strive against. To-day I felt somewhat able to tell the Lord that now I renounced it for ever ; and that I wish to live to Him and to be not at all distressed by being unnoticed by men. Lord, enable me to live under the smile of Thy love, willing not to be noticed upon earth, if so I may glorify Thee more.

Sabbath, 17th.—At the table sought for deadness to men's opinion. Had a good deal of distraction, but in the evening a flood of peace. My heart entered into Christ's peace upon which I was preaching.

Tuesday, 19th.—Heard of blessing attending my preaching in Huntly many years ago, in the case of two young men. ' Bless the Lord, O my soul.'

Thursday, April 25th.—Being at Edinburgh Fast-Day, a remarkable change of arrangement led me to preach in the morning for Mr. Moody instead of afternoon ; and no sooner was the service over than I was visited by a woman awakened that morning to deep sense of sin ; a woman not in the habit of coming to that church at all. A sin of thirteen years ago had been called to mind.

Friday, May 17th.—Feel to-day much impressed with this that at present there is no way in which I can so directly and really advance the cause of God as by much prayer.

June 4th.— Prevented by the meetings of the General Assembly from putting down anything. My birthday passed while I was in Edinburgh at the Assembly. Moses at this period of his life was purposing what to do with the people of Israel, and how he might deliver them. O that I were now sent to do more than I ever yet have been used to do for souls and for God's glory! I find that a fresh text or some fresh occurrence is the true way to help me to offer up fresh thanks and fresh prayer.

Saturday, 29th.—Our Communion season. My brother Horace heard of the illness of his little baby. We have heard of her death this morning. Such a stroke, and in such unexpected circumstances, makes me feel how much I was secretly trusting to instruments and to our own arrangements.

Sabbath, 30th.—Memorable day in many respects. Though much helped yesterday in preaching, to-day I preached with great difficulty, but when the Lord had thus humbled me, especially at the table, my bonds fell off, and the whole day after was very full [of] grace. The people, too, whom I could not look in the face before, were now all attention. Mr. Milne in the evening was most precious upon Psalm xxxix. 9—bringing before us the Lord's providences in regard to [what has happened] and in other aspects. May the Lord speak to my brother's heart and to Jane's [his wife], for He has withered their gourd. In the closing prayer this evening I felt greatly drawn out, and Mr. Milne's earnestness grew higher and higher while pleading for the unsaved. 'Mercy, mercy, mercy, Lord! Grace, grace, grace! Salvation, salvation, salvation!' Oh, surely the Lord has touched some.

Friday, July 19th.—Without being able to assign any cause beyond the feeling I have sometimes had in my head, it has more than once crossed my mind that the Lord may take me away suddenly. Great health is often thus cut down, and, knowing this, the Lord in His providence warns the healthy as much as if I were a sickly man.

August 8th.—Newcastle and London. Heard of Mr. Hewitson's death. How blessed are those who walk with God! I feel as if few of such were now left. What a consciousness there was in him of the realized presence of God! 'I will water him every moment,' seemed fulfilled in his case. Felt great sorrow at not having prayed for the Jews or spoken for them in public to-day.

Saturday, 24th.—A week of mercies. I heard of some good from my tract, *Real Joy.*

Saturday, 31st.—Home again; found all in peace. I wish I could pray for something new every day, while there are so many things in the Treasury of God.

Saturday, Sept. 7th.—Tried this morning specially to pray against idols in the shape of my books and studies. These encroach upon my direct communion with God, and need to be watched.

Tuesday, 10th.—I spent most of this day in reading *Dr. Chalmers's Life*—two volumes. In the midst of my reading a man came in to ask me to go with him to settle a quarrel between him and his wife. The Lord does not use me, like His servant Dr. Chalmers, for great things, but my way of serving the Lord is walking three or four miles to quiet a family dispute! The Lord shows me that He wishes me to be one of the common Levites who carry the pins.

Saturday, 21st.—Yesterday, twelve years ago, was my ordination day. I now begin another year. I have set apart time at mid-day every day this week for special prayer in regard to my ministry and my own soul. On

Monday I was led to notice the necessity of getting texts from the Lord, a cup full of water from the Well of Life. During last year little fruit ; only one old man and something hopeful among young children ; but I have had encouragement in other places. I do not know this last season of one soul awakened in this place directly from my preaching.

Sabbath, 22*nd.*—Have been enabled during the week to pray every day for help by setting apart an hour in addition for this end ; the benefit appeared to-day in remarkable liberty in speaking to my flock about the past twelve years.

Saturday, Oct. 19*th.*—At a few minutes past one the servant hastily knocked at the door of my study to tell me that I had got a little daughter. Praise to the Lord ! Let this be an heir of glory, and then how are we honoured. Strange confusion still in thinking of my new relation.

Monday, 21*st.*—I see that, rightly understood, it is as solemn a thing to be crowned with mercies as to be crushed with affliction. With a parent's feelings now, and circumstances all new in some measure, I feel the blessedness of the verse, James i. 5 : ' Ask wisdom,' etc.

Monday, Nov. 11*th.*—Could not sleep for nearly two hours after going to bed last night because of vexation at the dull, dead state of all things here. I begin to think that my work may be closing. My prayer last night, with deep earnestness, was that either the Lord would awaken souls or send me to some place where He might do so.

Saturday, 16*th.*—Isabella was able to come to my study, and together we thanked the Lord.

Monday, Dec. 9*th.*—To-day, in the forenoon, our little infant Isabella is to be baptized, and I have been seeking grace to use this ordinance aright. Lord, take this little one under the shadow of the Great Rock. I feel

as if it were a special visit we are making with her to
the wells of salvation—Father, Son, and Spirit.

Evening.—During my brother John's address I felt
the ascended Saviour as if standing with me giving
power to the ordinance, and Father, Son, and Spirit
present in truth bending down over the child. Very
quiet solemnity over me, and I feel it still this night. I
have felt very happy in the thought that, while little
success has attended my ministry of late, here at least,
in my dwelling, is a soul which the Lord takes as His
own. Our little one is His. I realized for a little
while the presence of the Three Persons of the Godhead, as at Jordan when Jesus was baptized. I know
Godhead was present.[1]

Saturday, 14*th.*—In returning yesterday from Mark-
inch Fast-Day, found a letter waiting me which told me
the good tidings of a soul saved through reading my
Commentary on Leviticus—the captain of a steamer in
the Thames. My soul has been as glad ever since as
I was at the birth of my little daughter. I had been
mourning over the stagnation of the pools in the valley
of Baca, when this came to stir up my soul to praise
and thanksgiving.

Tuesday, 31*st.*—Have come from the prayer-meeting
which I had to-night. The last night of the year is very
solemn, like looking on the whole of the past at once.
A year of great family mercy, ' I will mention the loving-
kindness of the Lord ; ' a year wherein the wise virgins
seem to slumber and sleep as much, or more than ever ;
a year of danger overhanging the land from Popery.

[1] Replying to a request from Mr. Milne to come and baptize his little
daughter, Mr. Bonar says : ' Your request is what I would like to comply
with. I like baptisms. It was at a baptism that " the heavens were
opened," and so much of grace is seen exhibited there—Christ free to a
little child.'

We are silently advancing towards the Day of the Lord. 'Behold! I come as a thief.' The thought of leaving my people here has been much on my mind this year; but it may be a thought like Jonah's, fleeing from difficulty.

1st January 1851.—Fully convinced by Scripture, and past experience especially, and by the experience of all saints, that the best thing I can do, in my study and mode of conducting work, will be to give more time to prayer, and always to give it the earliest place in my employments. When I return from a journey begin with prayer before sitting down to read letters, etc., etc. Now, Lord, help me to fulfil this, this year.

March 16th.—Our Communion. Mr. Moody-Stuart assisted; preached in the evening with very great power upon, 'A goodly price I was prized at.' O surely there is to be fruit of this day! Lord, why wast Thou so plainly among us if no more souls are to be saved? Was it all for Thy few chosen ones? If so, O how Thou lovest them! my Lord and my God!

May 16th.—Sensible of long intervals in my communion with God. Shallowness, hardness of heart, self-regard, darkness in the understanding, are most obvious in my case. It is the simple element of the truth, '*Christ gave Himself for our sins,*' that keeps me up daily. Oh, Eternal Spirit, teach me more! for I am but a child, yet I am a minister, and ought to teach others by my life and by my words. Oh, Eternal Spirit! mould me to Christ's likeness.

Saturday, 17th.—Set apart this day till eight o'clock for prayer and self-examination. Reading, too, in the afternoon, dear and precious *Hewitson's Memoir*, which has just appeared. O to be at all like him in the unbrokenness of his communion with God.

Sabbath, 25th.—Learned to consult with God, and not with flesh and blood, having got much and special help in preaching in Tanfield, though tempted and urged to give up a sermon that I thought suitable.

August 2nd.—Had some pleasant thoughts by the way while journeying to London, on Psa. xxxii.—mercy compassing about like an elastic band ; I cannot go beyond its circle. I may be surrounded with sorrow and trial, but still I am within the band of mercy.

Sabbath, 3rd.—Death of William Hamilton—a truly wise and godly man fallen asleep in Jesus this morning.

Monday, 18th.—Met Mr. Jacobus from New York, who lately was in the Holy Land, and got to know the Samaritan who found my Bible in Jacob's well.

Thursday, Sept. 11th.—Home. Meeting at Rait with four of the brethren, fitted to give a deep sense of responsibility as to our living near God daily. The ' Spirit of Might,' as well as the ' Spirit of Counsel,' is a blessed name of the Comforter, and this we need that we may carry into effect what we desire. We agreed that we ought to ask our people's prayers ; that we should seek guidance in our public prayer ; then, that in private prayer we should ask and put up petitions, even if we felt not in the spirit.

Tuesday, 16th.—In prayer in the wood for some time, having set apart three hours for devotion ; felt drawn out much to pray for that peculiar fragrance which believers have about them, who are very much in fellowship with God. It is like an aroma, unseen but felt. Other Christians have the beauty of the Rose of Sharon ; these have the fragrance too.

Wednesday, 17th.—Again, to-day, spent my time in the wood for some hours, praying much that the world may see Christ's glorious beauty. Let them hear the cry, ' Eli, Eli ! ' let them see Thy countenance.

Thursday, 18*th*.—Again in Dunsinnane Wood. Led to pray for the anointing with power from on high, and the being filled with the Holy Ghost, as bearing upon the fragrance and peculiar aroma I was yesterday praying for.

Saturday, 20*th*.—Forgot till the day was begun that this was the anniversary of my ordination. Glad that this has been a week of some prayer. In beginning the fourteenth year of my ministry, I see that Hezekiah was sick that year, and that year God wrought wonderfully with Sennacherib. I feel bitterly that this year's ministry has been very fruitless. I have heard of three cases of good done, perhaps more, in regard to persons at a distance, but not one very decided case in this parish. I fear that I have studied more than directly sought my people's conversion this year.

Sabbath, Dec. 14*th*.—I have been led more than once to think if it may not be my duty to go to such a place as Glasgow, and there as a missionary dig out the wretched people of the wynds. I sometimes think that the Lord is making my way easier to leave this place, by various occurrences. But what matters change of place if the Lord go with us?

Saturday, 27*th*.—The old minister is dying, to all appearance. It was a solemn sight for me to see him on Thursday unconscious, and, so far as we know, no change upon him.

Sabbath, 28*th*.—Did not hear till to-day that the old minister died on Friday. Solemn ending of such a life to the old man. I saw him the day before he died, and have tried to pray much for him of late. But how feeble effort appears to be when the time of death comes! O my Lord! send me zeal, love to souls, pity, compassion. I felt a sort of fear to dedicate myself to the Lord, to give up myself wholly to Him, till in a moment I saw

that the Lord is love itself, and cannot but require me
to do what is best.

2nd January 1852.—Yesterday at the funeral of the
old minister. May I not spend my days as he! Lord,
cleanse me from blood-guiltiness in regard to him and my
people. I felt constrained to this prayer as I went along.

Monday, 26th.—Several circumstances have combined
to make me turn attention to the thought of death. On
Saturday I was with one who died whilst I stood by.
Often, too, has the consideration been pressed upon me,
' How shall I feel at that hour?' This leads me to cry
for stronger faith, clearer faith, entire leaning upon
Christ and very close communion with Him now. I
am persuaded that the other world is in a measure felt
when a soul is truly in the act of communion with the
Lord.

Sabbath, April 18th.—The ground seems very dry,
dryer than ever. Am I to leave this people? Are the
stakes of this tent to be pulled up? Oh, if I saw tokens
of blessing! Oh, if I saw any drops from heaven!

Friday, May 7th.—Was greatly comforted when in
Kelso, by hearing of a man awakened at a service many
many years since, and brought to Christ at another, the
year after. Also the case of the woman, more than ten
years ago, brought to peace by the truth of God seen in
the ' ears of barley' from Mount Zion.

Saturday, 22nd.—Cheered last night by finding out a
case of apparent conversion in one of my young communicants. This makes me know that the Lord has
not left us.

Monday, June 28th.—Frequently during this season I
have had closer drawings to things eternal than before.
I have now and then not only panted after them, but
felt as if I were going in within the veil to be always
among them.

Sabbath, August 15*th.*—Thinking of the few that seem to advance in grace, was cheered by this, *that touching even the hem of His garment is salvation.*

Sabbath, 29*th.*—A trying day to me. Such Sabbaths as this wean me from preaching, lest I should grow too fond of even that, and be unwilling to depart and be with Christ. I felt how easily the Lord could dispense with my service, and get other vessels to fill, far, far fuller.

September 18*th.*—More than once this week, in remembering this being the time of my ordination fourteen years ago, I have tried to have seasons of prayer. This year *omissions* have distressed me more than anything. I have had sorrow more frequently and deeply for the want of blessing in my ministry. I have had evidence of only one soul in my congregation blessed this year, and a few others hopeful. The Lord has helped me to write *The Gospel Pointing to the Person of Christ.* May He bless it!

Monday, 27*th.*—'Thou preventest us with the blessings of Thy goodness.' Scarcely had we time to be anxious to-day when the Lord sent us a little boy. 'Bless the Lord, O my soul.'

Saturday, October 2*nd.*—Have been trying to praise, having written a discourse upon 'Seven times a day,' etc., etc. Such mercies as mine call for much praise from as many as I can stir up to the blessed duty, as well as from myself. I should be a harper even now, and have the Lord's people to be the same.

Saturday, November 6*th.*—To-day Horace has come to help me, and baptize our child to-morrow. I set my face to seek the Lord by fasting and prayer till the afternoon. Had some freedom as the day advanced. I felt able to cry, 'God be *merciful* to me a sinner,' in the sense of sanctification and seeking holiness, just as when I

sought pardon formerly. I then set myself to see all
that is said in the Bible about baptism, with prayer and
confession and with praise. The Lord to-morrow take up
James in His arms and acknowledge him for His child.
I find that many of the Lord's people have found communion with God in the ordinance of baptism. I have
been seeking this. Isabella and I prayed together about
this matter.

Sabbath, 7th.—I had some communion with God in
the ordinance, specially while my brother spoke of
' Incarnate love Himself, saying " Suffer little children
to come." ' Altogether much of the Lord's dealing with
me and mine. In the evening we both experienced a
most remarkable deliverance while riding to Blairgowrie,
the gig being completely overturned into a field, and yet
both escaped. I have got no more than Jacob got to
remind him that he had been wrestling. I have got a
slight touch to keep me impressed with my deliverance.
Lord, show me what this means ! Thou hast charged
Thine angels to keep us this night assuredly. What
shall we render unto Thee ? O for more of the cup of
salvation.

Saturday, 13th.—It still looks a marvellous deliverance
that escape of ours. I have, however, had reason to
notice it especially, for my leg has kept me a prisoner
all week, though it is only a sinew that has been strained,
Psalm cvii. 43. The Lord teaches me to preach as if
I were never to preach again, and how thankful I feel
for my brother's entire escape. I could depart without
being missed beyond a narrow circle, but his would
be a general loss.

Monday, Dec. 27th.—I have found these hours of the
Prayer Union very sweet. Why do I not pray longer
always ? It is like pressing farther and farther in, to the
holiest of all.

Saturday, 1*st January* 1853.—My watchword this year be Hosea vi. 3 : 'Follow on to know the Lord.' ' Lead us not into temptation, but deliver us from evil ' is to-day's clause in the Lord's Prayer which we have been using in the Prayer Union.   I do love the Lord ; there is none in heaven but He, none on the earth whom my whole soul goes forth unto, and never may it rest but in enjoying Him.   Six ministers whom I know have died this past year.   Why am I left ?   I was nearly cut off ; was this a notice to be ready ?   My heart sinks within me still in looking back and seeing how little self-denial I have shown this year past, and how exceedingly little I have done for God.

Tuesday, 11*th* [*Jan.*].—This fortnight past there has been before my mind very much the thought of what has been occurring in the case of my dear and beloved brother John Milne.   He has offered himself for Calcutta. He has twice written to me saying that he believes I will be called upon to succeed him in his present charge. This has come quite suddenly upon me.   There is a call to fresh and earnest work while I am here, and prayer to know the Lord's mind as to the future.   It is remark-able that I heard of this during the Week of Prayer.   I feel as to my fitness, that it is not what Mr. Milne thinks.   I need not change of place nor people, but of heart, in order to be more useful.

The friendship that existed between Mr. Bonar and Mr. Milne of Perth was peculiarly deep and tender.   They had much in common, and their work and inclinations drew them much together.   Mr. Bonar's little notes to Mr. Milne from Collace are very quaint and often very beautiful.   One day he writes :

' We meet here on Tuesday next for prayer and fellowship one with another.   Will you be present ?   Do come, and stay to the evening meeting.   You are a *rara avis* in this region — a Phœnix !

May you be so, and may you flourish as the φοῖνιξ till you go to wave your βαία before the Throne !' [1]

Another time he writes :—

'Any marks of a rising tide ? I long to come into the tract of some trade-wind from heaven that would send us sooner homeward to breathe amid the realities of a better world. Is there not honey in this verse, "Christ is the end of the law for righteousness"? Hold him up as the true fulfiller of our ministry.

'Only get above the clouds, brother. We must think only of how the Lord may be glorified. "*None of us liveth to himself.*" Never mind vigour or want of vigour, comfort or want of comfort, in our preaching and ministry. All we have to do is to do our best as we get strength at the time, and, as Robert M'Cheyne used to say, "The Lord can show us how to catch fish with a broken net."

'"Be of good cheer." Our works do not save us, our ill-success will not destroy us, our corruptions and imperfections will only make us more indebted to Jesus for ever. "He that believeth shall be saved."'

In closing a short note about some preaching arrangements, he says :—

'I was meditating on two words to-day. "*He* was there *alone.*" It seems to me as if heaven would almost be sweeter if there were no multitudes even of angels, but *Jesus only* filling all.'

Mr. Milne on one occasion had been holding a service in a country village, and had been rather too lengthy. In reference to this, Mr. Bonar writes the following playful letter :—

'I am going to open up a correspondence with you on the subject of *length*. It is not to be a mathematical, but a doctrinal discussion. I heard lately an amazing story of your having kept a certain company on their feet by a *two-hours'* prayer ! A somewhat more certain fact, however, is, that you kept the poor people of Kettens till eleven at night ! It is the theory of length that I wish to discuss. I do honestly and conscientiously think that there is more of *gift* in it than of *grace*. And I have of late pur-

----

[1] The Greek word for Phœnix meant also palm-tree. βαία are the branches.

posed to be shorter than I generally am, on the consideration that half-an-hour's discourse, spoken in faith and preceded by many hours of prayer, will be as likely to be blessed as an hour. Quantity seems to me very unimportant. It soothes our conscience to have said so much to our people, it makes us think, " Surely, now, *they* are to blame for not being converted, and not I." Whereas, dear brother, it may be that " Follow me," spoken in self-denying faith, would be better far than " continuing our speech till midnight."

' Last night I actually slept sooner than usual from the feeling that now I had laid before the people as much truth and as plainly as might find entrance into their hearts, if only the Holy Ghost would now come. Was I right ? Tell me your views. " Reprove, rebuke, exhort." '

After Mr. Bonar removed to Glasgow, this friendship continued through many joys and sorrows, and the annual gatherings at the Perth Conference in September were always times of reunion and brotherly fellowship. The Conference owed its beginning to Mr. Milne, and for thirty years Mr. Bonar was present at nearly all the meetings.

Saturday, Feb. 26th.—An exciting week. At our meeting of Presbytery on Wednesday, we agreed to let Mr. Milne away to India. This leaves me more than ever a pilgrim. In a few years M'Cheyne, Cormick, Hewitson, away to glory, Patrick Miller away from Dundee, Cumming away from this neighbourhood, and now Milne.

March 21st.—Our Communion yesterday. As usual my consciousness of great help began when at the thanksgiving prayer, then increased at the table, and continued to the close. But I felt more of direct temptation, like Satan in the midst, than I have done this long time. Mr. Manson very vigorous. I have prospered, as to getting sermons and help in them, ever since I made it a rule not to fix thought upon a subject till I had prayed somewhat fully for particular help as to the subject, doctrine, illustration, and application.

Sabbath, April 3rd.—During last week, especially while at Greenock Communion on the Sabbath, I saw that I fall into a great snare often by my fondness for books, Satan and my heart agreeing in thus leading me off from prayer and from the Word itself also. To-day have been feeling that God must fill my soul with yearning over perishing souls, and clothe me with compassion.

Saturday, 9th.—More and more saddened as the day of John Milne's leaving draws on. It is to be on Monday evening that we take farewell of him in his church. It is like another death to me. What a different place Perth will now seem, just as different as Dundee now is from what it was. But one thing is ever before me, the thought that I have slighted the opportunity I had of getting good from him.

Tuesday, 12th.—Have returned from my final visit to John Milne. I preached yesterday forenoon on ' Jesus Christ the same yesterday, to-day, and for ever.' The evening meeting was crowded to excess, and was well conducted. Mr. Milne spoke strongly to me upon the likelihood of his people choosing me, but this is not likely at all now, so far as I can see. I felt a little humbled when I heard that they were already looking out for a man of gifts, but now I really feel no wish whatever to be there. O that in my own place the Lord would enable me to show myself a ' workman that needeth not to be ashamed.'

Tuesday, 19th.—To-day Mr. Milne is to sail from Southampton. It was so ordered that Alexander Somerville and I were on the top of Dunsinnane Hill in the forenoon, and there we prayed for him and ourselves. In praying for me, Alexander Somerville asked that I might be content without man's favour, and that this might be enough, '*I will love him.*' He came over this often, and I felt it given him of God. I feel that is my condition now. Very few need me or are benefited by me. But this is my comfort, '*I will love Him.*' Christ cares for me and will keep me to the end.

May 1st.—After my Communion I heard of blessing upon the *Memoir of Robert M'Cheyne* in the case of one in Edinburgh.

Sabbath, 15*th.*—I once applied Elijah under the juniper tree, sent back to his old place on Carmel amid his unbelieving countrymen, to my brother Mr. Milne. I suspect now it was myself that ought to have had that applied to me.

Friday, 20*th.*—Left alone in the house, and having previously, in prospect of this, got on with my preparation, spent most of this day in prayer and meditation with fasting.

Friday, 27*th.*—Tried again this day, but having let in some common business, and trusting to last week's help, I did not succeed so well. I prayed over the names of all my communicants.

Wednesday, June 1*st.*—Spent after three o'clock in fasting and prayer. Before retiring to rest have felt something of 'my soul longeth, yea even fainteth,' etc., and I lie down this night intensely desiring to feel constrained by the love of Christ.

Saturday, 4*th.*—'Your body is the temple of the Holy Ghost.' This has been in my mind. I felt for a week as if it were giving up all hope of freedom and comfort were the Lord to be managing everything even about my body, but to-day I rejoice! His will is holier, wiser, and more loving too than mine. Let Him be 'the Spirit in the wheels.'

September 7*th.*—Have been enabled these two days to go apart for some hours into the wood and meet God there. Less than I could have wished, yet still some success. For some time past I have been occasionally getting humbling, soul-melting views, and occasionally near insight into things eternal. Have been drawing up the book, *The Old Gospel Way*, and writing the tract, *Seeking the Way*. Sometimes I think my heart is drawn considerably toward working among the perishing multitudes at home in such places as Glasgow.

Friday, 9th.—The Lord has sent a young man from Dundee to speak to me about his soul, in deep earnest.

Sabbath, 18th.—In two days will be the anniversary of my ordination. Throughout this past ministerial year answer to some special prayers has been the most encouraging to me, so that I feel sometimes as if the Lord might come with His Spirit quickly. Then sudden deaths have been frequent, and there have been three removals of my brethren, and myself was nearly gone, and my brother-in-law, William Grant,[1] seems now sinking away. These things bid me gird my loins. Let me watch. It was in the sixteenth year that Uzziah fell. I have been enabled this year and lately to finish that collection of Gospel truths, *The Old Gospel Way*.

Tuesday, 20th.—My ordination day. Thought it best to spend some hours to-day in praise; my causes for praise are innumerable.

Thursday, 22nd.—As the fruit of my hours with God I have no doubt it was that to-day I had singular help of spirit when addressing Mr. Bannerman at his ordination before going to New Zealand.

Wednesday, 28th.—To-day heard of William Grant's death on Monday night. How very solemn!

Saturday, Oct. 8th.—One thing to-day struck me. I should seek to be earnest and warm in family worship

---

[1] Minister of the parish of Cavers in Roxburghshire. He was married to Mrs. Bonar's only sister.

as well as in public, and I must watch to be useful at table. Often my heart groans when I hear of the success of other men of God, while I preach from week to week and see my people so unmoved ; no movement among souls beyond a momentary seriousness, nor do I often now hear of much good resulting from my books.

November 8*th*.—Prayer, prayer, prayer must be more a business than it has been.

Dec. 5*th*.—Began our monthly concert for prayer among the few of us remaining. The words, ' Be not weary,' plainly show us that we were often to be left in a state that might make us so—want of present success, want of special encouragement. I have got on hand *Dr. Nettleton's Life* to revise and publish, which gives me opportunity of speaking on many points, and speaking for Christ to many. It came to me most unexpectedly as a request from the bookseller just when I had some time for it.

Saturday, 24*th*.—Crying for a revival in myself and others, and in the Church at large. Sometimes hope rises—sometimes my heart sinks and becomes cold again. Our meeting of brethren for prayer on Tuesday was very pleasant and strengthening. Surely seed is sown at these times, but why does He tarry in the answer ? I have been asking, and wish yet more to ask, solemnity in reading the Word, and in reading my text very specially.

Saturday, 31*st*.—I see this year past has been instructive to me as to my uselessness, and has stript me of several fancied possessions. O that I were living so as to be winning souls ! I have been helped in family prayer remarkably ever since that day in October I sought special assistance in this matter. Lord, think upon Isaiah lxiii. 10.

Some letters written during this year let us see how he was enabled to comfort others by the comfort wherewith he himself was comforted by God :—

TO HIS SISTER ELIZA.

'*Collace, Saturday.*

'MY DEAR ELIZA,—Many thanks for your nice long letter. I don't remember reading that life of father which you refer to, though I have gone over all the shorthand volumes of his life. I remember being so struck in coming to the few last weeks and days, at the unexpected stop in the diary, especially a few days only before his death. It was the breaking of the thread, the end of the web, as Hezekiah would say (see Isaiah xxxviii.). We were reading this morning, Joshua v., the manna ceased only when they really had crossed the Jordan, and as for the Cloudy Pillar no notice is taken of its ceasing excepting this. The Lord says : "As Captain of the host am I *now* come." It was as much as saying : " I have hitherto led you through the wilderness in the Cloud, but now the end of that is come, and so I appear as Captain of the host leading you all into the Land." Some day it shall be thus with us. We shall suddenly find Bibles, and ordinances, and living by faith (our manna) all ceasing, for sight has come and the realities of the Unseen Glory, and we shall find our God and Guide suddenly present to us in the Person of the Saviour, "whom not having seen we loved."

'Mr. and Mrs. Manson spent the day with us. Mrs. Manson one day spoke of autumn and said : " It was not to her now a melancholy season, as she thought when young," and added that in about seven years she had lost father, mother, two sisters, and two brothers. Such strokes help to make believers more thoroughly *pilgrims*, though it is faith and hope, not trial, that begins the pilgrimage.—Believe me, ever your affectionate brother,

'ANDREW A. BONAR.'

TO MRS. MANSON, DUNS.

(On her sister's illness.)

'*Collace, 1st July* 1853.

'MY DEAR MRS. MANSON,—Isabella and I have been sympathizing deeply with you. You will be ready to say, " Deep calleth unto deep," but you must not say " All Thy waves and billows are *against* me." These billows are helping you forward to a haven of unbroken rest, and by sanctifying you now are preparing a deeper rest in the end. As you sit watching at your sister's bedside may be tempted to say, " Has the Lord forgotten to be gracious?" but if you are so tempted you will look again to His holy temple and say, " Shall I not be subject to my Father's will? Shall I not think on my Forerunner and learn of Him to say, " The cup which my Father giveth me, shall I not drink it?" Perhaps you feel anxiety to be as difficult to bear as even the certain stroke of calamity. Well, your Elder Brother has felt the same. Did He not once cry in Psalm cxlii. 3 : " When my spirit was overwhelmed within me, then Thou knewest my way." At a time when I could not see the Lord's ways, and was perplexed and anxious and burdened, at that very time this was my consolation, " Thou knowest the path by which Thou art leading me." Were you even come to this, " Now is my soul troubled, and what shall I say?" I doubt not that the Comforter would enable you to follow Jesus and to say, not " Save me from this hour," but " Father, glorify Thy name !"

' Here is a message for your sister : " He is ALL my salvation." Christ is my obedience to the law, my satisfaction for having broken the law, my payment of the ten thousand talents I owe, my righteousness! " HE is all my salvation "—my feelings, my thoughts, my prayers, even my faith are no part of my salvation in coming for acceptance as a sinner. My soul is the dry empty pitcher. He is the deep well. Drop in, O my soul !—Yours truly in the Lord, ANDREW A. BONAR.'

TO REV. JAMES MANSON, DUNS.

'*Collace, 29th Dec.* 1853.

' MY DEAR BROTHER,—Has not the Lord dealt very kindly with you all? Ask Mrs. Manson to help you to remember the Lord's mercy in this matter. Did He not send you your beloved sister in order that under your roof she might spend the last days given her on earth? Did He not make these days her brightest and best? Were you not well rewarded for all your watching, and prayers, and kindness by the peace in Jesus which He bestowed on your beloved friend? Dear Mrs. Manson, let me be like " one of the elders" and ask you, " Who are these that are arrayed in white robes, and whence came they?" Shall I answer my own question? Well, yonder is Abel, yonder is Isaac, yonder is Samuel, yonder is Josiah, and yonder is Timothy, and Paul, and Thomas, and Nathanael, and Nicodemus. But yonder too is Martha, Mary, Salome, Lydia, and Lois. But who with them? You surely know yonder face! your own mother, and beside her, so bright and happy, your sister! one and all strangely blest in gazing on the Lamb. Your brother, too, beside them, and all so blest that they cannot remember even one of their sad nights below. How your sister sings! She tells how she set out for glory later than those she has left here, and has got soonest to the crown. Hallelujah! Say then as Toplady in one of his pieces :

> " Loved while on earth, nor less beloved tho' gone!
> Think not I envy you your crown ;
> No, if I could, I would not call you down.
> Tho' slower is my pace,
> To you I 'll follow on,
> Leaning on Jesus all the way,
> Who now and then lets fall a ray
> Of comfort from His throne."

' It is long since Jesus said "*yet a little while.*" This year, 1853, reminds us how long it is since then, and in passing seems to say, " It will not be another 1800 years ere He returns." No, it must now be a *very little* while, and then He comes to bring with Him all who fell asleep in Him. " Wherefore, comfort one another with these words." No doubt the Lord had grace to give you both by this long-continued trial, and He will not fail besides to soften your passage through earth's wilderness (more wilderness-like than ever to you) by shinings of His grace, by the Comforter's full presence. Be of good cheer, He knoweth your frame. You have still some work to do for Him which this late scene has been preparing you for. Pray for us. Isabella deeply sympathizes with you.—Yours truly in the Lord,   ANDREW A. BONAR.'

Saturday, 14th Jan. 1854.—Began the year with our week of special prayer. Is it in answer to that season, the beginning of an answer, that I found our servant and another young woman proposing a prayer-meeting, and in right earnest? O let the cloud increase!

Wednesday, Feb. 1.—Have been drawing up fifty-two pleas to be urged in prayer for the conversion of Sabbath-scholars. I have been feeling how possible it is to speak of this without being much affected.

Tuesday, 21st.—I find Toplady speaking more than
once of 'Saturday assurances;' the refreshing he got
in prayer and study, or in regard to help next day.
I think I can say the same.

Saturday, March 4th.—Last week finally declined a
call to Elgin. My heart is toward the perishing multitudes in towns, if ever I leave this place. Reading
to-day the Patagonian Mission, Williams' narrative;
was thankful that the Lord had made my book upon
Leviticus a means of comfort to him.

Sabbath, 26th.—At the close of the Sabbath services
in the afternoon felt for a time a bright realization of
Jesus in the flesh, and how it might affect me to see
Him as man, to behold the very countenance of Him
who sits upon the throne. It seemed to draw up to one
point every thought, and to help to make all truth
regarding Him to be felt as real—His smile, life; and
His remembrance better to us than life. I thought
were I now seeing Him thus, I could say, 'Lord, for
Thy sake I preach, journey, write books, hold meetings,
give up things which otherwise I would have chosen,'
and I thought He would look upon me and say, 'I
know it all. Not a cup of cold water did you give in
My name but I noticed it, and it will have its reward;
come in with Me.' Yesterday was the anniversary of
my father's death and of Robert M'Cheyne's. Too little
do I think upon these solemn memories. Yesterday,
too, my book of *Nettleton's Life* was sent out. It is
good for me thus to mark the day, by trying to do good
while my life lasts.

Sabbath, May 21st.—Last night had an hour of nearness to God. To-day helped so that I felt my people's
need, and lifted up my voice in proclaiming a coming
Eternity of blessedness or misery. We have 'begun
to have a few minutes of prayer at the close of the

afternoon service, after the rest are away. To-day
Mr. Moody-Stuart, being with us, spoke some striking
words at the close.

Friday, June 23rd.—The consideration that Agur's
prayer is best, perhaps, for me in spiritual things, as it
is in temporal things beyond doubt, has led me to-day to
feel much contentedness under less success and influence
than I desired. This is our Communion week ; the
Lord may give some new blessing. I see that the
Baptist's whole public ministry was little more than a
half-year. Well, the Lord may make all these times of
my life just a preparation for some one half-year of
usefulness in the future.

August 26th.—Have been seeking before taking any
text to study that I may be the messenger of the Lord
of Hosts, and so also in preaching over again old
sermons. This calls for constant prayerfulness. The
Nonconformist lives have been my study for a time of
late. What variety of gifts and graces, and the same
God and Saviour liveth still. Endue me for my work,
Lord, Thou Spirit of Christ !

Tuesday, 29th.—Got sudden notice of my mother's
death whilst in Edinburgh unexpectedly on other business.
She died this morning at half-past ten, having been out
of her usual health only since Sabbath. It has been a
most gradual sinking. She is now with Christ. I never
forget the firmness and regularity with which she kept
to herself the morning hour for being alone after breakfast, and the hour before evening worship. This struck
me when a boy. How much more might we have
done for her soul's comfort ! Lord, teach us to improve
time lent us now. There is a solemnity in the stroke,—
a strange calmness in the bereavement, fitted to deepen
greatly my thoughts of Eternity. Lord, wean me from
earth ! Lord, take me within the veil ! Let me see her

waiting with Christ on the mountain of myrrh for the day of Resurrection.

Monday, Sept. 4th.—Funeral of my mother. This day has been spent in retirement from all company. Much prayer, much meditation amid our sorrow. Sometimes Eternity has been very near. My own passing into it has appeared at hand. My thoughts have been again going out to the day of Christ, to the ages to come, leaving a present earth forgotten. It was asked at the funeral that those of us in the ministry might find at this time our souls so taught that henceforth we might preach more as dying unto dying men. I have been thinking much of Christ having the keys of death and Hades. I think the Lord has cast over me the shadow of the veil that separates the two worlds. Lord, let it continue thus.

Thursday, 7th.—To-day, in going out among my people, I was led to think that if the Lord uses me to souls, it is a higher honour than if He sent me to raise the dead! I may go forth daily in His name, and if I am blessed to awaken a soul, then I have done a greater miracle than raising the dead from their graves.

Sept. 17th.—Glad at being permitted to send out *Nettleton's Life.*

Sabbath, Oct. 29th.—Being at Edinburgh Communion, felt that it is pride that often makes me inattentive to the sermons and prayers of some people whom I think not very spiritual.

Sabbath, Nov. 26th.—Yesterday William Burns left us. He addressed a meeting the night before leaving, telling us much about China. His coming home on a visit so suddenly seems of the Lord. The effect of his very voice seems to be to testify to backsliders, and to remind saints to pray for the blessing of old days. The Spirit has been at work where he has been, and now the Lord sends him to remind us that the light may pass to others.

Saturday, Dec. 23rd.—Before seven o'clock this morning another little girl was sent us by the Lord. O how many mercies may be crowded into the short space of a few hours! Lord, cover us with the garment of praise, and make this child a 'corner-stone graved after the similitude of a palace.' Let Thy mercy, Lord, sanctify us, Thy kindness make us great. I feel to-night as if I and all the house were lying down to rest amid mercies on every side, as if the fragrance of the Lord's special kindness were spreading through every room in the house, quietly ascending back to the Giver.

Friday, 5th Jan. 1855.—The thought that every week there is something of Pentecost going on in the earth has been unspeakably sweet to me this evening. What if the Lord's people were no more than half-a-million, I see that to keep up that number there must be about two hundred souls saved every week! How busy is the Spirit of Christ! How God loves the world still!

Friday, Feb. 2nd.—Tried to pray in prospect of little Marjory's baptism on Sabbath. Set apart this forenoon for this end chiefly.

Sabbath, 4th.—During the baptism I felt what my brother John spoke of regarding Christ saying, 'Suffer the little children,' etc. The same stream of love is flowing out toward me and my little Marjory. These drops of water coming down upon her are a token of that love descending upon her in presence of us, the parents. I felt oneness with the child, and so also felt that I could claim for her all I got myself. Lord, give me to believe very firmly. It was sweet to sing Ps. ciii.: 'And to their children's children still, His righteousness extends.' I thought of my mother taken, and another Marjory raised up. My ingratitude to the Lord has been very great, so that His mercies have flowed to me like a river over a bed of hard stones scarcely worn smooth, even by the long-continued flowing of the stream, and my knowledge of Christ seems to me at this day like as if a man saw about his own length all round him, while mist rested as an atmosphere upon the horizon, the sun just faintly struggling through. When that mist rolls off, what a scene, what a discovery of glory !

Sabbath, April 15*th.*—In prospect of consulting to-morrow with Mr. Gray about removing to the Glasgow field of Evangelical work, took some time in the evening for special prayer. I have just finished going over the fifty-two pleas in prayer, one each Sabbath, in our prayer-meeting at mid-day. Is there a small cloud appearing ? Is it possible that going away may be the answer ?

Friday, 27*th.*—Enabled to set apart a good part of this day for prayer regarding Glasgow. In my ordinary reading, Jacob's going down to Egypt occurred. That seemed a word in itself. I lay at Christ's feet, trying to look up in His face and get from Him counsel, strength, knowledge of His will, all I need. I discover that very small distractions may become very great temptations. ' *Gutta cavat,*' etc., etc.

May 2*nd.*—Heard of the death of John Anderson, our missionary in Madras. He has finished his work. Some day I will finish too ; but O that I may do more before that time ! I have been at Glasgow considering about the proposal of my removing to that sphere. I feel I should work with all my might and lose no time. What masses of souls there ! Lord, guide me well !

Wednesday, 30th.—Yesterday was my birthday. This has led me to set apart some time to-day in the wood for prayer and meditation. O how I wonder now at the Lord's long-suffering, and the sovereign grace that drew me from many waters! If there is one thing for which I bless the Lord more than another, it is this, that He has so far opened my eyes to see that Christ pleases the Father to the full, and that this is my ground of acceptance. I look and look again at this sight. It was the Lord who kindled that burning bush, and it is the Lord who draws me out to look upon that great sight, and in that sight I live.

June 3rd.—Felt comforted, after a Sabbath day in which the people seemed unmoved, by reading Mark iv. 26, 27 : 'The seed should spring and grow up, he knoweth not how.' The Lord's plan, at all events, is moving on.

Friday, July 7th.—Our ministers' meeting for prayer on Wednesday was solemn and impressive ; and last night I was enabled to take a time in the church alone for prayer about my people and my ministry. I can urge this ; Thou hast not yet shut up Thy tender mercies like the door of the Ark.

London, Monday, 23rd.—Came up for four Sabbaths, and now have been two. Little likelihood of my going to Glasgow, and some are urging me to think of remaining here. I preach in the Caledonian Road Church.

Saturday, 28th.—Have already preached about twelve times. One night at Hampstead peculiarly helped while preaching upon Paul's thorn in the flesh. Twice preached in the open air. I have noticed myself specially helped on every occasion in family prayer since I came here. Much in Providence seen in small things about my visit. But what a city! What sin in it! How loud the cry in the ear of God! How loud the cry for compassion and prayer in our ear!

Monday, Sept. 3rd.—Home. The Lord has not left me without some token of being with me still. I have had twice now interesting letters from London, telling me of His blessing a sermon I preached to the children there. A young man has been blessed thereby. Last week many solemn thoughts were called up by the anniversary of my mother's death.

Thursday, 20th.—Memorable day to me, the anniversary of my ordination. The Lord so ordered it that this was the day for our ministers' prayer-meeting, and eight brethren of us were met at Rait. During this year I have completed the *Text-Book for Visitors*, the first proof of it arriving to-day, which is remarkable. O that it may be blessed to many ministers and elders! Also the reprint of *Emilia Geddie*. The Pillar-cloud does not move as yet. Glasgow seems to have been set aside.

Saturday, Nov. 3rd.—Have returned from Edinburgh Communion. The Lord has humbled me by what He is doing in St. Luke's, where souls are being gathered, and where I see how earnest some are, beyond what I feel. I am too literary sometimes.

Monday, 12th.—Led to-day to notice that all my books, my many suitable and profitable books that come to help my study and suggest what I might preach, as well as those papers, and the like, that stir up the soul, are all part of God's calling of me. By these He carries on what He began, and so by every verse of Scripture which He gives me the heart to feel.

Thursday, 29th.—Spent three hours this evening in prayer. Felt at the close, Ps. cxlv. 17: 'The Lord is righteous in all His ways,' etc., etc. Kept still watching unto prayer the rest of the evening, and intend, by the help of the Spirit, to do the same for a time to-morrow morning. I have joined fasting with prayer, as it always helps me to freedom from distraction. The matter of Glasgow will form part of my prayers to-morrow morning.

Dec. 31*st.*—Have been trying to pray more than usual at this season. My cry to-day has been for the Spirit of Resurrection, and for His gifts to the Church at large and to this spot. The consideration that this is probably my last year at Collace has not that rousing effect that it surely should have. Rather, I feel as if the Lord were making my way to remove to Glasgow plainer by the continued indifferent state of the people ; little done, little felt. Horace is now on his way to Egypt. Psalm xc. is the song and prayer with which I close this year.

3rd January 1856.—I have been endeavouring to keep up prayer at this season every hour of the day, stopping my occupation, whatever it is, to pray a little, seeking thus to keep my soul within the shadow of the throne of grace and Him that sits thereon. This opening year may be a solemn one to me, resulting perhaps in my leaving this place. O that I might see more blessing on my work ! O how bitter it is to perceive no impression made by the word preached ! It often leaves my soul in a strange state of despairing sorrow. But, as it was said of old, *Dolor est ingratus.* I am apt to forget God's mercies.

Sabbath, 20*th.*—On Thursday last my young people presented me with a purse of gold, and various things connected therewith have shown me that my testimony is felt in their conscience. May I not take it as Phil. iv. 17 : ' Not because I desire a gift, but I desire fruit that may abound to your account.'

Friday, Feb. 22*nd.*—After praying lately about my

books, heard of several encouraging circumstances as to several of them.

Saturday, March 1st.—Yesterday got a day to myself for prayer. With me every time of prayer, or almost every time, begins with a conflict, and often it is when I have been long done and am at my usual study that the tide seems to set in by way of answer, or earnest of an answer. For I scarcely ever have set apart special times for prayer and waiting upon the Lord without getting some such token of acceptance soon. O the folly of not praying more !

Saturday, 22nd.—Much, very much, struck with the hope there is of the conversion of Mrs. L——. Indeed she seems to have really received salvation. Many years ago I remember, in passing through the wood near Dunsinnane, to have knelt down upon the grass, with the clear sky and bright stars above, and to have prayed : ' Lord, Thou canst turn back the course of those stars, and Thou canst change the heart of that family ; ' and now it seems as if it were answered when I was forgetting my own prayer.

May 14th.—Have been at Edinburgh, and then at Kelso Communion. Thanks to the Lord for His great goodness. Enjoyed my brother's return from his journey. O what mercies mingled with the living waters flowing through the sanctuary !

Monday, 19th.—More than ever convinced that sanctification is carried on by the Spirit by means of our direct looking upon the face of Jesus hour by hour, not only once or twice a day. Heard of another encouraging case of anxiety.

Friday, June 6th.—Solemn news has reached us—my sister Eliza on her deathbed ; another sudden shock has brought her to this. It brings before me so much to regret, in the way of omission not least. The youngest

of the family now, as last it was the head.   I have tried
this evening to sit beside the fountain opened for sin,
and to throw into it my sins, personal and relative.   Lord,
send Eliza life, and life more abundantly.

Sabbath, 8th.—On Friday morning Eliza passed within
the veil.   Ever since I heard it there seems a strange
silence resting upon all things round.   Eternity comes
nearer every time I think of her lying still in death in
that room where mother died.   How great and precious
Christ seems now !   And what there is breathing from
the words, ' It is the Lord.'   What comfort, what sanctifying thoughts !   May the Holy Spirit visit me and mine
at this solemn season.

Tuesday, 10th.—In Edinburgh.   Sitting with my
sister's Bible before me, find it all marked throughout.
I was struck ; I thanked God for all the comfort, all the
light, all the grace, which this Book has yielded to souls
like hers ; also for all it has yielded to me.   But I sigh
for far more light and love and power to gather much
from every book, and to have my heart softened so that
I may feel far more deeply.   I once felt something of
this in seeing the Bible of David Sandeman all marked
through, and then part of one marked by a lad here,
and Mr. M'Cheyne's Bible I well remember.   It was
as if you could have read his soul's experience at the
time.

Saturday, 28th.—I have been feeling somewhat this
evening, before our Communion, that this (which may
be our last Communion here) is fitted to try me how I
might feel in prospect of death, and leaving my people
then to give in my account.   I feel just this one thing :
I must hide in Christ, I must be found in Him.   I will
point to His faithfulness as the covering for my unfaithfulness, to His tried righteousness as the complete
garment in which I may stand forth as having done all

things well. A good deal vexed, yet much helped in preparation. Something of prayerfulness to-night, but a lack of that through the week. Many people coming up to our feast. Master, come Thou. Master, come and do what Thou wilt. I cannot see what is to be the end and result of my expected removal. Thou canst work by it.

Monday, July 7th.—Last week, while at Abernyte, just after leaving the church, suddenly attacked with strange pain, not much abated till yesterday morning. I preached and then it returned till this afternoon. The doctor has given me some relief. It is a thorn in the flesh after privilege. It is a hint to me that the Lord does not need me now so much. I got a bright warm glimpse for a moment to-day of the fulness of one drop of mercy ; how great it seemed ! And for another moment felt the blessedness of having passed all trials, and having reached the haven, the storm changed into an eternal calm. What is sin, that needs to be thus chased away from the neighbourhood of God's people after it has been forgiven, by such pains ?

Wednesday, 9th.—Got permanent relief last night. I felt so full of thanks at the moment that I thought in my sleep I tried to indite a new Greek word, something like κύριος and καιρός, to express the Lord's seasonable mercies.

Sabbath, 13th.—The first time, so far as I can remember, during eighteen years in which I have been prevented by sickness from preaching. Dr. Bannerman preached. It was solemn to feel myself a hearer in such circumstances. Teach me, Lord, that it is in the multitude of Thy mercies that we *come* to Thy house. How much more to *proclaim* the tidings of Christ the Lord ! I hope and have strong expectation that down this channel of affliction is to flow some blessing for myself and my ministry, perhaps for my people here also, before I go to another sphere. Lord, what fulness is in yonder pasture ; Lord, what leanness in me ! But is not my leanness an argument for receiving ? O give, give ! I beseech Thee ; give, give, for I am poor and needy !

Referring to this illness, he writes to Mr. Manson, July 30th :—

' Do you know, for the first time since I began to minister in the Gospel, I was laid aside a Sabbath lately ? I took ill at Abernyte on the Fast-Day there, just after finishing my second service, or rather after concluding the service. You will smile and say, " Does he know what he has to be thankful for ? Only *once* ! What mercy he has had all his days ! " Yes, brother, and this mercy has followed me in spite of all my sin ! I try to sing Psalm ciii., but am as bad at it with my *heart* as with my *voice.*'

Wednesday, August 6th.—Remembered that probably to-day the Glasgow Presbytery would be considering my call. I set [myself] to pray specially upon the matter, and while so doing in the wood Isaiah xliii. 1-7 came before me. I could plead that God had redeemed me, therefore will direct me ; then could carry me through fire and water. ' Fear not ' sounded very sweet. Then, ' I will bring my seed from the east and gather them from the west ' made me notice that the Lord could work there as well as here ; and then, ' I will say to the north, Give up,' etc., how God could make my people here agree to what may be His will ; and then verse 19, ' which maketh a way in the sea,' etc.

Sabbath, 24th.—To-day announced my conviction to my people that if I did not go to Glasgow I feared I should be acting the part of Jonah. Nothing but the conviction of a call would have led me to leave this place. And I fear lest my work here would never prosper after-wards. My mind has been much led out to this sort of

labour, and I desire to bear witness to Christ's Coming
in the city of Glasgow.

Saturday, Sept. 13*th.*—I feel as to any plans for
Glasgow altogether in the state which Paul describes in
1 Cor. ii. 2, determined as to nothing except to know
Christ the Crucified ; οὐ γὰρ ἔκρινα τοῦ εἰδέναι [τι ἐν ὑμῖν]
εἰ μὴ, etc. This morning a young soul came to speak to
me, greatly awakened. Is this of the Lord ? He is not
frowning upon me, nor upon this place.

Wednesday, 24*th.*—To-day the Presbytery decided
that I should go to Glasgow. It was the most solemn
meeting of its kind I remember. During the prayer
before the decision I felt a strong hope arising in me
that the Lord would use this very event for great good
to all concerned.

Saturday, October 11*th.*—Encouraging letter from
a missionary in Karatonga, who has translated my
Commentary on Leviticus into that tongue.

Sabbath, 12*th.*—I had sought that the single rays of
light and love which at other communions had shone
in upon us, might this day be blent together. I was
greatly encouraged in every service, preaching upon
Psalm lxix. 20, 21. Sometimes I felt broken at the
thought of going away, yet I felt the presence of God
so really that I was enabled to believe He would not
go up from this place where He had so often been. My
brother John very edifying.

Thursday, 16*th.*—Setting myself to prepare for my
last service here I have set apart this evening for special
prayer and confession.

Saturday, 18*th.*—My preparation has been forwarded
so that to-night I have time to meditate and pray. But
oh, what I see in my ministry these eighteen years ! I
see myself selfish, hard-hearted, with very little zeal, and
still less pity for souls. I easily see awful wants in my

ministry, and awful omissions. I feel that I am clothed in the filthy garments. My only rest to-night is in the righteousness of Christ, and under that fold of it, viz., His having been a true and faithful Shepherd of souls. Lord, is not that fold of the robe over me? What mercy, too, what favour to this people! Every road in this neighbourhood, every house in this place, almost every tree I have passed, might witness to some mercy. Cleanse me from blood-guiltiness. Send me forth again to be a ' fisher of men.' But I fear and feel that because God has a favour to His own here, He may be sending me from them in order to bring a more zealous and holy man.

Sabbath, 19*th.*—In the morning much unnerved, but strengthened when the service began. Took for lecture Psalm xxxvii. 3-7. Preached to the children upon Rev. xxi. 6, 7, and closed my ministry with my people by taking the text I began with eighteen years ago, John i. 8. What a difference between the beginning and the end of my ministry! To-day one and another most kindly shook hands or wept beside me, souls whom God had spoken to by me. Never before did I feel so broken, grieved in spirit, needing the Lord's help. I asked my people to meet me to-night at the mercy-seat, where we might together pour out our hearts to God. We sang Psalm cxv. 12-end, and then all rose and joined in the last verse of the last Paraphrase. O what these eighteen years might have been had I only lived nearer Christ! May the next ministry I engage in be a thousandfold more holy and blessed. I sought a Bethany blessing for them all ; Christ had all His life been blessing, yet at the close gave blessing. So may it be with this place now. I cannot but give thanks for those who have fallen asleep in Jesus. I spoke of this, making our gathering together in Him more precious.

Tuesday, 21*st.*—Received to-day a present from my

people. In this I see the hand of God removing from my mind, and from theirs also, every idea of anger, so that now I go away with unalloyed remembrance of my people. But it was solemn to-night to sit here, not in my study, for that is all in confusion, thinking over my last night in Collace. What mercies have been received here amid many apparent hindrances! Strange, strange, after a ministry of eighteen years, to be leaving now. O for the pardon of sin committed in that study, with which I am now done, and of ingratitude for mercies received there! Answers to prayer offered there by myself, my brethren, some praying ones in the flock, make that spot holy to me. How often, as Sabbath drew near, has that room been the spot where mercy was sought, and mercy found. Lord, now may I live a holier life, far nearer Thee, my God and Saviour. What health I have had here, what health to my children also! We leave no graveyard enclosing any of our dead. Happy years have passed here, very happy; but we are pilgrims.

Wednesday, 22nd.—Left Collace this morning at half-past nine. Sad, solemn feeling spread over me as I rode along, and passed for the last time as one among them, those houses and roads so familiar to me. My heart was full. The sun was shining very sweetly as if to cheer and to remind me that my God has been, and will still be, my joy. Read Psalm xxiii. and sang Psalm cxxi. before coming away.

Edinburgh, Saturday, 25th. — Busy yesterday at Glasgow, then on the Fast-Day here. I still recall my last moments at Collace, in the church and in the house. Now, for a time, I am as one that has no house, no flock.

Monday, Nov. 3rd.—Though I find it difficult often to realize myself chief of sinners, yet I never feel that difficulty in another respect, I am chief of *debtors.*

Sabbath, 23rd.—Little help this evening in preaching ; ashamed of the Gospel apart from intellect, and this seemed to leave me very weak. A fresh feeling of it, a real taste of it, is necessary every time we go forth.

Thursday, December 4th.—This being the day of my induction to the work in Glasgow, I was struck with the appropriateness of what came in my usual course of reading, Psalm cxlvii. 2 : ' Who gathereth the outcasts of Israel ; ' many other verses, too, in that Psalm. Lord, go forth with me. To-day give me a baptism of the Holy Spirit that I may have new zeal, compassion, love to Thee and to souls, and, in visiting or speaking even a few words to any, may I be so filled by Thee that I might say, ' being full of the Holy Ghost I spoke.' Let my words come as water from the well that overflows. I know the bitterness of a hard heart.

Evening.—The service passed without much power, but to-night, while some friends and brethren joined in reading and prayer, the Lord filled me with desire, and made me feel that I must be as much with Him alone as with souls in public. Ezekiel ii. and iii. were read by Dr. Samuel Miller, and remarked upon. Fill me with new compassion, love, desire, O Lord.

Sabbath, 7th.—A day to be remembered, the beginning of another ministry to me. Lord, let there be prints of Thy footsteps upon the floor of our church to-day ! Mr. Macdonald (of Blairgowrie) preached upon John x. 28. I preached upon Matthew ix. 36 and xv. 32 : ' I have compassion upon the multitude.' Not quite at home, and yet I felt from time to time that surely the Lord was helping me. Now, Lord, clothe me with compassion, give me bowels of mercies, make me like Thee. I was led to begin by saying, ' It is my heart's desire and prayer that my ministry here may be a proclamation of the heart and ways of our compassionate

God to mankind sinners, and that I may proclaim His heart and ways in the mind of Christ.'

Tuesday, Dec. 9th.—Began to survey the district. Multitudes of souls, very few indeed that even seek to know the Lord. Unless I go forth among them, filled with the Holy Spirit, I see that all will be vain.

Thursday, 18th.—Last Sabbath preached upon, 'O Israel, thou hast destroyed thyself;' and then upon, 'O righteous Father, the world hath not known Thee.' Held my first meeting in the district on Tuesday evening, and preached upon Rev. vii. 14, 15. It must be a power like that which drew out the people to hear the Baptist in the desert that will draw out the people from these houses. Let me pray much for this. O Lord, be to me the breaker-up of my way.

Sabbath, 21st.—I have seldom felt more need of God's power. We begin a prayer-meeting to-morrow, viz., Mr. Cumming, Mr. Somerville, and myself. The uncommon unanimity and calm Christianlike acting of my people at Collace up to this point has been a great comfort to me. How the Lord has taken that flock into His own hands while He bade me come hither!

Sabbath, 28th.—Last Sabbath of another year. I lighted upon these words of Samuel Rutherford, 'The memory of the scattered flock once committed to me, and now taken off my hands by Himself, because I was not so faithful in the end as I was in the two first years of my entry, when sleep departed from mine eyes because my soul was taken up with a care for Christ's lambs!' Sometimes this is the thought that rests upon my mind regarding my removal to this place. The season of prayer has begun. Yesterday I was able to dwell chiefly upon the one word in Psalm li. 1 : חָנֵּנִי 'Have mercy upon me.'

Wednesday, 31st.—Encouraged by hearing of a soul

awakened through reading *Mr. M'Cheyne's Memoir* in Guernsey. Led this evening, just as the year is closing, to pray over the past, and in prospect of the future. Death has entered our circle this year, and I have been moved to this place this year ; these two things might well make me feel more of a pilgrim and a stranger. Yes, Lord, I am uprooted ; I try to be satisfied with Thy using me in any way during the years of my sojourning here. My cry for myself, for my family, for my congregation here, for this district which I labour in shall be, חָנֵּנִי ' Have mercy upon me ! '

''Tis not a cause of small import
    The Pastor's care demands,
But what might fill an angel's heart;
    It fill'd a Saviour's hands.'

CHAPTER IV

Early Years in Finnieston

1857-1864

In a letter to Mr. Manson, Mr. Bonar expresses his feelings as to his new sphere of labour, and the work to which he was now called in Finnieston :

TO REV. JAMES MANSON.

'*Glasgow,* 65 *St. Vincent Crescent,*
Jan. 2, 1857.

' My dear Brother,—Let me send to you and "Apphia" my best wishes for this year 1857. May you have reason to sing of the Lord's mercies,

"They are new every morning ! "

and have good cause to look back every evening on what He has done for you, and exclaim,

"Great is His faithfulness ! "

' I can scarcely venture yet to tell you anything of my work here. I am only beginning to be at home. About 110 seats are let, and in the afternoons we have always a considerable congregation, many or most of them "Zacchæuses," but these may be called down from their sycamore tree. It will take all 1857 to know the faces and the ways of the people of my district, and till I thus know them I can scarcely expect to see many of them come to the church. I am trying to learn to "wait" on the Lord. I did not come here in furtherance of any wish of mine, so I can the easier leave results in the Lord's hands.

' It is interesting to find that where we stay the five families nearest us are all Free Church, and what is better, all have family worship. We may almost say that we have as many apparently "righteous" near us as would have saved Sodom! Mrs. Manson may smile at my mentioning this; but it is in order to show that the Lord thus graciously makes up to us so far the want of our retired manse and quiet neighbourhood. I have *four* Collace people in my flock; but as yet none from Abernyte! Help me to be more simply desirous of setting forth the Saviour. Sometimes my heart pants to know Him as the hart pants for the water-brooks; but I seldom feel that I preach concerning Him one-half of what I think I know. Pray for me.'

The beginning of the work in Finnieston was difficult, and progress at first seemed slow. But it was not long before the power of the labourer began to be felt, and people were drawn out to hear the Gospel in the open air and in the new church. Mr. Bonar's faculty for recognising and remembering faces helped him in no small degree in his work all his life. Soon after coming to Glasgow he spoke to a little girl in the street, calling her by her name. The child ran home to her mother, calling out delightedly, 'Mither, mither, he kens me!' If one of the congregation were out of his place in church on Sabbath, the minister's eye at once noted the vacant seat, and the minister himself was sure to appear at his door during the week to ask the cause of his absence. He was everybody's friend. Little children would run up to him as he walked down Finnieston Street or Grace Street and put their hand in his, looking up to see the loving smile that always greeted them, and to feel the kindly hand laid on their head. One of his own sayings was that, 'if we are filled with the Spirit, God will bless everything about us, the tones of our voice, even the putting out of our hand;' and God so used him. No one ever knew better how to speak 'a word in season.' Going down a stair in Grace Street one day, he met the lamplighter coming up. 'David,' he said to him, 'have you the *inner* light?' The question struck the man, and was the means of blessing to him. By degrees Mr. Bonar drew around him a more than usually large band of helpers, many of whom are now gone, but some of whom are still working for the Master in many different parts of the world.

Tuesday, 6th Jan. 1857.—Have felt a sinking of heart in view of the indifference and uninterested state of the people of my district; it may be the Spirit of the Lord will rouse them. Twice I have got very marked answer to prayer when seeking direction before reading a passage of Scripture at worship, when a few friends were assembled; most marked direction. Why not in greater things?

Sabbath, 11th.—Last night, and when I awoke through the night and this morning, greatly distressed at the thought that as yet I have not heard of any soul impressed by my preaching since I came, though some of God's people give their testimony to being fed; I felt Psalm xxxviii. 9, 'All my desire is before Thee,' and not less what follows, 'My groaning is not hid from Thee;' but in this state of mind I read Samuel Rutherford's *Letters*, where he tells of bringing an action against Christ and libelling Him for unkindness; but his meek Lord took no notice and soon showed His love and paid him the hundred-fold and one over. His love is wise. I need to be kept humble.

Friday, 30th.—In hour by hour living in fellowship I greatly fail, and yet I prize it above all things. I would fain work under an ever open heaven, and say every hour with Stephen, 'Behold, I see the heaven open, and the Son of Man.'

Sabbath, Feb. 15th.—Felt to-day more at home in the services than any time since I came to Glasgow. My lips seemed opened to proclaim Christ all day.

Friday, 20th.—Enabled, after considerable difficulty, **to give about four hours** this afternoon to waiting upon the Lord in prayer for help and blessing to others as well as to myself. I dwelt as I have done before upon Psalm lxxvii. : Lord, remember this day.

Friday, 27th.—The death of [N. B.] a few days ago is to me a striking event. His whole life since he finished his study has been a blank, for, when along with Robert M'Cheyne and Somerville he might have gone into the ministry, his mind became unhinged, and thus has been ever since ; who made me to differ ? I believe he knew the Lord and is gone to rest. What a privilege in this life does work appear, to be allowed to work for the Lord eighteen years as I have been, while my former companion has been made to stand by, an unused vessel.

Sabbath, March 1st.—Led by reading of Saul, after his anointing returning to his work, to notice that even after God has called a man to a particular work he may not use him in it all at once. Paul was sent for to Macedonia ; yet for some time nobody seemed to gather round him ; it may be thus with me in my work here. To-night for a little season felt peculiar delight in offering thanks, and offering those thanks as if among the multitude of those who give thanks around the Throne.

Friday, 27th.—The thought of Robert M'Cheyne's death, the anniversary of which was two days ago, has been much in my mind ; why am I spared? and what work am I really doing, though spared? O my Lord, give me a double portion of the Spirit that Thou gavest him. Make no tarrying, O my God ! We are beginning to get into order as a congregation ; we have chosen elders and deacons, still there is little power, except so far as God's people seem to feel the want.

Saturday, April 4th.—For nearly ten days past have been much hindered in prayer, and feel my strength

weakened thereby. I must at once return through the
Lord's strength to not less than three hours a day spent
in prayer and meditation upon the Word. To-morrow,
our first ordination of office-bearers. Anniversary of my
marriage. I have got some glimpses of Christ in our
nature very near. I have felt as if I could speak face
to face.

Sabbath, 5th.—My first sermon to the children here.

Sabbath, 12th.—Our first Communion here: in
preaching, fencing, and at the table very great enjoyment. All seemed stilled into quiet attention. My
brother John in the evening. Heard from him of a
young lady awakened by my last sermon in Edinburgh
to the Sabbath scholars, at least in part. I have reason
to bless the Lord for all His kindness.

Saturday, 25th.—On Monday evening, for the first
time, I had here an inquirer who was struck by
something in the sermon last Sabbath, and so led to
come and speak about his soul.

Sabbath, May 3rd.—Began open-air preaching to-night,
a quiet attendance, with many that would not have
come elsewhere.

Saturday, 9th.—I see that one part of a prophet's
work was prayer and intercession; let it be mine: give
me the spirit of supplication.

Sabbath, 24th.—Dr. Burns of Toronto preached this
morning. Several thoughts were suggested to me while
he was preaching, that fed me and showed me too that
God's people may get by what the sermon suggests, as
well as by what it says. My part is to keep near,
very near, Shiloh who gathers, and in so doing He will
gather as it pleases Him. My part is to keep in the
company of Him who got the draught of fishes, after
the disciples had failed all night. He that has manna
for our wilderness way has it for every state of a minister,

and for all the weakness brought on by a minister's anxieties, as well as for every day's necessities.

Saturday, July 4th.—Have been at Collace Communion. Heard of a young person awakened at last Communion and by my going away, with whom I spoke ; very deeply concerned. Exhorted them, at the end of the evening meeting on Monday, to make the ten days, between that time and the ordination of the new minister, a Pentecost-seeking time. I was very very melancholy, I may say, on Saturday evening. The old scenes reminded me of my ministry, and this accompanied with such regret for past failures, and during the Saturday's service, as one after another came into the church, I asked myself,—is this one saved ?

Monday, 6th.—Dreamed last night that I was dying, and, at the moment as I seemed about to depart, I saw somewhere presented to me words that spoke of Christ's complete salvation. *Potentissimus*, I remember, was one, and it made me think upon Him able to save to the uttermost. There was another that spoke of His work for sinners, but I forget the word. It was a pleasant dream. May it be thus with me in stronger reality still when I come to die ; I try to live upon this day by day.

Sabbath Oct. 25th.—Awoke thinking of the shield of faith that quenches the fiery darts, and of that passage, Phil. iv. 6. It is rest to have 'made known' our desires to Christ. A day of God's presence ; at one time deepest silence. Surely He was with us.

Saturday, Dec. 5th.—Got such a sight of the impotence of my preaching that I felt as if I need never attempt it more. A remark of an author led me to see my neglect of little things. He says, 'God seems to bestow as full attention upon a blade of grass, or a flake of snow.'

Tuesday, 8th.—A solemn message from Brownlow North; he speaks because he believes. His address was like the flash of a sword, and then the thrust.

Sabbath, 13th.—The church crowded in every part to hear Mr. North, and the lower part left full when he asked any to remain who wished to be spoken to. It has been a day when God seemed dealing with men in unusual earnestness. Are these beginnings of revival times?

At this time, writing to welcome Mr. and Mrs. Milne home from Calcutta, he again refers to his work :—

TO REV. JOHN MILNE.

'65 *St. Vincent Crescent, Glasgow,*
14th Dec. 1857.

'MY DEAR BROTHER,—Your letter gave me great delight. It is so pleasant to think of renewing old days of fellowship. What would you say to help me in my new sphere on the last Sabbath of January? and then you could do something for Arnot and Somerville and Cumming. You are like one of our Clyde vessels when it comes up to the Broomielaw to be repaired. It is there some weeks and then moves down the river to undertake a new voyage. Our friend Manson has resigned, the doctor having assured him that the only hope for him was entire freedom from work and care. He is at Clifton—another vessel, you see, under repair! O sovereign mercy! How the Master assigns His tasks! To one, "Trade with health ;" to another, "Trade with uncertain health ;" to another, " Trade with debilitating sickness."

'Mr. Brownlow North is here at present. Yesterday he preached in Finnieston, every corner of the church crammed up to the pulpit doors, and very great attention. It revived in me the hope of former days returning—Dundee and St. Leonard's. I am getting on here gradually ; now and then the Master gives something to cheer. My last Communion roll was 136 ; my average attendance is between 400 and 500. Glasgow is *the world in its thirst* for *riches*, every man seeking to get. But the times of refreshing are coming, for the Lord is at hand.

'Isabella joins in kindest regards to yourself and to Mrs. Milne. Χάρις ὑμῖν καὶ εἰρήνη.—Yours affectionately in the Lord,

'ANDREW A. BONAR.'

Friday, 1st *Jan.* 1858.—It is now the close of the first day of the year. I have been busy with work ; too busy. I should have prayed more. What mercies have I received for myself and family, and what tokens of good for my work! Surely I have reason to be of good cheer and to trust the Lord still, that goodness and mercy will follow to the end. A year nearer the Lord's Coming also. How solemn !

Saturday, 30*th*.—We must ask the Lord for more power. A continuous asking is, I suspect, very rare ; few ministers ; few people. But there are some. The Lord has His remembrancers.

Monday, *Feb.* 22*nd*.—Have felt that I have been like Baruch in Jeremiah xlv., seeking great things for my-self, while the Lord, by my small congregation and limited influence over the people of the district and among brethren, has been teaching me to be willing to be least of all and servant of all. The soul of a ' weaned child ' is what I seek : meek and lowly in heart, with the eye upon the Lord alone. In this there is rest to the soul.

Saturday, *March* 20*th*.—Have been watching my state as to prayer for some time ; I am most of all deficient in family prayer ; the reason may be that I think there is less of sympathy there, and less required of express, particular asking ; but this is wrong.

Tuesday, 23*rd*.—At four o'clock this morning a son was given to us. The morning was breaking, and the birds were beginning to sing, and was not the Lord even by this calling for melody of heart and thanks from us, whom, in spite of our ingratitude, He is loading with His mercies ? Oh, if this were a child over whose birth many may have cause to rejoice, gathering many to Christ before the great and terrible day !

Thursday, 25*th*.—Remembering towards evening that

it was the day my father died, and also Robert
M'Cheyne.   Solemn feeling of getting nearer, very
much nearer, the shore of eternity.   My young son so
lately born will perhaps one day be thus marking his
father's death when I am gone.

Friday, 26th.—All this time I am only at the margin,
never getting out into the deep of the great ocean.
When shall I be sick of love, dwelling in the continual
presence of the Lord, enjoying the joy unspeakable and
full of glory from hour to hour?

Saturday, 27th.—What mercies this week! A son
given (for whose birth I feel no little thankfulness) and
his mother spared.

Sabbath, 28th.—At the table of Communion felt I
could acknowledge Christ as truly the source of all my
blessing, and felt Him near, so that I could give myself
up to Him altogether and for ever.

Monday, April 5th.—Sometimes yesterday I felt God
at a little distance; sometimes He seemed to help me
forward.   I am learning, when despised by men and
disesteemed for want of intellect and the like, to take it
as a call to go direct to the Lord, with whom is the
hiding of power, and by prayer move Him to work
upon men.   I never feel the want of eloquence or talent
of any kind making me ashamed at the mercy-seat.
Here then is a field of labour.

Monday, 12th.—Thanksgiving day, and the baptism
of my little Andrew.   1st Chronicles xvii. 27 and all
the context was in my ordinary reading; this is my
prayer: Lord, as the parents brought their children to
Christ, so do I.   But above all this, as I myself am
Christ's, so let my child be.   And yet more, this ordinance is Thine, Lord.   Father, Son, and Spirit, my God,
take my child, wash him and give him all that follows
upon washing, yea all that is in the covenant of which

this water is the seal. I yesterday took the covenant for myself; to-day I plead it over him and say, 'Lord, let it be his also,' and does not his mother cry, 'Amen!' Felt peaceful resting in the Lord as my brother spoke of ' Yea, He loved the people,' and showed that that included the children of His people. Our Communion has been a good time, a time to me of felt weakness and necessity. I had some time after the morning service alone in the church.

Sabbath, June 6th.—I was speaking of men stopping their ear from the good news by putting their own fingers in their ears. A sudden silence and deep attention. On Thursday I had had two hours in the church alone.

Sabbath, 27th.—Often thinking of Collace to-day, this being the usual time of their Communion. What days we have seen there at these seasons !

Kelso, Saturday, July 17th.—Why should I feel anxiety in leaving my flock any time ; my absence is a part of the Lord's way of feeding them. I am no more than shepherd for the time, or rather a tool which He dispenses with now and then. Meanwhile His eye is upon the work.

Monday, August 2nd, Evening.—While addressing the children, very remarkable stillness as I urged them to receive Christ now, *now*.

Thursday, 19th.—Revisiting Leven, after twenty-four years' absence, remembered how God was then leading me on, saving me too from evil that I knew not.

Friday, 20th.—Heard of the death of Horace's little child Lucy. It sent me to pray, for I feel like Job about my family often.

Saturday, September 18th.—Got notice of the death of Mr. Allan,[1] whom the Lord used in the work at

[1] Rev. James Allan, a licentiate of the Free Church of Scotland.

Hillhead. He died happy in the Lord, and sent me
a message of thanks. The Lord used me once to his
soul when it was turned from darkness to light, and
frequently after he spoke of the word always coming to
his soul from me with peculiar feeling. Why is he so soon
taken away? ' Help, Lord, for the godly man ceaseth.'

Sabbath, 19*th*.—When feeling somewhat cast down,
this night sent for to see a lady near death, not of the
congregation, but who had got blessing at the prayer-
meeting. Thus the Lord secretly revives our branches
when they are drooping.

Wednesday, 29*th*.—Returned from Aberdour, leaving
behind me the little tract, *Monk of Inchcolm*, as seed
cast upon the waters there. It is the ' Lord who keeps
thy going out and thy coming in ; ' here is the essence
of its sweetness : ' *thy*,' each one of us. I may say
this of my family and of myself : Glory to Thy name
Lord, Thou Watcher and Holy One, three Persons in
One Godhead.

Wednesday, *October* 6*th*.— Gave way to-night to
chagrin and a sort of melancholy indifference to friends
because of past neglect towards me. But I see there
is little in this that cherishes holiness, etc., only it
does wean us from earthly affection, though it does not
necessarily implant the heavenly.

Saturday, 9*th*.—Heard particulars of the death of
David Sandeman in China. Herein is sovereign grace ;
the Lord spares me and takes away one so truly devoted
to the work and so self-renouncing. How remarkable,
too, Mr. Allan and he, who both laboured at Hillhead,
taken so near each other. What a surprise to both to
find themselves together before the Throne, waiting
there on the mountain of myrrh and hill of frankincense
for the Lord's Coming !

Sabbath, *November* 14*th*.—Yesterday was tempted to

spend much time and then some intervals of study in a pursuit that did not bear upon the duties of this day, and so I awoke in a state of great uncertainty as to what I should preach. I feel as if I had not got my subject from the Lord. This whole matter has led me to search into my feelings toward my people, and I have discovered that I do not sufficiently think of them individually and pray for them ; nor do I feel sufficiently interested in the cases that occur : Lord, give a larger heart and a holier to me.

Sabbath, Dec. 5th.—Spoke to my people upon God's kindness to me during two years ; my text—' If thou hadst known, even thou,' etc. To-morrow I propose to spend the most of the day in prayer in the church. Lord, help me.

Monday, 27th.—Prayer-meeting calm and solemn. I came away looking up to the still same Jesus, and tried to converse with Him about the Spirit. Yesterday I read in the church 2 Peter iii. ; most suitable for the last Sabbath of a year.

Sabbath, 2nd Jan. 1859.—The Prayer Union has been of use to my soul ; I see that the beam in our own eye, in contrast to the mote in our brother's, is just our tendency to speak evil of others.

Monday, 31st.—To-day I am putting my book upon the Psalms into the printer's hands.

Sabbath, March 27th.—Saw in the morning how selfish I am in seeking souls, but was brought to ask the Lord to save many out of desire for their good and His glory in them. I was led also to ask for a work of God in which He might be glorified, while my name is never breathed in connection with it.

Sabbath, April 24th.—Have noticed, in regard to myself, an uncommon power in prayer and preaching. To-night, while Psalm lxxiii. was being sung, I could not help saying to Christ, whom I felt close by, ' Put Thy hand upon mine, and say " I uphold thee." ' It was a blessed time.

Saturday, 30th.—I distinctly see now that Satan's chief way of prevailing against me is by throwing in my way a great deal of half literary work, half biblical. He gets me to attend to things connected with the Bible which yet are not directly the Bible, and so often on study days he gets me drawn off to some point not bearing on souls. Now, Lord, let me get victory over him, and let me henceforth be able to keep Friday and Saturday as if they were always fast-days—days in which I engage in nothing but what bears upon the salvation of souls very directly. O may I be enabled to carry through these resolutions !

May 4th.—Some hopeful appearances in several cases. To-day completed the last part of my notes on the Psalms, or, *Christ and His Church in the Book of Psalms.* May the Lord use it to lead many to see their full provision in Christ !

Friday, 6th.—Tried to keep the forenoon of this day till two for prayer and fasting. Was interrupted several times, but nevertheless got help. I prayed over, and felt much, Job xl. 4: 'Behold ! I am vile !' קַלֹּתִי 'I am light, I am insignificant, I am mean and base.' Also Daniel x. and other passages. Above all, I sought to live not for myself, not to enjoy comfort and gladness, but for God, my God, my exceeding joy. Praise for recent tokens of blessing upon my people. It is not simply the being cumbered with many things and troubled that hinders blessing ; it is my being taken up with, and deeply interested in, many things that are not directly the Lord Himself. Whereas the Lord Himself is the one thing, fellowship with Him, delighting ourselves in Him.

Sabbath, 8*th*.—The girl, who was awakened during the Communion week, has spoken to me to-day full of peace. To-night, at a baptism of six children in one family, one of our elders said : ' If ever he was ready to judge of the Lord's presence in a place by blessing, He was there to-night.' I had uncommon liberty all day, so unlike last Sabbath when I was dark, straitened, at a kind of distance from the Lord.

Friday, 13*th*.—Have been at Kilsyth to-day at the funeral of the old minister [Dr. Burns]. He was the Moses, and his son William was the Joshua. Lord, may his death be like Elisha's bones to the people there, and to many more besides ;. and to me, Lord, to me.

Sabbath, 29*th*.—My birthday. How far on I am getting in my journey ! O that I could henceforth say that I live ' worthy of God.' Felt in the evening most bitter grief over the apathy of the district. They are perishing, they are perishing, and yet they will not consider. I lay awake thinking over it, and crying to the Lord in broken groans.

Monday, June 13*th*.—Last night could do little else at the close of the evening but converse with the Lord about the awakening of souls, and ask it earnestly.

Sabbath, July 3*rd*.—Again this night in sorrow of heart over the terrible carelessness, indifference, deadness of this ' valley of dry bones.' I have come to this again and again these two years : that unless the Lord pour out His Spirit upon the district, nothing will bring them out to hear and attend ; and now we hear that this is the very thing which God is doing in the towns of Ireland. O my God, come over to Scotland and help us ! O my Lord and Saviour, do like things among us in this city ! I thank Thee, Holy Spirit, for working there. I thank Thee with all my soul, and I count Thy work there as in part the answer to our prayers here. But O my Lord, come to us also, if it seem good in Thy sight!

Thursday, August 11*th*. — At Queensferry. Visited Cramond. In the church and at the grave of my uncle[1] and Dr. Muirhead, prayed for the grace given to them and for a mighty outpouring of the Spirit beyond anything in their time.

Friday, 26*th.*—Interesting news from the West. Some hopeful appearances among ourselves. Also two prayer-. meetings started in my absence. I begin to perceive two things : one is, that I too much think in preaching about how I feel, rather than how God can use what I say ; and the other is, I have really very little realizing views of what is meant by a lost soul being lost.

Thursday, Sept. 1*st.*—Back again to Glasgow. Last night a large meeting at home. Most encouraging now to witness the spirit of prayer. To-day at Saltcoats, where God is working much as in all the surrounding places. Surely this is a time of favour to us. I heard of two ministers also who have lately been remarkably touched.

Sabbath, 4*th.*—Very solemn to-day ; evidently much prayer is going up. Prayer-meeting in evening, at the close of which a great number of the Sabbath scholars waited behind to speak : six of them in bitter distress.

Saturday, 10*th.*—This has been a remarkable week : every day I have heard of some soul saved among us ; one on Sabbath morning struck, and now in Christ. Several on Monday in deep concern. On Wednesday several spoke at the close of the meeting. Last night again, where I found one of my class awakened that morning. The Lord shows me that it is not even

---

[1] The Rev. Archibald Bonar, minister of the parish of Cramond from 1785 to 1816.

impressive words, but it is His power going along with
the words. I have got some solemn teaching on that
point this week. δόξα Θεῷ. Things among us were
never so interesting as this week. I am getting my
fond anticipations, when thinking of the prospect of
coming here, realized in some measure.

Friday, 16*th*.—Still instances of blessing, but Satan
has been tempting me to ingratitude by underrating
these. Lord, enable me to take the position Thou
puttest me in, however obscure.

Saturday, 17*th*.—Praying last night and this morning,
and at intervals all day, that the God who drew out
Israel to the Baptist may draw out our men, young
and old. I am like the Baptist in one thing : nothing
attractive, camel's hair and leathern girdle. Breathe
upon them, O Lord, and they will go forth to seek rest
and to seek Thee. The Lord has poured over my soul
an unusually calm, solemn spirit this afternoon. He
is near.

Sabbath, 18*th*.—In the evening, all at once, without
intending it, led to a most solemn pause. I felt strange
solemnity. Surely the Lord was there.

Friday, 23*rd*.—This day twenty years ago I preached
for the first time as an ordained minister. I have been
trying to stand before God to-day like Isa. vi. to get
new blessing, and like Zech. iii. to get all my past failures
taken away. It is amazing that the Lord has spared
me and used me at all. I have no reason to wonder
that He uses others far more than He does me. Yet
envy is my hurt, and to-day I have been seeking grace
to rejoice exceedingly over the usefulness of others,
even where it casts me into the shade. Lord, take
away this Achan from me. Yesterday I felt peculiar
delight for a while in thinking that I was that day
going forth to work in the vineyard for Christ, doing

everything for Him. Remarkable that, just while beginning to seek an opening into some meetings among the
men, I was asked to go at mid-day to Thomson's
Foundry, where nearly a hundred listened. It seems as
if thus the Lord was saying to me that now begins a
new period of my ministry. Certainly this year is a
second harvest season to me, like that in 1840. One
thing I find this year, we must expect always to eat
bitter herbs with Passover food.

Saturday, Oct. 8th.—Felt this evening for a little as if
speaking directly to the Holy Spirit in the name of
Christ, and asking Him to work among us. Somehow
for the time I seemed nearer the Spirit than the Father
and the Son, and yet I felt it was all through Jesus I
had this audience.

Thursday, 20th.—Remarkable fulness and richness in
the ministers who helped us to-day. Once or twice I felt
very singularly carried away as into the near presence of
my Lord, and filled with hope and expectation of blessing. It has been our best preparation-day since I came
here.

Sabbath, 30th.—Have found out more of my corruptions in the form of jealousy and envy when others
are used and myself forgotten. Yet I see the Lord
may do in the time of revival with me as He did with
Jonathan, whom He did not use against Goliath. I see
that when I discover this my soul becomes chagrined
at God and is ready to say, ' Well, then, let me do as
little as possible, since it is needless ; He gives the blessing to others with less labour.' Such has been the unholy feeling of my heart. Lord, undo this corruption.
Lord, if it be Thy will, use me yet far more.

Sabbath, Nov. 27th.—What a sore night I have had in
my bed, tossing and in pain till morning, as well as all
yesterday. I see it to be a chastisement from my

Father because I was taking too much time for active
work, and too little for prayer. I see distinctly that
my bodily health goes along with my care to observe
times for prayer of some length ; it is a rest for soul
and body which the Lord wishes me to cherish. To-
day concluded the third year of my ministry in Glasgow,
and this fatherly chastisement at such a time, in order
to recall me to more prayer, is not to be overlooked.

Sabbath, Dec. 18*th.*—Called by an unexpected providence to visit Ferryden, where the Lord is working wonderfully. It is like the breath of warm sunshine upon ice
and snow ; the souls of men here are everywhere melted
down. In the evening while preaching felt uncommon
peace, joy, and fulness.

Monday, 19*th.*—Came home from church accompanied
by a band of children who sang hymn after hymn.

Saturday, 24*th.*—Home. To-day begins the Union for
praise and prayer. In my usual reading, in Gen. xxxvii., I
see how envy leads God to heap more blessing upon the
envied one, and to withhold from the envier. Now, this
has been my fault in regard to brethren who have been
blessed. I have sought to find reasons why they *should*
not ; like the men in the parable, murmuring against
the good man giving his money to them also. Lord, this
day may I lay this aside for ever. Give more and more
to those brethren whom I have despised or thought
unworthy of revival work, and O that I could praise the
Lord for His goodness in pouring out His Spirit ! O
that I could praise Him for His goodness to me and
mine ! Lord, why have I been made to share in this
blessing ? But, Lord, as yet we have had only drops ;
may we not this coming year have the Spirit among us
working wonderfully as in those other places ? One
night when at Ferryden I found it very startling to
myself to notice how coolly I spoke to people about faith

and unbelief, how hard-hearted I was in telling the men at whose side I stood, ‘ if you now this moment receive Christ, you are for ever saved ; if not, you perish.’ The awful difference of the two sides of the line, the sin, and folly too, of not believing ; why do I not feel deep, deep compassion for those that are deluded and perishing ?

Saturday, 31*st*.—O what a year this has been for conversions in many places ! But I close it with mixed feelings, for while I rejoice in the Lord, and in the hope of His appearing soon, I nevertheless feel regret unspeakable at my wants, omissions, failures. More than ever, therefore, I hide in Christ. Lord, take me and my family all in, and shut the door.

Saturday, 14*th January* 1860.—Very deeply sensible that I need what some call a second conversion, that is, such a quickening and opening of the eyes as will make me see and feel eternal things as if in a new way. To-morrow is our Communion ; and this is what I seek all this season.

Sabbath, 15*th*.—Felt for a time as if Jesus were very near, and I had such a view of Him as trustworthy and full of love that I felt I could ask, speak to Him, tell Him all I wished, and leave Him to care. More faith, more faith !

Wednesday, 25*th*.—I have been noticing two things. One is that the Spirit may as really show Himself among us by clothing believers with new graces or new measures of grace, as in conversions. Another is, that at no time and in no circumstances ought a believer to make haste.

Saturday, 28*th*.—I have been led to see that family worship is my opportunity of daily, as at prayer-meeting, directly speaking to my servants and children for instruction in righteousness, and for quickening for that day. It is not merely a worship together.

Saturday, February 11*th.*—Felt to-day that what I must be is simply this, a channel down which the water is to run. The Lord may send it by me, making my words a channel, or making my books a channel, or making my class a channel. But all is no more than this, He makes me a channel.

Sabbath, 12*th.*—Our little boy, James, very ill of scarlet fever—anxious time. It has summoned me into the Lord's presence to hear Him say, 'Despise not the chastening of the Lord.' Lord, he was given to Thee in baptism! In any case let him be Thine. My heart yearned over him as he continually touched my hand and stroked it this afternoon. Relieve him, Lord! If for Thy glory, spare him!

Tuesday, 14*th.*—James very ill. I got on his behalf this verse, 'I will deliver thee, and thou shalt glorify Me.' To-day he is very ill.

Wednesday, 15*th.*—This morning there is a decided change to the better. Now, Lord, may we return to give thanks, and knowing that a broken heart is the best thanksgiving, let us have this as ours.

Saturday, 25*th.*—Our little boy, Andrew, still very ill. It may be the Lord will give him back to us. I think I can give him up, unless he is to be yet used in after days for God's glory. Yet I well understand 2 Kings iv. 27 : 'Her soul is vexed,' מָרָה. Father of mercies, answer! Whatever be the event I can say with the woman, שָׁלוֹם. It will be peace to my little boy. The Lord will enable us to say, 'Peace, be still' to our sorrow. He will sanctify us by all this, so that others will be the gainers as well as ourselves.

Wednesday, 29*th.*—On Sabbath evening we began to have hope, and next day 'the storm was changed into a calm.' Andrew is recovering. Thus both my boys have been given back to us by the Lord. O may it be (as I asked) for His glory! But these two days have yielded me awful proofs of the coldness of my heart. I have felt my utter inability to rouse up grateful love. I have at times felt, as it were, sickness at the discovery of my selfish, unthankful heart.

Friday, March 2nd.—The doctor has little hope of our Andrew. I could scarcely have believed how this announcement has made my heart bleed. Yet I know He does all things well, and Christ is ' the Resurrection and the Life' still ; the Saviour of the soul, and the healer of the body.

Sabbath, 25th.—Anniversary of father's death, and of Robert M'Cheyne's, and this year made more solemn by our little boy's illness.

Saturday, 31st.—Last night sitting up, expecting every moment that little Andrew would breathe his last. How such a time of sorrow tries the soul ! discovering the vanity of all but fellowship with God. Isabella and I have tried to put the little lamb into the Shepherd's hands, as on the day of his baptism. It was all I could do at his bedside last night. This morning he still lies breathing in weakness, and his eyes dim.

Sabbath Morning, April 1st.—At half-past six our dear little Andrew died. O what a calm after a struggle ! Lord, is he not with Thee, following the Shepherd above? I have more than ever to hasten me on to that day of God. O to see him come with Christ, to recognise that sweet, sweet voice amid the company of the redeemed ! It was beautiful sunrise as he departed, and he has gone to better sunshine, both rest and refreshment. Though watching from 11 last night till 6.30 this morning, yet when the moment came and we saw his countenance suddenly change, and all struggle sink into calm, I cannot tell how it went through my heart. Lord, shall I not abhor sin that brought in this death, and shall I not long for resurrection ? Come and destroy death, be its plague and the grave's destruction. Come, Lord, and wipe away all tears. Come, Lord, cast death and hell into the lake. Come quickly. I was able to preach all day.

Tuesday, 3rd.—I still think upon the moment of his death, how suddenly the breath ceased, and all the tent fell down. I have been in the room praying beside the body, that my sins as a parent may be forgiven, and that I may be enabled to be a real parent to the rest. One has suggested that the prayers offered at our dear boy's baptism may be answered by the blessing given now to us through this affliction, and through us to others. Even so, Lord Jesus! Yesterday morning Horace got the gift of a son to his family, so that the Lord is giving as well as taking away.

Wednesday, 4th.—We notice God's mercy in not taking away one of the older children, about whom we could not have been sure. This, too, is an alleviation that it has come in the Communion week, when so many helps are at hand. This is the day of our dear little boy's funeral. I do feel to-day that I love my Lord more than ever, even for what of His ways I see, and the gracious love I can discover already in them.

Friday, 13*th.*—Our Communion week passed over with some tokens of blessing, though I was much broken and scattered in spirit.

Saturday, 14*th.*—I find that Knill's experience on the death of a child was like mine—that to preach was the best help to the soul in affliction. He preached after his child's death, and the sermon was blessed to one soul.

Saturday, 28*th.*—Returned from Edinburgh Communion. Helped remarkably last night in the first prayer. I felt as if within the secret place of His pavilion.

Saturday, May 12th.—Last week, remarkable awakening in my old neighbourhood, St. Martin's, Cargill, etc. I feel the blessedness and the necessity too of getting far into the very presence of God and standing under His shadow. It is then that we are prayerful. I think I distinctly see the answer to prayer in former days in what is now taking place at Cargill ; it is God giving what He enabled us to plead before I left, Jer. xxxiii. 3.

Saturday, 26th.—Have been all day amid old scenes. Came last night to Cargill to see God's work among the people of this neighbourhood. Spent an hour in my old retreat in the wood of Dunsinnane, the place which I used to call the ' Wood of Ziph,' where God has often strengthened my hands, my divine Jonathan meeting me there. I praised Him on that spot for the present awakening, and whatever there is in this of the answer to prayer. And there also I asked yet more blessing for myself and my present flock, as well as more for this neighbourhood.

Sabbath, June 10th.—Yesterday very sorely rebuked by the Lord sending me sickness and headache, so that I could not study, or scarcely think. I can see some natural cause for it in the new house and in my too great bustle this week. I see also that it is a call to me to be ' sober,' to ' watch unto prayer ; ' all the more as yesterday I got the papers of David Sandeman, a memoir of whom I am asked to write. But, Lord, I am very slow at learning Thy meaning in Thy providences. Lord, teach me.

Wednesday, 27th.—To-night at full liberty, as I was also unexpectedly during the day, when addressing the men in the Foundry ; it seemed as if to-day the Lord had breathed upon me.

Wednesday, July 4th.—Much humbled and much taught by perusing the papers of David Sandeman.

And I feel that such examples of what men in our day have been cannot fail to put me in a position of very great responsibility. Indeed it has been impressed since last night upon my soul that the Lord may say to me, if I do not gird up my loins more, and work for Him better, and live in His nearer fellowship, 'Woe to thee who hast had the example of M'Cheyne! woe to thee who hast had the example of Hewitson! woe to thee who hast had the example of Sandeman!' A threefold chastisement may be mine, though I know not a 'woe' in the same sense in which it fell upon the three cities of Galilee. Lord, mould me to Thy will. I want to live in the love of God, *for* God, enjoying God, glorifying God, and every day able to tell 'what new discovery I have made in the fulness of Christ.

Thursday, 5*th.*—Getting on with the memoir. Deeply interested and profited. It is remarkable to myself how often the Lord has forced me to take up work which I dislike or shrink from. This has been specially so with all I have written. I have been led into it, and some-times driven into it, by others. I was led to-day to pray that I might have a flame and fire of love to my Lord, not only like Paul's, but even more fervent and burning. 'All things are possible to him that believeth.' But oh! if this were granted me, what a man I should be, unlike what I am now, indeed.

Saturday, 7*th.*—I feel that 'I am prayed for,' as God's people have sometimes found. While busy this week with the *Memoir of David Sandeman*, many are asking for me, for I asked their prayers. Hence, when I began to fear that I was not myself praying enough this week, I was led all at once to remember Joshua fighting and Moses praying.

Sabbath, 15*th.*—Kelso Communion. My heart ever feels the blessedness of prayer, and yet prays little. A secret blessing in the form of help indeed seems just now to follow me, which I think comes from the work I am engaged in, *David Sandeman's Memoir*. At the Communion table, ' If Thou wilt, let not this cup pass from me ' became my prayer as to the cup of blessing ; changing Christ's prayer into one for myself. Nothing will do but every hour living as if at the Communion table.

Monday.—Prayed not to be allowed to turn aside from the real path of duty. Yet taking up some of my papers which I was writing at in David Sandeman's life, my mind wandered off all else, and the forenoon was consumed before I had any direct communion with God. A tenderer conscience would not have acted thus. I am sorely vexed too about my children. I do very little for their souls, and they are not concerned about their salvation.

August 1st.—Yesterday for a few hours enabled to seek the Lord's face in the church alone ; but it was only for about an hour or less that I seemed to get near, and surely for a time my soul was melted. I could not but shed tears of sorrow over my defects and sins and shortcomings.

Arran, Friday, 10*th.*—Spent two hours in trying to render thanks unto the Lord. I was melted and made to mourn as I reviewed the Lord's love. Noticed, in Psalm cvi. 7, the Lord's נִפְלָאוֹת, things that are often *terribly* remarkable : His providences. But it was ' Call upon His name' that most of all occupied me ; plunging into the depths of that great name ! ' Wonderful ' also came to my mind.

Thursday, 23*rd.*—The Lord's majesty in creation broke out upon me while on Goatfell. Remember, O my soul, Rev. iv. 11. It is for *His* pleasure, and not for *thine* only, that these things were created.

Glasgow, Monday, Sept. 10*th.*—Both last night and to-night many anxious souls waited at the close of our meeting. The Lord is working, blessed be His name !

Wednesday, 26*th.*—It is my deepest regret that I pray so little. I should count the days, not by what I have of new instances of usefulness, but by the times I have been enabled to pray in faith, and to take hold upon God.

Sabbath, Oct. 7*th.*—I see that unless I keep up short prayer every day throughout the whole day, at intervals, I lose the spirit of prayer. I would never lose sight any hour of the Lamb in the midst of the throne, and if I have this sight I shall be able to pray.

Thursday, 25*th.*—Our Fast-Day. Sometimes I get special nearness to the Holy Spirit, and feel as if I could address Him as I do Jesus at other times, full of sympathy, full of love, ready to breathe ; and I ask Him to come and breathe, to come over the mercy-seat and breathe upon us. Last night I felt much of this.

Saturday, Nov. 10*th.*—I see I have been declining much in personal love to God. I pled this morning to be able to love the Lord better far than I do, getting more joy from Himself alone, more than books, preaching, doing good, etc.

Thursday, 15*th.*—Sometimes these words of M'Cheyne come to me, amid so many things to attend to—' And when from life's fever my God sets me free.' This has been a week of most incessant business.

Saturday, 17*th.*—Got to-night from Holland a Dutch translation of *M'Cheyne's Memoir.* Praise the Lord, O my soul, that thus good is done in foreign lands by that book. The last proof-sheet of *Sandeman's Memoir* came in on Monday.

Saturday, Dec. 1*st.*—Thinking of the last four years past since I came to this city, to-morrow being our fourth anniversary. Very, very many mercies. I should be far more grateful and more holy. At times I feel I can take up the words of Cicero and say them of Christ, 'Quanto minus est cum reliquis versari quam tui meminisse.' Yet as to personal love toward Thee, Lord, mine is cold ; increase it, Lord, and let Thy Spirit fill this temple and glorify Thee in me.

Monday, 10*th*.—Last night, though I do not often dream what is helpful to me, I dreamed that I got such a view of God's kindness and benefits to me, that for some time my throat felt choked. I could find no way of giving utterance to my overwhelming feeling of wonder. When I awoke, the savour of this still remained with me.

Monday, 31*st*.—Coming in from our Children's Meeting and having despatched some business waiting for me, I corrected the last proofs of the *Memorials of Mr. Allan*, now in glory. Then prayed and finished the year, a year of mercies.

Tuesday, 1*st Jan.* 1861.—Weary to-day in spirit ; going forth toward the Lord in real desire, and not drawn aside by anything else than what is of Him. Lord, this may be a year of Thy working, our blessing is to come. Spirit of Life, work, breathe, create !

Feb. 2nd.—Have been this week at Abernyte. Heard of some remarkable conversions in that neighbourhood, and some few connected with Collace. What thoughts I had when visiting the flock at Collace ! By this time how far advanced I should have been in grace ! When Robert M'Cheyne died, seventeen years ago, I thought how far advanced I should be in the way if spared a little ; but I seem to be just about what I was then. My soul groans at the thought, and my only refuge from the pain of it is in 'Jehovah-Tzidkenu ;' I am complete in Him.

Saturday, 23*rd.*—Greenock Communion season; called to mind the past. I thought I saw how last year at this season the Lord rebuked and chastised us by our little boy's death.

Sabbath, 24*th.*—I had some peculiarly blessed and bright gleams from within the veil, a look into the Holy Place. My heart really yearned for God. O that I knew Him and possessed Him as my soul desires!

April 4*th.*—Have been sadly vexed by my thoughts of God's ways. Because there is not anything remarkable among us in the way of revival, my heart rises against a sovereign God, such is its wickedness. Lord, forgive. Lord, Thy way be taken, Thy will be done.

Sabbath, 7*th.*—A good day, two persons awakened. The evening meeting most useful, at which Mr. Hammond was present. Interesting conversations with a good many persons. We are to have such meetings all this week.

Friday.—I feel that there is prayer, or what is equivalent, in our resolve to seek the Lord's face, even though not saying much. It is the 'rod' held up to heaven against which Amalek cannot prevail. It is saying, 'Lord, our hope is all in Thee.'

Sabbath, 14*th.*—Last night before going to bed, my whole mind was tossed with dissatisfaction about what I was going to preach. I even sat down and wrote the sketch of another sermon. I believe this was a gentle rebuke from the Lord, because I had prayed far too little (partly through interruptions) before fixing what to preach. To-day I had no freedom till the sermon was done; then, very much. Much solemnity. My heart sore with longing for a work of God among the poor careless souls in this district round us. Some drops upon the congregation.

Monday, 15*th.*—Spent some time in the church in

prayer with our missionary for the district and congregation.

Thursday, 18th.—Every night this week some blessing, and to-night very remarkable. About twenty people remained in anxiety.

Saturday, May 18th.—Much refreshed by Song iv. 8, 'With me, my spouse,' etc. 'Thou *shalt* come, Thou *wilt* look (תָּשׁוּרִי) from the top of . . .' It is in the day when He shall take us to 'the mountain of myrrh.' Felt much, too, to-day in regard to, 'We shall live with Him,' as a present thing, since He has risen from the dead. He pours in life into us.

Friday, 31st.—Most of the day in fasting and prayer till four o'clock. Found myself much revived in prayer for the heathen and those far off.

Tuesday, June 18th.—At nine o'clock a little girl born, and all well. Peace and calm filled the hour of suspense. Lord, I have given this little one to Thee from her very birth. Lord, O that I and the children Thou hast given me be with Thee in the kingdom, walking together in the streets of the New Jerusalem, each adding another note to the heavenly song.

Sabbath, 23rd.—Noticing to-day that my envy would be removed if I could only make myself believe that whoever is working, it is *Christ* behind all work ; or Christ using that finger, that hand, but it is Himself that works. Also, I see plainly that at present we are like vessels in the harbour, jostling often, and running upon each other, but when we get out to open sea, no more danger of this. Heard of some cases wherein *Sandeman's Life* has been used.

Monday, 24th. — Keeping the recommendation of the Assembly, a week of special prayer, had a meeting of *four* of us in the church to wrestle. I go to Huntly open-air meetings to-morrow.

Saturday, 29th.—The meetings at Huntly have been much blessed. The second day seemed a day of prayer all along, and then there was such a vast assembly, not less than 10,000 souls, all so still, attentive, and at times moved with feeling. Many anxious ones in the tent. Several times, when all in prayer, I felt the Lord come very near both in the open air and in the church. How solemn and responsible did a minister's work appear. I have returned with some impression of this. The bright day, the open air, the sweet fragrance of the grass, the scenery of the hills and the old castle, and the trees on every side, all lent their aid to make the scene memorable, and profoundly interesting.

Sabbath, July 28th.—Our little daughter to be baptized to-day. I read in the morning, Job i. 5, to stir up my heart. It is remarkable to me, also, that Prov. xxxi. was my chapter [for the day]. May my dear little child exemplify that chapter in all things, and among the rest, 'rejoice in the time to come.' My brother John preached upon 'One baptism.' I felt as if Jesus were on the platform where I stood, and I was going up to Him to put my child into His arms. Lord, take her, seal her, she is Thine.

Sabbath, Aug. 4th.—Though expecting to be weary, was helped much to-day ; full of joy. A soul waited at night to tell me she had found the Lord on her way home last Sabbath night. I had found her sitting, when everybody was away, in a corner of the church.

Sabbath, Sept. 15th.—Saw last night from 2 Cor. xiii. 7, that I should learn, and have been learning of late, to be quite willing to appear as having no special power or blessing in my ministry. I must seek to rejoice in the *God of others*, though I should appear ἀδόκιμος. This was an apostolic attainment, and let it be mine.

Friday, 20th.—Trying to set apart some time to-day
to review my past ministry (this being the date of my
ordination). I was much interrupted, specially by [a
gentleman] coming in. But he told me that the reading
of *Robert M'Cheyne's Life* lately had led him to come
and speak of what he had found in it. Then another
came, to whom I was able to do a favour. And so the
day passed till my time for study required my thoughts.
Lord, it is still prayer, prayer, prayer that I am
deficient in.

Found that one person this week has been greatly
helped by my prayer 'that the shower may be sent
again, for showers soon dry up.' Another, by a word
in the sermon, 'that where God sends a living soul it is
because there is some soul to be found.' And another
told me that some time ago the sermon upon 'Meroz'
was the occasion of stirring him up to ask what he
could do, which resulted in the formation of the Young
Men's Association.

Friday, October 25th.—After some sore temptation
enjoyed yesterday's Fast-Day much. Had some little
hope of this, because of what I found on the day of
prayer before—on Tuesday. I hope to lead now more
of a Sabbath life every day.

Saturday, Dec. 14th.—To-day, news of the death of
Dr. Cunningham. O what a loss to our Church! the
greatest man in it, I believe. But the Lord Himself
remains the same. 'Help, Lord, for the godly ceaseth.'
I remember that psalm sung many, many years ago,
when I was a boy, on occasion of the death of some
eminent ministers, and yet how many remarkable men
has the Lord raised up since.

Saturday, 21st.—Last Wednesday went to dear
Cunningham's funeral. His complete composure and
calmness, when aware that he was within a few hours of

death, were most instructive. Evidently he was a man
who felt the rock beneath his feet. To-day preparing
for Sabbath, and wishing to make reference both to his
death and to Prince Albert's, was a long time perplexed ; and then was led to ' First-begotten from the
dead,' and to that other, ' Better to go to the house of
mourning,' etc. This I see, but have been long of
learning, that I should be like David seeking counsel,
every time I sit down to select a text. Then I can go
forward, believing the Lord will use it.

Wednesday, 1st Jan. 1862.—Another year nearer the
great eternity and the great day of the Lord. In our
prayer-meeting this forenoon in the church, I took the
subject of David inquiring at the mouth of the Lord
every time before he took any step of importance. I
have failed in this in the past. I have often chosen
texts, resolved on what I would do, etc., and then asked
blessing ; when I should have asked the Lord to direct
me in the choice. Many very solemnizing views of the
past year. O that this year my children were all
converted ! In looking back over last year I am struck
with noticing how comparatively little of conversion
among my people has been taking place during these
last four months. Lord, let this not continue so, for
Thy name's sake.

Wednesday, 8th.—This being· the week of the Prayer
Union I have been trying, amidst great interruptions, to
call much upon the Lord for His Spirit. That word in
Isaiah xliii. has been much in my mind—' Put me in
remembrance.'

Sabbath, 12th.—Have heard to-day of the death of a
true brother in the Lord, Mr. Gillies, very sudden. It
brings eternity very near, but somehow, too, it makes
entering within the veil less strange, when another friend
has gone in before me. May the Lord so bless this

stroke that it will increase in me all watchfulness, zeal, prayer. O Lord, do this!

March 26th.—Yesterday memorable in its thoughts of the past. I have been enjoying some blessing at Greenock communion; and in the quiet of a day's rest there recalling the events in our own family two years ago, when the Lord took our dear little boy to Himself. One of the days I thought myself sitting under the Plant of Renown, speaking to the Lord: not as Jonah under his gourd, but trying to say, 'Not my will, but Thine!' I read over the list of my communicants, which I took down with me on purpose. I sometimes remembered Job xlii. 10.

Saturday, April 12th.—Our Communion. A soul was awakened on the Fast-Day, and brought into the harbour of rest upon the Monday. It was a peculiar day that Thursday. Sabbath, too, was very good, and one soul seemed struck on that day.

Friday, 18th.—Have been enjoying the thought that every drop in the well of life is given to us. O what a possession! Everything in the Mediator is something I can claim. O that I had a heart to take more every day!

Rumours of his being nominated for a Hebrew Professorship had reached him this year, and he writes :—

TO REV. JOHN MILNE.

'*Glasgow, 2nd May* 1862.

'MY DEAR FRIEND,—It is absurd to speak of me for a Hebrew Professor's Chair. I do unhesitatingly assure you that neither my *conscience* nor my *heart* would allow me to take it, even if it were coming to this, that "Sparta had not better men." No, no. "I dwell among mine own people," and there are many who have both head and heart for such a work, who ought to be employed in their proper sphere.   My Hebrew is, like Thomas Boston's, merely a help to my ministry and a recreation at times.

'Do you know that I am getting into the "sere and yellow leaf"?   My eyes require spectacles or a glass!   You have no idea how this adds to my venerable appearance.   But what is far better, do you not know that both you and I will soon improve in our looks amazingly, for the Day of Resurrection-glory is fast coming on?

<blockquote>
"Still we for Salvation wait,
    Every hour it nearer comes!"
</blockquote>

'With kindest remembrances to Apphia,—Yours truly in the Lord,   ANDREW A. BONAR.'

Anwoth, Thursday, June 12*th.*—Came to the Fast-Day.   Struck last night with the thought when reading His rewards to the Seven Churches in the Revelation: if the Lord has so much kept for us, it is a token that also now He has much to give us.   Again this forenoon, the Son of Man nowhere to lay His head.   If Jesus had had possessions He would have been isolating himself from the rest of men, whereas He shares everything, gives away everything, keeps nothing to Himself.   The associations of this place have been very delightful.   It is like a visit to Palestine thus to trace the footsteps of such a beloved disciple.

Saturday, 21*st.*—Home.   Was enabled to spend part of Thursday in the church, praying.   Have had great help in study since then; but is there not still an absence of the power of the Spirit?   To-morrow is our Communion.   Lord, shall I find 'a place of broad rivers and streams'?

Sabbath, 22*nd.*—Many felt our Communion this day to be uncommonly precious.   I had to take all the service myself, and sought to set Christ before them in one aspect and then another, the whole day long.

July 4*th.*—Yesterday was visiting our little Andrew's grave.   Thought of the Resurrection morning with fresh interest. My sister Christian [1] seems very likely to be removed soon from us, and she too will join the company on the 'mountain of myrrh' till the day break.

Saturday, 5*th.*—Spent to-day praying for the presence of the Comforter to dear Christian, for now she scarcely speaks to friends, but lies so still. This evening in our course we came on John xi. : the deep interest Jesus took in such scenes ; written all for us.

Sabbath, 13*th.*—Kelso Communion. A solemn shadow rested over us, our sister's apparent nearness to eternity.

Tuesday, 15*th.*—My sister spoke on Sabbath a good deal, when led on to do so. Among other things she said, 'I have put myself in the hands of Jesus, and feel myself quite safe.' She has been unselfish and patient and kind, beyond almost any I know.

Saturday, 26*th.*—The Lord has singularly spared Christian still, though so low. He has lessons to teach us. Last night went to sleep repeating 'the Lord my Righteousness,' and feeling as if with this upon my forehead I could go into the New Jerusalem, and to the just.

August 9th.—We have now been at Girvan some days. This afternoon got a telegram telling that my dear sister had departed last night. I had gone out, almost expecting this from the morning's letter, and was walking on a beautiful sunshiny day, right opposite Ailsa Craig, which seemed (as it often has done) a symbol of the 'Rock of Ages,' calm, fixed, strong, in the midst of changing waters. I had been thinking too of that sky as the thin veil in front of the great temple above, into which we enter when we fall asleep in Jesus. I had spent the forenoon in prayer and meditation, and these were the tidings that met me on returning to the house.

---

[1] His sister Christian lived for nearly ten years at Collace with **Mr. Bonar**, before his marriage.

Thursday, 14*th*.—Last night most solemn and memorable. We, the five brothers, all stood round, and laid our sister in the coffin. Her face was calm, pleasant, restful. Much, much, did that form represent of family affection; and much deep sympathy which we shall never find in the same form here on earth. I could scarcely have thought that a sister's removal would have made such impression upon us all. To-day we laid her in the tomb, ' till the day break.'

Friday, 29*th*.—Back again to my home and to my work in peace. Now, Lord, put-to Thy hand!

Saturday, 30*th*.—I thought I saw to-night very fully in Zech. iv. how it is God takes men as instruments for His Church's good. Here is the candlestick, but the oil is brought out by pipes. Now the olive-trees represent instruments, such as men that have gifts, and their gifts are the olive-berries on yonder trees. The Holy Spirit pours the oil out of these trees into the pipes, and so the whole Church gets the good of these gifts. In this way I see how it is that good books are made use of by God, they are just those olive-trees and their berries. Lord, let me be such by all I write. I have a drawing of that vision in my room. Let it ever remind me of how God may use everything I write.

Tuesday, Sept. 16*th*.—The Lord speaks to us in common things. Last night I was altogether perplexed and at a stand about a passage in *Rutherford's Letters* of which I could not make out the allusion. I prayed, and was led to take down ' Christ Dying and Drawing Sinners,' and there a similar passage all at once shed its light upon the whole difficulty. Thus in the midst of common duties, the Lord speaks to our hearts by the answers He sends. Lord, give me what is meant in ' blessing ' and ' blessed ' poured out from Thy heart and soul.

Saturday, 20*th.*—Remembering my ordination day, this time twenty-four years since. I see matter for deepest humiliation and yet matter of greatest thanksgiving. But, Lord, pour out the Spirit upon me and mine. Awake, arm of the Lord ! I am ready to grow satisfied, and so to sit down content with the past. Lord, keep me. A piece of extra work this year has been an edition of *Rutherford's Letters*, which I fear has been a snare to me, inasmuch as it has sometimes shortened prayer, yet also it has helped me.

Saturday, Oct. 11*th.*—To-day seeing my children pass the window, going out to spend a few hours in a country walk, my heart yearned over them, and I sent for them to give them something to add to their quiet enjoyment. Afterward, in beginning to pray, this occurred to me : ' If ye being evil know how to give good gifts,' etc., and I urged this with the Lord, that He would see me passing and throw me some blessing.

Friday, 17*th.*—The name that most fully applies to me in my office is ' minister,' doing service, trying to be of use, though continually failing. Having now just about finished the edition of *Rutherford's Letters* that has occupied me for some months, I look back with thankfulness at the many lessons taught me during the time, not from the letters themselves simply, but from the providence of God in relation to this piece of work. Several times remarkably suitable information has been furnished, just when required. Sometimes delay in sending away, or in sending to me, has turned out a very singular means of preventing mistakes. Then the apparently accidental meeting in my other reading with some things that have been helpful has been remarkable. Once more ; I have learned patience and calmness under daily vexing things, which in the end revealed some good, so that now I begin better to see in small things, 'Count it all joy when ye fall into divers temptations.'

Saturday, 25th.—Last night, putting the finishing corrections to the proofs of *Rutherford's Letters*, I noticed that in this edition we have exactly 365 letters, the number of years lived in the earth by Enoch, that man of God of whom Rutherford often reminds us.

Sabbath, December 20th.—I notice now that continual omission of the Gospel in our sermons, or passing from it quickly, arises from self-righteousness. We feel as if there was not so much need of pressing this truth. Whereas, self-righteousness is such in ministers and people that nothing but incessant repetition of the Gospel can be right.

Thursday, 1st January 1863.—A good meeting in the church formed a hopeful beginning of the year. And there I was enabled alone for a time to pour out my soul in prayer before God.

Saturday, Feb. 21st.—Too much work without corresponding prayer. To-day setting myself to fast and pray a little. The Lord forthwith seemed to send a dew upon my soul. To-night I have been asking καρπὸν [καθ'] ἑκατόν in regard to my preaching, books, tracts, visits, meetings, classes.[1] I am convinced that living in the spirit of prayer from hour to hour is what brings down the blessing.

April 12th.—Our Communion Sabbath. At the close of the day I felt as if I had till now been kept in some outer chamber, while others, such as Robert M'Cheyne who twenty years ago passed into glory, had even in this life got far nearer God and brought away far more

---

[1] καρπὸν ἑκατονταπλασίονα, Luke viii. 8 : ' Fruit a hundred-fold.' Quotations from the Greek and Hebrew in the *Diary* are evidently made from memory.

of the fragrance of the myrrh, aloes, cassia, in the ivory palaces. Lord, lead me in ; far further in.

Saturday, May 16*th.*—Still I complain of prayerlessness : I see that saints should do spiritual miracles ; we should be from time to time (not always, for that never was God's way) raising the dead like Elijah, and bringing down fire and rain as he did ; that is, upon the souls of men. Also, I see more reason to be humble before other believers, however far behind they may sometimes seem, for that one spark of faith may be kindled into a bright flame any moment ; and then with Christ for the fuel of the fire, oh ! how these souls that seem now so low and feeble will burn and shine in the Kingdom of God.

Friday, 29*th.*—My birthday. Still I am far, far behind. My leanness, my leanness ; but my soul is more than ever fixed upon Christ, and my conscience satisfied with His obedience, from Bethlehem to Calvary, and His drinking the cup of trembling from the manger till He drank out its dregs at the Cross. Yesterday was memorable : the meeting of the General Assembly, at which the subject of union between our Church and the United Presbyterian was discussed. It was like one of the days of the Disruption time. There was something very remarkable in the spirit and tone, and in the whole aspect of things that day. It seems likely to bring about new openings, new views of each other, and probably will end in union. It is a solemn time. There was something in the spirit of the United Presbyterian Synod in their late meetings quite unusual ; and there was something of the like among ourselves. ' Unto the upright there ariseth light in the darkness.'

Wednesday, June 17*th.*—Spent a little while in the forenoon in prayer alone. Enabled to put forth earnest cries and utter some groanings with the Mediator in full view. My children come before me in prayer.

Lord, my children are long of seeking Thee! Prayed
in reference to the proposed Union ; prayed for other
objects, such as my people—every one.

Sabbath, 28*th.*—Our Communion. I was alone all
day, but helped, so that I had not a care. I got much ;
it was the bread multiplying as I broke it to the people.
Surely the Lord was in the place.

Saturday, July 4*th.*—I had finished my preparation,
but felt as if I had rather first gone through it, and then
turned aside to seek the Lord's blessing, than sought
the Lord to guide me in choosing it. But I came upon
Haggai ii. 19 : 'Is the seed yet in the barn ?' No ; it is
already sown, but not prayed upon. Well, seek Me
now, says the Lord, and from this day I will bless
thee.

Kelso, Sabbath, 12*th.*—Last night, in the wood near
the house, got liberty in prayer, and cried to the Lord
over the slain Lamb, on behalf of myself and all in
whom I am specially interested, and then I was enabled
to go on and cry for men at large—for perishing men.
Eph. iii., as usual, came much to my mind. The first
table to-day set my heart a-yearning again. God is
working in the country not far from this, and this has
also stirred me up.

Monday, October 12*th.*—Being again troubled after
service by the lurking fear that there must be something materially wrong in my preaching or in my state
of mind, because I find myself used more in the way of
guiding and helping God's people and inquirers, than in
awakening the Christless, I went directly in prayer to
the Lord about it. Soon after, though I did not notice
it at the moment, the text on one of my papers was
shaken out of my Bible, and I took it up and read,
2 Chron. vi. 7-9 : 'Thou didst well that it was in thine
heart,' etc. The Lord has different instruments, and

reasons for these too. This has quieted my mind very
much. I seek to go on saying, 'Even so as seemeth
good in Thy sight.'

Wednesday, Nov. 18th.—This morning unexpectedly
the tidings came of the death of James Crawford.[1] 'Our
friend Lazarus sleepeth.' Very, very few have been like
him in heart and life : so fervent in spirit, diligent in
business, serving the Lord, reioicing in hope, etc. We
have lost a real brother, but One is coming who will
wake him out of his sleep.

Monday, Dec. 21st.—Yesterday, on the Sabbath, John
Bonar,[2] so long the Convener of the Colonial Scheme,
entered into rest. Last night I had been dreaming a
great deal of being with M'Cheyne, Alexander Thain,[3]
and some others. Is the Lord wishing by this to excite
in me more intense earnestness? more prayer? more
faith? more zeal? more love?

[1] James Crawford, W.S., of Edinburgh, an intimate friend of the
family.

[2] The Rev. John Bonar, D.D., of Larbert, Mr. Bonar's cousin.

[3] Of New Machar Free Church.

'Suffering is the other half of our ministry, howbeit the hardest.'
Samuel Rutherford.

CHAPTER V

Ministry in Glasgow
1864-1875

THE great and unexpected bereavement which came upon Mr. Bonar in the year 1864 may be said to have formed a period in his life. Hitherto he had been blessed, and greatly blessed, to others, but the rich deep stream of blessing which was to influence so many of God's suffering and sorrowing people flowed more abundantly out of the great sorrow of his own life—the death of his wife. He spoke much of sorrow, but never of his own, save perhaps in letters to his more intimate friends, in which we get a glimpse of his sadness and loneliness. In the weeks that followed his bereavement it was touching to see him carrying his motherless baby up and down the room in his arms, softly repeating over her

'May'st thou live to know and fear Him,
    Love and serve Him all thy days ;
Then go dwell for ever near Him,
    See His face and sing His praise.'

Writing to his eldest daughter when she was in Edinburgh he says :—

'I wonder what dear baby's after-life may be. She has had a morning of clouds to begin with, but if she gets the blessing that came on her namesakes, " Mary" and " Elizabeth," she will have a bright, bright noonday, and I hope you are all to have this.'

Yet it was out of this sorrow that God 'distilled heaven,' not to himself alone, but to hundreds of other mourners by his means. He never let his sadness be felt by others. His sunny brightness was proverbial, and his unselfish gladness never failed to bring light and comfort. To those who knew him his life was an exemplification of words of his own written long before to a friend in sorrow :—

' I hope you have been going on your way singing some more notes of the " new song," tuning your hearts for the Hallelujah chorus at the coming of the Lord with all His saints. It is a small matter to make *heaven* ring with song, the glorious honour given us is to make this very *wilderness*, this valley of Baca, this earth under the curse, ring and ring again with our joyful burst of praise to our unseen but much-loved Lord, the King of Kings.'

Saturday, 30th Jan. 1864.—This week the death of my fellow-traveller to Palestine, Dr. Black, who has reached the *New* Jerusalem.

Friday, March 25th.—To-day at Greenock Communion. Remembered the anniversary of the death of my father and also of Robert M'Cheyne. Do those in glory above think of such times and seasons? Do they think of the time when they left us?

Sabbath, April 10th.—Communion here. A very very blessed day. I was carried easily along in discoursing upon 'the Rent Veil,' and sometimes got great power to reason with men on God's behalf. At the table which Moody-Stuart served I felt singular nearness to the Person of Christ. Moody-Stuart was setting before us the truth that God had given us all He had and left nothing behind, for He had given us Himself in Christ. How I felt for a little that I could wonder at it all, and speak of it all to Christ ; and for a time I saw and felt how foolish, how contemptible it is, to care about souls being brought to me, or any connected with me, or any other. The grand, grand question was, how shall Christ pour out His fulness into these vessels and fill them to His praise and glory?

Tuesday, 26th.—In reviewing the two past days in Edinburgh, can see how strangely the Lord guided me as to texts, and in various ways during my business, and that week I preached *twelve* times, yet have returned not much wearied in body, and refreshed in spirit. Also, returning from this work for my Master, I found a desire granted as to a matter of literary interest, a desire which has led me to ask everywhere for a year—the possession of the only book of Samuel Rutherford's which I had not, *The Survey of the Summe of Discipline.* To-day Isaiah lvi. has been very sweet. It stills all earthly ambition. ' A name better than of sons and daughters,' the Lord's own favour.

May 19*th.*—Often I have wondered that I did not feel the temptations of Satan more frequently and plainly. But now I discover his plan. For a long time, indeed for years, I can see that he has contrived very many days to prevent my praying to any purpose. His temptations to me lie in the direction of putting half-lawful literature or literary work before me, which I am led on to read at once, without having first of all fully met with God. In short, he succeeds in reversing in my case, ' Seek *first* the kingdom of God.' Lord, give me power to resist. Lord, from this day give me many victories where formerly I fell under him.

Monday, July 11*th.*—Staying with my family at Kirn. To-day I and my daughter Isabella have been visiting Inveraray, and are now at Killean with some friends. I got away alone in the forenoon to the hills, and spent five hours in meditation and prayer, sometimes by the side of the mountain tarns, sometimes on the heights that look toward Loch Awe. Some solemn moments by the side of that little loch in the heart of Ben-derg.

I opened John iv. : ' Worship the Father in spirit and in
truth,' etc., trying to get in within the cloud of incense,
and be enveloped in it, asking there that the Lord would
reveal Himself more and more to me.   Again and again
enabled to do this, and to speak to Him of my ministry,
my family, my country, this fallen world.

Wednesday, Aug. 17th.—Last night preached at Hillhead.   Interesting conversions there of late, three at least
within the first night.   I am now busy in leisure moments
with a little book for the Tract Society, *Palestine for
the Young*.   My desire in it is to show saving truth in
connection with cities and country.

Saturday, September 3rd.—Set apart this forenoon for
fasting and prayer.   I began my fast, and got in my
ordinary reading that word which followed me through
the day, Hosea iii. 3 : ' Thou shalt not be for any man,'
and in that case גַּם אֲנִי אֵלָיִךְ ' I shall be found bending
toward you ! '   But my studies tempted me, thoughts of
them coming in, so that a whole hour was occupied in
putting down things that suddenly occurred to me.
Lord, give me רוּחַ נָכוֹן, that I may not be thus disturbed
when seeking communion with Thee.   Writing the
Geography of Palestine has too much encroached upon
some other things, I fear ; although the study has been
profitable to my soul, as well as helped my knowledge.

Saturday, 24th.—This morning about eight o'clock a
daughter was born to us.   In our ordinary reading last
night *Christ at Bethesda* was read, and this took hold
of me ; the true Bethesda in the house, for body and
soul.   Lord, may this little one be another of Thy saved,
a precious stone in Thy breastplate, one in whom Thou
shalt be glorified.

Saturday, October 15th.—O what a wound !   Last
night most suddenly, after three hours' sinking, my dear,
dear Isabella was taken from me.   Lord, pour in com-

fort, for I cannot. It needs the Holy Ghost to work at such a time. Lord, what innumerable kindnesses Thou gavest me through her : a true wife, a true mother, a true mistress, a true friend. She passed away so gently that, till I held her and touched her cheek, I could scarcely believe it was death. I have needed this affliction. It brings to my remembrance sins of many, many kinds : neglected prayer, neglected thanksgiving, self-indulgence, my life too much a life for myself and family. Lord, let me not love Thee less, but more, because of this stroke, and from this day may I work more for the ingathering of souls. I had been reading between dinner and tea my usual verse. Nah. i. 7 was that for the day. 'The Lord is good,' etc. Oh, little did I think how I would need it half an hour after ! Lord, Lord, make this a time of the Spirit being poured out upon my family !

Sabbath, 16th.—Have been reading to my children Rev. vii. But oh, the shadow is deep ! The Lord made Robert M'Cheyne's death a means of great blessing to me ; may this not be less, is all my prayer.

I have at times felt it a happy consideration that fifty-four years of my life are over, and that I am necessarily nearer the entrance into glory. It will be more than ever present to me. And somehow I have more hope than I could before cherish, that if I continue praying for my dear, dear children, every one of them will be found in Christ. Dear, dear Isabella was a most true, sincere, unpretending believer. In *small duties* she was specially to be found careful and attentive. O what I have lost ! I have been thinking of her in glory, perhaps with little Andrew beside her, and how they will meet me !

Some people pass through life having touched the hem of His garment without any public demonstration.

Some again, like Bartimeus, openly follow Jesus in the way, so that all see their deeds. But both classes are alike safe. The domestic follower is of the former class, most heartily on the Lord's side, but not acting on every one ; though, if you come into contact, you find what a true, thankful, loving spirit is cherished toward the Lord Jesus. I see, too, when a believer seems to be doing little, it often seems to be just this, that that believer has not the same gift as others around, and so is not going forth in that direction. But the stream, being thus checked, does flow forth in some other ways ; if not by words, then by the life, the letters, the little acts, etc. My brother John said yesterday, ' What a surprise she would get, when she suddenly found herself not amid her family, but amid the redeemed above ! '

I have been thinking again, may the Lord make her memory to be to me and my children what Robert M'Cheyne's death was to the public. She passed away in three hours after we got alarmed, and, as our old family servant said, ' slipt into glory ' at a quarter to ten. I was bewildered. I said to her, a few minutes before she departed, ' I know you are leaning upon Christ.' She tried gently to say that she was, but was almost unconscious all the three hours. I had just prayed aloud, ' Lord, receive her spirit.' When life was gone, and we had had our fill of uncontrollable weeping (for all the children were there, and the servants) I prayed with them as I could. The time will never be forgotten. I am beginning this afternoon to be able to learn a little from it. There are many praying for me, I know. It is a relief to me to write down a little of what I feel and see as the hours of this solemn, solemn day pass on. My dear boy James has been with me most of the day. They all feel their dear mother's loss, with bursting hearts, so that I cannot often bear to think upon their loss. My Lord and Saviour is henceforth to be to me instead of what I have lost.

He is to take the place of my dear Isabella when I go into her chamber, or find her sweet look and converse recalled by the place she used to make so pleasant by her presence. Ezek. xxiv. 15 is my case. The Lord told me He was taking her away only a few hours before it was done! It was, indeed, a stroke! In the evening my wife died. Well does He know what has been blighted with her. But He does not forbid me to mourn. Nor will He forget to bless.

Tuesday, 18*th*.—Much interrupted yesterday, and yet helped, too, by the occasional visits of friends. ' Purged, that it may bear more fruit,' was given me by one. I felt it difficult to keep from some hard thoughts of God, or rather, from doubts of my being loved by Him. Now I am delivered from this temptation, and can stand upon the Rock and look at the waves. ' Ye have dwelt in this mountain long enough ' has been in my mind. Some very wicked letters sent me ten days ago now help me strangely. My enemies have been compelled to forward my soul's interest.

Wednesday, 19*th*.—A day I little thought to come to, the funeral day of dear Isabella. Mr. Somerville prayed, and read Song ii. 10-17, Matt. xxv. 1-13, and then Dr. Miller prayed very fervently and fully. To-day has been stormy and wet all through, and not less at the grave. There she lies beside our little boy. The occupation and the presence of so many friends prevented the true realization of the solemn and bitter fact that now she has left us to feel by experience of her absence all she has been so long by her presence. I was able to listen to the Word and join in each prayer. My brother Horace remained with us ; the rest went each his own way. Resurrection has been much before my mind.

I believed we were this day committing to the earth the 'seed' of an incorruptible body, glorious, spiritual, immortal. Saviour, be everything to me till that day come.

The very many letters of sympathy that have come to me are so many tokens of how the Elder Brother has been thinking upon me, touching these hearts and saying, 'Go, speak in My name.' I see this also, that with all but a very few, the place of the dead is soon filled up otherwise, so that it is our wisdom to live upon the smile of Christ *alone*. When I depart, let me be remembered by Christ my Priest, my Brother, my God.

Thursday, 20th.—Little comfortable rest last night. I see how this sore grief will recur in many ways. My dear children will feel it from time to time, I can see, in ways they little think of now. But what mercies mine have been in having such a wife, whole-hearted every way, without a single drawback to our affection during these sixteen years. How often I felt my whole heart resting in her sweet love and wise management! On looking back I can see very many lessons she has taught me as to how I should feel toward the Lord Jesus, and how truly He may come into the place which He has seen good to leave empty.

This morning I came upon the two books she was last reading in her bed. The one was Hill's *Deep Things of God*, the other, Bridge on *The Proverbs*. Doctrine and practice were both combined in her life. *Little things* were remarkably cared for by her. My brother's book, *The Way of Holiness*, had greatly delighted her at Kirn. Sitting at home to-day, though it was the Fast-Day, I have been going over the past and learning to bless the Lord for His marvellous ways. I sometimes tremble for future days lest I fail, or lest I do not live up to what this chastisement of divine love is meant to bring. One of the first hymns she enclosed to me, after we began to know each other and to correspond, had this verse marked with her pencil very strongly :

> ' Through many a danger, toil, and snare,
>   I have already come ;
>   'Tis grace that led me on thus far,
>   *And grace will lead me home.*'

And she is at home now ! Our marriage day was looked forward to with immense desire, but not less shall be (through His grace) the marriage day of Christ, when we shall meet together for ever.

Saturday, 22nd.—The torrent is now settling into a calm river. My soul is finding real sweetness in the Lord and in the hope set before me. Many most interesting notices of Isabella's state of mind have come to light. Many letters from friends speak of her so warmly, so tenderly, and with such assurance of her oneness with Christ. The Lord's kindness to me in many ways has been quite remarkable. I have had very many letters full of sympathy, and really most helpful, for they were just messengers from my Lord's presence to carry me cups of His new wine. About forty such I have received. And then, so many prayers ! My children too have drawn round me so affectionately, I have got access to them in a new way. James especially has never sought to be away from me this week, and many talks we have had. The Lord could not have done this thing more tenderly and with more alleviation. Besides all which, the personal and direct presence of the Holy Ghost, the Comforter, has been in my soul. Let me then gird up my loins and meet all that is in the future. The thoughts of resurrection have been unspeakably sweet and the most sustaining of all ; and that day is ever coming nearer and nearer.

Wednesday, 26th.—Reading Zech. iv. I was led to remember that all proceeds from the Lord's decree, an eternal purpose. And then I remembered, ' He doth not willingly afflict,' and when I compared that with ' These have quieted my spirit,' I thought I saw that the Lord in afflicting was doing what costs Himself some pain, and that when it was over He was glad and could truly pour out consoling love and tenderness. I think He is doing this with me. Our chapters in the Bible at ordinary worship have been remarkable. Yesterday was ' Out of the eater came forth meat.' To-day's was the Well, ' En-hakkore,' where thirst was relieved. In the evening they have been John xiv. and onward. Thus has God spoken to our heart. It seems this stroke has overawed many in the city, and if in this way it pleases God to bless souls, let me be willing to be in this manner useful to one sinner, and to stir up saints. Let me rather glory in the honour thus put upon me, of being so used. Lord, let this be the result.

Friday, 28th.—The other day I was led to think a good deal of so holding fellowship with Christ in the heavenly places that we might think of Him standing by the redeemed spirits, forming the heavenly Paradise, with the Second Adam there, filling them with joy and fitting them for the Resurrection-morning. If eternal gain to me, and perhaps to some others, is to be the result of this stroke, shall I not acquiesce and feel even sacred joy in it ? It should be so. May the Comforter bring me more and more to this. I notice that some have remarked that Abraham was not fully a pilgrim, even after leaving Ur, until his father Terah died ; and then the pilgrimage went on. Therefore, having given me my dear Isabella, He will certainly give her back to me in the kingdom. But again, I have been reading about Isaac offered on Moriah, and how

the Lord forthwith, after His servant had been enabled
to make that sacrifice, broke in with, ' Because thou hast
hearkened . . . therefore blessing, I will bless thee.' So I
have tried solemnly to give my full consent to this doing
of the Lord, and will look for the blessing following.
My surrender is not so full nor any way so difficult as
Abraham's ; but in measure it is what the Lord calls for
from me.   May He enable me to make it really without
reserve or regret, and to wait for the after-blessing.

Sabbath, Nov. 6th.—The baptism-day of dear baby,
Mary Elizabeth. My brother John most fervently commended her, as motherless, to divine care and sympathy.
He spoke of baptism preaching all the promises of God
to the believer. He spoke of our depositing the child
in the bosom of Godhead. There were circumstances
of deep solemnity. I saw my children were all deeply
moved. I came home feeling all the way an indescribable sadness, and yet as if a hand were underneath
holding me up.

Friday, 11th.—Just this day four weeks since dear
Isabella was taken home, without a parting word on
either side. But, blessed be the Lord, I have been kept
until now from doubting His love in the stroke, though I
have ' almost slipped,' ready to say, ' Lord, could it not
have been otherwise ? '

Thursday, 17th.—I fear Satan is watching me and
trying to get me to put sorrow in the place of prayer.
A word was sent me the other night in listening to an
address, namely, how the fruit of affliction may be lost,
just as when harvest is all ripe a windy night may shake
out the corn. This seems to be my time for glorifying
and serving the Lord by bearing and suffering, as
formerly by active doing. Lord, may I not fail now !
But still the sorrow comes from time to time with
sudden violence. I see it comes upon my children too

occasionally.   May the Spirit use it as His instrument for blessing !

Friday, 18*th*.—I have been thinking how one riding toward a city passes along, though vineyards with all their clusters (few of which he can reach after all) be on each side.   This is the believer's way through earth, at its very best ; but mine now is through the desert.   I have been thinking too of the greatness of God.   It is because He is so very great that He can and does attend to each one's smallest care and sorrow.   Each one soul is to Him as much as a world, and he can bend down with the same love and loftiness of sympathy on that one as if that one were all.   The very greatness of the ocean enables it to fill to the full every creek and bay.   It is thus that my littleness helps to set forth God's exceeding greatness, and His sympathy in my sorrow, and His marking every tear, all sets forth the immensity of His grace and compassion.   Therefore I can plead, ' For Thy name's sake, Lord, deal bountifully with Thy servant.'

Wednesday, 23*rd*.—Once or twice I have felt myself so helped to bear my sorrow that it was as if there had been a direct breathing of power or influence upon my spirit, it came so gently and so calmly bore me up.   ' It is the Lord.'   He is very pitiful, and I shall yet see the need.

Friday, 25*th*.—Occasionally I get confidence in that word, ' When father and mother leave me,' etc., and feel as if I could trust my children now to be brought up well in spite of an evil world, even ten times more than if their dear mother were with them always.   Sometimes the cloud covers this sky and my heart fills with sadness and almost fear on their account.   Lord, strengthen my heart !

Saturday, 26*th*.—Was able to fast and spend the day till near four o'clock in prayer and confession, with thanksgiving also. I prayed for sanctification now ; prayed against languor and sloth and everything approaching to hard thoughts of God ; to be weaned from earth, and never again rooted in it, yet to be willing to live and work so long as the Lord will. I prayed for my children and spread before the Lord ' when *mother* leaves them,' He Himself will become the mother, and they be great gainers. I prayed against Satan, lest he should spoil all this affliction to me by some snare. I prayed that my ministry and my personal state may be greatly improved. My heart often sank ; I felt myself unworthy of the least mercy, and saw that the Lord had loaded me with mercies in days past.

Saturday, Dec. 10th.—Days pass on. Nothing seems to me the same as it was. Not a night but I either dream of dear Isabella or think of her the moment I awake. This day was her birthday. She has now been two months in glory, and has been looking back to the 14th of October as her grand birthday into that better world. In reading a little book of *Consolatory Letters* which my father drew up, I find one in which Ralph Erskine tells his sorrow, and it is remarkably like mine.

Tuesday, 20th.—The other evening I saw all at once that I had some reason to praise and thank the Lord for the many, many mercies of our sixteen years together. It was after I had lain down to rest, and my soul tried to utter forth praise and thankfulness. But to-day I see still more ; it was suggested to me (I think it must have been from the Holy Spirit) that perhaps the Lord is dealing with me as with Job, in one respect, viz., Satan may have been saying, ' he did not serve Thee for nought ; but now, lay Thy hand upon his chief earthly comforts and joys, and see if he will go on serving Thee as before. See if he will not think hard thoughts of Thee.' This thought has been helpful

to me to stir me up to resist any tendency at present
to slothful discharge of duty. Yet still, O Lord, who
knowest our frame, my heart is very sore. Life seems
nothing except for my children's sake, and yet I do not
think this is a right state for me to be in.

Friday, 23*rd.*—To-day the Comforter has visited me
with more power than hitherto. He has so suggested
dear Isabella's happiness in the paradise of God, that I
have been happy on her account. I have been fancying
how she is taken up with Christ : seeing, drinking in,
listening, perhaps conversing with others upon it all ;
and I have been fancying how she will meet me when I
arrive, and just as once we used to talk together, after
an absence, of all we had seen or heard, so she will be
full of wonderful things to tell me, wonderful sights she
has seen, wonderful discoveries of the Redeemer's love.
O what a happy meeting, and never, never to part !

Saturday, 31*st.*—It is now evening, and just at the
close of the most memorable year since the death of
Robert M'Cheyne. I shall remember this year, in the
ages to come, as the year I came in a special sense into
the valley of Baca. My heart still fails me as often as
I realize my loss. But, Lord, make my beloved wife's
removal as blessed to me as was the death of Robert
M'Cheyne to the public through means of his *Memoir*.
Pardon my neglects, my insensibility to warnings, to
kindnesses, to privileges, to exceeding great mercies in
the family for sixteen years. Alas, how my ingratitude
rises up ; how my selfishness, self-enjoyment, self-
complacence appear to me ! Many, many are my
regrets. I did so little for her daily difficulties, I prayed
so little for her. I helped her so little. I see a thousand
things to be mourned over, and at this moment my
heart is selfish, unbelieving, unloving, unthankful. Awake,
awake, arm of the Lord ! Fill me with desire for souls,

and delight in Thy work, and in Thy fellowship. And
O my soul, bless the Comforter for all He has done
for me this year!

Sabbath, 1st Jan. 1865.—I took Josh. iii. 3, 4: 'The
way ye have not passed hitherto.' How solemn the
review of both the past and the future! But Lord, may
I follow the Ark, and may my children all do the same,
as did the little ones of Israel when passing the river.

Thursday, 5th.—It has been a comfort to me to think
that it is I who am left behind to bear sorrow, instead
of dear Isabella being left to mourn.

Wednesday, 11th.—I sometimes think it is likely I
may die as suddenly and quietly as my beloved wife.
I might some afternoon fall asleep, and never awake in
this scene again. This thought has more than once
been in my mind, but it is only a thought. Thy will
be done, my Lord and Saviour. Blessed, blessed Comforter, Thy will be done. Father, sovereign Father,
Thy holy will be done. Thy time is best.

Saturday, 14th.—How little impression our sorrow
makes upon other men has often struck me, so that it
is peculiarly our Father's discipline for us personally;
instead of thinking this sad, let me rather be pleased
and glad that my Father takes this special, peculiar
interest in me by myself.

Sabbath, 22nd.—Our Communion Sabbath. I never
almost spoke with more ease and more enjoyment,
while preaching on Isa. lii. 13-15, and then serving the
table, upon 'As Captain of the Lord's host am I now
come,' and was led to give up my address and read
Heb. x. 29-39. Very solemn. Mr. Milne, too, greatly
enjoyed it, and felt remarkable refreshment, he told me.
How sweetly he prayed for me that, when the Lord
bound up the stroke of my wounds, I might find what
Israel once found, that 'the light of the moon was as

the light of the sun, and the light of the sun become sevenfold.' There has been of late some impression on some souls. If I can only now pray more, it seems to me there should be something like a shower.

Thursday, Feb. 2nd.—I find that preaching the Word is one of my best consolations. I have of late preached a good deal in other places near, and have found always how my heart was drawn out to the Saviour in a more full communion than formerly. My passage this morning, Exod. xxxiii. 1-3, showed me that there are *two* ways of going forth to preach and to serve : one is, without the Lord Himself properly, only His *angel*, when the soul is living upon former grace ; the other is, when Himself is with us, as with Moses that day. I envied Joshua remaining in the tabernacle to hear all, and quietly to enjoy all.

Sabbath, 19th.—There has been a revival near us in Hillhead ; not less than forty souls, young and old, already brought in, to all appearance. To-night preached there. Though the night was quite wintry, the ground deep with snow, the schoolroom was quite crowded. It has gone on very much by one speaking to the other. I have found this my fullest relief ; it has drawn me so much toward Christ directly for the sake of others. Lord, come down to my house, and to my congregation here. I have thought of *two* things in connection with this awakening. When Jesus is passing by so near, quickening souls, it is a time for God's people getting more life. Lord, touch again my sight that I may see further than before—more of the heavenly eye-salve! The other thought that has been upon my mind is this : there is joy in heaven over one sinner repenting. If so, the news of this revival in Hillhead has caused much joy in heaven among the angels. And have they not told it to the 'spirits of the just made perfect'? And

may not my dear Isabella have been last night rejoicing
over the blessing when I was preaching there, and
perhaps remembering me?

Saturday, 25th.—The work at Hillhead still goes on ;
many more have been awakened. I have sought the
Lord to-day, by fasting and prayer, that the blessing
may come to my people in town also. How great the
Lord's goodness seems to me at times in looking back
all my life. Shall I ever have a hard thought of such a
Lord as mine? His afflictions are sent in deep love,
and then followed up by new mercies, as if He were
hastening to soften the stroke. To-day my little Janie
sat in the study playing with some little books, and, as
if sent by the Lord, went on repeating Psalm ciii. and
then the paraphrase, 'Take comfort, Christians, when
your friends in Jesus fall asleep.' Was she God's
messenger to me, lisping the message for my sake
though she knew it not?

Saturday, March 11th.—Reading Job as our morning
chapter in the church, brings often before me the
thought that Satan may be watching to see if now in my
cloudy day I will serve the Lord as readily as in my joy.
I do often think with calm satisfaction upon my being
so far on in life that my time is not likely to be long.

Saturday, 18th.—Hearing of blessing in several cases
attending my evening service at Hillhead last Sabbath
has quickened and comforted me. When the Holy
Spirit is filling me with clear and full thoughts of
Christ, my whole soul is lifted up above sorrow, pressing
into the Holiest. This month has been a solemn month
in years past, and its solemn memories are rising up
before me.

Sabbath, 26th.—[Greenock Communion.] For a few
moments, when my brother John was beginning his
sermon, there was a singular solemnity in his tone and

words that made my soul feel very near the Lord, and almost within the veil. At the table I took Christ very gladly as the Christ of the Upper Room, and then as the Christ who gives us His blood and body. Point the Father to that blood, and claim there every blessing. But at night my heart was not very true nor very living. Sorrow spread its hardness over my spiritual feelings. But nevertheless, ' we shall be like Him.'

Saturday, April 1st. — Anniversary of our little Andrew's death, but to-day his dear mother weeps no more over him, and my day of rest is coming. To-morrow, some interesting duties and privileges ; six young men from Hillhead to be baptized, fruits of recent awakening. Thus the Lord comforts under trial by showing His works advance.

Thursday, 6th.—Our Fast - Day. Many associations with past times are rising, as far back as this week seventeen years ago. How very different all things then ! But the Lord has been very gracious in calling my thoughts to His mercies. On Monday, anticipating an unpleasant meeting of Deacons' Court, while praying beforehand the Lord showed me how one drop from the Fountain of Life, one beam of His love, one thought of His holy presence, one text about Himself, could at once quiet and restrain every spirit among us ; and I prayed this in opening the meeting. The dreaded outburst passed quietly away, everything coming out in peace. To-night nineteen communicants, all brought to Christ within these few months at Hillhead, are among the other young communicants to be admitted. God has done great things.

Sabbath, 9th.—Another Communion Sabbath full of mercy, full of blessed truth. So calm, too, that I often thought of the rest upon the mountain of myrrh where my beloved Isabella has been basking in the sunshine of divine love.   It was truly revival time, too, for there were about twenty souls that have been born again since last Communion.   'O Lord of Hosts, blessed is the man that trusteth in Thee.'

Wednesday, May 10*th.*—I sometimes think that God has said to me, as in Deut. iii. : 'Let it suffice thee ; speak to me no more of this matter ;' and that He has at the same time bid me go and attend to duty for a little while longer, while He will give me glimpses of the Promised Land.   That passage, in 1 Peter i. 6, has given me delightful thoughts.   The εἰ δέον and also the ὀλίγον, and then the very trial itself being so 'precious' in God's sight (like the death of His saints) ; and the results in honour and all blessing at the great day of Christ's appearing.   It expressly promises that that day will reveal the blessing.

Monday, 29*th.*—My birthday ; and I am now fifty-five, so that beyond doubt my days of sojourn are coming to a close.   How little did I think this time last year what sore and irretrievable domestic loss would befall me this year !   My prayer still is, that it may affect my life and ministry to a degree that shall make me yet praise the Lord for it all in a loud song when I meet with dear Isabella at the Throne.   And now this very day we are leaving our house for another, 20 India Street, and who can tell the things that will soon occur there ?   Our tents are once more struck, and when I get away to the country for some weeks, our church being shut up, it seems as if the Lord Himself were saying, 'Come now to a desert place, and rest a while,' perhaps that I may recover strength ere I go hence.

Saturday, June 17*th.*—Some nearness and enjoyment in spending some hours alone with Father, Son, and Spirit.   It was basking in the beams of grace.

Wednesday, 28*th.*—A feeling of real delight at the

thought of being for ever in the communion of the holy
and Christlike ones.

Saturday, July 15th.—Most severely tried by the
request of that murderer P—— to come to see him
in his cell. Many things make it very unpleasant, but
it is one of the ways 'not passed heretofore' that the
Ark may be taking me.

Sunday, 16th.—Felt at the table and afterwards that
after much sweet communion, it became me to rise
and say, 'Lord, here am I, send me.' Many a solemn
thought to-day about my motherless children.

Thursday, 20th.—I have been seeing that murderer, a
real φαρμακεύς (Rev. xxi. 8), a singular instance of a
conscience that has no fear, to all appearance, and yet
no Gospel hold. All is cool, light, or easy-minded,
with a great desire to be thought well of by men.
What has the Lord been teaching me? *First,* self-denial,
not to be like Jonah, though I learned that my being
sent for was the result of the suggestion of the Governor
of Edinburgh Prison. *Second,* to impress upon me the
utter worthlessness of all means without the Lord. The
Word and prayer alone, with the Lord's immediate
presence, can be of use. *Thirdly,* it may be the Lord
wishes me at a future day to be a witness against that
man at the Judgment-seat; my domestic life and his
being so complete a contrast. O what would I not
have given to have saved the life of my beloved wife!
Fourthly, to teach me the deep, deep deceitfulness of
the heart. This may be a mirror in which to see my
own. *Fifthly,* perhaps to help me to be of more use
afterwards, and in this way among others, viz., by attention having been drawn to me by this singular request.[1]

[1] Mr. Bonar afterwards told how, on his taking farewell of him, the
prisoner said, 'I will meet you in heaven.' Mr. Bonar turned round and
said, 'I shall meet you at the Judgment-seat.'

Monday, 31*st.*—Reading in Luke xx. 38, ' He is God of the living,' led me to see how truly we are falling in with God's mind when we desire the resurrection of our friends.

More than once this year his sadness relieves itself in letters to his friends. He writes in the summer to Mr. Milne :—

' Will you send me two of your circulars [about the Perth Conference] addressed to 20 India Street, which is henceforth to be our home in Glasgow. We have enjoyed Joppa on the whole, but the summer skies did not this year seem to me like other years, though at times I saw beyond them the cloudless firmament of the " New Heavens." '

Again, after returning from the Conference in September, he writes to Mrs. Milne :—

' Safe arrived again at my *tent* (it is not *home* now, in spite of my dear, dear children). I cannot but write my thanks to you and John. What if I say, " To whom not only *I* give thanks, but also all the churches of our land " (Romans xvi. 4). Your beloved husband's care to hide *himself* amid the temple-furniture will find the Master's " Well done" on the day we long for. I have learned some valuable lessons, and never felt so saddened as now at various wants in my ministry. Pray for me and for my children's souls. One thing I can say now better than in former days, viz., " My flesh longeth for *Thee* (risen and coming Lord !) in a dry land where no waters be." '

Friday, Sept. 8*th.*—Just come home from the Perth Conference. We had three days of great interest, helpful in many ways to saints. I learned much regarding my weakness, hard-hearted indifference to souls, want of faith that takes hold upon God, and many other such lessons. The intercourse with brethren was very delightful. Coming home to my once lightsome and joyous home filled me with mourning, till I once more was able to think of being with the Lord before long in the great gathering together in Him.

Tuesday, 12*th*.—Saw my sorrow like a piece of a wreck upon the shore, and them came a glow of joy from the Lord, and I saw that He could make the tide rise and fill the shore so that fragments of the past might be absorbed in it.

Wednesday, 20*th*.—Anniversary of my ordination. The grace of God and His long-suffering have been exceeding abundant towards me. The omissions of the past are most painful, apart from innumerable failures in a more direct way. To-day I got a very marked and memorable answer to special prayer regarding my book, *Palestine for the Young*, which has lain aside for a year, and about which a few days ago I asked. It is beginning this week to be printed, and notes came to me after I had three days prayed about it several times. May the Lord use it, and may this be a token.

Saturday, 23*rd*.—Many remembrances to-day led me to spend it, from morning till afternoon, in fasting and prayer. Something of the Lord's presence enjoyed occasionally, and throughout a secret strength to continue in prayer more than for many weeks.

Saturday, *Oct.* 14*th*.—Tried to fast and pray, but was restless till the evening. The thought of how the Lord has supported me since this day last year was very strengthening. My evening chapter was John xv., where I met with ' Every branch that beareth fruit He purgeth, that it may bear more.' But I deeply feel my perverseness, not learning as I should. Lord, sanctify to me the memories of this solemn season ! I should never forget, also, that the Lord has shown me singular kindness, first, in regard to my children, they going on without their mother in a way that I could scarcely have believed. Next, my health, in never having had a

pain since this time last year. It is plain still that the
Lord, seeing it needful to take away the desire of my
eyes, has at the same time smoothed the affliction in
every way. Not one day has passed, since this time
last year, during which my beloved Isabella has not been
distinctly before me. Yet one thing ; I seldom sleep a
whole night now without awaking before the day breaks,
and then thoughts of what I have lost come up with
sudden power oftentimes.

Saturday, Nov. 18*th.*—My heart smites me still for
being unlike Epaphras, who 'laboured fervently in
prayers.' Sometimes I realize the 'departing to be with
Christ ;' and then I try to be willing to remain longer
in the vineyard under such a Master.

Saturday, Dec. 16*th.*—This morning felt powerfully
that if the Lord were to show us 'all His benefits' (we
had been singing or reading that psalm at worship) the
sight would be too much for us to bear, for the contrast
of our forgetfulness, ingratitude, selfishness, would rush
upon us with awful power.

Sabbath, 31*st.* — I have been alone this evening
since I came in from the service, and have read over
what I wrote last year about my beloved wife. How
fresh all seems still ! Others have forgotten her ; few
think much upon her ; but it was meant to be to me
personally and peculiarly, and so the arrow is left still
in my heart. Blessed be the Comforter, who has so
often upheld me this year, and given me at times
glimpses of my entering within the veil, and then, at
length, understanding all this dealing.

Friday, 5*th Jan.* 1866.—While at Perth Fast-Day was
humbled by hearing how much I may owe to the
prayers of others. A devoted Methodist minister now
in glory used to pray specially for me six years
ago.

Saturday, 13*th*.—We have had prayer-meetings every night this week—very calm and earnest. These are the seed of blessings to come, for the Lord gives a harvest to such sowing. As usual in such cases I have found two things: (1) Much temptation to be bustled away from prayer to other duties; (2) many pleasant suggestive thoughts coming into my mind more than at other times.

Monday, 15*th*.—Yesterday saw clearly from Christ's words, 'If it were not so, I would have told you,' that our apprehensions about dying and about meeting the Lord at His Coming cannot be just; our manner of meeting and getting through these scenes may be just the same as our manner of getting through common cares and great trials. If it were not so, He would have told us. He would have spoken some special things about these solemn parts of our history.

Saturday, 20*th*.—It came freely into my mind this morning that to realize myself as ready to pass within the veil this very hour is a good preparation for passing out to my people on the Sabbath. My eye cannot then fail to be fixed upon Christ, and I cannot then help speaking of Him with all solemnity.

Sabbath, 28*th*.—Our Communion. I felt myself as a minister not for a moment worthy to carry the message, nor at all able to declare the love of Him who died; but I know that the Lord can use me as the man who led away the scapegoat into the wilderness in sight of all the people. He can make me 'a fit man' to do that service if He chooses.

Friday, Feb. 2nd.—Returned from Collace and Abernyte; preaching in both places with some solemnity; but my very heart felt sadness at the sight of places associated with so much happiness in other days when Isabella was the light of my home. I was led to read

Joel ii. 25, 26 : ' I will make up to you (recompense you for the loss of) the years eaten by the locusts ; and my people shall never be ashamed.' Lord, forget not Thy word to Thy servant.

Saturday, 3rd.—A letter has come to-day telling of a soul brought to Christ in Collace on Wednesday evening. O blessed Lord, it is thus Thou comfortest the cast-down. Memories of the past have been flowing in to-day like water, and the Lord graciously sends in this message. ' Who is like God ? '

Friday, 16th.—Last Sabbath I nearly broke down in the forenoon ; but, though I was obliged to shorten the service, got through. I have learned several things from this dealing, and to-day it is as if the Lord would make up for that painful and distressing time, for everything in my study has been uncommonly easy, full, and plain ; but now and then comes in the pang of bereavement.

Saturday, March 10th.—I see and believe that I should deal with Jesus just as did the twelve disciples, and should pray for my fellow-labourers, as if I were one of those praying for the seventy gone forth to the villages and towns. And then I may think of dying as just returning to tell Jesus all things that I have done and taught, and may expect to find Him as gracious, overlooking all defects, and rejoicing in spirit over even the little done in His name. Reading *John Welsh's Life* just issued, found how his Lord measured out to him years of sorrow after a prosperous ministry.

Saturday, 17th.—In looking over my old sermons and expositions to-day, I at once perceived their meagreness, and that I have been only skimming the surface ; but this thought was of unspeakable comfort to me, namely, a mere simple touch of Christ makes whole. And in all these sermons and expositions I have been coming into contact with Him, however feeble, however slight; and so I have been getting healing and giving others the same.

Thursday, 29th.—On Sabbath last the Communion at Greenock. Remembered the death of my father, the first death I ever remember, and Robert M'Cheyne's too, wondering that the Lord has spared me twenty-three years since then. How my heart yearns at times to be within the veil! Sabbath was a helpful day to me. My brother discoursed upon 'Jesus wept,' and opened up much to my view. Sometimes all within the veil seems very near.

Sabbath, April 1st.—On awaking found it just such a morning as when, six years ago, little Andrew died. The sun was beginning to shine as on that morning. He has been now enjoying the Sabbath within the veil, and his dear mother has joined him since then.

Monday, 9th.—Yesterday our Communion. Another in the valley of Baca. We had some tokens for good. Three persons about this time brought to Christ; but my soul does not long for the opening of the windows of heaven as it should. Satan is evidently at work in many ways at present. Lord, keep me from him; when all is over, and we have been safely landed, I believe, as Mr. Moody-Stuart said the other day, 'Mine heart shall meditate terror.' But I also see our fellowship with Christ. He is our partner, and we have just to 'beckon to our partner' in the other ship in order to get help and deliverance.

Saturday, 14th.—Returned from Dundee, where I stood by Robert M'Cheyne's grave. I preached in his church, and met with some of the old hearers. Lord, a double portion of Elijah's spirit to me! I need it all, and I have not got it, and my night cometh.

Friday, 20th.—I have been seeking to realize again at this time that possibly soon Christ may one day lay

His hand suddenly upon me ; and the next thing I dis-cover is my Lord smiling over me, and saying, ' As He that has the key of death am I now come.' And so He will call me within the veil to join the saints that are upon the mountain of myrrh till the day when He comes as the Resurrection and the Life.

Saturday, 28th.—Sometimes of late I have felt as if I were almost standing on the step of the other world, my Father's house, with my face, however, towards this world ; and that I might any moment be gently touched and drawn in within the veil.

Saturday, May 19th.—Have been learning from Christ's stay on the earth during forty days after His resurrec-tion, all for the sake of others, that disciples ought not to be too eager for glory, but should, for the sake of others, their families, their friends, the world, desire to continue here a while.

Saturday, 26th.—The life of Henry Craik has helped me to-day in solemn meditation, fasting, and prayer. In him I see how the Lord enabled one of His own to go on continually doing all for God, in studying, preach-ing, writing, keeping him abounding in prayer, and in meditation upon the Word. He was also enabled to live, not before man but God, declining to do many things that might have been expected of him, because, if he occupied himself with them, he must neglect retirement, fellowship with God, and family duties. Now, I am apt to go wrong here. He was to have called upon me the last time he was in Glasgow, but was then ill of his sickness unto death. Well, my call will come. May I be sustained in death-bed trouble as he was ! If, how-ever, the Lord take me away quickly, without warning, it may be better still in some respects ; but I have no choice.

June 2nd.—A month of special prayer for the Spirit. Something will come of it.

Thursday, 7th.—My brother Horace's induction at Edinburgh to the new church at the Grange. This is another of the Lord's ways.

Abernyte, Saturday, 9th.—In the quiet and bright sunshine, in the freshness and beauty of the earth all round, in the sweet message of the birds, in the busy life of all creation the voice of my God spoke. He seemed to tell me that thus He was willing to lavish upon me new mercies, and so I must not think hardly of His ways in bereaving me, for that was a stroke that could not be spared.

Wednesday, 13th.—What thoughts of the past as I stood on Dunsinnane Hill, and then came down among the people, and at last stood where I used to pitch my tent!

Tuesday, 26th.—I find our Communion Sabbath has been one of the most impressive days we have had to God's people. One person gave thanks for it as 'wonderful.' Another felt so much that he afterward wondered that he did not cry out at the sight of Christ bearing sin for us. To-day I stood again at the grave of my dear Isabella. I have been trying to think more of her as among the blessed ones who dwell in the light and glory of God, and among the millions of those whom we shall soon know and love with a love as yet unknown to us ; while Jesus Himself shall be the chief among ten thousand. All this summer, Lord, supply with Thy presence the sad, sad blank.

July 2nd.—Setting off for Largo, where I am to spend some weeks with my motherless children. My heart never bounds now at the thought of leisure, but I trust to have a quiet time of much communion with the Lord there.

Largo, Sabbath, 8th.—Many solemn sad feelings about my loneliness now, but the Lord can enable me to bear the loss of my beloved wife so as to be more than conqueror. Every man has his burden from the Lord, and glorifies God in proportion as he bears it in the Lord's strength.

Wednesday, 11*th.*—Some glimpses of free grace, seeing the Lord to be giving, giving, giving, all around, from year to year, in things spiritual and temporal ; seeing that *we* do nothing but take, take, take. Lord, give a heart to perceive Thy giving.

Saturday, 14*th.*—Helped by hearing my little girl singing in the garden to herself.

Wednesday, Sept. 12*th.*—Last Sabbath preached in the afternoon upon 'the angels that sinned.' A good many were singularly struck with it. Two of my elders were so struck that they could not sleep for thinking on it.

Saturday, 15*th.*—Got time to pray and meditate almost all the day, my preparation being far on for Sabbath. This time twenty-eight years ago I was looking forward to my ordination. I tried to cast the ministerial sins of twenty-eight years into the fountain opened. I cried for more grace, the power of the Holy Ghost in me. Once, when the thought of my affliction crossed my mind, I remembered God saying to Moses, 'Speak to me no more of this matter,' and how, after that Moses was enabled quietly to sit upon the mountains opposite and look over to the hills of the land, and how after all that, he got the glorious reward of obedience, and in the Transfiguration night forgot the past sorrow for ever in that recompense.

Sabbath, 30*th.*—To-night prayed with my daughter Isabella, who is to go to Edinburgh to school to-morrow. This and the whole season has been bringing to my thoughts most sorrowfully much of the past, but the Lord has been sending comfort in the midst of all. Lord, I commit Isabella into Thy hands.

While his daughter was at school he wrote very often to her, telling her the home news, and all that was likely to interest her. In one letter he tells her how much she is missed, and adds :—

'Things go on with us as usual. I come in *sometimes* at ten minutes to five, but *only* sometimes. I am improving greatly! My chapter to-day was Isaiah xxx., and was yours too, I suppose. I will often pray for you as I read the chapter morning by morning, thinking you will be doing the same. Is not that verse well worth your deep consideration, " In returning (from all your wanderings) and in *rest* (upon the Lord) you *shall be saved*," and then verse 18, " *the Lord waits* to be gracious."

'You will remember what Sabbath the 14th [October] is the anniversary of? But it has been two years of joy and holiness to her.'

In another :—

'What a nice text in chapter xxxvii. 28 : " I know thy abode, and thy going out, and thy coming in." It was no doubt spoken to Sennacherib as a threatening or overawing word, but let us take it as a most pleasant and comfortable one. Our Lord knows all about you, your "abode" in the Grange House, your "going out" as well ; your "coming in" and sitting down to lessons, etc. His eye of fatherly interest is always on you, and His heart yearns over you. Think of Him saying, " Come out from among them, and I will receive you, and you shall be my daughter" (2 Cor. vi. 18). Through Christ you may thus find the Father altogether *your* Father at all times and for ever.

'A man has interrupted me about a marriage, and then I have to go to the Religious Institution Rooms to the daily prayer-meeting, but I wish you to get this to-night in case you weary. We are all well, and often thinking of you.'

Sabbath, October 14*th.*—Memorable night. Since this time two years ago I have never been able to pass one day without something during its hours recalling my beloved Isabella to my thoughts. I had much liberty in preaching upon 'To me to live is Christ.' This is what I would fain reach, a life full of Christ, full of this heavenly joy, all blanks filled up by His presence.

Thursday, 25*th.*—The Lord blesses us as a congregation with many tokens of His favour. We found this at
our Communion season. O my unthankful heart ! In the
midst of all I often find myself sad and sinking in spirit
when at home because of my widowed state. Yet I
know that the Lord is withholding no good thing, and
that very soon I shall meet my beloved wife in the
kingdom of God. Let me be far more heavenly-minded,
far more anxious to win souls, far more compassionate,
a better father to my family, as well as a better master
to my servants, and a better pastor.

Sabbath, Dec. 2*nd.*—Twice in my preaching to-day I
felt myself carried half within the veil for a moment ;
the one time was in the forenoon when speaking of the
possibility that within another ten years some sitting
there might be seeing Christ face to face in His glory.
The other in the afternoon, when speaking of the soul
just saved, scarcely daring to think it was now in
possession of such an infinite treasure as Christ.

Sabbath, 30*th.*—Yesterday worn out in body and not
able to pray much, so to-day did not get very close to
the Lord's presence, nor to the people's consciences.
Preaching to the children, I remembered these ten years
I have been allowed forty times to preach to them, but,
alas, very little fruit from these sermons. People think
I succeed in preaching to the young ; I very seldom
think myself enabled to get at their hearts and consciences. Lord, use me more. Thou canst make worm
Jacob thrash the mountains. I have my back upon the
world, I believe, but then I stand rather *looking* into,
than *going* into, the Holy of Holies.

Sabbath, 6*th January* 1867.—Tried to keep the Prayer
Union begun to-day. At night a fresh burst of sorrow
seemed for a time to assail my heart. Earth seemed
wilderness every way, 'all men are liars.' I noticed

God's way of saying, ' Your life will be given you for a prey,' and how it means you shall escape, but yet shall pass through great risks, almost gone. And then I notice how He says that He will not destroy, yet will not leave wholly unpunished ; hence our sore chastisements and often sufferings of body that seem to break in pieces.

Sabbath, 27th.—To-night and for some days past I have been feeling somewhat familiar with those that have gone within the veil, as if I could meet them and converse with them easily. 'For ever with the Lord ' is a word of joy; sometimes it comes upon me like a bright flash, opening up for a moment the world beyond.

Saturday, Feb. 23rd.—I find Satan very sorely assailing me, so much so that I was led to hasten to the Lord and cry that I might not be allowed to fall into his snare, or do anything that would bring down my usefulness. I thought myself on the brink of a precipice ; and then after that was over found Satan bringing me into a snare regarding some of our church arrangements. Is all this to drive me closer to the Lord as my shield and to keep me standing with the whole armour of God ever on ? There have been some tokens of greater blessing than usual, and Satan seems intent upon checking it all. O let the river of life rise higher in my soul, sweeping away corruption ! Let Satan flee at my cry, and at thy presence in power, O Lord.

Sabbath, March 3rd.—Last week went to Crossford to lecture upon the Tabernacle to the awakened people there, a most interesting assembly. Afternoon at three about two hundred women, and in the evening as many men.

Saturday, April 13th.—I sometimes feel as if there were two sides to my soul, the one looking earthward, the other heavenward. How the flesh shivers at times when missing its desired objects, and nothing relieves but getting heavenly and unseen objects to engage thought and feeling.

Sabbath, 21st.—I have been asking calm faith, burning love, deep peace, bright hope, true compassion for souls, glowing zeal for God's glory. From time to time the weight of my never-forgotten bereavement touches my soul, though it does not rest upon it ; and thus a present life has lost its power.

Friday, 14th June.—Though slow to learn it, to this very hour I believe that in the death of my beloved Isabella the Lord was saying to me, as He did to Abraham, 'Get thee out of thy country and from thy kindred into a land that I shall show thee.' My eye ought not now to look around for anything to stay me, but to look upward always for the glory there, and the Lord Himself who is to lead me in. My brother James's illness has again reminded me how soon comfort may pass away. But this very thing made me to-day almost envy him, and then made that passage in my ordinary reading very sweet : 'For surely there is an end, and thine expectation shall not be cut off.' Yes, an end of sorrow, an end of waiting for the unmixed rest in God.

Saturday, 29th.—To-morrow is our Communion, in preparation for which, as well as because an opportunity of special benefit to my soul, I spent till mid-day fasting and praying. Some considerable sense of nearness to the Lord at times. I sought as much to be drawn into His presence and to Himself as weaned from the world. I want exceedingly to be content with the Lord Himself alone, though I have continual temptation to try the employment of other engagements in a certain degree. How peaceful and memorably happy this season used to be at Collace, but I fear it was to me often the finding of a heaven upon earth ; but ' God liveth.'

Tuesday, July 2nd.—My brother James not better, staying at Juniper Green in the hope that a change of air may be useful. Very happy in his soul, full of a calm peace.

Tuesday, 9th.—James is weaker, but lies in peace waiting the issue. Felt after speaking to-day how much may be effected by a very few words when the person is filled with the Holy Ghost. We can afford to be short.

Thursday, 11th.—While quietly sitting in the house at Burntisland where my family are, a telegram came telling me of my brother James's death about five o'clock. He just sank to rest. A solemn stillness seemed to fill the air as I tried to think of him gone within the veil to be with the Lord. He has lived just sixty-six years.

Thursday, 18th.—The funeral-day. Very much of the Lord's presence among us, I think, and much of the Lord's providence seen in all the arrangements.

More of his feelings about his brother's death are expressed in a letter to Mr. Milne :—

TO THE REV. JOHN MILNE.

' MY DEAR FRIEND AND BROTHER,—You will have noticed the death of my brother James. He sank to rest—no struggle, no pain, only utter weakness. His soul was kept in perfect peace ; any cloud that passed was momentary. You said to me, you remember, that ' you almost envied him being so near glory.' I quite enter into this feeling It *is* blessed to be able to lift the banner we have borne, and, laying it at the Captain's feet, to say, " I have finished my course." It will be the Captain Himself who will on that day tell us, " Henceforth there is laid up for thee a crown of righteousness."

' I am on my way home to Glasgow to preach there to-morrow.
I hope you submit to good advice, and preach more by your faith,
prayer, and happy acquiescence in the Master's arrangement,
than by word and voice.

' Good-bye. The time of the singing of birds is not come, but
when it does arrive, I hope to sing well and loud and for ever to
Him who sitteth on the Throne and to the Lamb."

Friday, Aug. 23rd.—Returned home from visiting the
several congregations in the greater part of Breadalbane,
such as Lawers, Ardeonaig, Glenlyon, Fortingall, Aberfeldy. It has been a time of considerable labour, meeting with sessions and people, but sometimes very solemn
and very profitable. One man who had been at Moulin,
when I held a meeting there for the Jews in 1841, told
me the text preached upon, and also related the impression produced by a remark I made to an old man who
was in the churchyard leaning on his staff, by reminding
him in passing of Jacob leaning on his staff as a picture
of the soul leaning on the Saviour. Another told me
the good result of the visit made by Mr. Manson and
myself in 1849 to Glenlyon and other places, with the
view of helping on Sabbath-school work.

Saturday, 24th.—The Lord has been very gracious in
sending me on that evangelistic mission, for it has
helped my own soul. It has also had some effect in
making me think less of my sorrow ; indeed to-day I
was thinking on Gen. xli. 51, 52, noticing that God's
Lethe was in some degree fruitfulness in the time of
affliction.

Saturday, Sept. 14th.—Have learned something to
humble me. Have got a sight of my littleness in every
way. No grace above a mustard seed. Next week is
the anniversary of my ordination. What thoughts it is
fitted to awaken !

Monday, Oct. 14th.—Ever memorable day to me ! I

do not think there has been a whole day that has passed since this night last year in which I have not, at one time or other, called up my dear Isabella to memory. Blessed be the Lord for the many ways in which He has strengthened me, especially by filling my hand with work and showing me much of His Spirit's presence and power in souls.

Saturday, 19th.—Have seen my soul has of late been secretly declining. I think I have detected some of the 'grey hairs here and there,' and am a little alarmed. It has been quiet and deceptive this form of corruption that has made inroads upon me—self-indulgence, inclining toward the flesh. A remark of John Flavel came home with great power : ' How did the love of the creature, like a sluice cut in the bank of a river, draw away the stream of my affection from Thee !' That used, I fear, to be true of me, and in another form of late something of this was imperceptibly going on. I notice how often the Lord says in the Old Testament to His servants, ' Be strong ;' act in full vigour, energy, with all your powers awake.

Tuesday, Nov. 5th.—[My son] James has to-day fairly begun the college course. How rapidly time passes on. May the Lord prepare him to be a servant of His in very deed. I have been helped by noticing the difference between Num. xi. and Num. xx. In the former case Moses pours out to God all his thoughts, fears, unbelief, doubts ; and the Lord puts them away and strikes at the root. But, in the latter case, he comes out with all before the people, and does not carry them to God. Hence the chastisement in this latter case.

Tuesday, Dec. 3rd.—To-day thought I got new insight into the words, ' Ask and receive, that your joy may be full ;' as if the Lord had said to them, ' Now, make it your rule to ask as much, and to ask the very things

that will make your joy full.' Always ask till you get
your cup running over.

Tuesday, 31*st.*—It is now near the close of the year.
I deeply regret that I have not prayed more during this
year, nor been, like Elias, climbing Carmel from time to
time. The providences and events of the year, such as
my brother James's death, would have been much more
useful to me had I extracted the honey from the comb
by prayer and supplication. The great shadow in my
lot, my never-forgotten bereavement, continues to make
earth to appear all unlike what once it was. But there
appears to me to be a strange want of depth in my
experience. It is as if I did no more than touch the
hem, or scrape the surface, or get glimpses now and
then of the things which are freely given me of God.
What mercies have I had this year in respect of health,
my own and my family's! This has also been a year
wherein souls have been saved. The Lord has not left
us alone. Yet I feel as if the Lord had left me standing
by the Fountain of living water alone, after breaking the
cisterns out of which I used to drink.

2nd Jan. 1868.—Standing beside broken cisterns, and
at the Fountain of living waters, may I this year find
myself satisfied abundantly. Yesterday was a day of
solemn thoughts. Our watchword in the church was
' They that wait upon the Lord,' etc., joined with ' Wait
for His Son from heaven.' Lord, this year may the
Spirit fill my soul, revealing the fulness of Christ to me
from day to day.

Sabbath, 19*th.*—I am often like one sitting under the
shade of his cypress tree, with bright sunshine bathing
it, and cheering the scene. There is always the shade
of earthly sadness with me now, but yet the cheering
light of God's countenance. I praise too little, and let
thanks too often die away.

Saturday, Feb. 1st.—Last Sabbath, our Communion, was full of truth and grace. We thought 'the shout of the King was among us.' At the close of this week several matters have come up to vex us. Are those answers to prayer for more grace? Are those God's way of sending me more and more to Himself alone? They seem fitted to work in this direction.

Saturday, 15th.—I learned one thing over again, viz., that while the Lord seems to use evangelists to awaken souls, He keeps a place for older labourers, in the instruction and leading of the saved. We must all know our own place, and be satisfied. We are while here, like roots under ground with all the principles of life, struggling upward, and soon to shoot forth above many a leaf of beauty, and many a branch bearing fruit worthy of Him in whom our root is fastened. The clods of earth interrupt our upward growth for a time. What a burst of sunshine and glorious liberty awaits us !

Saturday, 22nd.—Spent the whole forenoon in fasting and prayer. A time of sadness at the review of unimproved seasons, especially my bereavement; unattained blessings; backsliding; lukewarmness; weak, feeble faith; unheavenliness of mind and walk. My appeal is to Eph. iii. 20. I ask, seek, knock at my Father's heart through the Beloved Son for the Spirit's larger blessing. I want fruit a hundredfold; 'life more abundantly;' 'all grace abounding toward me that I, having all-sufficiency,' etc.; 'abiding in the Lord,' with the unction from the Holy One; 'eyes opened, that I may know the exceeding greatness of His power,' etc.; 'rooted and grounded in love, comprehending height, depth, length, breadth,' etc.; 'filled with the fulness of God;' 'filled with the Spirit.' And as a minister, out of me 'rivers of living water,' 'turning many to righteous-

ness;' an earthen vessel to carry Christ's name, used as
Boanerges or as Barnabas. There was, I notice, use
made in the times of Pentecost of both Peter and John
together. Change me, Lord, from glory to glory, into
Thine image, till glory come.

Wednesday, March 25th.—Anniversary of father's
death and Robert M'Cheyne's. I am still spared, and
this week the Lord is working remarkably in our congregation among the children, under Mr. Hammond.
Last Sabbath at Greenock Communion. A thin mist
seemed to rise between me and the Lord Jesus during a
great part of the time, though during it all I saw Him
full of grace. But I could not get close to Him. The
world, ever since the death of my dear Isabella, has
been darkened, but I am getting accustomed to this
darkness, walking in the light of God.

Tuesday, 31st.—The awakening going on. To-night
both Isabella and Marjory came home truly speaking of
their having been enabled to rest on Christ. What a
joyful time this has been! Memorable night indeed. I
think, too, the young servant has found Christ. I had
my dislike as to the method of proceeding, etc., but the
Lord has enabled me to acquiesce in whatever may be
His manner of working: and now, here is the result in
my own family. Truly, His ways are not our ways.
For some time past I have seen that 'one soweth and
another reapeth,' and that it is even as it was with
Timothy, a stranger is sent to bring the work to a
point. Blessed Lord, I have asked Thee often to
remember 'when *mother* leaves thee the Lord will
take thee up.' I have asked Thee to be more than a
mother to my motherless children, and now indeed
Thou art giving me my prayer. Praise, praise, for ever-
more!

Saturday, April 11th.—To-night spoke and prayed

with Isabella in prospect of to-morrow, her first Communion. How happy her dear mother would this night have been at the thought! But perhaps the news has reached her in glory, for 'there is joy,' etc. Again let me cry 'Hallelujah!'

Wednesday, 29th.—The Edinburgh Communion has been, in some respects, very blessed to my soul. The Lord seemed to use me on Sabbath to several souls. Made my last visit to 15 *York Place.* Just before leaving Caroline [my brother's widow] asked me to pray with them all. It was solemn and sad.

Saturday, May 23rd.—Did not accept my appointment to the General Assembly. The thought of my brother James, and several circumstances of the times, led me to decline. To-day, coming from a funeral, felt great gladness at the thought of knowing Christ and being soon with Him in a day that may be like this funeral day. That passage in Rom. ix. 2, 'I have great heaviness and continual sorrow,' etc., finds an illustration in my ever-recurring heaviness and sorrow over my dear, dear Isabella. Were I holier, the thought of the unsaved would thus come back upon me from hour to hour. Lord, fill me with the Holy Ghost and the mind of Christ.

Friday, 29th.—My birthday. The funeral day of my oldest cousin, Christian Bonar.[1] One gathered after another. My life has been longer than many, and my ministry, but I am not 'full of the Holy Ghost and of faith.' O for a heart like a glowing coal, and an eye ever looking full upon the Lamb! The times are unsettled, and in our church the Union question is disturbing us greatly. We have come to the time when, even among believers, 'the love of many waxes cold.' It is a world of broken cisterns!

---

[1] Daughter of Alexander Bonar of Ratho.

Saturday, 30th.—Reviewing the past, I see this fact in my life, worthy of continual admiration and thanks, viz., that for more than thirty years (indeed, perhaps, since October of 1830) I have never been shaken in my quiet resting on the Lord Jesus. I have been many, many times unhappy for a time, but never led to doubt my interest in the Lord Jesus. The Lord has never let my eyes close to the one foundation. He has kept me from mixing up my feeling with Christ's work. It has been all of grace, the doing of the Spirit who takes the things of Christ and shows them. Shall I not love the Holy Ghost with my whole heart? There have been of late a good many conversions among us, among the children, and among the young people of my classes.

June 2nd.—Have heard that on Sabbath morning our fellow-labourer and beloved in the Lord, John Milne, died! To him what a calm after the storm! I almost envy him this evening, within the veil, with Jesus, amid the redeemed who are waiting for the Day of Christ. What peace, what joy!

This same day, June 2nd, on hearing the sad tidings, he wrote to Mrs. Milne :—

'I have just heard the tidings, your beloved husband, and our beloved brother, has joined the general assembly of the firstborn whose names are written in heaven. Will you try to think of him as I have been trying to do, viz., as now hearing the Shepherd's voice and seeing the Shepherd's face in the greenest of the green pastures, full of wonder, full of love, brimful, too, of the joy of the Lord?

'And will he not be thinking of those he has gone up from? I can almost believe he is saying to himself, " and Barbara will be here speedily, or else we shall be descending with the Lord to meet her and the saints left behind." *His* cup, I am sure, is running over now, and as for you, I am sure of this : " Goodness and mercy shall follow you all the days of your life, and you shall dwell in the house of the Lord for ever."

'I cannot resist your wish that I should preach on Sabbath forenoon, though I feel it one of the saddest duties I was ever called to. May the Lord make it a resurrection time to souls. Meanwhile you cannot but be upheld and strengthened, for many, many are remembering you in your deep sorrow.—Yours truly in the Lord, Who will soon come for His sleeping saints,

'ANDREW A. BONAR.'

Monday, 8th.—Returned from Perth, where I preached the funeral sermon of my long-tried, ever faithful, and loving friend. On Friday we laid him to rest in the Grange Cemetery, and then I was called to this mournful duty.

I have been learning my littleness. I see how little I improve affliction; this seed falls on my heart too like the seed on the rocky ground. How often I come back to Deut. xxix. 3, 4. Then I see John Milne was immensely beyond me in the consecration of himself to the Lord, and, as a consequence, his influence was proportionately deep and extensive. Besides, he evidently had communion with the Lord much more throughout the day than I have yet reached. But oh, how many thoughts of the past, in connection with the present state of my soul, crowded through my mind yesterday. 'Less than the least of all saints.' And yet to me 'grace has been given' to win souls now and then, and especially to help those that win souls. While at Perth, discovered several cases wherein I had formerly been blessed.

As to myself, whether I am to live a little longer, or suddenly be called, or wait till Christ's return, I cannot say that I have any ambition or idea. I try to act upon John xxi. 21, 22. But, on looking back, I feel distressed and ashamed, deeply ashamed, at my not sympathising more in my dear friend's depression and trial, and at not praying for him far more. Paul found time, in the midst of a thousandfold more to occupy

him, to pray for individual cases often and much.
Prayer should make time for itself. 'Unto me belongeth
confusion of face.' And the worst is, it is with me
always thus. I pray little for friends, and then I bitterly
regret that I did not smite on the ground, not three,
but seven times.

Saturday, 27th.—Last Sabbath evening. my sermon
to the Sabbath scholars was a season of unusual
power ; I felt the words going forth and coming down
with strength. A good many were impressed.

Wednesday, July 8th.—Heard of the death of William
Burns, one of Christ's great missionaries to earth in
our day. How many in one year! Why are such as
myself spared? I have been getting portions of several
days for retirement and prayer. Reading *Dying Thoughts*
of Richard Baxter, and do join with him in cries for
increase of faith till it be lost in sight.

Monday, 20th.—Have been at Crossford Communion.
A tender look upon the people, a blessed day every
way. Mr. Manson's subject was Isa. xl. 31, and I
tasted 'renewing of strength.' Let my will be one
with the Lord's, falling into that great stream as a
tributary.

August 19th.—From time to time have been getting
more like one that passes within the veil to speak there
with the Lord. After many conflicts too, with corruption in many forms, have been more weaned from
earth than formerly ; or, rather, have been more really
delighted at the prospect of direct communion in the
presence of the Lord.

Thursday, Sept. 3rd.—Have been two days at the
Perth Conference, and enjoyed it greatly, but it was
encompassed this year with associations of John Milne
that made me often wonder if before another year I
might be where he is.

On returning from the Conference Mr. Bonar wrote the following letter to Mrs. Milne in Edinburgh :—

TO MRS. MILNE.

' *Glasgow, 3rd Sept.* 1868.

'MY DEAR MRS. MILNE,—You will like to hear something of the Perth Conference. There have been not a few references to your beloved husband, all of them solemnizing, and all of them full of affection. I was asked to pray with special reference to our loss. It was scarcely fair to ask me, especially as I did not know till I came to the Hall. I felt it very difficult to do anything else than confess sin in regard to our improving so inadequately the great privileges we have had in the past, in having such men of God among us. For my part I do earnestly desire grace to use better far than I have done the opportunity thus afforded of learning much and being stirred up to run as fast in the race as they did.

'The meetings have been very fully attended, very pleasant, very profitable. I wonder if John has thought of us? You know memory is not lost nor impaired there. Truly he has been the means of a vast and far-extended and long-lasting blessing to very many, by the Conference which His Master empowered him to arrange so well.

'I have not waited to the third day, partly because I shrank from the Communion in Free St. Leonard's. It seemed so difficult to think of being there without the friend and brother who has gone upward to that higher Communion in which we hope soon to meet him.

'May your soul receive largely from the Lord who knows your heart's desire and prayer, a running-over measure of "faith, hope, love."

'Will you try sometimes to remember me and my children? O to be borne, all of us, safely through the perils and snares of the last days, and presented at last without spot to Himself at His Coming !—Yours truly, in the Lord Jesus,

'ANDREW A. BONAR.'

Sabbath, 20th.—It was this day thirty years ago that I was ordained to the ministry. What a long time I have been allowed to work ! But the retrospect humbles me to the dust. What would not Robert M'Cheyne have accomplished in so long a time ! I lie down to rest this night sorrowing over my leanness, my unprofitableness, the blood-guiltiness that ever lies upon me because of souls neglected, not prayed over, not spoken to aright, not dealt with. 'Spare me that I may recover strength before I go hence,' is my prayer. Shepherd of souls, hide me in Thy faithfulness. Thy faithfulness is the covering for my unfaithfulness.

Thursday, Oct. 22nd.—This evening among the young communicants admitted (and there were forty) were my two beloved daughters. I have been thinking upon the thanksgiving of David in 2 Sam. vii. 18, specially verse 20, 'And what can David say more unto Thee? for Thou, Lord, knowest Thy servant.' 'According to Thine own heart hast Thou done all these great things.'

Friday, Nov. 27th.—My brother [Horatius] has just published the *Memoir of John Milne*, and to-day I have finished the perusal of it. What seasons! what scenes! Strange to think of him within the veil. It made me feel somehow, as if myself, with others, were now brought down to the banks of the river, and might be called away any day to cross it. My life and its work has been feeble, full of self, no more than 'aimed at Him.' I do not live as one whom Christ overshadows, and who rejoices to abide under that shadow continually, speaking out of it, praying in it, studying there, always there.

Friday, Dec. 4th.—This day twelve years ago I was inducted into my present charge. From time to time my widowed state presses upon me. To-day I was glad to see how this may be part of 'through much tribulation;' 'tribulations and patience of Christ,' that precede the kingdom. Yet also gleams of joy, great joy, light up my path. I hope to spend to-morrow in fasting and prayer most of the day. I have got on with my study for that end. Lord, be with me 'of a truth.'

Saturday, 12*th.*—My longing is to have a continual groaning of the heart after God, and for continual communion, and yet I have not reached this.

Saturday, 19*th.*—Returned yesterday from Moffat. While there the things of thirty-five years ago came up to mind. I was just beginning to preach; was there on a Sabbath with the beloved missionary Robert Johnstone,[1] and with him prayed and wandered about. He has entered into rest, and a whole generation has passed away since then, and the Lord still keeps me alive at this day to preach the same Christ. This revisiting of places full of associations reminds me of Num. xxxiii. 10, where Israel comes again in view of the Red Sea, though from another point, looking, perhaps, along the shore to yonder place where they were led over by the Lord.

1*st January* 1869.—Last night closed the year with the congregation of Crossford, where the Lord has done much.[2] To-day, in our own church, met again for prayer. My heart went out in desires to be used as a vessel for God's glory being shown forth in me. There is a strange sadness and sense of some one absent in the house at such a season. It needs the Lord's own presence to make up my want. But, when I look back on the past year and see what He did for my children's souls, who am I that I should not wear the garment of praise?

Saturday, 16*th.*—Unexpectedly to-day found time to spend the most of the former part of the day in prayer and intercourse with my Lord. What a view I got of myself! I saw immense mercy, heap upon heap, all the way I have come—advantages, opportunities, open doors,

---

[1] See Diary, 13th June 1836.
[2] For more than twenty years Mr. Bonar spent a week at Christmas or New Year with his family at the Hut-on-Clyde, Crossford, where his friends Mr. and Mrs. Manson had gone to live.

means of progress without number ; and yet all these
have left me at this hour exceedingly little affected.   I
am unholy, unthankful, with little love, little faith, little
feeling.   All I can do for rest and peace is to hide
myself from myself in the merit of my Lord.   The
shadow of the Great Rock is over me.

Tuesday, Feb. 2nd.—Our Communion was a time of
gladness, though mixed on my part with many temptations.   I have profited especially in connection with it
by having been led to preach upon, and write out as a
tract, some helps to growth in grace ; or rather to illus-
trate, ' They go from strength to strength.'

March 25th.—Have been very busy in work.   This
day calls up to mind many things : the death of loved
friends is one ; but also, this time last year, the birth of
my two daughters into the kingdom of God.   I have
never sufficiently praised the Lord, and never can.

Greenock, Sabbath, 28th.—The shadow of death over
us.   Horace's little boy, Henry, died on Friday.   This
has helped to put earth somewhat at a distance and
enabled me to take the bread of life like one very near
the opening of the gates of heaven.   If only I could get
quite quit of the idea of merit, or of God giving in proportion to our qualities, and the like !   O that this root
of bitterness, which is ever springing up, were destroyed
for ever, and that instead of it my faith in the love of
God were made to grow exceedingly.   And oh that every
hour I were entertaining some fresh thought of the
Lord's ways and Word.   The everyday common duties
and occupations of life stand sadly in the way of progress.   As the old writers used to say, *Perimus licitis.*

Wednesday, April 14th.—Yesterday spent a day visiting
the graves of some martyrs, among the rest Skellyhill
and Priesthill, wandering in bright sunshine over the
moor.   At the latter spot we sat and prayed together,

Mr. Manson, my brother John, Mr. Elder, and Major Mosman. I have been feeling since something like deep solemnity at the thought of being privileged thus to enjoy the scenery and learn such lessons from our fathers. It might well help us to live more truly the life of faith upon the Son of God. As to myself, this repeatedly came into my mind : 'The Lord delights to give thee all that is really good, and therefore be assured that in all He takes from thee He meant thee only good and nothing else.'

Several tokens of blessing have occurred at this Communion. The Sabbath sermon, Josh. iii. 16, much felt—as much nearly as the sermon some time since upon the 'cup of red wine,' which produced more impression than any I have preached. The Lord was with us.

May 3rd.—Horace's daughter, Kitty, very delicate. Another cloud, Lord ? But if so, it will break with blessing, for Thou art ever making Thy people happy, or preparing them for being made happy.

Saturday, 22nd.—Having agreed to preach from home part of to-morrow, I took all this day till four o'clock for fasting and prayer. Not much distracted. Some precious gleams, some hopeful moments, while calling on the Lord to work by His Spirit among us in new ways and in great power. One of my chief reasons for agreeing to preach to-morrow out of my own pulpit was that I might get this day for prayer, and so might help my people far more than by ordinary preaching.

Saturday, 29th.—Solemnized last night when I got a quiet evening at the review of my past life. I have lived fifty-nine years in the world. The review presented causes of thanksgiving and praise without number, and on the other hand, reasons for deep humiliation, bitter sorrow, regret, self-upbraiding. 'Behold my shield,'

not me.   Three pictures in my study often rebuke
me—[those] of Robert M'Cheyne, William Burns, and
John Milne; and at times the photograph of Samuel
Rutherford's tomb suggests to me what coldness of love
is in my heart compared with such a man.   And the
little I have learned from affliction is a constant grief
to me.

I got a very awful view of my long life's sinfulness in
the evening.   I seemed to myself to be one standing
amid mercies of every kind, but specially divine grace.
The Spirit has been, since my conversion forty years
ago, nearly continually putting to my lips full cups of
blessing, and I have done little else than just take a few
drops and then set the cup by !   The Bible day by day;
precious sermons;   great books of truth ;   the lives of
holy and happy saints ;   events of providence ;   all, all
these, and my own preaching and the ordinances in
which I take part ; these, these have been each a full
cup of blessing put to my lips ; but scarcely ever have I
done more than merely take a sip.   O what I have lost !
O what I have lost !   My heart sinks within me.   I
can only once again put my hand upon the head of
the slain Lamb, and look up.   The words of Joel ii.
25 have been before now a comfort ; for in some way
the Lord will add that to all His other acts of grace.
' I will restore to you the years that the locusts have
eaten.'

Sabbath, June 27th.—Our Communion.   Like the disciples ' sleeping for sorrow,' I nearly lost the feast by
weariness on the preceding days.   But this morning the
Lord shone forth upon my soul with a new beam, and
the day was a blessed one.

Friday, July 2nd.—Last night preached at Collace
(after spending the day in visiting many), in the old
church where God began to teach me many things ;

scenes associated with remarkable dealings in grace and providences. Preached on John iii. 16, a testimony to the same unchanging truth as in early days. In the meeting was led to confess the sins of my former ministry.

Ardrishaig, Sabbath, 11*th.*—I see we are very like the disciples in this, we are apt to let opportunities pass by with very little got from them, as the three disciples in the Garden.

Monday, 19*th.*—Death of my brother's daughter Kitty summoned me to Edinburgh.

Sabbath, 25*th.*—Communion at Ardrishaig. By mistake I did not get the bread and wine. Felt somewhat strange, but I learned some things. Thus, it may be the Lord was thus gently chastising me, reminding me to take off my shoes because the ground was holy. Then, I learned sympathy with those who often, at this season, are not permitted in the providence of God to go. Then, also, I felt a hunger I had not felt for a long time—a hunger for the bread and wine. I see that I will need every day, more and more, in the morning, before any business begins, a cup of the new wine of the kingdom—fellowship with God ; and I must pray *oftener*, though but for a minute, during the day.

Thursday, Sept. 9*th.*—Yesterday, while at the Perth Conference, got the tidings of the death of my sister-in-law, Mrs. William Dickson. As I sat with William Dickson this forenoon in the quiet room, thoughts of my own time of dark sorrow came up again. '*God* liveth ; blessed be my Rock.'

Thursday, 23*rd.*—Trying to-day (the anniversary of my first sermon as ordained minister) to review the past, and to spend every hour, so far as I have leisure, in prayer for more grace. I am greatly struck with 2 Tim. iii. 2 : '*unthankful, unholy*,' as characteristics of professing formalists in the last days ; but as in another form applicable to myself. Shame and sorrow fill me at my unholiness, after all the kindness of the Lord, opportunities, privileges, seasons of communion, example of other saints, blessings sent, etc. Lord, give, give !

Thursday, Oct. 14th.—The anniversary of a never-forgotten evening. ' His ways are in the sea.' But He is all faithfulness and compassion. He has done much for me by my affliction, as well as *in* it.

Saturday, Nov. 27th.—By a singular providence, I have got special time to-day to fast and pray. In my ordinary reading of Scripture, I often get a single expression which serves as a key-note to my prayers, and sets my soul in order. It was thus a few days ago, when reading in Isa. xxx. 30 : ' *The glory* of His voice.' And now, 2 Cor. xii. 9, 10, the real pleasure and delight which the apostle was able to take in bearing crosses for Christ. That word ἥδιστα ; most sweetly relishing it as men do a banquet. And then that other word, εὐδοκῶ ; ' I am well pleased with it,' regarding it with great complacency and satisfaction. O for such attainment, Lord !

Wednesday, Dec. 29th.—At Crossford. Have been reading the *Memoirs* of W. C. Burns and of Dr. Hamilton. Many, many associations ; much to rebuke me and humble me. I see the only life worth living is to live for others. The single-mindedness, intense zeal, yet calmness, of William Burns, has often spoken to my heart with indescribable power.

1st January, 1870.—Feebly, very feebly, tried to be in the spirit of Psalm ciii. There is in these late years nothing of mirth attached to this season ; but there is at times a calm gladness in the prospect of coming glory. ' Nearer than when we believed.'

Sabbath, 30*th.*—A sore lesson to-day. Having been through much interruption and many occupations un-prayerful this past week, the Lord was pleased in the forenoon to straiten me most painfully. Perhaps the people did not perceive it much, but I felt the rebuke very keenly. How gracious in the Lord, at the same time, to keep others from suffering from my want of faith and watchfulness. In the evening, at the very close of our day's work, the Lord sent a person to tell me of the blessing that had attended the accidental perusal of my little book, *The Cup of Wrath.*

Sabbath, February 13*th.*—Had time yesterday to fast and pray till three o'clock. Got more humiliation than usual; felt inclined to return again and again to con-fession of sin, and felt an unusual indifference to honour, name, etc., or rather, a hearty wish not to have self brought into notice. Reading the *Life of William Burns* helped me. To-day dispensed the Communion at Hillhead, their first Communion in Anniesland. About eighty sat down at the Lord's Table. Very much of the Lord's presence. In the evening preached again, and baptized *sixteen* children, some of them the whole household of persons lately decided.

Sabbath, April 3*rd.*—At Greenock Communion saw the blessed truth, that a touch was enough to bring one into connection with the electricity; so with our believ-ing desires or thoughts. And when I am under tempta-tion, one look upward to Christ secures the victory. Remembered Andrew's death on the first of this month. What it brings back, too, of his beloved mother, so tender, so loving.

Saturday, 16*th.*—Our own Communion last Sabbath, quiet, helpful; but Jordan did not overflow its banks.

Thursday, 21*st.*—To-day the Fast-Day in Edinburgh. Heard of *three* cases wherein my sermon last year at this time, on John iii. 16, had been remarkably blessed. To-day some measure of God's presence.

Saturday, May 14th.—Having come to Abernyte on my way to the opening of the M'Cheyne Memorial Church [Dundee], I was left alone all day, and spent some hours in prayer; part of the time in the little church, and then with Mr. Wilson. Felt deep, deep sorrow at the thought of the past. What gales of the Spirit have blown, and yet my sails have been ill set, and caught little of the breezes in these great awakening times.

Sabbath, 15th.—Preached in the M'Cheyne Memorial Church in the morning, and St. Peter's in the afternoon. In the evening, finding a great crowd who could not get in, preached in the open air, right opposite the Memorial Church, while Mr. Macgregor was preaching within. I know that the God of Elijah still lives.

Thursday, 19th.—I see the Lord's providence in a remarkable manner to me as a minister here in a recent arrangement. A great deal of time used to be occupied occasionally in going out to Hillhead. Had that been necessary still, I do not see how I could have managed it with my large number of members. But it has become unnecessary now, for they have got a station and preacher of their own. It is thus the Lord rolls away the stone when we go on from day to day, not anxious about the future.

Now in public matters, our Church is near a crisis through the Union question. This meeting of the General Assembly is a very solemn one. I have been led to cry to the Lord as the ' Wonderful,' and then ' Counsellor,' and ' Prince of Peace.'

Thursday, 26th.—Got the opportunity of retiring to the church for three hours to-day, there pleading before the Lord the cause of our Church, which this day's debate in the Assembly will so influence; and then my own soul's state, which has been assailed by temptation, and is besides languid. It was good to be there.

Sabbath, 29th.—My birthday. My life looks to me since conversion as a sort of half-awake life, half-decided, never altogether and with full fervour the Lord's. 'To me to live has been Christ,' is what I wish I could say, but cannot. So much of self. The Lord has held me up from any open stumbling these threescore years! He will do more for me still, and my song will be. Jude 24: 'Now unto Him that is able to keep you from falling,' etc.

July 1st.—Settled for a month here at Greystonelees in Berwickshire. Our journey yesterday was remarkably easy and without trouble, because that morning we had specially noticed together the traveller's text, Ezra viii. 21.[1] Is this calm day a type of my rest at last, when all wanderings shall be over?

Saturday, 16th.—Noticed in Isaiah i. 18, when alone for some hours' retirement and prayer, that there the Lord means to tell that we who are His are *at all times* white as snow. Not at some time only. My not praying more for missionaries and missions in private may be a reason why my prayer is often hindered and delayed.

Friday, 22nd.—Some hours for prayer on Lamberton Moor. Spread on the mercy-seat my personal sorrows and wants, my congregation, etc. How often still am I led to say to the Lord, 'Lord, when Thou takest a dear wife away, art Thou not engaged to take the place?' Like Psalm xxvii. 10.

Glasgow, Sabbath, August 21st.—Somewhat sad that there is no more power than before in my ministry. But I met with a hint from Exodus xxiv. upon which

---

[1] Mr. Bonar used to read this verse at family worship always before leaving for his summer holiday.

some one remarks that Moses was left standing on the mountain, as if unnoticed, for six days before the Lord took him up to hold fellowship upon the business for which he was called. The Lord wishes us to keep from day to day in close fellowship, waiting upon Him. If Moses had wearied of waiting, and begun to wander among the rocks, or chase the wild animals, that would not have been the way to obtain his interview.

Sabbath, Sept. 25th.—In the evening when about to preach to the Sabbath-school children, just on ascending the steps of the pulpit I recalled to mind the upward look of King Asa when going into the battle ; I looked up to the Lord for grace and for His Spirit to breathe upon the gathered multitude of children, and cause a great calm. And it was so all through, though circumstances were against us. The children were strangely still as I preached of Christ calming the storm, and the little ships sharing in the calm.

Saturday, Oct. 8th.—Yesterday and to-day especially, though also for some more days, I have had upon my mind a very clear and strong impression of the necessity of the Holy Ghost taking the veil from the heart of the sinner before he can see sin, eternity, Christ, or any spiritual truth. From time to time this has been coming in upon me, leading me to cry to the Lord more than formerly for the presence and working of His Spirit, that individuals in my communicants' class, and individuals in the congregation, who seem blind and unmoved by the great realities of salvation, may be quickened. May to-morrow be a day of the Spirit's working, when I preach upon ' The things which are unseen are eternal.'

Friday, 14th.—Ever memorable because of the past. My beloved wife is never long out of my mind when the house is still. At our worship to-night, in regular course, we sang, ' Let faith exalt her joyful voice.' ' O grave, where is thy triumph now,' etc. What a day of meeting that will be !

Sabbath, 23*rd.*—Our Communion. Many blessed messages. To-day some fruits. My expectation about the sermon upon ' things unseen ' not disappointed. A woman who had not entered church for six years so deeply impressed that she tried to shut her ears. ' Why did your father preach that sermon ? ' she said to my daughter.

November 4*th.*—Being in the country at a Fast-Day yesterday, did not get time to mark down what I meant to do, viz., the trial I underwent on the Wednesday. It was our Presbytery day, and there the question of Union was discussed, and I took part against it as a matter of conscience. Our Church is very sadly divided. My session have strong feelings on the different sides. I sometimes think that the Lord has let this state of things come to pass in order to complete our weaning from all earthly things, from *church* as well as *self*. The future prospect is dark. My soul longs for the Church of the first-born. I have a mind that is often bewildered in regard to disputed matters, so that if the Lord did not Himself by providence and the help of friends guide me, I should often have gone wrong. But Psalm xxxii. 8, 9 is true.

Saturday Evening, Dec. 31*st.*—We have been spending the week at Crossford. It is solemn to find myself to-night just at the close of another year. My soul cries out ' leanness, leanness,' but my heart's desire is to be a temple of the Holy Ghost, full of Christ. The world seems more this year than ever to be unsettled, and every form of error to be making progress ; but, as I was preaching lately, Christ wishes us to be calm. ' See that ye be not troubled.' He sits upon the floods, He sits King for ever.

Sabbath, 1st January 1871.—I felt this to be a day over which hangs something of sadness, so many things in the past to mourn over. Now and then the beam of hope, things hoped for, lightened up the sky. Went to the pulpit in a half-desponding mind, but my bands were loosed.

I am too easily pleased with outward prosperity in my classes and congregation, and with freedom in my ministrations. Lord, send power. This is a season of prayer which I would fain join. What will this year witness ?

Saturday, 21st.—So helped yesterday in preparation that I got the first part of to-day for special prayer.

Saturday, March 4th.—Have been troubled these three weeks past by receiving a letter from the brethren who have the management of the Cunningham Lectureship, asking me to take the next course. I have been quite amazed at their proposal, and have refused decidedly, for they completely mistake the amount of my learning and my ability for such a work. May the Master use me in my true sphere and give me the grace of prayer in far higher measure. I have further seen this week that I have been most blameworthy in restraining prayer, for I have sought for reading, observing, studying, illustrating, and other such helps, in giving forth the Word to young and old, all the while not asking them of God from time to time.

Saturday, 18th.—On Wednesday, 15th, was present at, and took part in, the ordination of a minister at Crossford. The service conducted by Mr. Manson in a most powerful manner. God has wrought wonderfully there. Such a day always awakens in me some bitter regret and sadness, because it makes me remember how far I am from having attained what I once expected. I do wish to be Christ's fully, and not to be merely a laborious, painful, minister of the Lord.

Saturday, 25*th*.—I well remember twenty-eight years ago how this day the messenger came to my house in Collace to tell me that Robert M'Cheyne was taken from us. And I remember, though indistinctly, my father's death ; the first death I ever knew. The world is not more attractive now ; it is less and less so, and the Church not more hopeful. May I be found of Him in peace ! The night is far spent, the day is at hand. A slight touch of sickness to-day made me think the more of Psalm xxiii. This is the Greenock Communion season. How often has the Lord allowed me to minister here !

Sabbath, 26*th*.—With the blood sprinkled upon me (Exod. xxiv.), O may I get far up the hill and meet God !

Saturday, *April* 8*th*.—Yesterday agreed to put my name with Moody-Stuart's to a letter to Dr. Candlish on the present Union question. It seemed to me quite providential that this was proposed to me, the letter expressing my opinions so exactly. To-day read for a time the *Memoir of Duncan Matheson*, one of the labourers passed into glory. Lord, give me more power, more zeal, more love.

Saturday, 15*th*.—Thoughts of dear Isabella still come from time to time, though I try to overcome the feeling of want, yet it is a sore temptation to me often. More of Christ, Lord, that I may overcome this part of the world. The state of the land is not good. ' When the Son of Man cometh, shall He find faith on the earth ? ' Our Church is not what it was, and the Spirit seems not among us as in other years. At times I find myself glad that the time which remaineth is short, and the glory nearer and nearer.

Friday, May 5th.—Back from Edinburgh Communion, where, on the Sabbath, I enjoyed a season of singular calmness while speaking to those at the table. I never remember an occasion wherein I had myself more still-ness of spirit in speaking. The crumb of the bread of life which I got in hearing that day was this : Christ is at once the loftiest and the lowliest, so that He will often wait upon us and serve us. I have been asked to preach one of the sermons at the General Assembly. May the Lord give me grace to testify fully for Christ that day ! Yesterday I got two letters telling me of souls blessed, one by my tract on *Assurance*, the other by my conversation. These met me on my return home, not like Jephthah meeting a thorn in the flesh.

Saturday, 13th.—On reading Revelation iv. 8, it seemed to me clear that that glorious redemption-song is the continual utterance of all that company. As if it had been said, their hearts are ever full of that holy, holy, holy One, whatever they are doing, whether sing-ing, working, worshipping. They never cease in this, their hearts are ever pouring out this gush of love to Him whom they serve.

Sabbath, 21st.—Having been appointed to preach before the General Assembly in the Hall, I had tried yesterday to get time for more prayer and preparation, but was obliged to let myself be interrupted ; yet the Lord helped me. I preached upon Psalm cxviii. 22-24. At night my soul sang Psalm cxxxviii. from time to time.

Wednesday, 24th.—For the first time spoke in the General Assembly against the proposed Union. Very trying to the flesh. But it seemed to me plain duty.

Monday, 29th.—Another birthday. I have often this year wondered if my time for finishing my testimony may not now be near. I sometimes wish it were, and then I begin to think how in the future ages I shall be almost sorry that the days of trial and serving God in the midst of it are over ; the days of winning souls, sowing seed in tears. Lord, give me light, love, life, likeness to Thee.

Sabbath, June 25th.—Very much to occupy, and though I besought the Lord to make this a week of near communion yet it seems to me as if Satan had succeeded, whenever I was about to ascend the hill, in getting me to turn back quickly in order to attend to some matter down here. In this state our Communion found me.

Sabbath, July 9th.—Creetown, Wigtown Bay.

Monday, 10th.—Alone praying in the churchyard of old Kirkmabreck, where often Samuel Rutherford preached.

Tuesday, 11th.—At Anwoth with all my young people. The day was still and beautiful ; solemn quiet enjoyment, finding some little communion with the Lord, and delight in Him whom Samuel Rutherford used to set up on high here. We sang together in the old church; all my children seemed interested.

Wednesday, 12th.—To-day a great longing and yearning of heart for the time when the Lord shall draw all the earth to Him.

Sabbath, 23rd.—Preached at Anwoth, and in the evening in the open air at the monument, to a large assembly. Spoke of Christ the Carpenter.

Tuesday, Aug. 29th.—Have returned home. Glad to begin my own work here. Lord, open the windows of heaven. My soul has been going out to the Lord Himself of late more than before, and I have been led to pray from time to time for the Holy Spirit in a way that I have not often done. Is He coming among us in power ?

Saturday, September 16th.—Have felt a yearning after

more inward communion with God my Saviour for
some days. My plans seem never to be God's purpose
for me.

Sabbath, 24th.—Remembered that yesterday was the
day of the month when first I preached as minister of a
congregation, now thirty-three years ago. I forgot this
on Saturday, being in some things interrupted, and had
not my usual time of special prayer. But I had some
special desires kindled that day. It seems to me that
when I began my ministry I had a spark of love
to souls cast into my heart from Christ's great love
which has a most vehement flame ; but that spark has
remained a spark to this day instead of being multiplied
every year till I was all fire.

Thursday, October 12th.—More and more do I learn
that continual watchfulness unto prayer is essential to
right preaching, right visiting, right conversation, right
reading of the Word.

Saturday, 14th.— Anniversary of that memorable
evening on which the Lord took away the desire of
my eyes with a stroke. Got time to pray much
to-day. My heart yearned for the salvation of my
children. Going over the scenes of this time seven
years ago many solemn thoughts arose. O what might
I not have learned ! Many most precious mercies too
in connection, but life here is not what it was, more like
what I am to preach upon to-morrow, ' Foxes have holes,
and the birds of the air,' etc. My ambition now is very
feeble compared with other days. To win souls and to
know God more, and then to be in the kingdom is ' all
my desire.'

Sabbath, 22nd.—I was led to notice that 2 Peter i. 3
says ' divine power ' has been given to us in reference to
' all things which pertain to life and godliness.' This is
the indwelling of the Spirit. O arm of the Lord, awake

in me! And so Col. i. 29. Is there such power, such great ἐνέργεια slumbering in me? O would that it were put forth upon me!

Saturday, 28th.—Before the Communion Mark vi. 31 has been a great comfort to me in a busy time, showing me Christ's full sympathy; and to-day I have got a time for prayer and quiet rest, having been carried through my preparation yesterday with singular quickness.

Saturday, November 18th.—I have been trying to get a monthly day for special prayer, if not for fasting too. To-day got a good part of the day, and was drawn out to seek for a discovery, a setting before my soul, of things unseen, and of the Lord Jesus in the mystery of godliness.

Friday, Dec. 29th.—Psalm cii. 15, a token of God's grace to others for the sake of those that plead for them has been dwelling upon my mind and leading me on to urge my petition for my family. Being quite alone I have been able to keep a fast as well as pray all day. I have been thirty-three years in the ministry; the Lord Jesus will cover all the sins of that time and will claim favour for me by His life and death in the thirty-three years of the days of His flesh.

Sabbath, 28th Jan. 1872.—Our Communion. I sometimes think that to the Lord's people dying will be very like going to the Communion Table. There is a little anxiety, and sometimes a little bustle, about the going in to the table; but that is soon over, and all is calmness, and we do nothing else but keep looking upon the Lord.

February, 18th.—I find my Lord and Saviour more and more satisfying to my soul. In very deed He is all my salvation and all my desire. I am like a man standing upon the shore of the ocean and seeing that it

has immeasurable breadth and unfathomable depth, so
that I cannot search it out.

Thursday, March 7th.—This week three funerals, and
then an unexpected death in the congregation. This is
the Lord speaking. While I look onward, beyond death
to the Lord's Coming, and while I fully acknowledge that
great truth, ' In death there is no remembrance of
Thee ; ' ' The living, the living, they shall praise Thee ; '
yet oftentimes there seems to me great sweetness in
Paul's words, ' πολλῷ γὰρ μᾶλλον κρεῖσσον.'

Sabbath, April 7th. — Our Communion. Lord, I
touched the hem of Thy garment to-day in taking the
bread and wine. Surely there will be health flowing
forth. Lord, I claimed the promise of the new covenant,
holding up the wine which is the seal. Surely I shall
receive the fourfold blessing of that covenant.

Sabbath, 28th.—Thought of how Moses, in the cleft
of the rock, would leave alone every care, and give himself to attend only to the Lord passing by. Tried with
some success to-day thus in regard to my sin, and in
regard to our distracted Church. Thought of Psalm
xliii. 4 : ' God my exceeding joy.'

Saturday, June 8th.—Morning interruptions are a great
hindrance to continued devotion. I wonder if these
interruptions were overcome in early days ? How did
Daniel find uninterrupted time for his praying? (Daniel
x. 2.) Lord, give me more leisure for prayer.

Sabbath, 23rd.—The Lord made this a remarkable
day in my experience, as to freedom and utterance,
while I spoke upon ' Jesus Christ the same,' etc. Struck
with a remark of my brother John : ' The Holy Spirit
has always, so to speak, a human heart in His hand,
renewing it.' Such is the Spirit's love.

Saturday, July 6th.—Before the Communion at Abernyte. I thought the other night, in the quiet around,

that I was bidden, in a manner, review my ministry and
life. I did so, and one terrible failure confronted me
everywhere, viz., 'Ye have asked nothing in My name.'
Want of prayer in right measure and manner! But for
this, instead of the thirtyfold, might have been a hundred,
in myself personally; and, in gathering in souls, there
might have been the thousand instead of the hundred.
It was a humiliating, saddening view. 'My comeliness
was turned into corruption.'

Saturday, 13*th*.—To-day, in a retired spot by the side
of a wood near Southlatch, Abernyte, was enabled to
cry for the Holy Spirit with much desire, and to plead
for His blessing, for the young, and for this place
as well as Collace, where I am to preach once more
to-morrow.

Kildonan, Arran, Saturday, 20th.—A day much
spent in crying to the Lord. For myself, I could
ask Eph. iii. 17, 20, but what a thought! I myself
ἐρριζωμένος ἐν ἀγάπῃ, and then enabled to compre-
hend something of love's depth, length, breadth, and
to know the love which goes beyond knowledge. All
this I can plead for, and two grounds of pleading
came up before me; His riches of glory might move
Him the more by contrast to pity me in my poverty as
I speak with Him. Then also He can do this without
going beyond His already begun means, 'according to
the power that is at work in us.' But not less did I
plead for the revival of God's work. Isa. lxiv. 1 and
other passages were spread before me. Verse 4 shone
in a new light, יַעֲשֶׂה לִמְחַכֵּה־לוֹ, He will assuredly work
for the man that waits on Him, and who can tell what
will be the measure of that working now and hereafter?
All the while the load lying on me from privileges, opportunities, advantages beyond other men and ministers,
in the fellowship of so many now in glory, helps from

books, helps from the prayers of others, seemed very, very great.

At Collace last Sabbath, the first Sabbath I have spent there since a new minister came, I had a strange mixture of feeling. In the manse, and going out into the adjoining wood, my heart was full of old memories. Sorrow and sadness, with thankfulness and wonder at the Lord's grace, filled my heart at the remembrance of my selfishness in the days when my home was so happy; how I allowed domestic enjoyment to deaden my pity for souls, and my zeal for God's glory. No less did I grieve over the past when I reviewed my singular privileges in former days, when I had the presence, prayers, fellowship, and loving help of such men as M'Cheyne, Burns, Milne, as well as the heavenly atmosphere of 'the times of refreshing.' In preaching, my soul yearned over the people.

Sabbath, 28th.—The Communion here in Kildonan. What a quiet day : the sea like a mirror, the air clear. I got a glimpse of Christ as being lovely in His Person alone, without anything added ; the *heart of heaven.* The head of a family (when loved ; such as was my beloved wife to me) is missed when absent, so that the light of the house seems gone. Christ in the circle of His disciples would make them so happy, that none would remark upon the want of John or Peter. *Christ,* as 'Lamb in the midst of the throne,' is able to give intense joy to millions upon millions—His look, voice, smile, presence. O to see 'the King in His beauty'! We shall be sick of love, and yet find all health in that love. 'All my springs are in Thee.'

Sabbath, August 4th.—Job i. 5 is often in my mind when I see my family so full of spirits in the country. What if they have (for the time) bidden farewell to God in their heart (בֵּרַךְ) ! To-day alone with

God in a special manner, seeking to be taught of God and led by the Spirit.

Saturday, 17*th*.—Another time of nearness in prayer. And now may every sermon of mine be first laid on the altar of incense, and sent forth breathing its fragrance. May every tract be like the thought of David, 1 Kings viii. 17, 18. Some glimpses of eternal rest. Can it be that I am soon to be there?

Saturday, 24*th*.—Got about three hours for prayer this forenoon. Most truly did I join in Richard Baxter's cry, 'Must I sit down with so low a measure of grace when I am almost there where faith is exchanged for sight; Lord, is no more to be expected here?' I hope to have some hours of the like days all the year.

Monday, Oct. 14*th*.—Anniversary of that evening when the Lord withered my gourd. Isaiah xxviii. 23-29 came in course this morning.

Sabbath, 27*th*. — Our Communion. Some rich moments before the Lamb. When Mr. Wilson was serving a table, he spoke of Christ as bound by the many cords taken from each one of His people. O what a binding to the altar! like Isaac's cord taken to bind the ram. In the very beginning of the prayer in the church this morning, I felt a sudden nearness to the Lord which scarcely left me all day.

November 22*nd*.—At the Edinburgh Conference. A fortnight ago the Lord gave me help, so that my address on holiness was useful to many saints. I go on Sabbath to open the new church at Crossford, where God has all along been working for His glory, but my soul's cry is still for more acquaintance with the Lord Jesus, and the Father in Him. I often wonder whether I have more grace now than in the revival days of 1840.

In reading Isaiah lvi. 3-5, was made to see how the

Lord intends to make up to us whatever He withholds now of earthly comforts.

November 24th.—Opening of new church at Crossford. I preached all day. Knox's tercentenary also. Again and again I long to lift up my voice for Christ in another way than I ever succeeded in doing. I can only say with Samuel Rutherford, writing to his people, 'we put you upon the right scent and pursuit of Christ.'

Saturday, December 14th.—The incessant occupations, the bustle of even right things, the number of people who must be visited, take away from me very much time which I would willingly spend in prayer ; but, on reading Malachi iii. 10, it seemed to me that I might apply to my duties what is there said. I am bringing in to God my tithes when thus denying myself much in order to attend to these souls. My time of prayer will, therefore, be none the less important and profitable. My little tract *Greater Holiness*, drawn from me unexpectedly, seems to be useful.

Saturday, 4th January 1873.—The year has begun quietly with me, not enough alone for prayer. In the morning, preparing for the Workers' Meeting a few days ago, was furnished in a few minutes after prayer with a most interesting meditation upon ' Angels working,' which I gave to my people. It was a lesson in asking from God in all my services. It is strange how often this lesson needs to be renewed. Often, often did I learn it in the early days of my ministry, but it seems fresh still.

Saturday, March 1st.—This being a very bustling and busy week, I was very glad to notice that our Lord Jesus when so many were coming and going that He had not leisure even to eat, did not put forth any miraculous power to keep them from coming, but just spoke with them and dealt with them ; and then, when opportunity came, withdrew for a time. Some days He must have had very little time for prayer and praise. He knows a minister's care and bustle ; He will sympathize and help.

Thursday, 27th.—This week, after being at Greenock Communion, had been thinking on the memorable providences of the 25th, my father's death and Robert M'Cheyne's. To-night the very unexpected tidings came of the death of our dear friend Joseph Wilson at Abernyte. He is as great a loss to our Church as any one I can name : so devoted, single-minded, full of grace and truth. It is remarkable to me that this morning my ordinary reading brought me to 2 Samuel i., Jonathan slain on his high places.

Tuesday, April 1st.—The funeral at Abernyte. A day of calm and sunshine, like summer. Many a thought of the past, and many of what is coming. One after another is leaving us. Lord, what shall I do, when shall I be taken ? 'Follow thou Me. If I will that thou tarry till I come,' etc.

Saturday, May 17th.—Great anxiety prevails about the approaching meeting of the General Assembly. There is division feared, that will send away a good many ministers and people. Many of us, however decided against the proposed Union, will not separate on the ground of the present measure of Mutual Elegibility. I have been enabled to pray much to-day, and as usual found immediately almost greater clearness in my mind and the beginning of the answer to my cry. I often return to Jeremiah xxxiii. 3.

Friday, 23rd.—A time of very great anxiety and care among us as to the dreaded division in our Church. There perhaps has not been more solemn, humbling, broken-hearted prayer among us for years than there is at present in many places about the Church. Out of this there should surely come some result which will be worthy of the Spirit of supplication who has given this heart to cry day and night.

Wednesday, 28th.—To-night great anxiety prevails about the General Assembly. It is feared now that nothing will prevent the separation of a considerable number. I go to rest to-night calling on the Lord, and asking as we did this evening at our prayer-meeting that the results may be such as will make us take up Numbers xxiii. 23.

Thursday, 29th.—Deliverance has come! A most marvellous turn in the discussion after all seemed very dark. Both sides were led to an adjustment. It was as marked a sign of the Divine presence almost as in 1843. This is my birthday. Made more than ever memorable to me. Shall I not often take up Balaam's parable and say, 'What has God wrought!' We have had most powerful incitements to pray henceforth more and more.

Saturday, 31st.—Have felt very much, I suppose, like the good Shunammite (2 Kings iv. 37), not able to *speak* thankfulness, but only to *feel* it. To-day got time for prayer till the afternoon. I used Moses' prayer : ' Lord, Thou hast begun to show Thy servant Thy greatness and Thy mighty hand,' . . . therefore now pour out Thy Spirit largely. Thy mercy is like a river, flowing on when it is once begun.

Sabbath, July 6th.—We have come to Kirkoswald for this month. Yesterday I was for some time in the neighbouring wood near the manse trying to pray. Got a little access, but to-day, both before and after preaching, was tempted to be unwatchful.

Sabbath, 13th.—Some warm-hearted people ; but often the hearers of the Word are few in number. God, who sent me here for a month to preach, will surely give the increase. I remember ' He that overcometh shall inherit all things.' For somehow I cannot take in the beauty and the suggestions of peace and joy that arise; my heart just yearns for some inexpressible joy. But '*I shall inherit all*' yet.

Glasgow, Saturday, October 4th.—Got nearly the whole day for fasting and prayer, being disengaged from my own people on the forenoon of to-morrow. Again and again I laid upon the mercy-seat the words of Jeremiah xxxiii. 3. I now try to pray every Sabbath before leaving the pulpit, ' Lord, give fruit, forgive the sin, fill me with the Spirit again and again, and accept my praise.'

Tuesday, 14th.—Anniversary of my saddest, sorest grief. How the time passes on, nearer and nearer the Resurrection Day. Many solemn things occurring at present. Dr. Candlish is dying, and the scenes of old days come up to mind.

Sabbath, 26th.—Communion. Several words came home at this season, such as ' forgetting all behind' of things won, of souls we have been instrumental in saving; and as yet we have asked mere ' driblets' of blessing. I was seriously alarmed in reading the Epistles to the Seven Churches. I see how the sins of Ephesus, Thyatira, etc., may exist in *me* with all my work and busy ministry. Yes, and along with ' faith, love, patience, works many and increasing.'

Sabbath, Dec. 7th.—This day seventeen years ago I began my ministry in Glasgow. I have never been even once kept from preaching by sickness. I have been led through discipline, public and domestic, that has helped me to preach more usefully. The Lord has filled the church. The Lord has done for me some things like 1 Chron. xii. 17, 18, sending me such a band of ' helpers.' The Lord has used me to win souls. But I have been very slow in my progress, very feeble in prayer and praise, yea, I have rather fallen back in prayer than advanced. I have not reaped much from my afflictions, public and private. I am not personally holier than I was seventeen years ago. This sent me this evening in all haste to hide myself in Christ.

Wednesday, 17th.—Have been since morning in Edinburgh attending the remarkable meetings of Moody and Sankey. What a sight! Our great Assembly Hall crowded with eager, praying, listening souls from ten o'clock till four. It was as full toward the afternoon as in the great days of our keen debates; no possibility almost of getting in. This is the answer to the prayers since the Union strife was closed for revival and blessing.

Thursday, 1st Jan. 1874.—The tide of real revival in Edinburgh has been stirring up all of us.

Friday, 9th.—Spent part of yesterday and this day in Edinburgh, witnessing the remarkable meetings there: for God is at work over all the town.

Tuesday, Feb. 10th.—This city has been at last visited; Moody and Sankey, sent by the Lord, as when ' He sent them two and two to every place whither He Himself would come.' I think the Lord gave me a word at the daily prayer-meeting, viz., Numbers xi. 23. There has been much made of the 600,000 of Glasgow, and here there is the same number in connection with the question : ' Is the Lord's hand shortened?' What can our God do? My soul has begun to feel quickened, and the days of 1839-40 and onwards come up to view. But there is more now than then.

Saturday, 21st.—The work goes on. Not a few have been brought to Christ this week, among the rest several anxious among my people. I now begin to see the answer to a prayer the Lord enabled me to offer often of late, Jer. xxxiii. 3 : ' Things I knew not.'

Sabbath, March 1st.—The past week has been a time

of great blessing to souls among us. Every day I have met with some who have been blessed: to-night, three of my young men; on Friday night, at the Communicants' Class, three who have been brought in within these two weeks. My gracious Lord, give me myself at this time grace to hold up my empty vessel. Give me, O Lord, fresh grace, very abundant grace, a very large increase personally in all holiness. I fear oftentimes lest I let this season pass without myself being a great gainer. I desire that from myself and my people there may ascend such a cloud of prayer with the incense, such a rich cloud, that at length it will descend in heavenly showers.

Sabbath, 15*th.*—The work of God goes on among us in this city. This morning, at nine o'clock, a gathering of three thousand young men, and the lecture on Daniel was most memorable. In my own church, Mr. Moody preached on the Second Advent. A blessed meeting in the evening in the Free College Church. Every day for a fortnight past, there has been news of some one brought to Christ. Yesterday I set apart most of the day for prayer that I myself might at this season get a new baptism. I want δύναμις, but I want also love and zeal. And how little of Christ I really know!

Saturday, 28*th.*—Many among us are receiving blessing. I have a Communicants' Class of fifty-two. Most of them very distinct in their account of their conversion. My own soul is not lifted up in the ways of the Lord as it might be. I need more compassion for souls.

Saturday, April 4*th.*—Have had to-day four cases of the remarkable breathing of the Spirit at present, souls getting salvation so easily, and all so solemnly too. There is deep gladness; no excitement. It is a day of visitation assuredly. I have fifty-four coming to the Lord's Table for the first time.

Saturday, 11*th.*—Got the great part of this day for prayer and meditation. Greatly helped by the sight of mercies in the past, so many and various. Felt sad at not observing that this present season has lifted me up personally. My compassion for souls is small, and 'power from on high' does not rest on me in any great measure in my ministry. I have been calling on the Lord for 'life more abundant' (περισσόν) and some special blessing. This may be the last occasion when I may witness revival scenes. I see others far more really and constantly watching for souls, like true fishers of men.

Sabbath, 12*th.*—I had a peculiar sense of Christ's nearness all day, Himself in the midst. Every part of the Communion service seemed to go on under His smile, and I left Him to send forth the blessing on those present in the form He might please, and on myself also.

Sabbath, 19*th.*—On both parts of this day I felt the nearness of the Lord more than usual. At one time I seemed to myself to be so near Him that I might have passed within the veil.

Edinburgh, Wednesday, 22*nd.*—Came in to-day to receive my degree (D.D.) at the University.

Sabbath, 26*th.*—On the Fast-Day was much drawn out to fellowship with the Lord. The same to-day. Often I felt as if now I could leave the fles hand pass within the veil; 'absent from the body, but present with the Lord.' I have got some comfort from observing, in Psalm lxxxiv. 11, that 'walking uprightly' is walking in םֹתּ, simple-minded, or single-mindedness, in the believing soul.

Saturday, May 16*th.*—Last night the meeting of Convention was held in the Kibble Palace—young and old who profess to have been brought to Christ since the beginning of the year. It was most solemnizing and wonderful ; about three thousand present. At the close the vast audience became very still when I was praying, so that for half a minute we might have heard a pin fall. The Lord was there. But ' His arm is not shortened.' There may be yet greater things than these. All this week my own soul has been lifted up in the ways of the Lord. Sometimes I looked within the veil. And what thanks shall I render to the Lord for more than *seventy* of those under my care converted since the year began. In our Sabbath-school there have been not less than *one hundred* awakened, and most of them very hopeful.

Sabbath, 31*st.*—At the Assembly, which has been remarkable for the attention given to the awakening. Heard from a minister that his first impressions were made by my preaching to children in 1843, on ' O Jerusalem, Jerusalem,' etc.

Monday, July 20*th.*—Staying at Oban and doing some work there. Some time to pray and meditate, but distractions too.

Thursday, 23*rd.*—A happy day at Taynuilt Fast-Day, when I preached on Hebrews x. 19, 23. Some sweet meditation and prayer while waiting outside during the Gaelic service, right opposite Ben Cruachan. The thought that we can send up requests in the same way as did the friends of the palsied man, by yearning looks, and thus hold up the ' rod ' as Moses did, has been helping me much ; for many times a day we can do this, in the midst of company, and whatever be our outward circumstances.

Sabbath, 26*th.*—Preached only once. I was led to pray more, and these two days have found my soul drawn out to pray much. As to worldly joy, it seems to me that now it is to me as when the Romans burned their ships and made it absolutely necessary for them to go onward and win. I must now find out the riches of joy in Christ, for I have no other to fall back upon.

Sabbath, Aug. 23rd.—This will be my last Sabbath in Oban. I have had many opportunities of speaking the Word to small assemblies generally ; but I have had a quickening in prayer. This afternoon, after preaching on Psalm xxxvi. 6 : ' Righteousness of God,' I spent a quiet afternoon in solemn prayer in my room while the rest were at church. I felt great yearning for more blessing, something, as I thought, of the ' groaning that cannot be uttered.' All the time of my stay here my morning manna has been gathered in the Hebrew Psalms, and it has been very sweet and very nourishing.

Friday, Sept. 4th.—Again at home, preparing for Sabbath. The Lord has not sensibly given me more strength of late. My preparation has been with diffi-culty ; but I can perceive clearly that I have not kept from hour to hour in direct communion, nor praised Him seven times a day.

Sabbath, 13th.—The Lord near this day. In the morning, after eight, at the tent on the Green. What a sight ! What a blessed opening for preaching to souls who have sunk to the lowest. The Lord is still working in the city by His blessed Spirit. Dr. Henderson died yesterday.[1] Lord, before I finish my course, may I reach far further into the mystery of Godliness, and have more power with Thee to bring down blessing on earth.

Wednesday, Oct. 14th.—A day of solemn memories. How difficult to learn the lessons of affliction well ! In my ordinary reading to-day Prov. xxx. 8, 9 came home to me in a new light. This prayer is just what God has done for me, both as to my circumstances in the world

---

[1] Rev. Dr. Henderson of Free St. Enoch's, Glasgow.

s to my position in the Church. Neither quite
re nor very prominent; neither popular nor *un*-
popular; just Agur's request. The Lord chooses our
inheritance for us.

Sabbath, Nov. 8th.—As might be expected, after many
blessings such as we have had lately, several trying
things have occurred, and are not yet passed. These
are the 'thorns in the flesh,' needful for us. But I have
been remarking the Lord's kindness to me in my work,
carrying me through a multitude of duties, and that
easily, which I formerly would have dreaded. A good
deal of discussion upon 'sanctification by faith,' and
how far we may attain holiness here.

Sabbath, 29th.—Last night and this morning have
been enabled to see that circumstances are of comparatively little importance if the Lord be with me. Whatever be the want of sympathy, or expectation, yet if He
send out one spark from the holy altar, give one drop
of the holy unction that teaches all things, breathe one
breath upon us, this will be a day of joy and blessing.
Last Sabbath evening He gave me a soul.

Sabbath, Dec. 6th.—The anniversary of my coming to
Glasgow. I have now completed eighteen years in the
city, and I was exactly eighteen years in the country.
Who can tell what more remains? Christ is more than
ever precious to me in His atonement, righteousness,
merit, heart. Nothing else satisfies me. I only yearn
to know Him better, and preach Him more fully. His
Cross and His Crown never lose their attractiveness.
Day by day He is my rest, my heaven.

Thursday, 24th.—After a season of fasting and prayer
ten days ago, I found something peculiar in my experience; and last Monday, when seeking an appropriate
word for our Workers' Meeting, there was given me a
peculiarly solemn one, ' *The dead praise not God.*'

Friday, 1st Jan. 1875.—Met as usual for prayer and praise. Cheered at the close by one of our men wishing to speak, awakened by my little book, *The Cup of Wrath.* What a year the past has been! What is this to be?

Saturday, 30th.—Got time to-day to spend some hours in waiting on the Lord at the well of him that cried, עֵין הַקּוֹרֵא, very thirsty for blessing, feeling my poverty in all spiritual grace, longing to be able to pray more; seeking the opening of my eyes to see more than I do in every truth.

Feb. 12th.—Our 'All-Day Meeting,' calling up the beginning of the revival work here, was kept on Monday last. There I was unexpectedly called upon to take a special service, and the Lord at the moment gave me special help. Some one spoke of 'vessels prepared for the Master's use' as being ready at hand when needed. Now the Lord had given me in the morning some readiness of spirit. At another meeting spoke of some people's conversion being marked in its steps, while others cannot remember theirs, but can say rather theirs was 'like the flight of a hind which leaves no trace, but gets to the mark.' That seemed to me very much my experience.

Wednesday, March 24th.—Yesterday my sister-in-law[1] Isabella died, after many years' great weakness. To-morrow has not a few memories of the departed, and this month all through has many.

Saturday, May 22nd.—Yesterday got time for some more prayer, and waiting upon God. Ever since, I have had a yearning after more than my soul can grasp. This morning, at the Breakfast for the poor in the Drill-hall; felt some assistance there. Then in my own church I longed for 'the resurrection from among the dead,' on which subject I was lecturing. I think we are fed upon

[1] Mrs. Bonar of Greenock died on 22d March 1875.

crumbs very much.   We cannot bear more.   Each saint gets his crumb.

Saturday, 29th.—My birthday.   Always some sadness about it from the thought that I seem never to advance really beyond other days.   In studying the writings at present on 'Holiness by Faith,' what I see is simply this, that some have of late been enabled, in a very remarkable degree, to realize their union to the Lord, and to let Christ 'fill' their heart.   It is old truth expressed in a new manner : believed, felt, acted out in a new degree.   Many people carry these views to a very hurtful application, as if we ever could get beyond falling into sin and defilement in this life.

Saturday, July 10th.—Have been with Mr. Moody again in London.   Immense crowds, wonderful sight, and more wonderful impression.   Had time to-day for prayer.   Saw how simple confidence in Christ had helped me in the past very often, and sought to be able to have this *always*, as well as often.   There is great talk about 'Higher Life,' and much movement in that direction, and, though there is error mingled, this may be the Lord's way of answering the prayers which some of us have long sent up, asking more holiness for the saints, in their life more likeness to Christ.

Sabbath, 11th.—At Camberwell Hall not less than 9000 assembled, morning, noon, and night.   In the morning, before eight o'clock, I was summoned away to preach to the overflow in the neighbouring church.   But the most memorable part of the day was our Bible-Reading with Mr. Moody in the forenoon ; about thirty Christian friends present.   We were like Acts xx. 7, talking for two hours, and then dispensing the Lord's Supper.   Mr. Moody closed with prayer.   Most solemn scene, never to be forgotten.

Monday, 12th.—The last of Mr. Moody's meetings

here, an assembly of ministers and friends at Mildmay :
I thought upon Rev. vii. 1, 3.

Two letters to his eldest daughter, written during this visit
to London, give an interesting account of the meetings and
Dr. Bonar's keen enjoyment of them :—

TO HIS DAUGHTER ISABELLA.

'11 *Sussex Place, Kensington,*
10th July 1875.

'MY DEAR ISABELLA,—Did your newspapers give an account
of the Thursday evening meeting at the Camberwell Hall? The
crowd was immense, about 10,000 crammed into the building, and
for five minutes at the beginning there was a little confusion.
But all was still in five minutes and not a person was injured.
Mr. Moody quietly said, "There must be quietness, and there is
no need of anybody fainting! If you just make up your minds
that you will not, there will be none!" A Methodist minister
beside me whispered, "Isn't that Arminianism? You can keep
from fainting if you like!" Mr. Moody shook hands with me in
going in, and then, in giving out the first hymn, said, "Dr. Andrew
Bonar is here with us, and I daresay he would scarcely feel at home
if he did not hear a psalm! Let us sing the Hundredth Psalm."
'I feel it already somewhat melancholy to think of the meetings,
"this is the last here," as to-day at the Prayer-Meeting in the
Victoria Theatre.'

The other letter contains an account of the Bible-Reading
he refers to, on July 11th, which he often used to speak of
afterwards as a remarkably solemn and memorable one :—

'After the morning meeting Mr. Moody arranged a little Bible-
Reading, where about thirty intimate friends of his were gathered
at the house of Mr. Denny. We talked on and on for two hours,
it was like Acts xx. 7, Paul continuing his speech till midnight—
in a conversational way, very likely. We talked over Christ the
"Priest," turning from Old to New Testament, and then we got
into the Judges, and at last came to the backsliding of Samson, and
from that to Peter's backsliding, on both which Mr. Moody said

some very solemn things. Then he asked me some questions on Joseph of Arimathea, and when we had got into the theme of Christ's death and sepulchre, he proposed (as beforehand he had suggested) that we should now keep "the Lord's Supper," and so we did. I prayed and handed round the bread and wine, and, after saying a few words when the solemn silence had given us time for meditation and communion, Mr. Moody closed with prayer, in which he most touchingly sought to be kept from falling or bringing any reproach on the Lord's name. The benediction followed, and so we went away to the afternoon meeting, after being about three hours together.'

Saturday, 17*th*.—Still in London. Prayer to-day, alone for some hours, seeking after love, knowledge, and all holiness. Also I see that often I have prepared sermons for my people in the outer court, when I might have been in the Holy of Holies, sitting before God. For a few moments I seemed to get very near God, and far into the Holy Place.

Lochranza, Arran, Saturday, August 7*th*.—Set apart some hours to-day on the hill to pray and inquire about holiness.

Sabbath, 15*th*.—How I long to be holier! There is such a sad feebleness in my grace! After being in much perplexity for a text, got it given me like a real message, when I simply asked the Lord to choose for me.

Thursday, 19*th*.—By a singular providence left alone. The evening came on, and still I had prayer and meditation. I was trading with the talent of prayer. Some nearness. I spread out Eph. i. 18, Eph. iii. 18, 20, Col. i. 9, 10, etc., power to preach with new life. When all was over I remembered Rom. viii. 26, as promising that, in addition to express requests being granted, my groanings for my family, etc., would all be taken up.

Sept. 20*th*.—[Home.] At the meeting of elders in my house to-night, recalled the day of my ordination. Prayer for holiness went up.

Thursday, Oct. 14th.—The Convention in the [Kibble] Crystal Palace. Not less than 7000. Memorable day. With me, the hour when 'the power of the Spirit' was the subject was the time when most blessing came. George Müller spoke.

It is this δύναμις that my soul is greatly exercised about. Why not to me 'Spirit of power' as well as of 'love, and of a sound mind?'

Monday, Dec. 27th.—Yesterday, as well as Saturday night, was drawn out in prayer for intensity of grace and real nearness to God. Preached on 'Be filled with the Spirit.' O my soul, shall this temple be filled with the Lord's presence, so that self shall melt away?

'I beseech Thee, show me Thy glory.'—*Exod.* xxxiii. 18.

CHAPTER VI

Labours More Abundant

1876-1888

Saturday, 1st Jan. 1876.—The whole past week, as well as to-day, has been one of aspiration, rather than study or meditation. Some prayer, and a deep persuasion that I may be this year a great benefactor by praying much (אֲנִי תְפִלָּה)

Sabbath, 9th.—Tried to be in sympathy through the week with those that keep the 'Week of Prayer,' but much hindered as to time. Yet I had occasional moments of nearness. ' O that Thou wouldst rend the heavens,' etc.

Sabbath, 23rd. — Our Communion. Many times to-day, when I had the whole service myself, my soul felt borne along as one upheld, and many glimpses of things within the veil were given me. But, as yet, I think His love has only touched me ; not penetrated and possessed me.

Saturday, March 25th.—Very busy of late. This week, amid many distractions, had very peculiar help. To-day is full of the memories of the past, and being Greenock Communion, brought much before me. ' God liveth ; blessed be my Rock.' A woman in the district seems to have been saved at our annual meeting this week.

Sabbath, April 9th.—Our Communion. Lord, on the ground of all that has been brought out concerning Jesus, Thy beloved Son, let there be a great flood of

blessing sent! Because the house has been filled with
His name, let the glory of the Lord the Spirit fill it
now!

Saturday, 15*th*.—Fast-Day in St. Peter's, Dundee, on
Thursday. A flood of memories; and in the house
where I stayed, finding above the mantelpiece the text
in large letters, ' Jesus Christ the same,' etc., was led to
long and cry to the Lord for something of the same
spirit and working as we witnessed more than thirty
years ago.

Sabbath, May 21*st*.—Awaking early, saw myself very
far from being in the frame and state of mind which the
Lord might use. But as I mused I was led to seek
something of the coal from the altar for my lips, some
drops of the oil of gladness for my own refreshing:
much compassion like 'the bowels of Christ,' some
sparks of the fire of His zeal; the garment of praise,
the rod that God can use to open the rock; and the
breath of real prayer, and supplication, and intercession,
and strong crying. Over all this, the faith that sees
eternity, above and below, heaven and hell, and the
intense compassion of a holy God yearning over sinners.
May I travail in birth for souls!

Sabbath, June 25*th*.—Our Communion. The tide in
the afternoon was very full. Young and old were
deeply interested for half an hour as I was closing the
service. My own soul was greatly enlarged.

July 2*nd*.—Got of late some some sight of Christ as
partner for my soul, and have noticed that I do not
pray in secret for Christ's Coming as I ought. Have
found myself receiving new strength when I thought
I was to be weary and languid. Praise to the Lord!

Glen Sannox, Arran, Sabbath, 9*th*.—Reading Payson's
Life. Some of the Hebrew Psalms have been peculiarly
sweet and full of late.

Thursday, 13*th*.—A minister from America cheered me greatly by telling me how *M'Cheyne's Memoir* has been used there.

Monday, 17*th*.—Some seasons of prayer in the glen.

Thursday, 27*th*.—Felt sadness that men should have such wonderfully grand scenery all around, and so very few praise the Lord for it all.

Thursday, *Aug.* 17*th*.—The Lord is teaching me more prayerfulness. I do love the Lord : I love the beloved Son, His Person, His Word, His ways, His work, His will. I love the Holy Ghost, sometimes with great affection.

Sept. 9*th*.—At Perth Conference. Great enlargement when speaking of ' the rest,' followed by a time of impotence rising from want of much prayer. Nothing but constant intercourse with the Lord will carry on the soul. I got last Saturday set apart as a day of prayer ; and I trace much of my help to that day. I hope this winter to get such a day of prayer and fasting once a month.

Monday, 18*th*.—Yesterday the Lord gave me opportunity and strength of body and soul for more than ordinary work. My usual services and my young men's class, and then after, a sermon at the Seamen's Chapel, and then another in the tent. Have now just about completed thirty-eight years of my ministry. What wonderful kindness, what sovereign grace in giving me such time for service !

Saturday, *Oct.* 14*th*.—Time for prayer and fasting. Specially led back to the day of my great bereavement. My heart's desire is that the sweetness of divine communion may to me be such that it will make all other wants forgotten. Come near, Lord. Come very near.

Saturday, *Dec.* 30*th*.—I fear much that I have been sliding into easy-minded contentment with the truth and the work going on without seeing souls added every day. Delight in the Word read and preached is not the same thing as the light shining upon the dark world.

Sabbath, 31*st.*—The year is just ending, and I am thankful for the text I preached upon to the young people to-night, Isa. xxvi. 20. Lord, I come into the chamber, do Thou shut me in. Yes, and let me be found in the secret place, if this year be my last on earth.

28*th Jan.* 1877.—Our Communion. A time when my soul has learned a new lesson in regard to the helpfulness of trying to pray every hour of the day, though only for half a minute, and to praise in the same manner. To-day I was like a man standing in full sight of plenty at the door of a well-stored granary, all of it mine ; but I took little of it.

> ' One more day's work for Jesus,
>   How sweet the work has been !
>   To tell the story,
>   To show His glory
>   When Christ's flock enter in.
>   How it did shine
>   In this poor heart of mine ! '

Saturday, April 7*th.*—Our Communion to-morrow. Specially interesting to me as the time when my daughter Janie comes to the Table.

Wednesday, 25*th.*—Last night Alexander Somerville gave his farewell lecture in the Kibble Palace previous to his going to Australia. About 5000 present. To me it was remarkable, after nearly fifty years of acquaintance and friendship, that I should be at his side asking prayer for him.

June 8*th.*—Let me look back upon a few days past. My birthday was 29th May ; memorable this year,

because it was the day in the General Assembly when
Professor Smith's case came on. Very anxious time.
Then, next day, the 30th, altogether unexpectedly and
out of my usual course, I spoke in the Assembly in
proposing Robert Simpson for the clerkship, and was
congratulated on all sides, as he gained the cause. Our
troubles with broad theology are not over. I am compelled to read and take part in discussions about these
things, which to me are very wearisome and trying ; but
I see that a little of ecclesiastical occupation may be
real discipline to the soul. It is like the drought of the
desert which makes the water of the fountain more
delightful ; and as to these times, I find Job xxix. 3 to
be a grand word : לְאוֹרוֹ אֵלֶךְ חֹשֶׁךְ.

Thursday, 14th.—Preached at Stirling. Heard of one
converted under my ministry in Glasgow, a few months
ago, and now back there. In the evening got a letter
from the North telling me of a student brought to
Christ by reading *Robert M'Cheyne's Life* seven years
ago. The Lord most clearly let me know these two
things this week, when, more than for many days, my
heart has been distracted and worn out by most dangerous error in the Church at large and within the
bounds of our own presbytery.

Wednesday, 20th.—This evening the memorial-stone
of our new church was laid.

Saturday, 23rd.—Last night lost a whole hour in
seeking out a reference which I had mislaid, and so the
time which should have been spent in prayer was gone
before I was well aware. It is ever thus that the evil
heart departs from the living God.

Kilmarnock, Sabbath, July 1st.—Communion. Lord,
give me for my hire some lost pieces of silver.

Collace, Sabbath, 22nd.—Greatly moved by the sight
of the people. Had some almost overwhelming sense

of sins of omission in the days past. If I had only prayed more! Lord, how I might have won souls for Thee!

Oban, Saturday, August 4th. — This day, and also Monday and Tuesday, as well as Sabbath, a great deal of prayer for hours together.

Saturday, 11th.—Some more season of special prayer. O how I thank the Lord for the Holy Scriptures through which He speaks, and by which He stirs up our souls.

Wednesday, 15th. — Season of memorable prayer. Next Wednesday, prayer very much for discoveries of Christ.

Sept. 20th.—Anniversary of my ordination. Remarkable that I was at the presbytery, presiding as Moderator, when a letter was sent me telling of the death of Mr. Joseph Davidson [1] on Thursday, at the very hour when a call was under discussion for one of our ministers to be his successor. Well do I remember my days with him as minister at Collace, when the Lord brought him to Himself. He is taken. I am left still.

Saturday, 22nd.—The same day that Mr. Davidson died, one of my old people died in the Lord, in Collace. She and he had met that same day in glory. Both of them were brought to Christ under my ministry, and both have gone in within the veil. Will they not, both of them, remember the past?

Saturday, October 6th.—Have been able, amid much business, to get much of this day for prayer and meditation, having got preparation forward yesterday in great measure. Such a time is like climbing up the mount, and looking all around in calmness, seeing what our inheritance is, and thus better able to ask many things. O what a sense of poverty comes over me, looking at

[1] Minister of the Free Church at Saltcoats, then at Rothesay.

that wealth! Heard of a soul brought to Christ by my instrumentality forty years ago.

Sabbath, 14th.—The memories of this season, thirteen years ago, have been coming to-night. Holy Spirit, sanctify me by old sorrow. O sanctify me quickly, too, for my days may be few now! Holy Spirit, come and breathe upon me.

Saturday, 20th.—Heard yesterday of the death of John Purves, with whom I began my ministry. My mind has been wandering back to old days ever since.

Wednesday, 24th.—Yesterday at the funeral of Mr. Purves. Jedburgh called up very many memories, and as I was coming away from the manse, the full sight of the Dunion Hill met my eye, at once recalling the Lord's mercies to me as a minister of Christ. It was as if the Lord had brought me full in sight of that hill all at once, in order that I might remember how prayer offered there on 5th July 1835, has been wonderfully answered ever since.

Saturday, Nov. 17th.—Got notice from Dr. Moody-Stuart that I am to be named for the Moderatorship of the next Assembly. I have written to him, entreating him to arrest this proposal. I feel like Judges ix. 9. May the Lord overrule all.

Saturday, 24th.—This week have got notice that I am nominated to the Moderatorship, and every letter that has come insists upon the call of God through the Church to me. This is very trying to me : a real cross. I have been thinking how I prayed during the summer, more than once or twice, in the words of Jer. xxxiii. 3. Can this be one of the 'great and mighty things'?

Sabbath, Dec. 2nd.—Our anniversary. What mercies during these twenty-one years! I have been constrained to let the brethren nominate me to that office after all. How very strange are the Lord's doings! I am obliged to go back and read Exod. iv. and then Jer. i., and pray the prayer of 1 Kings iii. 7, 8, 9. In all this I know my brethren have respect, not to myself so much as to our family descent, and the work done by those of our family on present and former occasions. Assuredly ' He leadeth the blind by a way they know not.'

Sabbath, 6th Jan. 1878.—Heard of a case of awakening through my visit to Edinburgh, preaching on the 'dying thief.' Heard of another in former days, of one who at this hour is serving the Lord in a parish far from this. I am still pressed with the feeling that my failure in prayer is very great. Lord, Lord, give me this year the Spirit of grace and supplication ! I might pray so much at intervals, in journeys, even in my bed.

Saturday, Feb. 9th.—Taking time for prayer in prospect of coming duties, and because I find myself low.

Sabbath, 10th.—Preached upon a very full subject, Acts v. 42, but I had an ulterior object in view rather than the present salvation of souls, and the result was, I did not preach with either clearness or power.

Wednesday, 13th. — Death of Dr. Duff yesterday. Nearly fifty years of missionary labour.

Thursday, 14th.—Have come out to Crossford to spend three days quietly in preparing matter for my work at the General Assembly.

March 16th.—Have been noticing that it is not so good to reserve prayer and praise for such times as the beginning and end of work as it is to *interweave* those into the work as it goes on. The heart is thus kept continually watchful, looking upward.

Tuesday, 19th.—Encouraged in prospect of the Assembly by reading in Gibbon (ch. 70) how the consciousness of power can elevate the manner of a man to the station, imparting a dignity even where it was unknown before ; Rienzi, Cromwell, etc. But, above all, the consciousness of the presence of the Lord with me will carry me through my work in the Assembly.

I was invited to be present and take some part in the ordination of John Sloan in the Park Church. During my prayer I felt a deep solemnity had fallen upon us all, especially when I referred to Isaiah vi. 3 : ' Holy, holy, holy.' Surely the Lord was in the place.

Tuesday, 26th.—Yesterday had its many memories ; the dark cloud of many deaths this month. But that cloud can drop down its rain.

Sabbath, April 7th.—Communion. Drawn out by the words, Θεέ μου! (Matt. xxvii. 46) the intense earnestness. May I find Thee at the table to-day in new manifestation and nearness. I can truly say this morning, Ὁ Θεός, ὁ Θεός μου, πρὸς σὲ ὀρθρίζω (Psalm lxiii. 1). Several times through the day I did see allsufficiency in the Lord—to an immense extent. I seemed to get for a moment to the mighty source and fountain of life, joy, holiness. It was all in Thee, my Lord and my God.

Wednesday, May 8th.—Resting at Crossford in prospect of the Assembly. To-day a time in my study of humiliation and prayer. I had not a few causes of very deep sorrow ; so little real and continued communion with God ; slightness in my exposition of the truth ; altogether leanness and meagreness in my spiritual life ; and a sad presence of corruption from time to time. Even as regards this matter of the Moderatorship, it is surely important to me that I view it solemnly, considering how it may be used, day by day, for the good of souls and the glory of God, led on, and leading others on, to higher attainments. I meditated upon ' the ten talents,' upon Isaiah vi., upon Acts xx. 31, and like passages.

Thursday, 23rd.—The meeting of Assembly.[1]   In the morning my meditation was Psalm xxiii. before I rose, that clause coming home to me : ' Led in green pastures, and though I walk in the most difficult and dark valley,' etc.   He will be with me to-day.   I have had assurance of the prayers and sympathy of very many of God's people in all parts.   It has quite surprised me and humbled me.

Came home from the Assembly at 3.40.   I did not feel bold, but was enabled to speak out all I had written, longing to touch the hearts of all present.   The Lord has His own way of answering prayer.

Wednesday, 29th.—My birthday.   How strange are God's ways !   To find myself Moderator of the Assembly seems so completely unlike anything I had thought of.   These six days have been days of some difficulty and trial ; but all has been a time of help.   Psalm ciii.

Friday, 31st.—Came home full of thankfulness, because the most perplexing case we have had, that of Professor Smith, has been so far dealt with well, and that without any difference of any consequence in the Assembly.   There is evidently much prayer, and many answers to prayer.   There was calmness and solemnity among us.   Another thing calls for praise.   I think I have been led to conduct the breakfasts, which I did not relish at first, in such a manner that they have been a kind of preparation for the day's work, and a time for prayer.   It was often a grand sight to-day to look upon more than three thousand in that crowded Hall, mostly men, all intensely interested, listening most eagerly.   The sun shone brightly, all was quiet order, both during the discussion on Professor Smith and that on Dr. Dods, and then the result so satisfactory.

Tuesday Evening, June 4th.—Returned from the Assembly, where my closing address was received with

[1] Held that year in St. Andrew's Halls, Glasgow.

great attention. Indeed, there has been a singular calmness and solemnity in the meetings that has made us say, ' The Lord has been among us.'   What a load of care is lifted off my mind to-night ! my fear being more that I should not prove a blessing to the church and people of God. יוֹדוּ לַיהֹוָה (Psalm cvii. 8).   The Lord has shown kindness to my father's house, as well as to myself, in this whole matter.

I think I have sought the Lord's glory, not my own honour.   In going out to-night, that passage in 1 Cor. ii. 3 was much upon my mind.   I know something of this.' weakness, fear, and much trembling,' and it led me to seek ἀπόδειξις πνεύματος, the Spirit to move the hearts of all present, and thus there be also ἀπόδειξις δυνάμεως.

Friday, 7th.—Have been resting, reviewing these memorable days, now over.   As to health, I had not even a headache, though often very tired.   Then, as to care and anxiety, I found Psalm cxviii. 5 became true,

Dr. Bonar's feelings after the Assembly were those of great relief and thankfulness, and, though the work was to him uncongenial, he often looked back to it with gratification. He felt that much of the blessing experienced was owing to the prayers of many in all parts of the world who were remembering him at that time.   One of his friends, Mrs. Milne, he writes afterwards to thank :—

' It was very kind of you to acknowledge what I sent.   I thought *I* ought to acknowledge in some way those who prayed for me, as I know you did all along.

' I go with my family in August to Anwoth, to enjoy the twittering of the " blessed sparrows," and, if possible, pick up some of Samuel Rutherford's grey hairs that may be somewhere found !

' My last Bible biographical study has been " Eutychus."   I am prepared to show that he was a blameless young man, in spite of his falling asleep. Highly-favoured youth! one of only *two* Gentiles that have been raised from the dead.

'Entreating you to pray often for me as " poor and needy," with many of the stains of Sardis and Laodicea, and a flame as low as that of Ephesus on the altar of love to Him who has *so* loved us,—Yours truly, elect lady,　　　ANDREW A. BONAR.'

Monday, 17th.—Some good news. A young man awakened and brought to Christ by my closing address in the Assembly!

Saturday, 22nd.—Yesterday so busy that there was exceeding little time for prayer. I have tried this forenoon to ask much, for this is the way to grow rich : ' Call,'—' I will shew thee,' etc.

Sabbath, July 7th.—I feel wearied, needing rest. But the Lord has twice of late gladdened me by blessing me much : once when I was preaching the other evening on the South Side, and Sabbath evening last week in our own church.

August 8th.—Gatehouse, near Anwoth, after a season of journeying from place to place, having been in England, Gateshead and Haworth, where William Grimshaw laboured ; then at Jedburgh, Kelso, and other places in that neighbourhood. Visited Kirkton and Bedrule, where I preached some of my earliest sermons, perhaps to the smallest congregations I ever addressed in regular churches. Much of old times came up to mind. Preaching here last Sabbath, I was more like a man deserted than I have been for many years. I had come from the Inverness Conference, and was very prayerless, I fear, during the week. I see that the Master teaches the necessity of such times of continued waiting on God as a stay in the country presents, for in Luke v. 16 it is written that He was in the habit of thus withdrawing : αὐτὸς δὲ ἦν ὑποχωρῶν ἐν ταῖς ἐρήμοις, καὶ προσευχόμενος.

Tuesday, 20th.—To-day went up to the wood above

us, and, after looking at Disdow from the top, sat down and had two hours' meeting with the Lord in prayer and praise. The Lord came near, that same Lord who used to fill the heart of Samuel Rutherford. I see that faith is high just when our thoughts about our Lord Himself are high and great and satisfying. It was thus with the centurion, and he went away with his prayer fully granted.

Wednesday, 21st.—Memorable. Enabled to spend nearly the whole day in prayer, praise, and confession. The day was fine, not too warm, and I wandered among the woods near old Rusco, quite alone, speaking with the Lord. In the evening I spread out Dan. x. before the Lord. I was led to give great thanks for the whole circumstances of last Assembly. I was led to deep humiliation for our Church, and prayer for the outpouring of the Holy Ghost on my people and on the Church at large. I spread out several promises before the Lord, and my heart was sore with desire, and yet glad in expectation of what this very day may obtain for me. But I find true what Samuel Rutherford wrote : ' A bed watered with tears, a throat dry with praying, eyes as a fountain of tears for the sins of the land, are rarely to be found among us.'

September 1st.—Felt deeply that I do not sufficiently go forth in the spirit of Elisha, who said, ' Where is the Lord God of Elijah ? ' Is He not as much with us as with him ? as near ? is not this mantle able to do as much now as in his hands ?

Saturday, 21st.—Yesterday was the anniversary of my ordination ; but many interruptions came in my way, so that I had little leisure for the proper use of such a day. To-day I have more time and quiet ; and oh! what a review of forty years' ministry. In infinite mercy the Lord has used me for winning souls, but I see to-day

with awful fulness that if I had lived *nearer God*, if I
had prayed in the Holy Ghost more, instead of winning
five I might have got fifty or five hundred year by year.
To-day my omissions seem very terrible, as they have
sometimes done before ; my little improvement of immense advantages and my feeble appreciation of the
privilege of being spared so long in the ministry. I have
been trying to draw deeper from the fountain of the
water of life, but my thirst is soon slaked.   To-day this
has been much upon my mind, viz., that *just because* I
have been filled in some measure, I should be deeply
humbled ; for that measure of blessing was an incite-
ment to seek more from the Lord, and I was not caring
to go on and take more. 2 Kings xiii. 19 : ' Hadst thou
smitten five or six times, then thou shouldst have smitten
Syria to destruction.'   I am ashamed at the fact that
there are in my congregation a good many who have
sat under the Word for many, many years, and they,
with their families, remain unblessed.   Lord, give me
words for them !

Saturday, Oct. 12*th.*—This evening we welcomed home
with great joy our brother Dr. Somerville, whom God
has wonderfully blessed.

Monday, 14*th.*—Saw much of the wilderness as past.
This day, fourteen years ago, earth became to me a
real wilderness, and I wondered how I could journey
through it.   But the Lord's presence, and plenty of
work for Him, have borne me on.

Sabbath Evening, 27*th.*—Our Communion.   The last
of eighty-seven such occasions in the church we have
so long occupied.   There have been tokens of deep
impression this afternoon and evening.

Sabbath, Nov. 24*th.*—Last Wednesday our last prayer-
meeting in the old church, and the last meeting to-day
for worship in the old building.   It is somewhat sad, and

it was very solemn. 'Drops from heaven' have fallen there, but it is no less true, 'He could not there do many mighty works because of their unbelief.' Humiliation and thanksgiving went together to-day in our farewell. My subject in the forenoon was Exod. xxxiii. 15, 17.[1]

Sabbath, Dec. 1st.—Our anniversary, and our anniversary in our new church. Services conducted by Dr. Somerville and Dr. Robert Macdonald; old friends. Together we have preached Christ for *forty* years, the same Gospel of the grace of God. Great attendance. At the close of the evening service we had a thanksgiving for twenty minutes, blessing God for the day and for all the past mercies; also blessing God that no accident had occurred in the building, and seeking blessing on the architect and the workmen. It was a day made more solemn still by a death in the morning of one of our young people, just as there had been last Sabbath, in the evening, the death of one of our members—both somewhat suddenly. My text was Prov. xi. 30: 'He that winneth souls is wise;' our banner, I trust.[2] The first psalm sung in the new church was Psalm xcviii. 4: 'Let all the earth' . . . 'Before the Lord; because He comes,' etc.

Sabbath, 29th.—I preached to-night my first sermon to the children in the new church, and took for my text the subject with which I began in the old church when preaching to the children: 'We would see Jesus.'

Wednesday, 1st Jan. 1879.—Our prayer-meeting was to-day in the forenoon, and very fervent and solemn. I have to-night completed a revisal of an edition of the

---

[1] After pronouncing the benediction at the close of the afternoon service, Dr. Bonar stood for a few moments with uplifted hands, and solemnly added, amid great stillness: 'And, if Thy presence go not with us, carry us not up hence.'

[2] This text in Hebrew is engraved over the door of Finnieston Church.

Scots Worthies, that for a month has given me considerable care. It took off my time for prayer, and yet it was for God's glory, and the examples there often struck me to the heart.

Saturday, 11th.—In spite of considerable interruption this has been more than usual a week of much prayer. We begin next week a series of evening meetings, and I have had, from time to time, great freedom in praying that the tract which I drew up in connection with these meetings may be blessed. *Expectation* of blessing in such work as this is like *assurance* in the personal matter of our own salvation. It is a high degree of faith, arising from a clear, steady, full view of certain promises and declarations of God. Jeremiah xxxiii. 3.

March 20th.—This is a month of memories, so many friends have passed away this month, and this evening another has gone to glory, Mrs. Manson of Crossford. What a desolation!

Sabbath, April 13th.—Before the evening service, when I was to give a lecture on Prophecy (the fifth seal, Rev. vi. 9), found myself exceedingly dull and weak. I cried to the Lord as He who 'gives power to the faint,' and was wonderfully helped, so that I could not but sing in the evening Psalm cxxxviii. 3 : 'In the day I cried Thou didst answer me, and strengthenedst me,' etc. I have been revising the proofs of *The Brook Besor*, and also finishing the editing of the *Scots Worthies*, during these few weeks past. I purpose to keep Tuesday as a day of prayer and study of my sermon for the General Assembly in the vestry.

Friday, 25th.—Have been to London, travelling homeward quite alone, and so got time to read and pray. Some helpful thoughts from the Lord. Psalm xxxvii. 18 among the rest : 'The Lord counts the *days* of the perfect man,' every day of his ordinary life, what it is, how it is to be spent, what it requires. When the Lord is with us in His fulness it is the ocean sweeping away all that was unholy, and bringing in all that is pure. Every craving of the soul is met and filled.

Saturday, May 17th.—A time this day of prayer, with special reference to the approaching Assembly. I tried to realize myself as one with Christ, and in this position to pour out my heart, confessing sin, seeking favour, pleading for the Church, for the world. Psalm lxxiv. throughout.

Sabbath, 25th.—Was carried through my sermon to the General Assembly with a good deal of calmness and some enjoyment, Isaiah vi. 8 being the subject, 'Whom shall I send,' etc. In several other duties also I have found help. It was a time of new discipline to me.

Tuesday, 27th.—The most important day of all, the case of Professor Smith. With very short preparation I was called upon to propose the motion against him. I took Psalm lxi. 1-3, and then I remembered my own sermon, Isaiah vi. 8, and I thought of Mordecai to Esther, 'If thou holdest thy peace' (iv. 14). I was not at all at ease, nor had I much power, but I was able to state the case. Fain would I have escaped the duty.

Friday, 30th.—Yesterday my birthday. I am nearing my threescore years and ten. Through those last days in the Assembly I have been rather humbled in my own eyes; but now I am free from all that public work which my connection with the Moderatorship brought me into.

Sabbath, June 1st.—Came home and spent a quiet Sabbath with my own people, and in the evening stayed in the house reviewing the Lord's ways. My little book, *The Brook Besor*, has been already found comforting to some of God's saints.

Friday, 27th.—Our Communion was quiet and helpful last Sabbath. Here in London I have been dispensing the same ordinance to a great congregation at Mildmay [Conference]. Not less than 1800 communicants at one time this afternoon, and all so still, so deeply earnest. In about twenty minutes the bread and wine were distributed to all those, the arrangements were so well carried out. I had proposed a subject in my mind, but after the prayers in the adjoining hall was led to take up the 'upper room;' its memories of Christ. The Lord's presence seemed to be felt. To me it was a time of sowing seed of which we shall yet hear fruit.

Wednesday, July 23rd.—The Communion at Crossford on Sabbath last was a time of great quietness and some desire. To-day has been set apart by me for praise and thanksgiving. I have had a good deal of liberty at times. Isaiah lxiii. 7 was my starting-point. I kept very much to the mercies of the past year, and it was wonderful how they rose up one after another. The valley of Berachah was not forgotten. The time passed quickly till it was two o'clock. The mercies of the Assembly time, the mercies of all my various meetings and services, the mercies of my home too, and my study, myself spared so long and health so remarkable. And then the prospect of more and more according to the prayer, Eph. i. 18 and iii. 14-21, and my text in Jer. xxxiii. 3, that has so often encouraged me and been so often realized. In the evening a thanksgiving service after the Communion gave opportunity to speak of the Lord's mercies, temporal and spiritual.

Sabbath, Sept. 28th.—Let me record it to the praise of the glory of divine grace and infinite mercy that for many years (indeed, as many as I can remember), since my first discovery of the sinner's way to God by Christ, I have never been allowed to lose my way to the mercy-seat for a single day. I have not always had bright sunshine, but I have every day had sunlight, and not darkness, in my soul. 'What shall I render to the Lord?'

October 18*th.*—Very strangely the memorable day (14th) passed by before I remembered, my hands being quite full of work. I often now feel as if I were finishing my work, so that I need not distress myself about matters that might have been a care to me. The Lord leading me to give once a month a lecture on Prophecy is one of the things that seem to me to be the finishing of my works.

Saturday, Dec. 13*th.*—Have been reading again the memoir of an American missionary, Mr. Stoddard, whom God used much among the Nestorians. Having some time to-day I set myself to pray more, confessing sin, asking, thanking, and praising. I am ashamed of my shallowness in knowledge, feeling, and desire. Most humbling. On the other hand how astonishing has been the Lord's kindness to me, mercies like waves of the sea, bright mercies like the stars of heaven, mercies to my soul, mercies to me a sinner in every possible way, crowned with the unspeakable kindness of putting me into the ministry, and using me to win souls. But I long more and more to be 'filled' with the Spirit, and to see my congregation moved and melted under the Word, as in great revival times, 'The place shaken where they are assembled together,' because the Lord has come in power. My lecture on Prophecy this month has been blessed to impress several persons.

Saturday, 17*th January* 1880.—On Thursday evening my sister-in-law, Mrs. Grant,[1] passed away. A most motherly, unpretending, gentle Christian woman. Have been writing a leaflet upon the terrible disaster at the Tay Bridge. Come nearer, nearer, O my Lord!

[1] Widow of the Rev. Wm. Grant of Cavers.

March 1st.—Last night dreamed that I was dying; I thought I felt the breaking of the cord of life. I gathered in all my thoughts upon the all-sufficient Saviour, and found the kind of trepidation, with which I had regarded the prospect, was abating, when I awoke. There is, no doubt, some lesson in this dream.

Sabbath, 21st. — To-night preached to the young people; but felt, as I have done of late several times, that my preaching to the young has little power, and even little interest. The fulness of the Spirit might remedy this.

Saturday, April 10th.—It is a time of great political excitement. But I am less moved now by all such changes; my own time on earth may be soon finished. The atoning blood is more than ever precious to me. The righteousness of Christ is more than ever glorious in my view. *Christ Himself* is altogether lovely. A slight touch of sickness to-day, with a little pain, solemnized me, and led me to regard the possibility of my entering within the veil before long. Every time this is before me, my regret is the omissions of my past life in a peculiar way. But Christ is my all.

Wednesday, May 19th.—Alone to-day in the country, Crossford. I see it is one thing to speak the truth in the love of it, and another still greater to speak it thus, 'in the majesty of the name of the Lord of Hosts.' It is one thing to bring truth from the Bible, and another to bring it from God Himself through the Bible.

Thursday, 20th.—In a glen, spent some hours in meditation and prayer. Looking up to the open sky, I spoke with God as a blood-washed sinner warranted to come to Him. I spread out the sad facts: no revival; our Church tainted with rationalism. In the evening again, a time of prayer.

Tuesday, 25th.—The most anxious time since the

Disruption. From time to time my prayer was for the Church and General Assembly. I felt bitterly the state of things among us, in regard to our young ministers especially. Prayed for the outpouring of the Spirit, and the checking of the evil at this Assembly. For Satan is trying to wile ministers and people away from the great, glorious Gospel.

Sabbath, June 27th.—Our Communion. At the close this evening, the most solemn time was of prayer after all the services. I felt as if I could not let the Lord go till the blessing came; the blessing of an outpouring of the Holy Ghost.

Sabbath, July 4th.—Got a great view of Rev. xxi. 6, Christ standing at the fountain and giving forth blessing δωρεάν ('freely'). It was last night in reading the passage I saw Him so gracious. We have come to Him and been made righteous, and now He is continually giving, and will hand out to us blessing upon blessing. If we wonder, He will smile and say, δωρεάν. If His love to us be expressed in marvellous fulness, and my soul feels it is utterly beyond expression why He should thus love me, He will smile and say, δωρεάν. To-day I may stand with Him at the fountain, and ask 'life more abundantly,' and He will give it δωρεάν. I may ask joy and peace in believing. He will at once give it δωρεάν, not because of anything in me, but because of His own grace. Lord, I ask at this moment to be filled with the Holy Spirit, who will be in me always, showing the things of Christ, and raising intercession for others, and who will be to me 'eye-salve.' Thou wilt give all I ask δωρεάν. Thus, when I further ask blessing on my people, and upon my family, and upon the land also, even a new revival, will He not do it? I have no argument but one to use, and that is this most gracious word, δωρεάν. When I get the crown from Him, the crown of righteousness, δωρεάν will be written upon it.

Saturday, 10*th.*—Kirkpatrick-Fleming. Spent some time in the church, praying for 'the fulness of the Holy Spirit.' Much distressed at the review of my life, so little in it of the 'power' of the Spirit. Very humbling to one now in his seventieth year. Heard of the death of John Walker of Perth.[1]

Iona, Sabbath Evening, August 22*nd.*—Came here to the Communion : a memorable day. Very bright sunshine, and the deepest calm upon the sea and all around. As we crossed the Sound on our way to the church, those in the boat sang hymns from time to time, going and coming. I preached on Exodus xxxiv. 29. After the first table we gave place to the Gaelic congregation, and took their place in the open air, on the spot where the last of the Druids were buried. There were present a minister from the English Presbyterian Church, an Episcopalian minister, an Established Church minister, and a United Presbyterian minister.

Thursday, 26*th.*—We are staying at Craignure, Mull. Delightful retirement. Some seasons of prayer. Instead of being addressed by the Master ὀλιγόπιστε, fain would I be called πιστεύειν ἐπὶ πᾶσιν (Luke xxiv. 25). It is wonderful that now, for fifty years, the Lord has kept me within sight of the Cross. One day alone here I found hid treasure in the words, 'The very hairs of your head are all numbered.' All my family, all my classes, my texts, my writings, my sermons, my trials and cares.

Glasgow, Friday, Sept. 17*th.*—Last Sabbath evening a minister from Reigate spoke to me. He got blessing when I preached in Bristol in the year 1845.

Monday, Nov. 15*th.*—Reading the *Life of Dr. Candlish*,

[1] Minister of Free Kinnoul Street Church in Perth.

which has just come out, my thoughts went back to my early days when a missionary in his congregation, and then my early years as a minister. I got a view of my self-conceit and my self-confidence in those days in recalling circumstances and failures that humbled me most deeply. Indeed, I trembled ; because it may be I am just as much deceived as to myself about some things else at present. ' Search me, O Lord ! ' ' Hide me, O my Saviour, hide ! '

December 23*rd.*—Our Workers' Meeting. During the addresses that night I got a most humbling discovery of two things, viz., that I had exceedingly little of that quality of a true minister—' *beseeching* ; ' and exceeding little real belief or realizing of the greatness of eternal death, and the judgment upon sinners.

Saturday, 8*th January* 1881.—There has been something felt at our meetings for prayer. Each evening the attendance was small, but the Spirit was present. This morning I got a most humbling view of myself in connection with family worship, how that has been with me very much a formality for a long time, not preparing my heart for it, not expecting to gain blessing, not intent upon getting blessing, as I continually set myself for in a series of meetings in the congregation. Revive and quicken me, O Lord !

Saturday, 15*th.*—Most unexpectedly a few friends in Edinburgh have kindly sent £1000 to help us as a congregation to clear off our debt. This is the beginning of the answer to many prayers on this matter. We have on hand a scheme which extends over some years, and which has been prayed over much. ' Cast thy burden upon the Lord ' applies to a congregation, Ezra vii. 27. I myself have been every day praying about this for some months past, and now the Lord has begun to own the prayers.

April 10*th.*—Have not written for a long time in this record. And yet I might. For there have been many remarkable cases among my young communicants, and some providences that should not be forgotten. This Communion morning got some view of how deep may be the holy peace of a soul that sees the vastness of the Saviour's grace.

Wednesday, 20*th.*—Have been troubled by being pressed to go to America for two months by Mr. Moody. My way is far from plain, however.

Saturday, 23*rd.*—Greatly delighted by an interview with a middle-aged man from Musselburgh, converted by my tract, *The Near Way to the City.* He has not had a desire for strong drink since that day, one and a half years ago.

Saturday, May 7*th.*—Have decided to go to America, as being an opening for preaching the Word such as I will never have again ; it is the Northfield Conference. I have had little continuous prayer for some time through excess of bustle and meetings ; but now and then, in the midst of these, I have had some thoughts and glimpses of God, and also of the Cross, shedding its influence over all worlds, all beings, all ages.

Thursday, 19*th.*—Last Sabbath at the opening of my brother's new church in Greenock. We three brothers each took a diet, and preached upon Christ's offices, prophet, priest, king. All of us spared to preach Christ about forty years ; all of us now above seventy years of age. ' The Lord of us hath mindful been, and He will bless us still.'

Friday, 27*th.*—Yesterday and Tuesday were days of very great anxiety in the Assembly, but have ended well. We are praising the Lord. I was enabled, remaining at home, to give two nights to simple prayer for those fighting in the valley.

Tuesday, June 14th.—This evening rather unexpectedly, though she had been long very feeble, our old
and faithful servant died in the Lord. She has been
with me forty-three years, and had been many years
with my mother. It was very solemn to come in in the
evening and find she had been taken away very quietly to
be with Christ. Lord, speak to us all, Thyself hast done it.

Friday, 17th.—The funeral of our faithful servant. It
fills me with memories of the past. She is buried beside
our own dead in Sighthill. If there be communion
with each other before the resurrection, how she will
delight to meet friends in glory and speak of the past.
How the resurrection gives us joy at such a time.
Meanwhile it is as Gen. xxxv. 8, Deborah's grave and
the sorrow.

Sabbath, 26th.—Our Communion. During the whole
day and every service felt myself strengthened and
upheld by the Lord's presence and Spirit more than
usual. There were moments of great nearness. At one
time in preaching I felt persuaded that the Spirit was
working by me in the souls of some that were listening.
I saw myself and my people dwelling under a canopy
of blessing stored up in Christ, more abundant than the
rain in the cloud. Lord, let these skies pour down their
torrents!

Wednesday, July 6th.—A large and solemn meeting
of my people to-night on occasion of our setting off for
America on the morrow. Psalm cxxi.

Tuesday, 19th.—Montreal, where I took the prayer-
meeting. I had preached at Quebec. Friends met us
on all sides. It was like Paul finding out disciples in
every city where he landed.

Tuesday, 26th.—The Falls of Niagara. Learnt there
to stand still and wonder. Prayed over Isaiah xi. 2, 3
very specially.

Friday, *29th.*—Chicago.   Elsewhere I have noted down particulars of this visit, the meetings held, persons spoken to, lessons learned.   Major Whittle here met us (myself and Isabella), and became our guide.

Thursday, August 4th.—Northfield.   Yesterday began, but specially to-day the Conference took shape.   Was requested to open, which I did from Exodus xxxiv., communion with God.   A gathering of God's people from every quarter.

Saturday, 13*th.*—Much exercised about getting power from on high, about which much conversation.   I am rather disappointed that there is not more prayer throughout the day, but the atmosphere is delightful, so much brotherly love, so much Biblical truth, so much delight in whatever exalts Christ.

Sabbath, 14*th.*—Preached on John iii. 30.   Very many spoke to me afterwards about that service as much blessed to them, both ministers and others.   And it is most interesting as well as humbling to me also to find how many ministers and students and others spoke about *Robert M'Cheyne's Life* as very useful to them.   Should I not praise the Lord?   Should I not let the Lord use me any way He pleases?   My daughter Isabella is much appreciated in her singing of gospel hymns.   Mr. Moody as kind as possible, and most earnest in all work.

Saturday, 20*th.*—Visited Northampton, where Edwards laboured and was blessed, where Brainerd also prayed.   Blessed be the Lord who has led me hither.   It is a place of sacred memories : ' Is the Spirit of the Lord straitened ? '

Wednesday, 31*st.*—The˙ Conference closed.   Everything has been pleasant, very pleasant, and there has been blessing to God's people all along.   It was not meant to be preaching to the unconverted, but a time for sharpening the sickles of the various persons who cut down the harvest-fields. About a thousand such have been attending these meetings, taking them all in all.

Saturday, Sept. 10th.—Set sail. Calm.

Saturday, 17th.—Enabled to pray some hours every day in the ship.

Monday, 19th.—Liverpool, and then home at night. Psalm cvii. 28-30. But I have a good deal to reproach myself with. I have failed to use opportunities which the Lord might have made openings for my winning souls. And I have noticed the Lord (who has kept me in health, and kept my daughter also in health) reminded me that I had been ungrateful by some touches of discipline. Just when about to arrive heard the news of the death of my sister-in-law, Jessie [Mrs. William Bonar]. Lord, with this solemn shadow over me let me resume my work at home, and be more blessed than in all past time. There were three of my sermons that seemed to be specially blessed, Exodus xxxiv. 29, John iii. 30, and that upon Exodus xxiv. 7 ; specially the one on John iii. 30. I learned something of my leanness, for I found how few sermons I had that were full of Christ.

Saturday, Oct. 15th.—It took some time to settle down and calmly look at all these months past. Last night and this morning I have been meditating upon my past sorrows. It is wonderful how the Lord has carried me on these seventeen years since my beloved Isabella was taken to Himself. I see now how it was myself that was the necessity for that separation to save me from self, and compel me to live not to myself, but for Christ and the winning of souls. I thought I had been more tender, more teachable, these seventeen years, the clay softer and more impressible. I want some discovery to-day of my inexpressible worthlessness, impotence, weakness. That God has used me is nothing else than the merest sovereign grace.

Sabbath, 23rd.—Our Communion. Never had I a surer view of this truth, namely, that while we are keeping the ordinance of the Supper the Lord Jesus quietly pours in more life into us, whether we feel little or much.

November 23rd.—The day of the funeral of John Thomson, minister of the Mariners' Church, Leith, with whom I passed through High School, College, Divinity Hall. The Lord took him away to Himself quietly and gradually, in a sense, in a few weeks' time, and still I am spared in sovereign grace.

December 13th.—Yesterday evening my desires were : one drop of the atoning blood to give me continuous deep peace ; one drop of the oil of gladness to give my heart all the gladness I could wish ; one look of His uplifted countenance to strengthen and sanctify, drawing me to Himself; one breathing of His Spirit to pour in fresh life through my whole being.

Wednesday, 21st.—We kept this evening in our congregation as an evening of thanksgiving and prayer for twenty-five years of work and blessing in our congregation and district. I tried to tell the story of the past twenty-five years and was followed by several of the office-bearers. There was much that was fitted to draw forth wonder and praise ; but little did some of them know, when speaking in praise of the minister, how he saw in himself and in his work a shallowness and meagreness in every grace that filled him with sorrow before God.

Sabbath, 1st January 1882.—Last month my office-bearers insisted on an evening meeting, the semi-jubilee [of Finnieston Free Church]; [1] but to me it was, and has been, humbling, almost saddening.   There is a *littleness* about all my doings that distresses me.   I would fain have a full heart, fervent love, burning zeal.   But in all these I am wanting.   O for a Day of Pentecost this year, to make me as much unlike my former self as were the apostles before that day of the Spirit's out-pouring !

February 5th.—Beyond question now another. wave of blessing has come.   Mr. Moody's meetings are more than ever before full and overflowing.   I hear of several of our people touched and hopefully changed.

April, Thursday, 6th, Fast-Day.—The two last even-ings have been remarkable for Mr. Moody's meetings. Church crowded.   The impression is great, more in the form of 'thirst' than of alarm and deep sense of sin. These are solemn times.

Tuesday, 25th.—Left the Assembly because they were discussing Disestablishment, and visited Ormiston and the neighbourhood where George Wishart had preached, etc.   Many thoughts of God's ways with our country. ' Lift up Thy feet to this Zion wherein Thou hast dwelt.'

Friday, June 9th.—This week Mr. Moody closes his five months' work among us.   It has been a time to be remembered in very many ways.   And, on looking back, I think it was the Lord who inclined me to go last season to America, and thus help to engage him to come to us.   Also, I thank the Lord for my being used in some ways to help him in knowledge of the word and truth.   It seems to me plain that the Lord shows His sovereignty by making that man a vessel through which the converting power of God may be poured out on various classes of men.   The drunkards have had their ' day of visitation,' and many others of the work-

---

[1] This meeting was held on Wednesday, 21st December 1881.

ing men especially. Δόξα Θεῷ. I can now see in the great blessing among us a great answer to the times of prayer which I was enabled to keep on board the ship both in going and coming from America. Jer. xxxiii. 3 has been fulfilled to me. He has shown me great things which I knew not. One marked effect upon ministers here has been the state of expectation in which they now are, looking for real results of their work.

Saturday, 17*th.*—Tried to take a special time for prayer to-day, but failed greatly, so much wandering and depression. Saw myself to be not more than a skeleton of holiness, not a holy man. Desire fills my heart ; but I am rather like one panting for the water-springs than reaching them and drinking.

Sabbath, July 2*nd.*—In the evening baptized the Jew, Marcus Buck. I bless God that I have had this privilege in my ministry before its close.

Dr. Bonar's holidays were spent for four successive summers, at Craignure, in Mull. His letters from Craignure show how much he enjoyed the solitude and retirement, and also how much he was alive to the humorous side of everything, enjoying all as only one of his happy and childlike nature could. The following letter to Mr. Manson is a sample of many others in the same strain :—

TO REV. JAMES MANSON, CROSSFORD.

'*Craignure, Isle of Mull,*
Monday, 24*th July* 1882.

'MY DEAR MR. MANSON,—Here we are, in this island of the Western Main, where are no streets, no shops (except one), no tramways, no cabs, no gooseberries, no blackbirds, no noonday-meetings, no "songs and solos." And yet we are comfortable, and could make you comfortable, probably, if you could be persuaded to take a sail hither.

'Yesterday, there being no English service here I undertook to give it, and accordingly reached the spot (Lochdonhead), got into the pulpit, and essayed to read the first psalm—but, ah me ! I had forgot my spectacles and my eye-glass too ! What was to be done ? I acted on the old principle engrained into us in our study of the classics :

"Tu ne cede malis sed contra audentior ito."

I therefore *repeated* the psalm, and then descended from the pulpit to the seat where my four daughters were sitting, piteously begging the use of Isabella's eye-glass. But, alas ! it gave me no help, and so after the prayer I repeated a few verses of a chapter which I contrived to find out correctly, and found out my text by a sort of instinct. It was all right now, for you know I do not use paper ; otherwise, what a fix ! Had you ever such an adventure in a pulpit ? By the bye, my four daughters were "the precentor." Had they been absent, the raising of the tune would have been left to me. How I would have sung !

'How are you progressing as you look out from your "loopholes of retreat" ? What do you think of the Eastern question ? Egypt is still "the basest of kingdoms." We surely hear the cry, "Overturn, overturn, overturn, till *He* come whose right it is to reign." '

Saturday, Sept. 16th.—For some days this week have been kept very troubled about our relative, George Dodds of Paris, who has been cut off very suddenly. His death will be a terrible loss to the mission as well as to us, his friends. Two things I long to be full of before my ministry ends, viz., fervent zeal for the glory of God in Christ, and tender compassion for souls.

Saturday, 23rd.—It is now forty-four years since I was ordained to the ministry. I have been trying to review the past. I was ordained on the 20th, and preached on the Sabbath following, the 23rd, taking John i. 8 as my first sermon : 'I know whom I have believed ;' how earnestly I wish sometimes that I could speak of Him with a tinge of fear ! I wish I could find myself in the cleft of the rock, and preach out of it every Sabbath. How little of the harvest have I cut down!

Friday, 29th.—Various things combine to make me feel like a tree which is soon to be transplanted. The Lord is loosening my roots. I sometimes get moments when I seem to realize myself as face to face with Christ within the veil, walking with Him.

Saturday, Oct. 7th.—My review of past work and service rouses in me a feeling of deep sadness because of what has been wanting. And now my cry is, that every visit I pay, every sermon I preach, every tract I write, may be like a spark from a seven-times-heated furnace ; that furnace being my heart, filled by the Holy Spirit, and ever burning within me. It has not been so in the past.

Thursday, 26th, Fast-Day.—Our attendance at church more than ordinary. Our evening service, when admitting fifty-one young communicants, a most solemn and profitable season. I feel almost alarmed now at my congregation, the number being about 1030. The Lord is peculiarly gracious to me above others, and yet I know that I fail exceedingly in prayer and nearness to the Lord.

Saturday, 28th.—For some time past my great conflicts have been with small matters in the congregation, the session, the circle of friends ; small things comparatively, which fret the spirit. I see that overcoming these completely is a test of my nearness of communion with the Lord. For these are exceedingly apt to hinder close and constant fellowship.

Friday, Dec. 22nd.—Last night the Lord encouraged me in an interesting manner. I was at a Workers' Meeting in Whiteinch. The superintendent of the Sabbath-school and meeting told how my words had been the means of his awakening years ago. Then a great helper among them told how, eight years ago, I led him into rest. And the minister spoke of my words having been so useful to him in guiding his ministry. These things have a strange effect upon me oftentimes, they make me feel ashamed, so to speak, of being so honoured by my gracious Saviour.

Saturday, 6th Jan. 1883.—In reading in my ordinary [course] about the various work in the temple of Solomon, it struck me that these details manifest God's wonderful interest in His people's work for Him ; and we may say that our own doings for Him, speaking, giving, visiting, are all as interesting as those in the temple. For they concern the building of the great heavenly temple ; the carving of stones for it ; the preparing them ; the different parts, etc.

March 9th. — A new providence. My daughter Isabella is engaged to Mr. Oatts of the Christian Institute. I feel it solemnizing thus to be called upon to help her to look forward to a lifetime of another kind of life. My ship now sails into a new region. New experiences will be given me, new anxieties, sorrow, joy. Job i. 5 comes up.

March 25th.—Communion at Greenock. My brother has now passed his eightieth year. To-day he enters on his eighty-first. He receives his degree as D.D. next month. How gracious the Lord has been to our family !

April 8th.—Communion Sabbath. Our numbers now are too large for one man, being to-day 1040. We had with us friends from various quarters—Collace, Elgin, Nairn, Liverpool, London, two Swiss students, as well as persons from the neighbourhood about the city. I got some glimpses of eternal things and of *Christ Himself*. Never felt more than now that earth's sources of comfort are ' cisterns that can hold no water.' Sympathy, on the part of some of my nearest friends, seems to have decayed.

Friday, May 4th.—This morning awoke from a dream, in which I thought I got an amazing view of the greatness of *one sin* against such a God. How it made the atonement appear wonderfully great !

Tuesday, 8th.—Unexpectedly got some considerable help for the debt of our church, after special prayer in the matter. Still distressed at the fact that my fellowship with the Lord throughout the day is so broken, instead of being constant and continuous.

Thursday, 24th. — The opening of the General Assembly. My brother Horace chosen Moderator. Our family has been dealt with wonderfully. This is the *fortieth* year since the Disruption. All these years in the wilderness the Lord has been with us, though we have passed through fire and water.

Saturday, June 2nd.—This evening gave a closing prophetic lecture on Isa. lxiii. 1-5, the last of forty on these subjects, of which six only have been by any but myself. I do thank the Lord for this opportunity of so long and so often testifying to the Coming of Christ, and the blessedness of looking for that day.

Tuesday, 19th.—Yesterday came out to Crossford for a day. Got quiet in the church alone for prayer, calling on the Lord for revival here, Eph. iii. 18, 19. Also, heaven in my soul ; for I seemed never to get really near it. ' My soul breaketh for longing that it hath ' was my feeling for a time.

Craignure, Mull, Monday, Aug. 6th.—Tried to pray over the list of all my people. As I did so, I got several discoveries of my negligence, and of the great want of the power and presence of the *Holy Ghost with me* in my visiting.

Sabbath, 26th.—Startled while reading Luke xiii. 30. It seems to warn some of us older ministers that it may be we may become self-confident, thinking that because of the past time we must of course stand out still superior to others.[1]

Saturday, Sept. 22nd.—Pondering the past years of my ministry with deep concern. ' Have I been so long time with you, and hast thou not known me, Philip ? ' has been running in my mind. To-day have been spending time in prayer and fasting. The Lord can use me as I use a pen ; but no thanks to me.

Wednesday, 26th.—Very memorable. Isabella, my daughter, married to William Oatts. Everything passed off pleasantly. The Lord with us.

Sabbath, Dec. 16th.—Have been led to ask that the Lord might make my sermons sometimes like ' quivers full of arrows, dipt in love,' while the Heavenly Archer Himself carries them to the mark ; and sometimes, like a tree of life, from which I am enabled to shake down the fruit and the leaves of healing upon all beneath its shadow.

Crossford, Tuesday, 25th.—Time for prayer till the afternoon. I sought specially to know the *love of God*, of which as yet I am persuaded I scarcely feel anything; and I sought the presence of the Spirit in prayer in our congregations, as in days of old revival.

It is interesting, as bearing on this last entry for 1883, to read part of a letter which he wrote on the following day, Dec. 26th, to his son, showing how the subject was occupying his thoughts :—

' I wish to make you my " Magnus Apollo " in regard to the Greek of a verse in Eph. iii. 17. As an impartial critic say what you think of this proposed rendering. The grammatical con-

---

[1] Dr. Bonar used to tell, with great solemnity, what was said to him at the beginning of his ministry by an old friend and minister : ' Remember, it is a remark of old and experienced men, that very few men, and very few *ministers*, keep up to the end the edge that was on their spirit at the first.'

struction is difficult, but I suggest that verse 17th may be (like
1 Thess. i. 4) in the *vocative*, to be thus rendered, " *O ye who are
rooted and grounded in love !* " Just as in 1 Thess. i. 4 Paul writes,
"O ye brethren beloved of God!" Some day, at your leisure,
give me your opinion.'

Tuesday, 1st Jan. 1884.—I have been thinking of the
Spirit bringing to our remembrance past things.   Lord,
remind me of the mercies, the gifts, the blessings, of the
past year.[1]

Saturday, March 15*th.*—Have been more and more
led to be unwilling to speak of work done by myself or
my congregation.   It is so difficult to escape from
self-importance.   But the mote in the sunshine is
our position.   Perhaps I am less bound to earth than
I used to be ; the many ' broken cisterns ' make ' the
Fountain of living waters ' very, very sweet.   Matthew
xviii. 4 lately made a great impression upon me.   It
shows so clearly that our great doings are the *little
things* which not a creature knows but *Christ*, which we
have done heartily because it was to Him, in some of
His people or such like.

Thursday, 20*th.*—Last night our annual meeting, one
of our most pleasant and useful for many years.   But
the Lord is making me feel very weak, and further, He
is teaching me to be ashamed of myself in His sight,
because of the absence of prayer, love, and zeal in His
service ; and still also my feebleness in prayer alone
often saddens me.   *Lord, fill me with the Spirit.*

Tuesday, 25*th.*—A day of many memories.   Friends
in glory ; and some of us spared wonderfully.   I have
been noticing, among my many mercies in contrast to

[1] In a note to his youngest daughter he says, ' Are you very thankful?
You know the difference between *gladness* and *thankfulness*?   Gladness
looks at the kindness and takes it all ; but thankfulness looks at the
Giver, and loves Him for it all.'

several of my brethren, that I have been 'kept in secret from the strife of tongues.'

Saturday, 29th.—Much struck with the remark of Flavel : ' The devil is aware that one hour of close fellowship, hearty converse with God in prayer, is able to pull down what he hath been contriving and building many a year.'

Monday, April 28th.—Occasional glimpses of Christ, each touching my heart much : a little of His glorious greatness; a little love ; something of my own exceeding littleness.   Altogether, I see myself simply a vessel into which the Lord can pour what He chooses.

Thursday, May 1st.—The Fast-Day at Torphichen, where the memory of other days crowded upon me.   It is very remarkable, yet a call to intense thanksgiving and praise, that my bodily health has continued so complete and unbroken for many years, perhaps ten at least ; I have not known a headache even. ' Who maketh thee to differ?' often occurs to me, specially when I see brethren in the ministry breaking down.

Sabbath, 25th.—Saw plainly this morning that my own deceit of heart, and Satan working thereby, had yesterday kept me from any lengthened diet of prayer. Just what an old writer says happened to me ; Satan, like the lapwing, drew me away from the real object (prayer and fellowship with God) by suggesting every now and then something about some other part of my work, or something to examine about my lecture, sermon, etc., and so the best hours of yesterday were in a great measure lost, so far as ' prayer and transfiguration ' might have been.   But, Lord, act Thou to me on the principle of Joel ii. 25 : ' Restore the years that the locust hath eaten.'

Saturday, June 21st.—Stunned by several unexpected

disappointments, but above all, by clearly seeing that I am falling behind in the heavenly race. 'Many that were first shall be last,' is true of me. I am not used in conversion work as I was in early days. Perhaps I rest on this, that God used me at one time very much ; forgetting that after all I may be like Jonathan, who could at one time take a garrison and defeat an army, and yet was found soon after unable to face one giant. Lord, use me yet! Lord, I love Thee and Thy work! give me souls still, before my sun has set, and give me more grace and knowledge of Christ. My light in daily life is very dim, I fear ; and my preaching of Christ is not with a tinge of fear. But I shall see Christ glorified by the multitudes He has saved by others, and I shall rejoice in His joy.

Saturday, 28th. — A most solemn day, being the funeral of James Scott.[1] An immense crowd in the hall, and then at the grave. I spoke a little on Rev. xiv. 13, 14. This was my preparation for to-morrow's Communion. ' In death there shall be no remembrance of Thee.' Now, now is our time for bringing in souls to Christ, and it may be the time for very close fellowship with Him. Very much of prayer, like that at Peniel, very much love !

Craignure, Mull, Aug. 2nd.—Preached last Sabbath, and again the same blessed opportunity set before me. I think I see Rom. viii. 16 in a new manner. The Spirit enables me to take firm hold of the truth. I need to be freed from what I consider to be something like *the shadow of fear* and uncertainty at times. Have heard lately of *two* cases in which the *Memoir of Robert M'Cheyne* has been blessed : one here, another in England. Of late I have not found persons speaking to me about salvation, but I have found five or six persons

[1] Rev. Jas. Scott, of the Glasgow United Evangelistic Association.

reported to me as the fruit of my preaching, of whom I had no notice before.

Sabbath, 10*th*.—Drawn out to pray for this island by seeing the calm contentedness of the people in their indifference. Led back in my experience to the days when Isabella was taken from me. At that time how dreary, how truly empty, everything seemed on the side of earth. A constant want was what I felt at home and in every corner. But yet the Lord has led me on, and has quietly taken the place of all, by His own blessed presence and fellowship.

Monday, 18*th*.—Have been preaching at Tobermory and Loch Aline, as well as here. Sometimes I get near the Lord and can speak to Him as a son. Several hours of prayer here, but as yet no day of prayer.

Sept. 10*th*.—Home. Got some blessing at Perth Conference yesterday. Lord Polwarth remarked that perhaps the greatest service John did for his Master was *leaning on His bosom* in such perfect confidence. May I reach this high attainment!

Saturday, 27*th*.—The meetings held here by some of the brethren for 'deepening holiness' have led me to consider what it is that they think they have got beyond others. I am persuaded that what most of them mean is this, viz., that acquaintance with the personal Saviour and constant fellowship with Him which imparts fresh life and unction to prayer, conversation, preaching, etc. All this, however, is not any second conversion, but is the Spirit breathing through the heart in a new degree. The Kilsyth awakening was a time when many ministers were remarkably blessed in this manner. Others of us had this from the beginning of our ministry, more or less. And if any make this something by itself, instead of just the Spirit bringing in more of Christ, they are in great danger of mysticism.

One of my brethren got such a 'stirring up of the gift that was in him' in the early days of his ministry. And often this occurs again and again in the course of our Christian life.

Saturday, Nov. 1st.—All week the sweetness of last Sabbath's Communion has been felt among us. Some were greatly melted. Prayer was answered, and some things which we had feared might vex, were not allowed to come to us.

Saturday, 8th.—I have been truly hindered in prayer and meditation by the multitude of people who call. I have been speaking to the Lord about these interruptions, and have been ready to use the language of the Psalmist, 'Be merciful, for man would swallow me up: he oppresseth me daily.' 'Save me from the reproach of him that would swallow me up.' Paul's experience of this appears in 2 Cor. xi. 28, but I remember the Lord's words, '*My grace is sufficient for thee.*'

Friday, Dec. 5th.—The funeral day of my brother Horace's wife, after three days' illness taken home. The two last hours she was able to speak to them all, just like a calm Sabbath evening conversation, with occasional prayer. She is buried in the Canongate Churchyard ; and when there, I recalled the memory of my father's funeral, the first funeral I ever was present at. Sixty-four years since then, and yet I am spared !

Thursday, 1st January 1885.—When 'leaning on the Beloved' we can afford to look back upon the past part of the wilderness, with all its failures, imperfection, unbelief, etc. The Beloved looks back with us, and, as we speak of these humiliating views of the past, He tells us that all is forgiven, and whispers into our ear something like Joel ii. 25 : 'I will restore the years that the locusts have eaten.'

April 1st.—Have passed through some days of feebleness and under something like a cloud between me and the Sun of Righteousness, so far as regards direct comfort and joy. Some removals in the congregation and other discouragements have had this effect. But Isa. xl. 31 remains true.

Thursday, 23rd.—Jubilee of Free St. Luke's, Edinburgh. It was, indeed, a solemn evening to me to be present at St. Luke's, and hear so much of the days of old, like Psalm lxxvii. 11, 12. I am one of the handful left behind still on earth. Many were the prayers, many were the Gospel proclamations here, in days of revival, etc., which came perhaps in answer to those prayers very specially. It was there that in old days conversion was expected ; it was. there that minister and people asked and received. William Burns was there often, Robert M'Cheyne, Alexander Somerville, my brother Horace, Dr. Duncan, and many others. The God of Elijah liveth still.

Sabbath, June 28th.—Our Communion. It seemed to me that at this season it was as if the river were full of water at all the meetings, and in all to-day's services, from morning to evening. We were like people sitting on the banks of the river calmly enjoying ourselves, and receiving an order afterwards to rise and work.

Tuesday, July 21st.—Thinking on our being the temple of God, was led to notice, that this being so, we may have the Holy Spirit's groaning desires for prayers ; and the cry 'Holy, holy, holy' for praise. Then, also, the kingdom of heaven is like the small mustard-seed, all the little sense of sin, discovery of the power of the blood, little insight into the mystery of the Gospel, and the ocean of love ; little joy, peace, compassion, zeal, all these are mustard-seeds which have the promise of growing till they be, each of them, a great tree ! And then, too, the leaven will permeate every faculty—affection, thought, desire, motive—the whole being of the soul !

Thursday, August 6th.—For several days I have had time and freedom in the forenoon to spend two hours in prayer. To-day, when thus engaged, I was led forward in thought to realize myself standing before the Lamb, without a single sinful tendency, and without one drawback in the way of the slightest uncertainty. ' For ever with the Lord.' For ever with all those holy, happy friends ! For ever, for ever, holy and without blame, like the Lamb Himself.

Friday, 14*th.*—While taking another season of prayer was greatly drawn out for a little. I see that, just as where the glass is prepared, a moment of the sun's light gives the photograph, so it may be with a moment of Christ's shining in my soul. ' Changed into the same image.' Also I see that, in Eph. iii. 18, it is as if he had spoken of our survey of Christ's love as John walking through New Jerusalem, height, depth, length, breadth. The very walking where this immense and wonderful love is spread out before us may be to us what that walk was to John, in its effects never to be forgotten. Even one such walk, what may it do for us ?

Tuesday, 25*th.*—Got another forenoon for prayer, and got some nearness. I laid aside other things for this. It is resting.

Saturday, Sept. 12*th.*—To-day got the last proof of my brief *Memoir of James Scott*. May the Lord use it much.

Sabbath, 20*th.*—It is this day exactly forty-seven years since I was ordained. My ministry has appeared to me to be wanting in so many ways, that I can only say of it, *indescribably inadequate*. ' Tekel ' may be written upon it. On the other hand, the Lord's goodness to me seems surpassingly strange, and can be explained simply by this, that He wishes to show what He can make out of the most unlikely materials. He is thinking of what He will put *into* this vessel, and what He will put *upon* it. He loves me because of what He is to make me.

October 15*th*.—Yesterday was the memorable day in my domestic history ; and to-day I found leisure to take the larger part of the day in the vestry for meditation and prayer. I have learned, in some measure, that the Lord can fill the soul with *Himself*, when He takes away what seemed indispensable to our happiness on earth.

Friday, Dec. 11*th*.—This evening a telegram, telling the sudden death of David Dickson, my brother-in-law, this forenoon. He was, indeed, ' a good man and a just.' Many, many will miss him as well as we. This afternoon, just after coming home, all at once I felt myself giddy for a few minutes. It may have been the excessive cold. But, at any rate, the Lord speaks by this thing, and it is blessed to be able to say, I know Him who has the keys of death ! I shall be found in Jesus. Meanwhile, in these my latter days, the Lord is teaching me John the Baptist's lesson : ' He must increase ; I must decrease.'

1*st January* 1886.—' So much the more as ye see the day approaching ' has increasing significance. Every effort more earnest ; prayer and praise more intensely an outpouring of the heart ; love more really a flame.

Sabbath, 24*th*.—A blessed Communion day. Dr. Robert Macdonald with us. Deep attention. The Lord was there. Desire has been quickened ; the world has lost something of its power ; prayer has been more real. Christ Himself seems more than formerly dwelling among us, and using such as myself to be instruments in His work.

Friday, March 12*th.*—Comforted this morning, when a multitude of cares were laid upon me, interrupting study and prayer, by being enabled to use Ps. iii. 1, 3, 4, and then the loss of some hours by persons coming led me to Joel ii. 25, 'restoring the years that the locusts had eaten,' for the principle is in verse 26 : ' My people shall never be ashamed.' Many things tell me that I must sit very loose to earth in every aspect.

Sabbath, 28*th.*—Greenock Communion. My brother John entered his eighty-third year three days ago. Very greatly emptied at this season ; got not a few humiliating views of myself. Sometimes it seems to me as if the Master were quietly saying to me, ' The Lord has not much need of you now.'

Saturday, April 10*th.*—Our Communion week. I was able to get time on Thursday for prayer in the vestry for some hours. My soul was in a languid state ; I was again brought to this, ' All men are liars,' but the Lord Himself is more than ever glorious. The Fountain of living water feels most satisfying when other waters fail. When I was very much inclined to fear that the Lord had set me aside, a little girl came with a message. After settling the message, I asked her if she knew Christ. She said ' Yes,' and then told me it was one forenoon when I was at Maryhill Industrial School and said a few words to the young people.

Sabbath, 11*th.*—Our Communion. My brother Horace seems much stricken down in health. I got remarkable glimpses of Christ's love as I preached upon 2 Cor. v. 14. They were but passing glimpses, but they helped me much. The Lord was with us indeed through the day.

Wednesday, 14*th.*—To-day had the privilege of sending a letter to the minister of the congregation at Natick, near Boston, promising him my copy of ' Eliot's Bible.'[1]

---

[1] A very rare book in the language of an extinct Indian tribe.

There is a college for ladies there, of a missionary kind, built within half-a-mile of the oak under which Eliot used to preach. I had gone over the ground when we visited that part of America. How strange to have this link of connection with the region of Eliot and Brainerd and Tennant, whom we so reverenced in our early days, little thinking of having the opportunity of visiting their country, and still less of being any way useful to their descendants.

Tuesday, 20th.—Have been solemnly reviewing the Lord's recent ways in our city regarding revival work. I see the answer to prayer in ways that we were not looking for : (1) I and others prayed that the richer people of this city, young ladies and young men, might be reached in some way. The Lord has been doing this remarkably by sending a new instrument, George Clarke, from England, and by using W. A. Campbell very largely among the young men. (2) We asked that in our usual congregations there might be seen the manifested power of God, and this has been shown for some months in the Cowcaddens Church. (3) It is natural that now, as in the case of Levitical priests, at my time of life I should stand aside, praying more than working. But one thing, O shine, shine forth in my spirit, that I may feel *Thy love to me* filling my heart ! With this cup of blessing I shall go on my way full till Thou comest or callest.

Saturday, May 29th.—My birthday. I find there are only now *ten* Pre-Disruption ministers in full work. Of these I am one. What kindness in the Lord to spare me thus ! But I know He may well say to me what was said to the disciple Philip, ' Have I been so long time with thee, and is this all thou knowest, and all thou hast done for Me ?'

Saturday, June 26th.—Our Communion week. Found

myself much comforted in the consciousness of my doing
very little useful work for the Lord by the consideration
that I may really take part in all the work done throughout the world, if I pray much in full sympathy with
them.   This I have been more than formerly enabled to
do yesterday and to-day.

July 18*th.*—It is solemnizing to me this summer to be
visiting a dying brother, George Mills, who has so often
helped me in summer months.   Then also to see James
Manson so unfitted for work.   All the while the Lord
keeps me well and sends me forth to labour.

Sabbath, August 1*st.*—Ardslignish, near Ardnamur-
chan.   Preached in the kitchen of the farm to about
thirty.

Sabbath, 22*nd.*—A good deal of that which Rom. viii.
seems to speak of, a yearning indescribable.   For about
an hour this yearning was very strong on behalf of
myself and my people, and sometimes for all the
unsaved.

Saturday, September 25*th.*—Connecting Gal. v. 22 with
' the fulness of the Spirit,' I have been praying much for
fulness of love, fulness of peace, fulness of joy, fulness
continually, fulness of goodness, fulness of long-suffering,
fulness of faith (faith that sees things unseen, especially
the Lord Himself), fulness of meekness, fulness of temperance, fulness of ἀρετή, fulness of knowledge, fulness
of patience, fulness of godliness, fulness of brotherly love,
fulness of charity.   The meetings of the Convention for
deepening spiritual life, though sometimes a little mis-
leading, have been helpful.

November 29*th.*—Yesterday was at Dundee.   It was
the celebration of the jubilee of St. Peter's.   When I was
preaching in the forenoon, Acts ii. 47, what attention
and solemnity !   The church was crowded in every
corner, and when, near the beginning of the service,

sudden gleams of sunshine several times lighted up the faces of the people, it was a most striking sight.   As for myself, the Lord gave me unusual liberty and calmness and enjoyment ; even my voice seemed to have got back its early power.   The whole day—morning, noon, and evening—cannot but be memorable to me the rest of my life.

Friday, Dec. 31*st.*—A few days ago George Mills of Kilpatrick-Fleming died.   We have lost a most prayerful man and most devoted pastor.   My prayer is, ' Open mine eyes.' . . . ' I am a stranger in the earth.'

Monday, 10*th January* 1887.—We have had a week of prayer, night after night.   In this way we have quietly sown the seed of prayer upon the soil of divine grace, and there may be a blessed harvest.

Tuesday, 11*th.*—This evening, reading Rev. xxi. 14, was led into a very helpful train of thought.   These twelve apostles, what an honour is bestowed on them by each of them having his name on the foundations of New Jerusalem !   Now, such as Simon the Zealot, and even Matthias, were very common men, very commonplace believers, we might almost say ; and yet the Lord is not ashamed of them, but has prepared for them this city so glorious, and this position of dignity there.   Should not this help my faith ?   Even *me* He can in like manner love and delight to honour !

Tuesday, 25*th.*—Last Sabbath was our Communion.   The Lord gave me glimpses of special nearness.   In the service I felt for a few minutes uncommon exultation in the Father's love while giving out

> ' Bring forth the fairest robe for him,
>   The joyful father said,
>   .   .   .
>   A day of feasting I ordain—
>   Let mirth and song abound.'

Several persons noticed the presence of the Lord to be at that moment very marked, as if He were stirring us up to leap for joy.

March 5th.—It is now a somewhat familiar thought that I am near the goal! But still 'looking unto Jesus,' and running.

Saturday, 19th.—The giving up of Fast-Days is another sign of the times; and then, also, it necessarily breaks off a good deal of ministerial fellowship, such as used to be at these seasons. No more preaching on Fast evenings to children in Edinburgh, no more in Greenock; then, also, no more going to assist Dr. Laughton in Greenock, he being laid aside; and Horace no more able to come and assist us here at our Communion. 'The sands of time are sinking.' Each of these changes is a particle of sand falling out of sight. This month has already been memorable for the death of friends— my father, Robert M'Cheyne, Joseph Wilson, several relatives.

April 17th.—Our Communion. My brother Horace has been unable to come. Many things have made earth to me more than ever a wilderness or a land of broken cisterns. But the Lord Jesus is more than ever a full heaven to me.

Sabbath, 24th.—The Communion in Edinburgh. I preached my Children's Sermon in Lady Glenorchy's last Thursday. The Fast-Days being now given up, that sermon also will cease. I have been forty-two times there, and was thinking with much sadness on the few results, when Mr. Cusin told me of one of his young communicants awakened two years ago by my sermon on 'Christ carrying the lambs in His bosom.' One who gave no name also in the evening of to-day sent me a letter of thanks.

Friday, 29th.—How much have I to be thankful for!

Domestic peace and love have never been interrupted. All of us are of one heart toward each other from day to day.

Sabbath, May 8th.—The Lord gave me a gentle rebuke. I had not taken much time for prayer on Friday, and I found myself in the forenoon to-day confused and almost at a loss. I had trusted to my familiarity with the subject.

Sabbath, 29th.—My birthday! I have been led to inquire if perhaps it may be the Lord's will to use me in my old age rather for prayer and praise than for direct work. I was noticing the importance attached to 'thank and praise' in 1 Chron. xxiii. 30: 'Stand every morning to thank and praise the Lord, and likewise at even.' Lord, give me the heart for service, make me *Asaph* as well as *Epaphras*. But I have been taking a solemn view of the Sabbaths of my life. Leaving out seven years, and beginning where I might be fully expected to make right use of God's holy day, there have been in my seventy years no less than 3640 Sabbaths! What use have I made of these at all adequate to the privilege? It is a most solemnizing, almost an appalling question. Through that time I have enjoyed about ten years of Sabbaths!!

Sabbath, June 26th.—Psalm ciii. 1, the mercies of this Communion Sabbath! My brother John, now in his eighty-fourth year, assisted in his usual way, and preached on Galatians ii. 20 with great power.

Sabbath, July.—Lismore, near Oban. We are now resting here for six weeks. To-day have been led to much meditation upon the Lord's sovereignty; and Romans xi. 33: 'riches of wisdom.' What shall we not yet say of the Lord's providences, plans, all His ways and thoughts towards us! Election seems to me a most blessed truth this day, for therein I discover how I may cast off every lurking idea of my unfitness standing in the way of infinite fulness being mine. The poorer the materials, just the more thereby will He display His 'wisdom' in forming out of me a wonderful vessel of glory! So, also, I find it good to connect this wisdom with all the little events of daily life; out of these the Lord brings such grand results from time to time. This is the only Sabbath for many years in which I have been quite silent, not preaching even once!

Saturday, 23rd.—Every day this week have been able to keep a special hour for prayer, for the outpouring of the Spirit on the congregation and district, and all the churches in the city. The missionary and Bible-woman are keeping the same hour, and we go on for other three weeks.

Saturday, 30th.—Occasionally I write a letter or send some little book to some overlooked person who may be in sorrow, and thus try to claim the reward of a 'cup of cold water to a disciple.' Have kept the hour of prayer, and strange to say, the first result, in regard to congregational work, has been the death of the most useful worker in the district, Robert Cairns. 'His ways are not our ways.' The friends in America are to sail for home to-day. 1 Thess. iii. 11.

Saturday, August 13th.—Absent ones from America arrived all safe, and with much that has been pleasant.[1] Psalm cvii. 29-31 was our evening song in family worship.

Friday, 26th.—The best thing I have found in this quiet island has been seasons of prayer. My intense desire and prayer has been that I and my brethren may be 'full of the Holy Ghost' every time we preach. Why not?

---

[1] Mr. and Mrs. Oatts and his daughter Janie, who had been at Mr. Moody's Conference at Northfield, Mass.

Tuesday, 30*th.*—To-morrow we return to Glasgow. To-day have been led to pray about sin and right views of righteousness. My fasting here has been chiefly giving up all else in order to pray. One good token is found in this, viz., my dreams of late have been full of comforting thoughts.

Thursday, *Sept.* 15*th.*—Perth Conference. The night before once more went out to Collace and preached in the church, staying all night in the manse I used to occupy. It was on the 20th of this month, forty-nine years ago, as I reminded the people, that I was ordained among them. My heart sank in me at the review of the past, lest the Lord say, τὴν ἀγάπην σοῦ τὴν πρώτην ἀφῆκες. For more than a year oftentimes I have been troubled at the Lord not using me to awaken sinners, though He uses me to build up the saved.

Thursday, 29*th.*—Have been getting blessing at the Convention for deepening holiness, and was much assisted in speaking there on the first day. But it seems to me that I have not got *the Spirit of power* to any extent.

Saturday, *Oct.* 1*st.*—What I have had deepened in me by these meetings has been the blessedness and necessity of realizing the presence of the Lord Jesus everywhere, at all times. ' *Thou art with me.*'

Friday, 14*th.*—Memorable to me as the anniversary of my beloved Isabella's sudden departure to be with Christ. And now my son's son, a child of three days old, has been taken from them. Broken cisterns, broken cisterns all around ; but the fountain remains full.

Wednesday, 26*th.*—Our Communion last Sabbath has been felt remarkable. Many spoke of the great impression in the congregation, and the large numbers remaining till the very close. I felt myself very greatly helped all the time, and had glimpses now and then within the veil.

December 3rd.—To-morrow is our anniversary, but oh! I am troubled in spirit because of the very few souls that come to me seeking the way to Zion! I have been thinking of John in prison, receiving Christ's message, 'Blessed is he that is not offended in Me;' and have been pondering also John iii. 30: 'I must decrease.' But my fear is that there is some secret cause why the Lord does not use me more, and so I have been speaking to Him much about this matter.

Saturday, 31st.—The year about to close, and in reviewing it I wonder that I have not been filled with the 'spirit of grace and supplications.' The seed might have been a hundredfold more fruitful. And if I had *praised* more I could not but have *prayed* more, for my whole soul would have gone forth to Him who has all fulness of grace for us who come. To-night I think upon the atoning blood, and upon Himself who shed that blood. He is my peace, and all my 'springs' of water are there. I lean upon this fountain as the year closes.

3rd January, 1888.—Keeping the Week of Prayer all over the world; God's elect are crying to Him in a special manner at this season. Some of my petitions are in Christ's censer.

February 3rd.—Incessant work seems to me to be more than ever a snare, hindering prayer in several ways. There is great need of 'watching unto prayer.'

Saturday, 4th.—I was like Joshua with the Gibeonites to-day, hastily listening to a person whom I thought I knew, and not asking counsel of God. I lent him £2, which I see now have been got from me by a clever trick.

Saturday, March 3rd.—At Dundee last Sabbath; day cold and snowy. I remembered and saw the use of 2 Sam. xxiii. 20, and took courage, because the Lord can give me victories in the most unfavourable season.

April 6th.—Last night was my brother Horace's Jubilee. It was a singular gathering. Every one testified to the hymns which the Master had given him for the Church. The Lord helped me to say a few words about the very uncommon fact that *three* brothers of us had each for about fifty years preached the same Gospel, etc. O what a privilege! What an honour to each of us! But O that we had always been full of the Holy Ghost!

Monday, 16th.—Yesterday our Communion. Partly through a slight cold, and partly by interruption, I had little time for prayer in the end of last week, and Saturday night I dreaded exceedingly the prospect of being left to myself in the services of the day. But the Lord was very gracious; He ' filled the pools,' and we had a remarkably solemn and happy day.

Monday, 30th.—Yesterday much helped three times, but kept humble by finding in the evening, when I preached, that no anxious souls waited behind, though there have been a good many such for many weeks previous. The Lord is no doubt teaching me some lessons by this. On the other hand, He has cleared up to me a critical difficulty in Rev. xxi. 16 on which no commentary casts light, as if he would say, ' Thy part is to teach and build up rather than awaken.'

May 7th.—It pleased the Lord last week to lay me aside for four days by an attack of giddiness and sickness. I was able to preach only once yesterday. It was a quiet hint to me that my work may come to a close perhaps sooner than I expected. If so, it will be exchanging service down here for service before the throne above! Much struck with all Mr. Spurgeon is passing through, because of his faithful testimony for the truth. Just like the Lord, however, in the case of one so abundantly honoured and used; the ' thorn in the flesh,' such as Paul needed, such as Moses at Meribah, and often,

often in the case of others of his most honoured servants like Jonathan Edwards. These must rest wholly on the merits of another to the very last, and have no complacency in their own works.

Saturday, 12*th*.—Found time to give the whole of this day entirely to prayer and meditation. There will be fruit of it to me and my people.

Tuesday, 29*th*.—My birthday. It came upon me with great awe, the thought that I have been now seventy-eight years in the world, and am now near the world to come. When I look round it is like a battle-field ; many old friends gone ; and then I see brethren like men wounded in the fight, such as Manson, Moody-Stuart, Macdonald, both my own brothers, laid aside from their former work. Besides, such as Laughton, Thomas Brown, Alexander Luke ; and yet the Lord spares me to be one of *five* Disruption ministers who are still in full work. But I have often of late solemn thoughts about ' finishing my course and the ministry I received of the Lord.' Imperfection stamped on everything I ever undertook ; omission running through my life. My place is under the shadow of the Righteous One.

June 24*th*.—Our Communion. My brother John unable to be with us, just as Horace could not come in April. This threw a solemn shade over the time ; for thus there is a close to the long, long continued fellowship with one another, as well as with the Lord and His people, at these seasons.

Saturday, 30*th*.—Lochgoilhead, to which I had come to preach to-morrow. A telegram came in telling that my brother [William, in London] was gone ! I believe he has entered into rest. He sank away very quietly, my son James, and my nephew John, from Greenock, at his bedside. It was at 5.30 on Friday evening. It will not be at first, but a while after, that we begin to learn what the Lord intends to teach us in this bereavement.

Wednesday, Aug. 22nd.—Heard of a Brahmin getting light and helped into Christ by reading my book, *The Gospel Pointing to the Person of Christ*, and now that little book is to be translated into the native language.

Thursday, Oct. 11th.—We have had three days of a most remarkable Conference on Prophetic Truth, in Edinburgh, and the Free Assembly Hall too.   Fifty years ago, those of us that held this truth were very few and much despised.   But these three days have been days when, from all sections of the Church of Christ, there have been brethren brought together and the place nearly filled.   I myself was conscious of remarkable help from the Holy Spirit, so that I thought of those passages in the Acts where mention is made of the Spirit filling him that was about to speak.   Just as I began to pray on Tuesday, my voice gathered strength and my heart was glowing.   I prayed, ' Father, glorify Thy Son this day while we speak of His kingdom and crown.   Blessed Saviour, who art gone to the mountain of myrrh and hill of frankincense, impatient in Thine own way till the day break, fill us with the same holy impatience ! and O Holy Spirit, who hast shown us the *Cross* in some measure of its power, lead us into the truth regarding the *Crown*.   Let some rays of its brightness fall upon our souls now.'   Both that day and then again to-day I was helped beyond all I have almost ever experienced, speaking so calmly, and yet the while with much delight, and gaining the attention of all present.   And then, this afternoon, we kept together the Lord's Supper, ' till He come.'   O how the presence of the Lord has been felt among us !   We shall long remember this day.   The whole time has been such that one of those who spoke (Mr. Grant) said that he felt as if this season were part of the cry at midnight, ' Behold, the Bridegroom cometh.' I never remember having been so calmly joyful at any Communion as this day. It seemed to be a foretaste of the Feast in the Kingdom. All this, too, I felt to be the true oil for the wounded, bereaved (1 Thess. iv.), thinking of my own time of mourning, now so soon to end.

Sabbath, 14th.—This time, twenty-four years ago! *Himself* with me has been quiet consolation in the day of sorrow.

Sabbath, 21st.—Our Communion. ' It is good to be here' was my feeling. After I came home for a few minutes, I had great joy in the thought that it was *almost the time* now for my finishing my course and being with the Lord, and then coming with Him in glory.

November 24th.—I have lived this month in the feeling that I should set my house in order. My Jubilee, to be kept next week, has led me to a most solemn review, especially as to omissions. O that I had prayed a hundredfold more !

Friday, 30th.—Last night's Jubilee [1] passed over very pleasantly in one way, but was to me at the same time very solemn and humbling. I see in the retrospect so much that was altogether imperfect, and so much that was left undone. But it was a great gathering, and most hearty on the part of all the friends who came. ' Bless the Lord, O my soul, *and forget not all His benefits.*' May the Lord save me from the danger that lurks under praise and laudation of friends. I had no idea that I had so many friends in various parts, and that the Lord had been pleased to use me in so many

---

[1] The celebration of Dr. Bonar's ministerial Jubilee, held in the Queen's Rooms, Glasgow, on Thursday evening, the 29th of November 1888.

ways. They have given me a great sum of money, £4000.
Collace has sent £51. There has been sent a quilt, beautifully wrought, with 213 names on it. Some very kind and
unexpected letters from various friends. It is all of the
Lord. He can enable me to do more for His name.

After this memorable meeting was over, he wrote to Mr.
Manson, who was unable to be present :—

'MY DEAR FRIEND,—I *was* glad when last Thursday night
was over. It was a most hearty meeting ; but don't you think
that we are on such an occasion in danger of being like Herod
when the people flattered him? " He gave not God the glory,"
etc. In speaking of my first charge I took them away with me to
Dunsinnane Hill, and bade them look half-a-mile yonder ! There
is famous Abernyte, where Dr. James Hamilton began his
ministry, and where *James Manson* won souls for Christ, and
where Joseph Wilson carried on the work. As our old friend
and brother, John Walker, said to my first stable-boy, who met
him about Perth some years after, "Ah, these were days when
drops from heaven fell."

' No doubt you and Mary helped us that night, you being the
Aaron and Hur, while we were only the feeble host that were
trying to fight. But " I add no more at present," hoping soon to
see you face to face.

' Your affectionate, aged, frail, poor, unworthy, feeble, stupid
brother, and fellow-servant of a glorious Master,

'ANDREW A. BONAR.'

Sabbath, Dec. 2nd.—Our anniversary. Carried through
in a way that interested the people, but as for myself,
when I returned home and sat in the evening alone, I
felt deep and bitter regret at the thought of the past. I
think I felt what is meant by ' being ashamed before
God,' as Ezra expresses it. And all this aggravated by
the immense kindness of the Lord to me and mine. I
have been thinking to-night that perhaps my next great
undertaking may be this, ' *appearing at the Judgment-seat
of Christ,*' when I give an account of my trading with my

talents. I wish to hide in the shadow of the Plant of Renown, and be found there when the voice says, ' Where art thou ? '

Saturday, 22nd.—Last night we had our Children's Jubilee Meeting in the Queen's Rooms, but I feel relieved now from a series of exciting meetings which have had their use, and yet are not altogether helpful to the soul. This year throughout has been a time of meetings and various distractions.

Sabbath, 23rd.—Stayed at home to-night for prayer and meditation. I have been getting remarkable glimpses of divine love, in answer to earnest prayer, that ' I might know the love that passeth knowledge.' Yesterday and to-day I have stayed astonished over ' *God manifest in the flesh,*' in the infant Jesus in His flight to Egypt, under yonder shady tree, watched over by His mother, with only Joseph near ! The universe might gaze on that sight with unutterable amazement. At times, these two days, it has come upon me with indescribable wonder. I am kept humble very much by what was Cecil's consideration, viz., that when I shall see fully what Christ is, I shall be so ashamed of the poor service I have rendered to Him that I shall never be able to forgive myself for not having served Him better. ' I know not how to separate the idea of self-reproach from heavenly enjoyment.'

CHAPTER VII

Closing Years

1889-1892

Saturday, 5th January 1889.—Busy with too many meetings at this season, leaving me too little time for prayer.

April 5th.—Last month had many memories of friends taken away, and now to-day another is gone, my brother-in-law, William Dickson. He has seen 'the King in His beauty' this morning.

May 25th. — Yesterday evening at the General Assembly of our Church, that being the exact date of the time when, fifty years ago, the deputation to Palestine began their journey from Egypt to the Holy Land. Having been requested to be present and tell reminiscences of that time, I was helped in doing so. And then Dr. Saphir spoke most profitably. I am the only survivor of the deputation, and very few of those that took much interest in the Jews at that time, are now alive. But how wonderfully the Lord has blessed this work! And how kind He has been to me in connection with it. 'O for a well-tuned harp!'

Wednesday, 29th.—The Lord has enabled me to lean upon Christ day by day, for sixty years, or rather fifty-nine. He took hold of me that year [1830], and has never once left me in darkness as to my interest in Him all that time. I have been meditating upon His marvellous grace; and I see it in this light, viz., He promised that day I found Him that I would have rest in Himself always as I went along, and then nothing less than a whole eternity of blessedness. All this for accepting the *Gift of Christ*! The first moment of faith rewarded by everlasting ages of blessedness!

June 23rd.—Our Communion. The Lord is kinder to me than ever, the nearer I come to the end of my journey. Psalm ciii.

Seaforth, Liverpool, Sabbath, July 14*th.*—While here with Mr. Collie I got some very blessed glimpses while reading the chapter Rev. i. 17. Christ, after sixty years, coming to give John 'the touch of a long-vanished hand,' and make him hear the 'voice that had long been still.' Near views of the Lord's person.

Blackwaterfoot, Arran, Thursday, 25*th.*—Fast-Day before Communion. Found myself led somewhat far into the holiest for a little, while seeking to observe the day as a time of confession of sin, and longing after more grace.

Wednesday, 31*st.*—This afternoon a telegram tells that my brother Horace has entered into rest. Certainly I had been expecting it; but, when the reality comes, there is something of awe in it; the gates of the unseen have opened to take him in.

Wednesday, August 7*th.*—The solemn days of my brother's funeral have passed. In the forenoon of Sabbath I sat in the vestry of his church listening to the prayers and singing of the congregation assembled for devotion. Once or twice I almost realized what it may be to hear the great congregation singing together as they welcome a brother arrived in glory! I wonder if there is full recognition during this period of separation from the body; and, from the parable of Lazarus at the feast, I am inclined to believe there is.[1]   When Horace entered, and was led to his place by the Elder Brother, what a moment!   '*Denique Coelum!*'[2] And soon he looks round, and there, father, mother, sisters, brothers! And then beloved companions who went before, M'Cheyne, John Milne, William Burns, Dr. Chalmers, James Hamilton, and hundreds of such!   The singing of 'A few more years shall roll,' and then, 'For ever with the Lord,' was intensely impressive.   He was laid in the Canongate Churchyard, 'gathered to his fathers.'   I do not know where I may lie, but I suppose it will be in Glasgow, though it is of almost no moment, since the time is so near when the Lord shall come and the Resurrection Day!   Dr. Moody-Stuart, in a letter of sympathy, speaks of the funeral as 'our sowing the seed that is to ripen on that day.'   Over and above, let me bless the Lord for the gifts He gave to His servant.

Thursday, 8*th.*—All forenoon spent in special prayer, that my latter days may be days of rapid progress in the knowledge of Christ, and times wherein I shall see the Spirit poured out remarkably upon our church, our congregation, all missionary labour.

Tuesday, 13*th.*—Another time of three hours' prayer and meditation upon the Spirit.   Humbled, even while in a sense envying him, at hearing that that one book of my brother's, *God's Way of Peace*, has had a circulation of 280,000, and very greatly blessed.

Sept. 18*th.*—Most unexpectedly, though he has been

[1] Writing to Mr. Robert Young in Edinburgh to thank him for his book, *Trophies from African Heathenism*, Dr. Bonar says : ' I like such a book as yours for many reasons, and among the rest for this, viz., I find it is like making new friends ; and even in heaven (don't you think) we shall take more interest in those we have been thus introduced to, than in those we never heard of when we were on earth.'

[2] The family motto, ' *Heaven at Last.*'

of late very ill, Dr. Somerville taken home　When I heard it at his own door, I thought of Ezekiel xi. 13. He is leaving me behind without almost any one of the older days.

Friday, 20th.—I am much exercised about one thing, there are so seldom any coming to me who have been awakened under my preaching. The Lord has used me to help and build up, but not much to awaken. Why is this?

Saturday, Oct. 5th.—Last night our twelve days of meeting finished. Major Whittle has been remarkably clear and earnest in setting forth the Gospel every night. Last night was felt to be more than all impressive. Some evident fruits have already appeared. But no outpouring in a general way.

Monday, 14th.—Got great joy when reading Proverbs xxiii. 16, as the word of the greater than Solomon addressed to us preaching His Gospel: 'My son, my reins shall rejoice when thy lips speak right things.' Christ listening to our sermons!

But now add to all else Exodus xii. 42 : 'That night to the Lord' twenty-five years ago. It was then the Lord sent for my beloved Isabella, and began to teach me that I could go on without her, if Himself was with me.

November 16th.—I see very plainly that the Lord has been teaching me, and that I needed the teaching, that I was not necessary as an instrument when revival work was spreading in the city. I fear I had secret conceit of my importance, and the importance of old friends. But the Lord works by independent instruments in this place and that, in this person and in that.

Saturday, 30th.—To-day heard of the birth of a little granddaughter in London. Why do I not give more praise and thanks?

1st Jan. 1890.—A calm day amid a great many meetings. But the stream of life flows on, and I seem borne down to the ocean without very much concern. Holy Spirit, fill me!

More carefully than ever I hope this year to give two hours before going out every day, to meditate on the Word and prayer. And in this way there shall go out of me *heavenward* ' rivers of living water ' that will bring down refreshing rain-showers.

Last year very few persons called on me, seeking to be guided to Christ. One reason for this may be that at present almost all awakened ones go to meetings, and there speak with those that are watching for them. But, besides, I think the Lord is giving me something of the experience in Isaiah xxviii. 24-28, employing me rather to build up and feed His own.

It is a very great privilege for me to find members and office-bearers of my congregation carrying on work in the evening all over the city. William Oatts, in the Christian Institute; William Ralston, in Bethany Hall; Mr. Mackeith, in James Morrison Street; Mr. Ferrie, in the Mizpah Hall; Robert Munsie, in his hall; Miss Jones, in Cowcaddens; Mrs. Oatts, up and down the country—all this apart from work done in our congregation every week. Oh, if I could only pray like Moses in Rephidim, while these are fighting in the valley! Lord, make me satisfied, and yet also lead to more searching inquiry as to why I am not used more directly in awakening sinners from their sleep. Sometimes I have an awful fear of becoming a backslider! Lord, Lord, wilt Thou so keep me that I shall be one of those in Luke xii. 35, 37.

Feb. 9th.—My oldest friend, James Manson, seriously ill. But the Daybreak is near.

Friday, 21st.—James Manson died this morning.

For three days in great weakness, but no pain ; and so passed away. I saw him on Monday, when he spoke to me very pleasantly, and I prayed with him. I saw him yesterday, but he seemed unconscious. He has entered into rest. O blessed to be able to say with the apostle—

> τὸν δρόμον τετέλεκα,
> τὴν πίστιν τετήρηκα,
> λοιπὸν ἀπόκειταί μοι
> ὁ τῆς δικαιοσύνης στέφανος.—2 Tim. iv. 7. 8.

Sabbath, 23rd.—A peculiar day. I preached in the forenoon on Heb. xi. 14, every now and then looking in within the veil, and thinking of *five* of my dearest friends who have passed in within these twelve months. Not one of them had bodily strength to give any dying testimony ; and it was not needful : 'All these died in faith (κατὰ πίστιν),' lived under the shadow of the Great Rock, and fell asleep there quietly, as I expect some day may be my lot, unless the Lord come quickly.

March 2nd.—My last visit to Crossford. Preached funeral sermons. What memories ! How fast the Lord seems to be breaking up our circle of friends ! I preached in the morning upon Aaron's death on Mount Hor, and in the evening upon ' Abraham's bosom.'

Tuesday, 4th.—The vexation of Presbytery matters was like coming down from the Transfiguration Hill to find that the devil was busy among us still.

Wednesday, 26th.—Got a remarkable answer to prayer at a meeting where I found myself utterly weak and impotent ; but I asked, and that same hour got, the ' word in season.'

April 22nd. — The Communion has just closed. There have been some special tokens of the Lord's

presence ; so much so, that I never remember so many
individual believers speaking of what they themselves
had received through the feast.   And the Sabbath was
the brightest day of all ; and yet, when I went to bed,
and when I awoke on the Sabbath morning, I felt
myself exhausted, unprepared, and feeble.   Like Livingstone at Shotts I would fain have gone away from the
work that day.   The Lord emptied me first, then
blessed.

May 20th.—Funeral of Dr. G. R. Davidson, minister
of Lady Glenorchy's, Edinburgh, the last link of a chain
that bound me to that congregation.

Friday, 30th.—Yesterday I finished my eighty years !
I have to-day begun my eighty-first.   O that like Moses
this new period of my life may be full of the Lord's
interviews with me ! and perhaps some more blessing
to the Church through me, just because I am 'the
worm.'   Wondrous grace thus to spare me !   Increas-
ingly solemn to know how near I am advancing to
Eternity.

June 21st.—I have been much impressed with two
things to-day, viz., the Lord has given me 'all Christ,'
a most incomprehensibly great gift ; and then Deut.
xxix. 4, on the other hand, I have not understood it
all these many years : ' The Lord has not given me
eyes to see and a heart to perceive until this day.'   O
that He would do much for me to-morrow, giving me
eyes to see and a heart to take in the immensity of
blessing, ' all Christ.'

Sabbath, 22nd.—Got occasional glimpses of the glory
passing by, and snatches of the great truths of the
Word.   But my soul was full of cravings all day and to
the end.

July 4th.—After eight days' work in London, at the
meetings in Mildmay, and then at Greenwich and

several churches, have reached home again.[1]   The hand of the Lord has been upon me for good, though I have found much that has made me know that the Lord is making me 'decrease' in order that Christ may in me more *increase*.

Sabbath, *20th.*—Aros, in Mull.   Last Sabbath was the first *Sabbath* through a whole year in which I have been altogether without some public work.

Reading *Brainerd's Life*, it seemed to me that he did not hold fellowship with the *living Saviour* as he might have done, and did not see himself covered with Christ's merits whereby God's eye was turned away from his imperfections, corruptions, ignorance, failures, because the obedience of Christ was imputed to him.   I would be like Brainerd every day, mourning and sad, if I did not see myself so covered with the obedience of Christ that the Father saw me in Him to be beautiful and attractive, because of the garment of righteousness.

Thursday, *31st.*—There is a simple spring of fresh water, on the shore near our house here, overflowing ; but, when the tide comes in, quite covered over.   Still, the moment the tide recedes, there still is the ever-fresh spring. This is exactly what I find with myself.   The influx of common things and various duties seems to lead my soul apart from the fellowship of the Lord ; but still the spring is there, and flows out again.   But I grieve exceedingly at finding myself, when I awake at morning, like as if the tide had all night overwhelmed the spring, so that I have to seek for it and clear it out again.   O when shall this cease and the flow be uninterrupted ?

Saturday, *Aug. 2nd.*—Back again to-day to Eph. iii. 17, 20, that most wonderful prayer.   These three

[1] While in London at this time he baptized his little granddaughter, Marjory Caroline, at Hampstead, on the 28th of June.

days have had some special moments of prayer that took me within the veil.

Wednesday, 6th.—Got a most helpful view of our King, how the sway of His sceptre extends to the simplest thing that concerns us. His heart and hand together care for everything of His children. 'Not a hair of your head,' not a breathing of prayer despised.

Thursday, 14th.—Greatly strengthened by hearing how more than a year after his death the prayers of George Mills are manifestly begun to be answered at his old field of labour, where he saw little while living. A word to us ministers.

Sept. 11th.—I see distinctly that my Lord is teaching me to 'glory in my infirmities,' and to be willing to be set aside. My voice fails; some of my people, specially the younger part, going elsewhere; my class melts away. Some very mortifying cases of ingratitude on the part of some; my influence with brethren manifestly declines—all this is saying, 'He must increase, but I must decrease;' and thus I am prepared by Him, whose 'way is perfect,' for finishing my ministry, and removing to the service within the veil. But I have some cases of peculiar blessing to set over against these discouragements. I have been trying to set down elsewhere some of these. I know 'He doeth all things well.'

Saturday.—Only *three* young communicants came last night to begin my class. I have had no anxious ones coming to my house for many months. They go to meetings to be spoken to there. I have been musing upon Paul left alone in his last days; 'all men forsook me;' and upon John the Baptist left in prison without a visit from his Lord. Surely, in those two cases, evidently it was the 'thorn in the flesh' to prevent reliance on any past favour.

Letters from time to time telling of blessing from what I have written have been cheering to me, and meeting with God's people who are built up by my preaching. All else I must consider as discipline, and will seek to 'glory in infirmities.'

At his annual congregational meeting this year, Dr. Bonar touchingly referred to his age and growing weakness. 'Some of you,' he said, 'don't hear me very well now. I think there may be something that may be a sermon to you even in the *sight* of an old minister who has for over fifty years been preaching the Gospel, and has found it *perfectly satisfying*, and has no desire to change it. If an angel from heaven were to tell him another way would be better, he would say, "Get thee behind me, Satan."'

Sabbath, 21st.—My very soul has been pained and distressed by clearly perceiving that very, very few souls have been awakened under my preaching for some time. The work among us is at a stand, except that some of God's people are growing in grace.

Tuesday, 23rd.—Last night another died in the Lord most peacefully, after long illness, Tennant Sloan. To-day got some heart-searching lessons at the meeting for deepening spiritual life. Myself was helped to speak solemnly, with some impression, though before-hand weak and confused.

Oct. 14th.—Ever memorable. This time twenty-six years ago, what a night to be remembered! And now another change may soon come. A Committee of our Deacons' Court arranged with me to-night the matters connected with calling a colleague. I read with them Num. xxvii. 15, 18, and prayed with thanksgiving, and the business went on pleasantly.

Sabbath, 19th.—Some felt the Action Sermon—'well pleased for His righteousness' sake'—to be wonderfully impressive. I myself got blessing all the day. Three old friends took part, Dr. Laughton, Dr. Baxter, Mr. Pinkerton [Kilwinning]. The people at all the services seem to have found peculiar pasture. My people thought I was specially helped, and that my voice had got back its power so far. If so, it is the answer to prayer I have been sending up.

Sabbath, Nov. 30th.—Sometimes, as this morning, I get most painful discoveries of my soul's barrenness and coldness, when I awake and find myself without any real compassion for souls; without any real burning zeal for God's glory; with very shallow and poor apprehension of the doctrines I preach, at no time more than when I lie meditating on Sabbath morning, before rising, do I feel humbled and almost alarmed. I wonder if this is the Lord's way of emptying me of self, before He sends me forth to minister? And all this when so many labourers around me have been removed, and so many intimations given to me that I need not be surprised if I be the next. The blood that takes away all guilt, the obedience that covers me with merit, O how precious! And the Holy Spirit's work within makes my soul a temple!

Sabbath, Dec. 28th.—Have had two or three inquirers in the past week; very interesting. Some other tokens of the Lord's gracious answers to my prayers. This is the last Sabbath of the year; very solemn to be drawing nearer, and nearer, and nearer to the great ' *Eternity.*'

Saturday, 24th Jan. 1891.—It was very solemn to me on Thursday to stand looking toward the Braid Hill, near Morningside, Edinburgh, at the foundation of Mr. Salmond's Church there. The days of youth when we so often passed this way on our walks, with fancies of what the future might be, so unlike in many ways to the reality! and how few companions of these days now remain! I am struck to the heart often with wonder that I have so little communion with Christ.

Saturday, Feb. 7th—Much humbled in reviewing my ministry to find how many of the young men of my congregation have been to this day unconverted. O Lord, shall their blood be upon me in any sense? I tried to set a full Christ before them always, but I fear that I failed to wrestle in prayer on their behalf. It is a sore fact in my ministry.

Saturday, March 28th.—I have been thinking of myself as one of the redeemed ; and as such I am just like one drop in the River of Life, altogether like thousands and thousands of others, but not higher than any one of them. I like to think of myself thus rather than as a mote in the sunbeam, for the river's drops have much clearness in them, and the distinction of those that have 'turned many to righteousness' will be this, they will be the drops nearest the bank where the Lord stands, and may from time to time touch His feet.

April 12th.—Just finished what may be my last literary work, an edition of *Samuel Rutherford's Letters.* Got much from it to my own soul all the time ; the love of Christ that filled his heart throws out its sparks as we read.

Friday, May 29th.—Spared to another birthday! I begin my eighty-second year to-day. Scarcely any of my early companions in study and in the ministry left in the field. I preached on '*Death—ours*' last Sabbath, led by many circumstances to think upon it as not unlikely to come soon. For it has presented itself to me continually as just like a busy and tired man at the close of the day becoming sleepy, and ere ever he is aware finding himself in the region of rest, with Christ in the midst!¹ Of late I have had many answers to special petitions, and I have found thereby my fellowship with Jesus the Intercessor greatly helped.

June 11*th.*—Last night at a congregational meeting Mr. D. M. M'Intyre was chosen as my colleague. I do rejoice in this, and only hope that nothing will hinder his coming to us.

Sabbath, 14*th.*—In various ways I feel with the Baptist ἐμὲ δὲ ἐλαττοῦσθαι, 'I must decrease.' Old friends away, my voice fails, so that strangers do not hear me or come to hear me ; but never was Christ more fully to me a portion and a refuge. The weaning from earth is going on, I feel, but I long for deeper communion, and more continual.

Aberdeenshire, Tuesday, July 7*th.*—Have been at Crimmond, and Brucklay [Aberdeenshire], where I met with people who remember M'Cheyne's visit. In coming away, got a telegram telling of my brother John's death. He was in his eighty-ninth year, and was taken away most gently ; really like ἐκοιμήθη. I am now the only one left of our family. My father, mother, sisters and brothers, all gone before me (six brothers, four sisters). I hope to meet them all in the kingdom, but meanwhile it is very solemnizing to be left thus alone. There may be some purpose of the Lord with me, which I do not see ; but I will be satisfied with this, viz., that it is the Lord that will work out His own plan through me.

Greenock, Sabbath, 12*th.*—Spent the day in the house with the family and a few friends. In the forenoon I gave them notes of some of my brother's preaching

¹ It is remarkable how often he spoke of death in this way, and how his anticipations were fulfilled. More than one friend remembers hearing him say ' I should like to die this way. I shall preach on Sabbath, take the Prayer-Meeting on Wednesday, and on Thursday night people will be going about saying, ' Do you know that Dr. Bonar is dead !'

forty years ago, and in the evening gave an address to them from Num. xx., the death of Aaron.

Wednesday, 22nd.—Have been a week here at Fortingall. Heard to-day that Mr. Sinclair, minister of Kenmore, who translated the *Memoir of M'Cheyne* into Gaelic, received more than one letter telling that it had been blessed to the reader.

Tuesday, 28th.—Found a quiet time to pray for my elected colleague's decision and the Presbytery's.

From Fortingall Dr. Bonar wrote to Mr. M'Intyre in prospect of his coming to Glasgow, and in his letter refers to the death of his brother, Dr. John Bonar of Greenock.

TO REV. D. M. M'INTYRE.

'*Fortingall, near Aberfeldy*.
15*th July* 1891.

'MY DEAR MR. M'INTYRE,—We continue praying that you may be sent to us "in the fulness of the blessing of the Gospel of Christ." At this season we are a somewhat scattered people, so many go down the Clyde, or off to some other part of the country for change and recreation.

'My brother John at Greenock was taken from us last week in his eighty-ninth year. He was much interested in your coming to us, and would have given you a hearty welcome, but it seemed good to the Lord to call him home. His end was very peaceful and gentle—no pain, simply weakness and old age. He really (as Acts vii. 60 expresses it) ἐκοιμήθη.

'We are in great hope that Mr. Spurgeon may yet be spared. He may not be able to preach or write, but (higher still?) would he not intercede upon the top of Rephidim, joining the company of Moses, Aaron, and Hur, whose prayers and faith brought down victory to the fighters below?

'Do not think that we are indifferent to your trial in prospect of leaving an attached and prayerful flock. I passed through such a trial when I left Collace for Glasgow. But I have never for a moment regretted it, though no minister could have parted from a more affectionate people. It was in order to win more

souls that I left them, and the Lord gave me what I sought.   O
what a prospect, "joy and crown of rejoicing in the presence of
the Lord Jesus at His Coming!" in the midst of "the children
whom He has given us."'

Saturday, Aug. 15th.—Asked to help in sending a
supply of my *Visitor's Text-Book*, translated into
Samoan by Dr. Turner.

Friday, 21st.—Was gladdened to-day by finding that
Mr. M'Intyre had been led into fulness of the Gospel by
my preaching.   And God is giving me many encouraging tokens.   A young woman, who had not been in
church for some weeks, has been awakened by a text.
Was not this in answer to the prayers we have been
sending up for the Spirit to work among the people
here?

Friday, Sept. 25th.—Home again.   Last night the
Induction Services.   Mr. M'Intyre is now among us,
all settled happily.   It was this week fifty-two years
ago that I was set apart for the ministry in Collace,
and now I have arrived at a new stage of my journey,
the last stage of it.   O what a comfort to me that, if
I be soon called away, my successor will be a man
of God, most earnest to do faithfully the whole work
of the ministry, and holding fast the old truth, the
everlasting Gospel.   Many prayers have been answered,
and many more prayers are going up, here and elsewhere, for me and my beloved people.   Lord, hear!
Yesterday and to-day I have had some glimpses
within the veil, as if to prepare me more for what may
now soon come.   It is very solemn to find myself near
the threshold of Eternity, my ministry nearly done, and
my long life coming to its close.   Never was Christ to
me more precious than He is now.

Sabbath, Nov. 15th.—Have been feeling that word,
'Despise not the chastening of the Lord;' making light

of insignificant trials and vexations. There is a message in the lesser as well as greater.

Sabbath, Dec. 6th.—To-day our anniversary, my soul was drawn out toward my people in regard to our easy indifference, when we think of, and read of, the unsaved, not least the millions and millions among the nations. In the evening my heart was sore, very sore and sad : I have been partaker in this neglect, I fear. I must, through grace, never more let a day pass in which I have not called on the Lord to pour out His Spirit upon us, and upon the nations abroad, wherever the Gospel is preached. This is the least return I can make for the wonderful kindness of the Lord to me and my people, these thirty-five years !

Thursday, 21st January 1892.—Yesterday memorable because of the funeral of the prince (the Duke of Clarence), all the nation feeling it as a calamity. But in another way yesterday was memorable (like ' the year that King Uzziah died ') ; we had a remarkable meeting with Moody and Sankey at Edinburgh, and a day of prayer for the Holy Spirit. We were seeking that like Isaiah vi. ministers especially, but also all God's people, might be visited by the outpouring of the Spirit. This is our Communion week. The Lord helped me greatly yesterday at Edinburgh when called upon quite unexpectedly to take an overflow meeting. It was a time of great blessing.

Saturday, February 6th.—This week very memorable because of Spurgeon's death. Another Psalm xii. 1 cry. There is among us some breathing of the Spirit, but it is at present chiefly under Mr. M'Intyre and his helpers, I fear. As for me, I can see these things in myself : (1) unwatchfulness in using privileges, (2) a kind of sorrow, chagrin, because I am not more used, and (3) a trifling with souls in my hasty preparation for the pulpit.

It is a time of John iii. 30, ἐμὲ δὲ ἐλαττοῦσθαι.   These four lines have been running through my mind :

> 'That Thou shouldst think so much on me,
>   Being the God Thou art,
> Is darkness to my intellect,
>   But *sunshine* to my heart.'

But I have been saying to myself, 'What, are you like Elijah, or like Jonah, displeased at God's ways ? '

Sabbath, 21*st.*—Two more of our ministers taken away. Have been passing within the veil in my thoughts, and fancying the meeting I may soon have with these and others, and especially how, when we sit at the Table there, reclining, like John, on Christ's bosom, we may by a look and a desire convey to Christ our question, while He sends back the answer by a secret touch and by a look.   At another time, when the scene is Rev. vii., we shall personally, each of us in turn, converse with the King, and be taught by Him, etc.

March 10*th.*—Considerable movement under Moody and M'Neill. We find also in our congregation, in our district, souls saved.   The meeting to-day has been remarkable : especially the evening one, when 4000 persons filled the place, and all seemed so attentive. ' Awake, awake, O arm of the Lord ' is our cry.   It was a most fascinating sight, that great multitude of people so eagerly listening to the Word.   This is the third great wave of revival in my life.

May 9*th.*—Have been humbled, and have seen myself dreadfully behind in real love to the Lord, and in the blessing and apprehension of His love to us, as stated in John iii. 16.   My soul was in a state of pain to-day because of this discovery of my terrible shortcóming. It may be the Lord is preparing me for more usefulness.   I know that I must 'decrease.'

Saturday, 28*th.*—To-morrow will be the anniversary

of my birthday, and as I read this morning Deut. ii. 7,
'The Lord thy God hath blessed thee in all the works
of thy hand : He knoweth thy walking through this
great wilderness : these *forty years* the Lord thy God
hath been with thee ; thou hast lacked nothing.' As I
read this, I said, 'Yes, not forty only, but *eighty-two
years*, more than twice that time ! לֹא חָסַרְתָּ דָּבָר, for since
the year 1830, when I first knew that He had found
me, I can say, 'The Lord thy God has been with
me,' יְהוָה אֱלֹהֶיךָ עִמָּךְ.   My son James picked up for me
the other day a fine old copy of Richard Baxter's *Dying
Thoughts*, which has reached me to-day, as if thereby
the Lord would send me a message to have my lamp
burning and my loins girt.

On receiving this book he wrote to his son :—

'*Glasgow*, 28*th May* 1892.

'MY DEAR JAMES,—It was very mindful of you to look forward
to my *eighty-second year*, and to send me such an appropriate book.
Yes, if spared till to-morrow, I shall have finished the eighty-second
year of my pilgrimage.   When I read the other day that verse in
Deut. ii. 7 : "The Lord thy God hath blessed thee in all the works
of thy hand : *these forty years He hath been with thee*, thou hast
lacked nothing," I said to myself, "these *eighty and two years* He
has been with me !" twice the time mentioned there, and I can
truly say, "The Lord my God has been with me.   I have lacked
nothing."   More than that, He has given me "that blessed hope,"
the prospect of being for ever in the kingdom with Him who has
redeemed me by His blood.

'My dear James, it was in the year 1830 that I found the
Saviour, or rather that He found me and "laid me on His
shoulders rejoicing," and I have never parted company with Him
all these sixty-two years.   Christ the Saviour has been to me my
true portion, my heaven begun ; and my earnest prayer and desire
for you and Mary and little Marjory, will always be that you may
each find not only all I ever found in Christ, but a hundredfold
more every year !—Your affectionate father,

'ANDREW A. BONAR.'

On the 26th of September he wrote again to his son on his birthday :—

'MY DEAR JAMES,—Another birthday so soon! Saturday was your sister Mary's birthday, and to-day is yours. *"Forty years!"* Moses would have said (Deut. ii. 7), "The Lord thy God hath blessed thee in all the works of thy hand : He knoweth thy walking through this great wilderness : these *forty* years the Lord thy God hath been with thee ; thou hast lacked nothing." Mary and you must tell this to little Marjory and teach her to sing Psalm ciii.

'I wish I had something worth sending on such an occasion. At any rate I send up my prayers in your behalf to the great Intercessor.

'We are all well, and all unite in most affectionate greetings to you all.—Your poor, old, frail, but affectionate father,
'ANDREW A. BONAR.'

Another little birthday note to one of his daughters, though written in a former year, may come in appropriately here :—

TO HIS DAUGHTER JANIE.

'*Glasgow, 17th June* 1873.
Eve before Waterloo.

'MY DEAR JANIE,—I hope this will find you well on your birthday. You were born on a day memorable for victory. May you have new victories to celebrate every returning year. Your Captain is the Lord Jesus, 'the Captain of Salvation.' Your flag or ensign has this inscribed on it—

"Jehovah-Nissi."

And the speech which your Captain makes to you has this for its sum and substance—

"Be of good cheer, I have overcome the world."

'The various medals you will get as the memorials of your battles and victories are mentioned in Rev. ii. and iii., with this superscription on each : "To him that overcometh ;" and on the other side, pictures of the "Tree of Life," "Hidden Manna," "White Stone," "A Throne," etc.

'Many "Waterloo" days and years to you, dear Janie.—Your affectionate father,   ANDREW A. BONAR.'

July 20th.—Have been now some days at Portpatrick. I have taken time to go back upon former days, and have learned to praise the Lord more, and to seek that Christ may be more than ever yet my chief joy.

August 1st.—O that I may preach a hundred times more fully and gladly concerning Christ Himself and all His righteousness. I turned to read the Memoir of dear Dr. Somerville, and found Christ in every page. Blessed be God for such a friend as he was, and for all the grace given to him.

Wednesday, 3rd.—That verse in Romans viii. 26 may well afford us great joy, for it tells that, apart from our direct prayers, the yearning we feel toward the unsaved, and the sorrow we carry about with us even when engaged in other things, are understood by the Holy Spirit, who stirs up our heart in these 'groanings that cannot be uttered,' and Christ takes them up to His Father as strong cries and prayers.

Tuesday, 16th.—Got yesterday for a moment a view of God's love that melted me and drew me. O that I had this always! Much in sympathy with Richard Baxter's *Dying Thoughts*, which this week have been much in my thoughts.

Sabbath, 28th.—A blessed day because of prayer answered. Open-air services.

Sept. 15th.—Perth Conference. Speaking near the close I referred to the thirty years of its existence, and the very few that now are with us. We tried to get a glimpse of the waiting company on the other side, in the manner of Toplady, who sings—

> 'Saints in glory perfect made
> Wait thy passage through the shade,
> Ardent for thy coming o'er
> See, they throng the blissful shore.

Perhaps by another year I may have gone in among them.

Sabbath, October 2nd.—Some blessing from the Convention for Deepening of Spiritual Life ; and to-day felt as if listening to Paul, when hearing Warszawiak telling of 'the glory of God in the face of Jesus.'

Saturday, 22nd.—Have been hearing how Spurgeon frequently through the last days of his life spoke of not caring to fall asleep, because he had such fellowship with the Lord Jesus as he lay awake.

Tuesday Evening, Nov. 1st.—Last week another of our most devoted brethren has been called home, Andrew Inglis, of Dudhope, Dundee. Passed away quietly and most unexpectedly in his sleep. O what does the Lord say by this to me who am left a little longer? I am asked to preach his funeral sermon next Sabbath, as I have done for not a few of my brethren whom I hope to meet with soon in glory. Why am I spared when so many have been called away? I have been going over the names of at least *nine*—Cormick, M'Cheyne, Milne, Joseph Wilson, Joseph Davidson, Manson, Armstrong, Somerville, Inglis. On each of these occasions I have been called upon to speak to the congregations.

December 4th.—Anniversary of opening of our church. I had something of shame before God, humiliation, and the feeling, not of ' I must decrease,' but of this having come, ' *I have decreased.*' So very much of self has been in all my ministry, so very little of Christ's compassion for souls. Testing myself even by family worship I can discover real backsliding ; for it has been often a service without earnestness, without delight, almost a form.

Was glad to hear of one soul at any rate who got into the kingdom while I was speaking at last Communion. This week there have been six or eight conversions coming to our knowledge, as if the Lord meant to mark this anniversary. Very solemn.

Tuesday, 6th.—I find that just at the hour when I

was deeply exercised in prayer on Sabbath night, Mr. M'Intyre felt a remarkable impression in the Mission Hall, though he was not speaking anything but the plain truths of salvation.

This is the last entry in the Diary, and it may be interesting to read a letter written that same evening to Mr. M'Intyre :—

TO REV. D. M. M'INTYRE.

'*20 India Street, Tuesday Evening.*

'MY DEAR MR. M'INTYRE,—I am keeping at home to-night, but am with you in spirit. I have been told by more than one of the peculiar solemnity of the Sabbath evening meeting and of the undoubted impression in the case of six or eight of those present.

'Might you not go again on Sabbath next without intimating yourself?

'Thanks for your note to-day. When at home last Sabbath evening I felt for about an hour an unusual weight on my mind that led me to special prayer for the Spirit's working. I trust these are tokens of the Lord's presence among us—" a movement in the top of the mulberry trees."—Yours in the Lord,

'ANDREW A. BONAR.'

Shortly before he had written a note to his little grand-daughter in London, and the letter following to his grand-nephew at school, must have been one of the last he ever wrote :—

TO HIS LITTLE GRANDDAUGHTER.

'*Glasgow, 25th Nov.* 1892.

'DEAREST MARJORY,—This is grandpapa's answer to your letter which you kindly wrote to him :

'" May'st thou live to know and fear Him,
    Serve and love Him all thy days ;
Then go stand for ever near Him,
    See His face and sing His praise."

'Give my love to papa and mamma, and bid them look at the beautiful pictures on the next page.—Your affectionate grandpapa,

'ANDREW A. BONAR.'

TO HIS GRANDNEPHEW, HORACE DODDS.

' Glasgow, 28th Dec. 1892.

'My dear Horace,—I have been thinking of you and speaking of you, for cousin Janie is going to Nile Grove for two days. You seem to be getting a long holiday at this season. Improve the time by reading some general literature, and some such book as I send with this long epistle.[1] I am glad you like the place. Like ourselves here you seem to have intense frost, that sends us to the fireside—too much, perhaps—and makes us lazy in rising at morning.

' Dear Horace, here is the rule given us for our everyday life by Christ Himself : " *seek first* the kingdom of God—other things shall be added." I knew [this] youth, whose life was brief but busy, always kind, and cheerful, and happy ; for he was indeed a disciple who found delight, day by day, in Christ's fellowship.

'You have the advantage that not many boys have, viz., *the prayers of father and grandfather in your behalf still to be answered.*—Believe me, my dear Horace, your affectionate uncle,

'Andrew A. Bonar.'

On Sabbath, the 25th of December, Dr. Bonar preached a Christmas sermon on Luke ii. with more than usual vigour and animation. After service he took part in the little prayer-meeting which was always held in the session-house, and went over the subject again with great interest, saying as the meeting broke up, '*Next* Sabbath each of you must bring a promise for the New Year.' It was noticed how he stopped some of the people as they left church that afternoon, and spoke an earnest and solemn word as they passed him. The days that followed were days of fog and intense cold, but he still continued his afternoon visiting. On Tuesday evening he went with his daughter, Mrs. Oatts, to Mr. John Anderson's Bible-lecture in the Christian Institute, and closed the meeting with prayer. On Wednesday he visited as usual in the afternoon till half-past four, and was present at his prayer-meeting in the church in the evening, where many noticed the earnest-

---

[1] *A Bright Sunset: Recollections of the Last Days of a Young Football Player.*

ness of his prayers, specially in regard to the Watch-night Service, which was to be held on the coming Saturday night in the Mission Hall. On leaving the church he said to his church-officer, who was in the habit of calling at the manse every morning, 'You need not call to-morrow, I am going to give you a holiday.' He went to bed well, apparently, and bright and happy as usual, but woke next morning with a chill, and was ill all day. On Friday, 30th Dec., he was no better, and continued to grow gradually weaker, sinking very rapidly as night approached. His mind was clear, and full of his much-loved work. In the morning he spoke of several things to be attended to on the coming Sabbath, and remembered that a collection for the Jewish mission was to be taken that day. He often put his hand to his head, but when asked if he were suffering, he said, 'No, only very tired.' About six o'clock he called his family all together for family worship beside his bed. After singing Psalm xxiii., which he tried to join in as usual, Mr. Oatts read Psalm lxii. and was just beginning to pray, when Dr. Bonar folded his hands, and in a clear, distinct voice began his evening prayer, taking up the words of the Psalm, 'O Lord, Thou art *our* Rock and *our* defence.' 'Thou wilt be our Sun and Shield.'[1] Then followed confession of sin and prayer for acceptance 'through the merits of the Great Intercessor,' with a committal of us all to the Lord's care for the coming night. As he finished he bade each of his children 'good-night,' and composed himself as if to sleep. He did not speak of dying; he did not say 'good-bye.' The only words he spoke that seemed to show he knew that death might be near, were when the doctor came about nine o'clock and asked him how he felt. He looked at him, and said with great solemnity, 'We never know how our ministry will end. I have had a long life of perfect health.' To those around him he said nothing

---

[1] These words of Psalm lxxxiv. had evidently been in his thoughts for some time, for in his Bible were found notes upon them, in preparation for a sermon or address.

of death. He was in the dark valley and did not know it. Living or dying, he was the Lord's, and He was with him.

For a time his weakness and restlessness were very great, then he grew more quiet, and lay gently breathing his life away. At half-past ten he closed his eyes and fell asleep so quietly that those round his bed hardly knew when life was gone. A look of inexpressible peace, almost of delighted surprise, rested on his face, as if he had suddenly and unexpectedly found himself in the presence of his much-loved Lord and Master, with whom he had been walking all these years on earth, and who now 'received him into glory.'

On Wednesday, the 4th of January 1893, men and women and little children who loved him followed through the snow to Sighthill Cemetery, where he was laid to rest beside his wife and his little boy. Within sight of the great city where so long he lived and laboured, he lies waiting for the day of 'our gathering together unto Him'—that day for which he longed and prayed.

'We bless Thee for the quiet rest Thy servant taketh now,
We bless Thee for his blessedness and for his crownèd brow.
For every weary step he trod in faithful following Thee,
And for the good fight foughten well, and closed right valiantly.'

List of Dr. Bonar's Works Referred to in his Diary

	DIARY.
NARRATIVE OF A MISSION TO THE JEWS.—	7th March 1842.
MEMOIR OF REV. R. M. M'CHEYNE.—	23rd Dec. 1843.
COMMENTARY ON THE BOOK OF LEVITICUS.—	2nd Oct. 1845.
REDEMPTION DRAWING NIGH.—	26th Sept. 1847.
THE GOSPEL POINTING TO THE PERSON OF CHRIST.—	18th Sept. 1852.
THE OLD GOSPEL WAY.—	7th Sept. 1853.
NETTLETON AND HIS LABOURS.—	17th Sept. 1854.
THE VISITOR'S BOOK OF TEXTS.—	20th Sept. 1855.
CHRIST AND HIS CHURCH IN THE BOOK OF PSALMS.—	4th May 1859.
MEMOIR OF REV. DAVID SANDEMAN.—	July 1860.
MEMORIALS OF REV. J. ALLAN.—	31st Dec. 1860.
RUTHERFORD'S LETTERS.—	17th Oct. 1862.
,, ,, (new edition).	12th April 1891.
PALESTINE FOR THE YOUNG.—	20th Sept. 1865.
THE BROOK BESOR.—	13th April 1879
SCOTS WORTHIES (new edition).—	13th April 1879.
LIFE OF REV. JAMES SCOTT.—	12th Sept. 1885.

REMINISCENCES OF HIS LIFE

The succeeding chapters of this book have been written to bring out in detail some parts of our father's life and character, to show, not a perfect man, but one who more than most around him bore on his forehead the impress of holiness. As they read, his old hearers and those who remember his life as portrayed in these pages will recall the words of the beloved Apostle; 'And now, little children, abide in Him; that, when He shall appear, we may have confidence, and not be ashamed before Him at His coming.'

Marjory Bonar

Glasgow, October 1895

CHAPTER VIII

A Minister of Christ

THE events of a ministry are not easily recalled after the lapse of sixty years. Two generations have passed away since the days when Andrew Bonar went in and out among the people of Jedburgh, but his name lingers in and around the old town, for 'the memory of the just is blessed.' There are still some who remember that their father or their mother belonged to 'Mr. Bonar's class.' It was in Jedburgh, in 1835, that he preached his first sermon, after passing through the regular course of study in the Divinity Hall of Edinburgh. There his first ministerial experiences were gained. The visitation of the prisoners in the jail gave him an insight into the evil of the human heart which he never forgot;[1] and his intercourse with Mr. Purves, his senior minister and friend, seems to have been the means of stimulating him in the study of prophetic truth, as well as in other ways. He never forgot those to whom he had ministered in Jedburgh. When staying at Hawick in 1878, he spent a day along with the Rev. Duncan Stewart in revisiting his old field of labour. Some who professed to have come to Christ during his ministry there were dear to him, and he spent a great part of the afternoon in climbing stairs and finding them out. ' He remembered every one

---

[1] ' An absent God and a present Devil ' was one prisoner's account of her experience in the jail.

well, their name, their spiritual history, etc. Some had not shone for Christ so brightly as they might have done, but he did not pass them by. He had a word for each as he thought they needed. He seemed to have far greater delight in looking after these sheep that afternoon than in viewing the pleasant scenery round Jedburgh.'

One of his reminiscences of the people was a story of a half-witted man whom he used to visit. This poor man had found Christ and had learned to rejoice in the thought of His return to earth. He went to Edinburgh on a visit, and came home much dissatisfied with the ministers. When asked why, he said, ' Oh, they a' flee wi' ae wing ! ' They preached Christ's First, but not His Second Coming.

During his work as missionary in St. George's, Edinburgh, to which he removed at the close of 1836, Mr. Bonar's interest in the Jews was quickened by contact with several of them both in public and private. Hardly had he begun to feel at home in his first charge at Collace when he was appointed one of the four who formed a deputation in the year 1839 from the General Assembly of the Church of Scotland to the Land of Israel. This event gave a colour to all his future ministry. A stone from Mount Sinai, an olive-leaf from Gethsemane, a shell from the shores of the Lake of Galilee, a piece of Desert shittim-wood, were texts by which he made the scenes and incidents of the Bible real and living, and from which he preached the love and faithfulness of ' that same Jesus ' whose feet would one day stand again upon Mount Olivet.

A beautiful incident, which he often related, occurred at Kelso when Mr. Bonar was on a visit to his brother Horatius. He was addressing a meeting there, and, when showing some ears of barley which he had plucked on Mount Zion, he said, 'If God keeps His threatenings so faithfully (Micah iii. 12), will He not keep His promises?' Next day, an old woman sent for him, and, as soon as he entered her house, she held up her hands and exclaimed, 'Oh, those ears of barley! those ears of barley!' He asked her what she meant, and she said she had just thought when he was speaking the night before that if God kept His word about ears of barley, would He not keep it about the salvation of a soul? And all her doubts fled.

The parish of Collace in Perthshire, where Mr. Bonar was ordained in 1838, lies at the foot of the hill of Dunsinnane, where once stood Macbeth's Castle, and from which there is a wide view over several counties of Scotland. The associations of the place were all in harmony with the young minister's love for everything of antiquarian interest. On the hill of Bandirran, close by Dunsinnane, are remains of a Druidic circle. A farm in the neighbourhood bears the name of Balmalcolm, and not far off is the hamlet of Cairnbeddie—'the cairn of Macbeth.' Tradition says that a green mound on the farm of Lawton is the spot where Macbeth used to administer justice. Over the doorway of the Dunsinnane burying-place in Collace churchyard is a small Saxon arch, said to have been taken from the little village of Thorngreen,[1] where once stood a house adorned by the stones of Macbeth's Castle.[2] The first Protestant minister of Collace was the Rev. James Anderson, who was ordained to the ministry of that parish in the sixteenth century. He wrote a poem entitled 'The Winter Night,'—a warning to his flock against Popery,—and dedicated it to John Erskine of

[1] Thorngreen, Sachar, and Kinrossie, were little villages in the parish of Collace.

[2] These details are extracted from a note-book in which Dr. Bonar has collected everything of interest connected with Collace.

Dun. When Mr. Bonar came to the parish, the old minister to whom he acted as colleague had already been there for nearly fifty years, but there was only one woman who was known to have received any good from his ministry.   He was very much afraid of some one coming who would preach the 'new doctrines.'   Mr. Bonar was presented to the parish through the influence of Mr. Nairne of Dunsinnane, who continued always a true friend to him and to the cause of the Free Church in the neighbourhood.   Mr. Nairne, it is said, asked Mr. M'Cheyne if he would leave Dundee and come to Collace. He said 'No ; but I will tell you of a much better man,' and named his friend Andrew Bonar.   On hearing of his presentation to the parish, Mr. M'Cheyne wrote to him :—

'*Dundee*, 17*th July* 1838.

'MY DEAR ANDREW,—I have several times been on the very point of writing you to wish you joy of your presentation to the church of Collace. May it indeed be a gift from His hand who hath done and will do all things well. There are many tokens for good about it, so that you must feel yourself very much called by God. "Before I formed thee in the belly I knew thee ; and before thou camest forth out of the womb I sanctified thee, a prophet unto the nations." "Paul an apostle, not of man, neither by man." "*Certainly* I will be with thee, and this shall be a token unto thee that I have sent thee." All these are sweet words, for just as there is no greater misery than to run unsent, of our own private motion or self-esteem, so there is no greater joy than to be called of God as was Aaron, to receive not only "grace," but "apostleship."

'Now then, dear Andrew, we are ambassadors for Christ, as though God did beseech men by us. We, then, as fellow-workers with God must beseech men not to receive the grace of God in vain. May God count you faithful, putting you into the ministry, and may the arms of your hands be made strong by the hands of the mighty God of Jacob. For a while you were like Moses. It "came into your heart" to be a minister of God's Word to deliver Israel out of Egypt, for you supposed that your brethren would have understood how that by your hand God would deliver souls.

But they understood not, and so you fled to the land of Midian and called your name " Gershom," for you said " I am a stranger here." But when the set time was expired the Angel Jehovah of the Bush that burned, yet was not consumed, has met thee in the wilderness—" and *now*, come, I will send thee into Egypt." Dear Andrew, forgive thy younger brother speaking to thee as if he were an elder—one that must ever sit at thy feet and walk in thy footsteps, following thee in as far as thou followest Christ. God has also visited your friends with sore bereavement, to remind you that it is no permanent connection you are going to form,—that you must have the same faith as Abraham and Isaac and Jacob, who all dwelt in tents in the land of promise, declaring plainly that they seek a country. . . . I hear of your preaching, and am refreshed by the very echo of it. . . . My people have a great attachment to you. . . . I long to know all your feelings. I heard from Mr. Nairne, who says that all the godly people of the country-side are rejoicing. I long to have an open door to preach in these rural retreats. May the Lord appear to you saying, " Fear not, for I am with thee—for I have much people in this parish." Good-bye. May He keep you in perfect peace. Peace upon Israel.—Yours affectionately, ROBERT MURRAY M'CHEYNE.'

It is interesting to find Mr. M'Cheyne in the same year giving his friend kindly advice about his style of preaching and how to improve it : ' Dear Andrew, study to express yourself very clearly. I sometimes observe obscurity of expression. Form your sentences very regularly. . . . It sometimes strikes me you begin a sentence before you know where you are to end it, or what is to come in at the end.'

Once, when referring to the first sermon he ever preached, Mr. Bonar said, ' In looking over my notes I find I made a great mistake. I had no " heads." When we are young men we are apt to think this is the right way to preach—going straight on from topic to topic ; but the hearers need pegs on which to hang the truth.'

The people were not greatly impressed by his first sermon, and this inclined the old minister the more in his favour. Years after an honest man said to Mr. Bonar, 'It's a gude thing, sir, we didna like ye at first, or we wadna hae had ye noo!'

The country is one of great natural beauty. The village of Collace lies half-hidden among trees and hedgerows in the rich, level lands of Strathmore. To the north the long dark line of the Grampians throws a distant grandeur over the soft Lowland scenery. Near the scattered cottages of the village the square tower of the parish church peeps out from the trees. Dunsinnane House was Mr. Bonar's first home at Collace, and then he came to the Kirkton, an old-fashioned, ivy-covered house by the roadside, close to the church. The garden was separated from the churchyard only by a wall, and one day, not long after their arrival, the servant rushed into the parlour exclaiming, 'Eh, sir, they're buryin' a bairn at the back door!' His sister Christian came with him to this house, and it was a frequent resort of his mother and the rest of the family. The Kirkton is associated with the visits of Robert M'Cheyne, who often rode over from Dundee to give his services at Collace. As he came to the door one wintry day, he said, 'I have been riding all the way to-day through the pure white snow, and that verse has been in my mind all the time, "Wash me, and I shall be whiter than snow."' One of his sayings is still remembered in Collace: 'Bethany was known in Scripture not so much as Bethany, but as "the town of Mary and her sister Martha." I wonder who in this place gives the name by which it is known in heaven? It will not be known there as Collace, but as the town of—perhaps some bedridden believer up in the hills.' While preparing the 'Narrative of a Mission of Inquiry to the Jews,' Mr. M'Cheyne and Mr. Bonar exchanged work for a few weeks, that they might have fewer interruptions in their writing. Some one asked the old minister then how he was getting on with 'that wild man from Dundee'? and his reply was, 'Mr. Bonar is bad enough, but that man is ten times waur!' Of a Sabbath-day during that time Mr. M'Cheyne wrote, 'I preached on "Jesus loved Martha" in the morning. The old minister spoke much on *popular arts, and handling the word of God deceitfully*; but I did not mind. I preached in the afternoon in the church—nearly quite full—on "Give us of your oil."'

Mr. Bonar's old servant used to tell, years afterwards, of Mr. M'Cheyne's last visit to Collace. He preached in the church, and 'the folk were standin' out to the gate, and the windows were pulled down that those outside might hear. Mr. Cormick (of Kirriemuir) spoke first, and then Mr. M'Cheyne preached on "Lest I myself should be a castaway." I had to come awa' after he began, and I could see from the house the kirk lichted up, and oh, I wearied sair for them to come hame! They stayed at the kirk that nicht till eleven. The folk couldna gi'e ower listenin', and Mr. M'Cheyne couldna gi'e ower speakin'. I mind the time when Mr. Bonar couldna get his tea ta'en for folk comin' and speerin' if conversion was true. Oh, to hear Mr. M'Cheyne at prayers in the mornin'! It was as if he could never gi'e ower, he had sae muckle to ask. Ye would hae thocht the very walls would speak again. He used to rise at six on the Sabbath mornin', and go to bed at twelve at night, for he said he likit to have the whole day alone with God.'

A servant-girl, in a house where he stayed, described him as '*deein'* to hae folk converted.' A minister in the north was so impressed with his daily life of holiness that he said, 'He is the most Jesus-like man I ever met with,' and went to his room to weep. Dr. Candlish remarked to Dr. Moody-Stuart, 'I can't understand M'Cheyne; grace seems to be natural to him.'

One or two of Mr. M'Cheyne's letters to Mr. Bonar, both before and after the settlement of the latter at Collace, are full of interest. One is dated, Dundee, 13th September 1836 :—

'MY DEAR ANDREW,—Your kind letter has just found me, and rejoices me much. I have often, often wished to see your face in this the scene of my labours and trials. Indeed, I need much to be refreshed by you, and I do hope that God will give you not a prosperous journey only, but a full heart, that I who tarry at home may share in the spoil. . . . Oh, to be kept lying in the dust while we work for God! I am often given up to feel the desperate wickedness of my heart, and I believe it is all to keep me in the dust. Now, my dear Andrew, be sure to make out your visit to me and refresh me with your presence. . . . On Thursday evening is my prayer-meeting, which you must join us in. I shall be so happy to get a word from you that will encourage me and my people. On Thursday I will take you round my parish. On Friday I will make you write a sermon, on Saturday commit it, and on Sabbath preach it; and you shall have one from me. Do consent to this if you can, and we shall have another from you in the evening. I must not write any more, as it gets late. It quite lightens me to think you are coming. . . .

'And now farewell. "I have many things to write, but I will not with ink and pen write unto thee. But I trust I shall shortly see thee, and we shall speak face to face. Peace be to thee."—Your faithful friend, ROBERT MURRAY M'CHEYNE.

'I subjoin a map that you may find the house where I live; it is about five minutes' walk further west than the church—the westmost lane in Dundee going down to the sea.'

Another was written when Mr. Bonar was working as missionary in Edinburgh, without any prospect of being sent to a sphere of labour of his own.

'*19th January* 1838.

'MY DEAR ANDREW,—I am sorry this is Friday night, or I would have written much more at length. Yet a word may convey my kind wishes to you for this year we have begun, and may remind you of your feeble brother in the north, who needs all the encouragement you have to spare—and specially needs to be carried upon your shoulder and on your breast when you are within the veil. I return you your sermon on "Lord, my heart is not haughty." I had no intention of carrying it away with me when I asked it from you, or would have got your leave first. I hope you did not need it. It has been a sweet word to me, and I have often thought of it. My soul is far from being like a weaned child. I sometimes tremble when I think that afflictions will be needful to wean my soul. . . . You would hear that Mr. Reid is to remain at Chapelshade. . . . Dear Andrew, God is keeping you in the hollow of His hand. When a warrior begins to fight, he never throws his best dart at the enemy first. He throws some weak arrows among them, just to begin the contest; he keeps his polished shaft for the hottest of the fight. Your day is coming, or, if you be lifted away from the scene of conflict to the land of peace and triumph, we will both adore the Sovereign Father of our Lord Jesus, who loves some so well that He must have them to minister to Himself in praises rather than in conflicts. I send you your tract on the Jews, of which I have made large use. I last night gave the substance of it to my prayer-meeting, and engaged their interest very much in behalf of the dearly-beloved of God's soul. I quite agree with you in thinking them the first object of all missionary exertion, and hope hereafter to devote more and more of my thoughts and prayers to them. . . . Tell me when you will come over and see me and preach to my people. . . . Do write and tell me the meaning of any parts of the Bible. I am very ignorant, and thirst for knowledge of the Word—but most of Jesus Himself, the true Word. May He abide in you—you in Him.—Yours affectionately,   R. M. M'CHEYNE.'

A letter which shows another side of Mr. M'Cheyne's character, is one which he wrote to his doctor, who had refused to send in a bill for his services. Mr. M'Cheyne enclosed his fee, along with these lines:—

'Dear Doctor, I fear you will think me too-merry,
But it strikes me you're making two bites of a cherry.
You know when a patient won't swallow a pill,
You never consult his sweet mouth or his will,

You say, "Take the physic or you may depend on 't
You 'll never get well, come, drink—there 's an end on 't."
Dear Doctor, allow me to borrow a leaf
From your book of prescriptions, commanding and brief.
"Hoc aurum et papyr," mix—pocket—call "Dust !"
And swallow it quickly. Come, Doctor, you must.
I had rather want stipend, want dinner, want tea,
Than my Doctor should ever work wanting his fee.
Forgive this intrusion—and let me remain,
In haste, your affectionate R. M. M'Cheyne.'
        'Dulce est desipere in loco.'

Dundee, April 4, 1838.

Mr. M'Cheyne's early death, though regarded as an irreparable loss to the Church of God, was destined, through the publication of his *Memoir*, to effect perhaps a greater work than his prolonged life could have accomplished. Mr. Bonar's love for him was touchingly apparent in his after-life. The 25th of March was always remembered as the day on which Robert M'Cheyne went home. In 1873 he writes, after a visit to St. Peter's, Dundee, 'There is still some peculiar fragrance in the air round Robert M'Cheyne's tomb!'

When in America in 1881, his thoughts went back to his friend through all the long years since 1843, when looking on scenes of which they had often talked together. He writes :—

Saturday, 20th August 1881.—'How deeply interested would Robert M'Cheyne have been to-day had he been with us ! he who used to speak of this place. It was really strange to me and wonderful that this morning I should be on the way to North-ampton where so much work was done for God in other days. The day was beautiful, everything bathed in sunshine. . . . We came to what was the old street where Jonathan Edwards' house stood. . . . The two great elm-trees in front of the house are remarkable in themselves. It was under these the man of God and his wife used to sit, so that the spot became like the oak of Mamre, God meeting them there ; and in those days the ground all round was a grove of pines where Jonathan Edwards used to walk and pray.'

His thoughts were still dwelling on old memories of his friend, when next day he writes again :—

'Filled with alarm and regret in reviewing the Lord's mercies to me, in using me to write the *Memoir of R. M. M'Cheyne*, for which I am continually receiving thanks from ministers. Why was I commissioned to write that book? How poor have been my returns of thankfulness. Oh, when shall I attain to the same holy sweetness and unction, and when shall I reach the deep fellowship with God which he used to manifest?'

The history of the *Memoir of M'Cheyne* would in itself be enough to fill a volume. The wonderful blessing which has everywhere followed its circulation was always attributed by the author to the prayer offered at the time of its publication ; and is also owing, doubtless, to the prayer which has followed its course ever since.

The members of the Deputation to the Jews in 1839, returned into the midst of scenes of revival in their own land. The blessing reached Collace as well as other places, and the pastor's heart rejoiced to find souls seeking Christ in all parts of his parish. There was great depth and reality in the work of grace, deep conviction of sin, and correspondingly clear apprehension of the way of salvation. Many remarkable conversions occurred among old and young. One man who had been a drunkard was brought to the Saviour and became afterwards an elder in the church, and a consistent follower of Christ. On his death-bed he said, ' I am going to the God of the Bible to enjoy Him. I know that my Redeemer liveth.' Another describing his conversion, said, ' Havena I been stoopid, sir? It was sae simple, just as if I had stoopit down and lifted up a clod at my feet.'

A sawyer, who was busy at his work when the light broke upon him, was so filled with joy that he began to preach to his fellow-workman, and had to cry, 'Lord, keep back some o' the licht, for this poor vessel is not able to contain it.' One who was very anxious dreamed that she saw a wide river rolling between her and Christ. She looked and looked at Him on the other side, and as she looked, she suddenly found herself beside Him! She awoke, and saw the meaning of her dream.

A man in the village of Sachar was so terribly awakened, that for many days he was almost ready in his misery to take away his own life. He became a useful member of the church after his conversion, and his frequent prayer at their prayer-meetings used to be 'Wauken them up, Lord, wauken them up!' A very sad case occurred of a man deeply awakened under William Burns' preaching at Dundee, and for days in great agony of mind. After a time all his concern passed away, and he lived and died in indifference.

Coming out of church one Sabbath, Miss Bonar met an old woman weeping, and in great distress of mind. 'Many of the sermons,' she said, 'had grippit her before, but none had grippit her sae sair as this.' She found peace in believing, and along with some others, began a prayer-meeting in the village of Sachar where she lived. A little company of factory girls used to walk seven miles from Stanley to attend the services at Collace. They had to cross the river Tay on their way, and, when they were returning home late one night, the ferryman refused to take them over, so they lay down cheerfully to sleep among the bushes till the morning.

The thirst for the word of God was very great. Not only did the people walk long distances to hear, but they never seemed to grow tired of listening. One evening, Mr. Milne had come from Perth, and Mr.

Manson from the neighbouring village of Abernyte to take part in a meeting at Collace, and it was agreed that each of them should give a short address. Mr. Milne spoke first, and became so interested in his subject—'a well of water springing up to everlasting life'— that he went on for two hours. The people sat motionless, and, quite unconscious of how long he had spoken, he turned to Mr. Manson as he finished, and said, 'Now, brother, you will say a word!'

When Mr. Bonar came to Collace there were perhaps not more than half a dozen living Christians in the place.[1] From those days of revival the parish began to assume a different aspect even outwardly. Few, if any, idlers were to be seen outside the cottage-doors on a Sabbath day, and family worship was conducted morning and evening in nearly every household. 'Drops from heaven fell' on every side, yet still the pastor longed for more. 'Oh that Collace were full of prayer like Kilsyth! Oh that the church were full of people weeping for sin, and oh that there were needing to be psalms sung to drown the weeping of the people as they get a sight of their sins!'

'It is truly encouraging,' he writes to his brother Horatius, 'to hear of souls awakened, and yet it is also alarming that there should be so few,—alarming to ourselves who preach, since we have a promise. I often feel quite certain that my own prayerlessness is the reason why so few of my people are awakened. The thought fills me with pain, and excites me to a new course of prayer.'

[1] He used often to quote the old rhyme which before those days was not applicable to Collace :

> 'Truth and grace cam' by Collace,
> And by the door o' Dron,
> But the coup and the stoup o' Abernyte
> Mak' mony a merry man.'

'There have been some interesting cases of conversion. But when is the heaven to become black with clouds and winds, and the rain to fall in a Carmel-flood?'

'I rejoice with you,' he writes to Mr. Manson, '[at tidings of revival]. I try my own soul by this test,—can I be as glad at this news as if my own parish had been the scene of these wonders?'

He closes a letter asking Mr. Manson to come and preach, with the words, 'I wish you would bring out with you the trumpet that awakes the dead.'

Dr. Bonar's memory was full of recollections of the preachers and preaching of those times. He used to tell an anecdote of Mr. Burns as an instance of how God overrules for good what seem to us the mistaken impulses of his people. He went one day to Perth to attend a meeting in St. Leonard's, at which Mr. Burns was to preach. When Mr. Bonar arrived at the manse, Mr. Burns exclaimed, 'Oh, this is most providential. I have a strong impression that I should be in Dundee to-night. You and Mr. Milne will take this meeting.' 'But,' they remonstrated, 'you are advertised to preach here.' 'Oh, you two will do it,' he said, and left the room, returning bag in hand to say good-bye. There was nothing for it but that they should go to the church and conduct the meeting. Mr. Bonar gave the first address, and Mr. Milne followed. Some days after, as Mr. Milne was riding to Bridge of Earn, a woman ran out of her house to speak to him. 'Oh, sir,' she said, 'I will never forget Monday night. I was awakened by the first address, and led to Christ by the second!'

Mr. Burns preached one evening in Sachar, and his prayer greatly impressed the people. He asked for the young minister that the Lord would put a sharp sickle in his hand, that he might gather in many souls to Christ, and for the old minister he prayed, 'Lord, bless the old man who has been so long in this parish. May his flesh come again like that of a little child.'

When Dr. Hamilton was minister in the neighbouring village of Abernyte, a man in his parish used to walk over to Collace to church. He apologised for doing so and said, 'It's because Mr. Bonar is no sae learned as you!' A good woman, who used to worship in Abernyte church in Mr. Manson's time, said to a friend one evening, as they walked home from church to her house at the foot of Dunsinnane Hill, 'I wish I had a memory like Mr. Manson.' 'Toots, woman,' was her friend's reply, 'if you were to be a minister you would have a memory like him, but you're no' a minister, and ye dinna need it!' This woman came to live in Perth in her old age, and, when attending the Conference meetings, Mr. Bonar always went to see her. On the last visit he paid to her, she did not know him, and did not even look up when told some one had come to see her. At last he began to speak, and, at the sound of his voice, she started up exclaiming, 'It's my ain auld minister!' and flung her arms round his neck!

After the Disruption of 1843,[1] the Free Church congregation met for some time in a tent near Kinrossie, and many a remarkable scene was witnessed there. People came from miles round to be present at the Communion services. Long after, Dr. Bonar looked back to those times with peculiar tenderness, and often on the morning of the Summer Communion in Finnieston (held on the same day as in Collace), remembered his old flock in the country. 'Our Communion was very sweet,' he writes in June 1843, 'immense crowds of people.

[1] Some one met the old minister after the Disruption and asked how he was getting on. 'Oh fine,' was his reply, 'opposition's the life of trade!'

About sixty of the St. Peter's people came from Dundee. I have got great comfort in my young communicants. Six of them I believe to be really new creatures in Christ Jesus.'

One who used often to hear him preach in those days, and who afterwards became an elder in his church in Finnieston, Mr. J. H. Dickson, has given some recollections of these Communion services. 'My remembrances of Mr. Bonar's ministry in Collace are mostly connected with Communion seasons. There were no conferences then, but, after the great revival of 1840-41, groups of people used to come from the surrounding districts—not because the gospel was not preached in those places, but the new life which the revival brought, made Christians long for the fellowship of these Communion seasons in Perth, Blairgowrie, and Collace. Great blessing was received, and earnest prayer went up for weeks before such seasons. The one most fixed in my memory was held in June after the Disruption. The congregation met in a large canvas tent. The day was bright and sunny. Mr. Bonar's closing address after the Tables was on Song iv. 6 : "Until the day break, and the shadows flee away." He referred to Mr. M'Cheyne as standing on the "mountain of myrrh" till the day break, and, as he pointed to the bread and wine before him as shadows that would flee away, there came a great hush over the congregation, and then the sound of sobbing from the Dundee people who were present, at the mention of their beloved minister's name. Mr. Bonar himself was much affected ; indeed it was a weeping congregation.' Of other such days Mr. Bonar writes :—

'It was a good day yesterday, brother, especially at eveningtide. Mr. Cormick was very lively and solemn, the Supper itself a time to my own soul when I felt oneness with Jesus. . . . When breezes from Lebanon blow, what a world the eternal world appears, and what a Lord is the Lord of glory !'

'Yesterday I felt a little of "abounding grace," and the blessedness of being sure yet to be holy, holy, holy. It seemed a very short day—"the sun hasted to go down," I thought. We would need a *long* eternity, or heaven would be no heaven, it would be so soon over.'

'I rode up to Blairgowrie to the Lord's Supper. I felt that there the gift of God to sinners, and the heart of God to sinners, is so fully and exclusively set forth that the Lord's Table is really the *stereotyping of the Gospel.*'

After a Communion season an elderly woman, who had lately been converted, said, 'I canna say much, but my heart's like a burnin' coal !'

' Chosen not for good in me,
  Wakened up from wrath to flee,
  Hidden in the Saviour's side,
  By the Spirit sanctified.
  Teach me, Lord, on earth to show,
  By my love, how much I owe.'—*R. M. M‘Cheyne.*

CHAPTER IX

The Good Pastor

AMONG the thatched cottages of Kinrossie, with its pretty village green and antique market-cross, stands the Free Church of Collace. Not far distant, on the edge of Dunsinnane wood, is the manse, hidden from view more than it was forty years ago by the growth of trees and hedges. A vine and a fig-tree climb up on either side of the old study window, and over other two windows are carved the Hebrew words, '*He that winneth souls is wise*' and '*For yet a little while, and He that shall come will come and will not tarry.*' The path from the manse through Dunsinnane wood became a spot hallowed by prayer and communion with God. One day a man going along that way heard the sound of voices in the wood, and found Mr. Bonar kneeling there in prayer with two young men. The manse was finished a few months after his marriage in 1848. An old woman in the parish, when Mr. Bonar told her that he was going to be married, remarked with more plainness than politeness, 'Weel, sir, I hope it's a' richt, but we women are awfu' cheats!' This same old woman said of a minister who had come from the other side of the river to preach to them, 'He wasna worth his water-fraucht!' In those days it was no uncommon sight to see one and another in church stand up during the sermon to shake off drowsiness, and sometimes Mrs. Bonar would touch a sleepy hearer with her parasol.

Mr. Bonar thought nothing of preaching twice and then riding several miles in the evening to preach somewhere else, or to visit a sick person. Every Sabbath morning at ten o'clock he conducted a Bible class for young men and women, which was attended with much blessing, and was the means of stirring up many to search the Scriptures, and of leading them to Jesus, the Way, the Truth, and the Life. An old woman, who had learned to love God's Word, said to Mr. Bonar, 'I wonder how God's people get through the Bible, for I am often stopped a whole day at one verse.' A young woman said to him, 'I often wanted to die after I found Christ, for I was afraid of sinning. But one day I remembered Christ's words: "I pray not that Thou shouldst take them out of the world, but that Thou shouldst keep them from the evil that is in the world;" and I don't want to die now.' The experience of another was very peculiar. She was so sorely tried by the Tempter that she went out into the fields alone, hoping to get rid of his evil suggestions. But Satan followed her and told her that the Old Testament was not true. She turned to the New Testament, but he said that was not true either. When she came as far as the Metre Psalms he told her *they* were not true, but she got a little rest at the paraphrase: 'Behold the Saviour on the Cross.' At another time the devil tried to persuade her that there was no God, and that she had no soul. When tempted at last to disbelieve everything, she sat down and told him that the places mentioned in the Bible were real, for Mr. Bonar had seen them when he was in Palestine. But the Tempter said, 'Mr. Bonar is a liar!'

Many interesting incidents occurred in connection with his visitation. He went to see an old bed-ridden man who reminded him of a sermon he had preached ten years before. 'I mind,' the old man said, 'you spoke about the Cave of Adullam. "Do you like the Cave, and do you like the Captain? Then come in— come in—no other condition." My, *it sank into my heart like oil.*' He asked a boy to hold his horse one day, while he went into a cottage. As he was re-mounting, and putting his foot in the stirrup, he turned to the lad and said, 'Do you ever think you have a soul?' The question was never forgotten. Coming home one night from a meeting at Rait, he lost his way, and as he wandered about he said to himself, 'Can I give thanks for this?' In a short time he came to a house, and was just going to the door to ask direction for his way home, when a girl came out and exclaimed, 'Mr. Bonar! you're the very person I want to see.' He found she was in great distress of mind, and was able to give thanks that, in losing his way among the hills, he had been led to find a soul. Returning home late one night from a meeting, he heard of the serious illness of one who had been formerly in his service, and at once had his pony saddled, and rode three miles to see him. After this he continued his visits every day till he recovered. He fixed a certain night for calling on a young married couple, when he was likely to find them both at home. The night came, and with it a storm of wind and rain. They said to each other, 'There will be no minister here to-night,' but, true to his word, the minister appeared at the hour appointed.

One winter evening, when walking to Scone to preach, he overtook a woman on the road, and began to talk to her, giving her a tract when they parted. Some time after, he noticed a widow in church, who waited after service was over, and said to him, 'I am the woman you spoke to that dark night on the road to Scone and never saw. You gave me a tract. My son at home, long ill, had been troubled about himself, and that tract

was the very one for him, and brought light to his
soul. He made me come over from Kinnaird to tell
you.'

It was his habit in the country to rise at six o'clock
in the summer mornings, and seven o'clock in winter.
'You'll be thrashin' your strae the nicht, sir,' was the
remark of one of his people on a Saturday evening, for,
even then, Saturday was carefully set apart for prayer
and preparation for the Lord's Day. His sermons
were not always fully written out, and in the pulpit he
only used little pieces of paper on which the 'heads'
were jotted down in shorthand. When preaching one
day in the tent at Kinrossie, a puff of wind blew away
his notes, and the people had such a horror of sermon-
reading that nobody would lift them up. It is needless
to say the minister continued his sermon without
them.[1]

Mrs. Bonar's letters and his own give bright little
glimpses of their life at Collace. Three children were
born in the manse, and, until after their removal to
Glasgow, death did not cast its shadow over their home.
The first Sabbath in church after his marriage Mr.
Bonar gave out these lines of the Sixteenth Psalm
to be sung :—

> 'Unto me happily the lines
>   In pleasant places fell ;
> Yea, the inheritance I got
>   In beauty doth excel.'

His quiet humour showed itself in various ways. A
good man in the parish maintained that, because he and
his wife were believers, their children would be born
without sin. Mr. Bonar tried to reason with him, and

---

[1] As Moderator of the Free Church General Assembly in 1878 he read
his opening address with the greatest difficulty. This was the only time
he was known to read a sermon or address.

then said in his quiet way, 'Wait and see!' When his
child was a few months old the man came back to
him and said, 'I see, sir, you were quite right!' His
description of a brother-minister, who had not his
own bright hopefulness, was, '—— is like one of the
Emmaus disciples : " he walks *and is sad.*" ' One of
his elders used to recall his visits with him to a neighbouring farm, where he went to hold a meeting in the
evening. The road was full of ruts and holes, and sometimes Mr. Bonar would be standing in mud up to the
ankles, laughing and making fun of his droll appearance.
In one of his letters to Mrs. Bonar from Collace, he says:—

'I am enjoying myself to-night by the fireside alone, for it is
very cold. Nothing new to tell you. . . . Our people think " Mr.
John (Dr. Bonar of Greenock) was uncommon lively" this time.
. . . I happened to meet L. P. at her door to-day. She has been
"complaining," and here is her account of herself : " You see I
pu'ed neeps when they were frosty without my gloves, and so the
cauld grippit my two hands, and spilt all the bluid, and raised the
influenza." '

Another time he writes to Mrs. Bonar in Edinburgh :—

'A taste of solitude helps to make you and anything of yours
more prized than ever. The cuckoo is sending his note through
the woods now, and the young grass is appearing. Part of the
walks are gravelled. The corn is breering.[1] . . . Watch (the dog)
has imitated you—that is, he is away seeing his friends. . . . Take
a farewell look at Minto Street for me ; I 'll never forget it—the
houses down to No. 49 [2] are all familiar to me, and your green
before the door, and the rooms where we used to sit. If we get
so fond of an earthly abode, what shall we feel to a mansion in the
Heavens, or to a place in the New Earth where no decay shall
ever enter ? Meanwhile, live on Him who is " the same yesterday,
to-day, and for ever." Take this as your text, and think on it all
the time of the flitting.'

---

[1] Appearing above ground.
[2] Mrs. Bonar's home in Edinburgh where her marriage took place,
April 4th, 1848.

During one of his visits to Ireland, before his marriage, in very stormy weather, he wrote the following little allegory and sent it to 49 Minto Street :—

'There was a pilgrim whose lot it was to cross the sea and go up and down the land of Israel. He had been in many perils by sea and by land, from robbers and from burning heat, and yet was no way injured. He could still sing, "O that men would praise the Lord for His goodness." He sat down one day, and, no doubt thinking of the storms that often toss the little boats on the Lake of Galilee, he told the following story:

THE STORY

'I knew a daughter of Zion who feared the Lord and trusted with all her heart in His grace. She had herself been brought through a land of deserts and of pits, and never had found Him a wilderness. She read and believed the words written in Matt. vi. 25-34, which Levi the son of Alpheus was commanded to write by the Holy Ghost. But still, through temptation and a fearful heart, she often forgot *the Person who spoke those words* : and always in such seasons care arose in her soul. One dark night there arose a strong wind; it tore down the boughs of aged trees, it raised the waves of the sea to a great height, it shook many dwellings, and it roared loudly over all. This godly daughter of Zion heard it, and her heart grew fearful in behalf of one for whom she often prayed, and who loved and prayed for her. No doubt she believed that her God cared for him, and that not a hair of his head could fall without our Father ; but still she feared and was very "careful." She imagined him to be on the sea, very pale and sick, the ship heaving on the waves, and its planks creaking as if they would break, the sky dark, the rain falling in torrents. There was nothing sad, but she thought it possible. In this state of mind she could not praise the Lord, her harp lay unstrung. She could not pray ; she had no sweet meditation. Nay, her body was worn out with sleeplessness and care.

'Morning came, the sun shone peacefully all around. A messenger arrived. She heard that the object of her care had never set foot on the ship, but had spent, and was to spend, some days on land in more than usual rest. Upon this she began to remember Ps. cxxvii. 2, and said to her soul reproachfully, "Alas, I might have all that time been engaged in better thoughts ! I might have prayed, praised, and exercised faith in the care of my High Priest. Even my body might have been the better of this, as well as my soul." From that day forth (says the pilgrim who tells the story, and who often to this day thinks upon that daughter of Zion) she learned to be less anxious, I trust, and to be more satisfied with *the Lord's knowing how to keep His own*, whether *she* knows or not.'

'A good story for next *Christian Treasury*, and a good motto would be Luther's words to Philip Melanchthon : "Philip must be told to cease from the attempt of *being himself the ruler of the world*." '

Mrs. Bonar, when Isabella Dickson, was brought to Christ during the times of revival in Edinburgh in 1842. Along with her friend, Miss Gifford (afterwards the wife of Dr. Alex. Raleigh), she attended a prayer-meeting for the Jews, held in St. Andrew's Church. Mr. M'Cheyne spoke at this meeting, and what he said interested her, but it was the impression of his personal holiness, rather than his words, that most deeply affected her. 'There was something singularly attractive about Mr. M'Cheyne's holiness,' she told her husband afterwards. 'It was not his matter nor his manner either that struck me ; it was just the *living epistle of Christ*— a picture so lovely, I felt I would have given all the world to be as he was, but knew all the time I was dead in sins.' On reading a letter in the last chapter of *M'Cheyne's Memoir*, from one who had been impressed in a similar way, she felt startled, it was so like her own experience. Mr. Bonar's acquaintance with her began during the long and trying illness of her mother, whom she nursed with unwearied devotion till her death in 1847. During this sad time the Twenty-third Psalm was her never-failing resort. She once said, in reference to it, 'O, if you only knew all that I have got by it ! Sometimes when they sing it in church it is too much for me. I don't know what I would have done without it and the orphan's verse, Psalm xxvii. 10.' When, years after his beloved wife's pilgrimage was over, her husband lay down to rest at the end of his long life-journey, the words of the Twenty-third Psalm, sung by his dying bed, calmed the hearts of his children as they watched his gentle passage through the valley of the shadow of death into the Father's house beyond.

Often during those eighteen years of seclusion Mr. Bonar wondered what might await him in the future, and if his work might not some day lie in a wider field. Several invitations came to him from other places, but he did not see God's call in any of them. It needed a very clear indication of His will to make him think of leaving his beloved flock. While in London at one time, he wrote to his brother-in-law, Mr. William Dickson :—

'Many an upbraiding do I meet with for what they count the "folly and absurdity" of continuing to feed a few sheep at Collace, rather than agree to plunge into the mass of misery among souls here. But, nevertheless, I am not moved from my belief that the Lord may mean to work more in a very small spot than in a great city, while, at the same time, He may use country shepherds to go up now and then to the city, and tell what things the Lord has made known to them.'

In regard to a definite call to London, he wrote :—

'As to London, I shall be slow to move in such a matter. I sometimes think that Satan may occasionally try in such ways to extrude a minister—it is not always the moving of the cloudy pillar.'

When his removal to Glasgow began to be seriously talked of, he wrote to one of his friends :—

'I am much pressed to consider the subject of Glasgow evangelisation—in short, to agree to be called to a district and church about to be erected in Finnieston in Glasgow. I have prayed, considered, and in every way reviewed the matter as impartially as I could, and the result is I am feeling my way toward it. The thousands in that part of Glasgow (it is quite like a district of London) made me yearn; so few to care for them, and every day more houses built, and more souls arriving, richer and poorer. What think you? To leave Collace I have always thought would be like Abraham leaving Ur of the Chaldees—that is, nothing but the clear call of the God of glory would effect it; but this seems to me like His call.'

The affection which united minister and people was often touchingly manifested after their separation, as well as during their long intercourse. It is more than thirty years since the pillar-cloud led him away from Collace on another stage of his journey heavenward, but his memory is lovingly cherished by those who still remain, and he is mourned for as if he had left them but yesterday.

'Little as I am acquainted with the Lord, I will leave it as my testimony that there is none like Him. God has been good to a soul that but poorly sought Him. Often, on riding home on Sabbath evenings, I have felt "Whom have I in heaven but Thee? and there is none upon earth that I desire besides Thee. . . .' Believer, is He not all this to you? O sinner, O unsaved ones of my flock, He might be more than all this to you! Young people, whom I greatly long for, remember what James Laing[1] said to one, 'Remember, if I see you at the left hand, I told you to come to Christ.' Shall I see any of these faces on which I have so often looked, and those which have so oft looked up to me, on the left hand? Shall any one here gaze on an angry Judge? any hear Him say, Depart? I beseech you, receive Christ . . . to-day. I beseech you, by remembrance of past Sabbaths, by the many witnesses that the Lord sent among you from time to time, by the messages of

[1] *The Lily Gathered*, by Rev. R. M. M'Cheyne.

grace so many and so varied, by the joy that your salva-
tation would give above as well as here and to yourselves, by the thought of approaching death, by the
thought of the Lord's speedy coming, by the opening of
yonder veil, when eternity shall receive you, and time
be for ever gone, receive Christ now.' [1]

[1] Mr. Bonar's Farewell Sermon at Collace, preached on the 19th of
October 1856.

CHAPTER X

In the City

IT was on a dreary December day in 1856 that the
first congregation assembled in Finnieston Free Church,
Glasgow, for the induction of the minister. He is
described as being at that time a 'tall, straight, and
somewhat spare man, about forty-five years of age, with
hair just tinged with grey.' The addresses were long,
and one of the members of Presbytery on the platform
made a sign to him to sit down, and even pushed a
chair forward with his foot ; but he remained standing.
The incident was a trivial one, but to those who knew
him it was characteristic. Ten or twelve people formed
the nucleus of the congregation, and three elders from
Free St. Matthew's Church kindly gave their help to
the new Territorial Mission Church, until it was able
to stand by itself. One of these elders, Mr. Andrew
Nielson, remained in the congregation, and became one
of its best and truest helpers.

The attendance on the first Sabbath was large, but
for many a day after there was only a sprinkling of
people in the church. The district round was closely
populated, and circumstances altogether combined to
make Dr. Bonar feel 'like a missionary to the heathen,
who has to spend months in learning the language and
habits of the people.' . . . 'I must be content gradually
to get acquainted with the faces and characters and the
ways of my poor district, and to seek openings among

the indifferent, the drunken, the lazy, the ignorant, the practical atheists, the bitter Papists, the formal professors, the young and old, sick and healthy.'

' I have plenty of work, but few Jacobs are finding the ladder between heaven and earth. Most sleep on, and then journey on to eternity with their staff in hand, and nothing more—little comfort on earth, and none at all beyond earth. O for the Spirit's outpouring ! '

The devoted teacher of Grace Street School had been carrying on work in the district before the church was built, and many others—office-bearers, tract-distributors, Sabbath-school teachers—now added their help. At the close of 1857 the roll of communicants was 136, and the usual attendance at church from 400 to 500. Dr. Bonar used to recall the first inquirer who came to his house—a young woman dressed in deep mourning, and in great distress. He asked her if she had met with some bereavement lately. She replied, ' Yes, I have lost a brother, but I am not mourning so much for him, but that I can't find my Saviour.' It was two years before the work really began to tell on the neighbourhood ; then the wave of the American revival swept over Scotland and touched Finnieston, and days of blessing followed. A gentleman one day asked, ' How are things doing with you ? How are you getting on ? ' ' Oh, we are looking for great things,' was Dr. Bonar's reply. ' You must not expect too much,' said his friend. ' We can never hope for too much,' he responded. He sowed the seed unweariedly, and always in hope, carrying the word of life into the lanes and dark closes, day after day, and week after week. Some who remember those days speak of him as being then in his fullest vigour of mind and body. Nobody escaped his notice, and his quickness in recognising faces was remarkable.

Not unfrequently he was asked by Roman Catholics in
the district to perform the marriage ceremony for them.
He always accepted these invitations, for they gave him
an opportunity of setting forth the simple gospel to the
company—mostly Roman Catholics—who assembled
on the occasion. He was invariably well received,
and welcomed with the words, 'Come along, yer
Riverence!'

The first meeting of workers in the congregation
numbered only twelve. Long after, in reviewing the
past, Dr. Bonar referred to their small beginnings and
said, 'We can say with Jacob, With our staff we passed
over Jordan, and the Lord very soon made us two
bands. We will hear a great deal in the day of the
Lord of how the workers found the lost pieces of silver.'
He used to say about different methods of work, 'There
is more originality in a full heart than in anything else.'
At one of the yearly workers' meetings, which became
so memorable in the history of the congregation, he
spoke specially to visitors and collectors, quoting Isaiah
xxxii. 20, 'Blessed are ye that sow beside all waters,'
etc. 'You know that the ox is the symbol of laborious
strength, and the ass is not a little remarkable for its
stubbornness. If you would be persevering and successful in your work, including as it does among other
things such weary climbing of stairs, you will have need
of this strength of the ox, and this patient stubbornness
of the ass!' When reminding collectors of their opportunities of speaking a word for the Master as they went
from house to house, he said, 'God blesses those who do
more than they are required to do.' At a workers'
meeting in later times he read 1 Corinthians xvi. 16,
'Submitting yourselves one to another'—'accommodat-
ing yourselves—specially *singers*—falling in with other
people's ways of working. We are not to look for

thanks from men. Christ says if we do we are no better than the publicans.' 'If you say your hands are full, it is just what they ought to be!'

'I never like to hear any one say, "I never trouble others with my religion." A believer *must* trouble others with his religion.'

'If you shine as lights now, and cast your light on the shadows around you, you will hear of it in the ages to come. If you do not, God will get others to do it.'

'I have come to believe this to be almost invariably true, that seldom is anything good proposed to us but we have something to object to in it at first. This seems to be the reason for the expression used by our Lord—"Thrust forth labourers." We are all unwilling to go. The truth is, we are all a little lazy. We need to be "thrust forth."'

'Remember,' he said, 'the Lord never uses angels to preach the gospel. It must be sinners that tell sinners what it is that takes away sin. God sends His people, —"You know every bush in which the sheep hide—go you and seek for them." God knew what a wrench it would be for Philip to leave the great awakening in Samaria and go to meet *one* soul in the wilderness; so He sent His angel to tell him to go. It was as if Christ said to him, "*I* left the ninety-and-nine in the wilderness, to go to seek the one lost sheep. Go *you* and find that lost one in the desert."'

'"Without Me ye can do nothing." Christ has willed that the world should be influenced through the instrumentality of the Christian; so that, as we say, Without Him *we* can do nothing, He, as it were, says, Without you *I* can do nothing, as if He needed our services.'

'You said you had no time,' he writes to a brother minister. 'Have you not time for all *duty*, and this was a *duty*?'

It was not the minister's fault if any of his people stood idle in the vineyard. If a stranger came from the country to join Finnieston Church, Dr. Bonar's common practice was to take him with him to the Bible class, then to see the Sabbath-school in Grace Street, and generally, before many days had passed, he found himself installed as a Sabbath-school teacher or a district visitor, or in some way a helper in the work of the congregation. 'The way to rise high in Christ's kingdom is to serve much;' and he carried out this axiom in his own life, and taught others the secret of the same blessedness.

'Lengthened life should be lengthened work.'

'Some good men are very peremptory in asking God to give them souls. That may not be the best service you can do for God. The best service you can give Him is *to submit to His will.*'

'The best part of all Christian work is that part which only God sees.'

'Service for the Master that everybody praises is very dangerous service. Perhaps in the day the Master returns the name of one we never heard of in the Church of Christ may be the highest, because he did most, simply for the Master.'

To those who were prevented from doing active work, but were serving God amid the small duties of daily life, he used to say, ' Remember, there is a reward for " thinking upon His name " (Mal. iii. 16). That is a quiet way of doing good, and open to every one.'

'We are to be rewarded, not only for work done, but for burdens borne; and I am not sure but that the brightest rewards will be for those who bore burdens without murmuring.'

'Burdens are part of a believer's education.'

'Self-forgetting work is heavenly work.'

'Christ's obedience was His taking up our undone work.'

A friend wrote to him, telling him that he felt discouraged in his work. He replied, not by letter, but by a parable :

'While tunnelling the Alps, one of the workmen began one day to think upon his arm, and to speculate on its feebleness. Comparing it with the greatness of the work to be done, he forthwith sat down, sad and depressed. "Stronger men are needed here. Who am I to bore through Mont Cenis ?" He uttered this moan aloud, and a voice was heard, a voice from one who was watching over the work and the workmen. The voice said kindly, but at the same time half upbraiding, "Did I not know what your arm could do, and what it could not do, when I sent you to propel, by careful attention to your steam apparatus, that wedge of steel ? Think of that little wedge of steel *tipped with diamond.* Why moan over your feeble arm ?" A friend of yours, Jeremiah of Anathoth, was asked to carry God's message to a people whom he thought he could in no ways impress, and so he wished to refuse, saying, "Ah, Lord God, I cannot speak, for I am a child (נַעַר)." "Very well," replied the speaker, "a mere boy can carry a message. Go on— go at once. *I am with thee.* I will make thee an iron pillar and brazen wall against the whole land." Up, up at once, and forget your feebleness. *Think of Him whose power accomplishes the mighty work*, and how He asks you simply to see that the wedge of diamond-tipped steel be in its right place.'

'God can do anything,' he said, 'by or for a man in Christ.' A minister, who was having a time of revival in his country congregation, expressed a wish that some of his city brethren would come and help him. Dr. Bonar said quietly, 'I thought you said the Master was with you. Why do you want any of us ?'

Every Sabbath was a time of labour from morning to evening, but, though not outwardly a day of rest, it was to him ever 'a delight.' Beginning at half-past ten with the Elders' Prayer-Meeting in the vestry, his labours went on till nine o'clock at night. Sometimes he left home earlier in the morning, hoping to find some one at that hour whom he might induce to go to church or to the Bible-class. Besides conducting the two regular services, he generally went into the little prayer-meeting held during the interval of worship in the session-house. On the day on which the church was opened, a band of godly people were present from Jordanhill, near Glasgow, and met together to wait for the afternoon service. The only place they found in which to wait was beside the stove of the church, and there they gathered to spend the hour in prayer. This was the beginning of a prayer-meeting which has ever since been continued. At half-past five the young men's Bible-class was held, and when that was over, and a visit paid to the Sabbath-school, there was always an evening service in church or mission-hall. He was fond of open-air preaching, and sometimes preached from the steps of the church to a crowd reaching to the other side of the street. It was not without many regrets that the church in Finnieston Street was abandoned, in 1878, for a larger and more commodious place of worship near the West End Park. Uncomfortable and badly ventilated as it was, the old church had many hallowed associations, and more than one could point to a seat in one corner or other, and say, ' I was born there.' Even the old bell had a mission of its own, calling in careless dwellers in the streets around to hear the words of life and salvation. Over the door of the new church are carved the three Hebrew words, לֹקֵחַ נְפָשׁוֹת חָכָם ' He that winneth souls is wise.' They were put there as an indication of the object of the church's existence, and also in the hope that some Jews passing by might see them, and come in to worship the God of Abraham. Dr. Bonar preached from these words on the day on which the church was opened, explaining

that 'winning' was the word used to describe a hunter
stalking game, and reminding 'soul-winners' that their
work must be done in a wise way. 'How carefully
David prepared to meet Goliath! He chose five
smooth stones out of the brook. He did not assume
that one would be lying to his hand when he needed it.
Never go to the Lord's work with meagre preparation.'

At the close of that day's service he referred to the
comfortable place in which they were now met, and
said, 'We read in the New Testament that our Lord
made the five thousand sit down "because there was
much grass in the place." That is why we have provided cushions in the pews. We believe the Lord Jesus
is not indifferent to your comfort.'

In connection with the new church an incident occurred
which he always referred to with deep thankfulness to
God and gratitude to his friends. The cost was very
much greater than had been anticipated, and the debt
which for some time rested on it was a cause of grave
anxiety to the congregation. Many suggestions were
made as to how it was to be cleared off, and among
other things a bazaar was proposed, of which he strongly
disapproved. He suggested delay as to further plans
until the matter had been made a subject of special
prayer. A full meeting of elders and deacons was
called, and the time was spent in earnest prayer for
God's guidance. About a fortnight afterwards, one of
his elders called upon him one morning. He was busy
in his study, and looking more than usually bright. 'I
have something to show you this morning,' he said, and
taking a letter from his pocket, he added, 'Here is our
bazaar! This contains a cheque for £1000. The Lord
has heard and answered our prayers.'

This gift was sent by friends of Dr. Bonar's, and
transmitted to him by Dr. J. H. Wilson of the Barclay

Church, Edinburgh, who had been the originator of this generous scheme for lightening the burden which lay upon both minister and people. In sending it he wrote to Dr. Bonar :—

'I only wish I could convey to you the expressions of grateful and affectionate regard with which the letters abound ; and while the object is not a personal, but a congregational one, I need not say that it is on purely personal grounds that the whole thing has been done, in the belief that it would be a small contribution to your comfort and freedom in working, in having this burden somewhat lessened.'

Dr. Bonar wrote in reply :—

'*Glasgow, 15th January* 1881.

'MY DEAR DR. WILSON,—"It is more blessed to give than to receive"—may this blessedness be yours ! I cannot tell you how this most brotherly act of kindness surprised me and filled me with thankfulness. You could not have done a kinder thing to myself, as well as to my people, for this debt has been of late a most serious burden, and a hindrance to efforts in various directions. And let me mention that it cannot but have an effect on us spiritually ; for it is the answer to special prayer begun. I strongly opposed the scheme of a bazaar when one or two of our Deacons' Court proposed it, and we at last agreed to set apart an evening for prayer on the whole matter. On the appointed evening we had a very good attendance of elders and deacons, and the prayers were fervent and hopeful. And then, we, as a Court, set ourselves to form a scheme which, in the course of a good many years would, if successful, leave us entirely free. This most unexpected and generous gift will wonderfully stimulate our efforts. We do heartily thank the disinterested friends who have taken part in this movement, and will use the words of Ezra, "Blessed be the Lord God of our fathers which hath put such a thing as this into thine heart."

'Meanwhile, reminding yourself, Colonel Young, and all the other unknown friends, of Matt. x. 42 and Heb. vi. 10,—Believe me, dear brother, yours affectionately and gratefully,

'ANDREW A. BONAR.'

There was much pleasant intercourse between the minister and his co-workers. The office-bearers have happy recollections in early years, of evenings when they used to convoy him home from the meetings to his house in St. Vincent Crescent. Many a helpful talk they had as they walked along, till they reached the door, where they still stood chatting together till Mrs. Bonar's quick ear caught the sound of voices, and she came out to welcome her husband home. It was at such times that he poured out one incident after another of his work and rich experience, often conveying a deep lesson, and in some cases a lifelong impulse to those who listened.

He took a loving interest in all parts of the work of the church, and his sympathy smoothed away many difficulties. He would slip quietly into one of the little kitchen-meetings, taking his seat among the hearers, then rising to give a word of cheer and encouragement at the close. His presence in a meeting acted at all times like a charm. As he came in, overflowing with brightness and kindliness, his progress, as he went from one to another shaking hands, could be traced by the ripple of light that passed over every face. Not unfrequently at a tea-meeting or social gathering, the opening was delayed, and the explanation given, 'The minister has not finished shaking hands with the people yet!'

He once told as an illustration of the words in Heb. x. 24 : 'Let us consider one another,' etc., an experience of his own when in the country. There was one man who always sat in the front seat in the gallery, and kept his eye fixed on the minister as if to help him on. If he said anything this good man liked very much, he would look at him with an expression which said 'That's good! come on!' and it cheered the preacher's heart. He thought this was an example of 'provoking to love and good works.'

His readiness to learn from others was very remarkable, and he had the faculty of drawing out what was best in every one. ' A true disciple,' he said, ' is always learning. Every believer we meet with has something for us if we could only get it. We are wrong if we are not trying to draw out of others what God has given them. Never think you can be of no use to another disciple. God does not give everything to one. Aquila and Priscilla could do a good deal even for Apollos.'

At a meeting in the church one evening, two good men had spoken who were rough and uneducated. Dr. Bonar listened to them with evident enjoyment, and when some one spoke of it to him afterwards, he said, ' If you are very thirsty you will not be particular about the dish you drink out of.'

The work of the Holy Spirit went on silently from week to week, making the ordinary services wells of salvation to thirsting souls. Every Sabbath, to use an expression of his own, there ' was more joy even in happy Heaven, because lost ones were being found.' Each time of revival in Glasgow left its impress more or less on Finnieston. Dr. Bonar did not always approve of all the methods employed by those who were sent to carry on the work, but that did not hinder him from identifying himself with any such movement. He believed God could work even where there might be much imperfection, and he and his people were never left unrefreshed when heavenly showers were falling. The revival under Mr. D. L. Moody in 1873-74 was a marked period in his city ministry. He threw himself into it with his whole heart, helping and sympathising in every possible way. In no congregation were the results of the work more apparent than in Finnieston, and never was the pastor's heart more full of joy. One instance among many others of the Lord's presence at these times, occurred after Mr. Moody's visit to Glasgow when services were continued in Finnieston Church. As Dr. Bonar came into one of these meetings after it had begun, he walked to the front of the platform, and, laying his hand on the rail, he said, 'I feel the breath of the Holy Spirit in this place to-night.' The words, and the solemn way in which they were uttered, were the means of awakening a young woman who was present.

The news of 'a sound of abundance of rain' in any part of the world, specially in the mission field, Jewish or heathen, gladdened his heart, and made him long to hear the same 'joyful sound' at home. When writing to Dr. J. H. Wilson, in 1859, he says :—

'You will have heard of the good news from our Jewish school in Constantinople—ten in one week brought to Christ's feet. I hear, too, of some real work in Aberdeen. The Lord is coming near us. I feel often like Isa. xxiv. 16, on which I was preaching lately. When news comes of "glory to the Righteous One" elsewhere, it goes through my heart with something like a chill, and makes me cry "My leanness ! my leanness ! Woe unto me !"'

When news came of revival work in the fishing-villages, he used to say, 'The Lord Jesus has still a warm heart to the fishermen !'

'Tell it everywhere,' was his advice on hearing of blessing in any place, 'that is the way to spread it.'

CHAPTER XI

Echoes of Spoken Words

THE congregation that gathered round Dr. Bonar in Finnieston Church was attracted, not by the eloquence of the preaching,[1] but by its simplicity, and the fresh light the preacher threw upon the Scriptures, making them appear to many like a new book. Strangers had to grow accustomed to the peculiarities of his voice, and his habit of letting it suddenly drop just when the hearer's attention was fixed. A good lady in his congregation once remonstrated with him about this, and told him how provoking it was to his hearers to lose some of his very best things. 'How do you know they are the best, if you don't hear them?' was his retort. He liked to tell of a worthy couple who joined his church and told him where their seat was. The woman said, 'I hear you quite well, but he (meaning her husband) says he does not; but *I* say, *are ye sure ye attend?*' The most ignorant among his hearers could understand his simple unfolding of truth, while many a striking saying fell from his lips as he leaned in his characteristic way over the pulpit, and talked quietly to those before him. The most fearful felt their faith strengthened by his joyous confidence in the things of which he spoke. Eternal things came very near, and unseen things became real, as they listened to one who spoke as if already among them.

[1] 'You know I am no speaker—only a talker,' he says in a letter to a friend.

'Suppose that I, a sinner, be walking along yon golden street, passing by one angel after another. I can hear them say, as I pass through their ranks, " A sinner! a crimson sinner!" Should my feet totter? Should my eye grow dim? No; I can say to them, "Yes, a sinner—a crimson sinner, but a sinner brought near by a forsaken Saviour, and now a sinner who has boldness to enter into the Holiest through the blood of Christ."'

'When Jesus tells us of the glory and beauty of the New Jerusalem,—lest we should think it incredible that feet like ours should ever tread the golden streets, or hands like ours ever pluck the fruit of the Tree of Life, or lips like ours ever taste the water of that pure river,— He says, "John, write: These sayings are *faithful and true*."'

'If you ask me "What is glory?" well, I can't tell you, but I know that it is a hundred times better than grace.'

'We are like children trying the strings of the harp which we expect yet to use.'

'Never be offended at Christ's providences. He will recompense all to you, even in this life. O believer, *keep Him to His promise!*'

'"The Lord is my Shepherd, I shall not want." Then you have everything but heaven!'

'We have more to do with the world to come than with this world.'

'The nearer you come to Him the better, for you will then be further from the world, and the world will have least power over you.'

'"No man could learn that song,' etc. (Rev. xv. 3). Because there is something in each one's experience that another cannot borrow.'

'What a happy thing it is that it is the "kingdom of

God our Saviour" (2 Peter i. 2). We know *Him* so well. It was He who put our robe of righteousness on us. We would be lonely in the great company if we did not know Him so well. Would it not be a great comfort to the dying thief that Christ said, " To-day, . . . *with Me* in Paradise ! " '

One Sabbath, when preaching on the image of God being restored, and the time when 'we shall be like Him, for we shall see Him as He is,' he suddenly exclaimed, 'O my people, you won't know your minister on that day ! '[1] 'It will be ecstasy,' he said at another time, 'to have made this attainment—to love the Lord our God with all our heart, and soul, and strength, and mind.' To those to whom that time seemed very far off, and to whom the trials and difficulties in the way were very great, he would point out the strength and the sufficiency of His grace who had promised to complete the good work He had begun.

' Faith keeps us, but God keeps our faith.'

' If the Father has the kingdom ready for us, He will take care of us on the way.'

' God will not give us an easy journey to the Promised Land, but He will give us a safe one.'

' We do not need new swords, new spears, new arms. We only need more eye-salve to see Who is on our side.'

' Jesus left His disciples in the little boat on the Lake of Galilee purposely, that He might come to them in the fourth watch of the night and deliver them. I think He would have come to them sooner—perhaps in the first or second watch—*if they had trusted Him.*'

[1] A stranger—a young careless girl—sitting in his church one Sabbath, smiled as he suddenly and seemingly irrelevantly exclaimed, 'Come, blessed resurrection morn !' In after years the words, in the very tones in which they were uttered, came to her over and over again with such power that she marvelled at God's mercy in using what had only excited her ridicule at the time, to quicken and refresh her on her dying bed.

'None of God's pilgrims fall by the roadside.'

'It is the mark of every quickened soul,' he used to say, 'that he feels his heart going *upward*, as, after His resurrection, Christ would be thinking of *going home.*'

'If you have not *two* heavens, you will never have *one*. If you have not a heaven *here*, you will never have one *yonder.*'

'Judah had a rich land for his inheritance, but Levi had a rich God.'

'Lot would not give up Christ, but he would not give up much *for* Christ.'

'"The world" is all that is outside of the soul's spiritual life.'

'The world is so blind that it did not see the Light of the World when He came. How, then, can you expect that it will see His people?'

When preaching in Collace Church in 1842 he reminded his people of the many offers of salvation they had had during four years of faithful ministry, and said to them, 'These walls are a witness, and their lingering echoes will be witness when I am in the grave. Angels have seen the cup of life held out from this pulpit and put to your lips.'

The same faithful earnestness characterised his preaching at all times, and made his declaration of the love of God in Christ peculiarly sweet and persuasive.

'O men and brethren, look at that Cross, and listen to what it says: "He that hath the Son hath life." I often think, when the Lord is thus pressing you to accept Christ, He has not only stood at the door and knocked, but He has, as it were, opened the door a little to try to persuade you.'

'"Weep not for Me, weep for yourselves and for your children." It is so like Christ to dry up other people's tears, and let His own flow.'

'The Lord left our Saviour in the grave three days that no one might dispute the reality of His death—that there might be time, as it were, to count the pieces of the Ransom-money. When His disembodied spirit was in Paradise these three days, it was like uttering "Finished! Finished! Finished!" over the hills of Paradise.'

'We are asked to accept this salvation—to let this love into our heart, without shedding a single tear, unless it be a tear of love and gratitude.'

'Look into the Fountain, and the very looking will make you thirsty.'

'Take the water of life "freely," though you cannot allege a single reason why you should take it. Yet take it "without a cause."'

'No one who is anxious to have a Saviour has committed the unpardonable sin.'

'What God does in saving Gospel-hearers is to show them *with* power what they have previously known *without* power.'

'Our unwillingness is our inability.'

'"There is no man that sinneth not;" this truth is the hypocrite's pillow, but the believer's bed of thorns.'

'Christ is the lever by which God moves a world of souls.'

'God does not say, "Pay what you *can*," but "Pay what you *owe*."'

'A cloak of profession will make an awful blaze in that day when He burns the stubble.'

'God is a sin-hater, but a soul-lover.'

'The natural heart keeps no record of sin; it is only God's law which does so.'

'The Shepherd can number His sheep, but the sheep can't. Christ's favourite expression, when speaking of His saved ones, is "many." Our Shorter Catechism

should have said, " elected *many* to everlasting life."
I am not sure but we shall be in the majority yet when
we are gathered into the kingdom.'

' The Ransom-money is the only current coin at the
court of heaven, and it has the resurrection stamp upon
it. We used to speak of a " king's ransom," but guess,
if you can, what the value must be of a ransom that
sets free nations, kingdoms, peoples ! '

' Lord, we bespeak blessing for to-morrow ' was often
his prayer on Saturday evening at family worship ; and
he went into the pulpit in the expectation that this
prayer would be answered. Many of the worshippers
were brought, by his opening prayer in church, into
the very presence of God, and felt that they needed no
more to strengthen them for that day's journey through
the wilderness. Some of his petitions are graven on the
memory of his hearers :—

' Good Shepherd, gratify Thyself by saving me ! '

' Remember us, O Lord ! and when we have said this we
have said everything, for Thou knowest what to do next.'

' Thou dost not give away the children's bread.
Surely, then, thou keepest it for the children. Give it
now to us.'

' Give us a taste of the grapes of Eshcol that we may
long for the Promised Land.'

' Lord, before we put in the sickle, we ask Thee to
whet it.'

' When we pray in the morning to be filled with the
Spirit, may we expect to be filled all day with thoughts
of Christ.'

' Let us be as watchful after the victory as before the
battle.'

' When we are forgetting Thee, recall us to communion with Thyself by some text, some word of Thine
own.'

'O make us sincere to the core of our heart by the help of Thy Holy Spirit, for it's not natural!'

'Awake, awake, put on strength, O arm of the Lord! that arm that has plucked many a brand from the burning, and has been folded round many a lamb!'

'"Visit us with Thy salvation"—for there are folds and folds of the robe of righteousness that we would fain have Thee to unfold to us.'

'We ask for conviction. We do not ask that it may be very deep, for we make idols of so many things that we might make an idol of our conviction. So we do not say anything about the depth, but we ask for the reality.'

'If our hands that should grasp the heavenly treasure are kept closed because they are filled with earthly things, *deal with us*, Lord, until we stretch out empty hands, suppliants for Thy blessing.'

'If Thy people cannot say they have come to the land where "they hunger no more, neither thirst any more," they can at least say they neither hunger nor thirst while the Lamb is leading them through the desert.'

'Let us seek to be delivered from trifling prayers and contentment with trifling answers,' he once said solemnly; and at another time, 'Is not this a lamentable state of things that there should be so much to get and so few to ask!' Closet prayer he considered as 'an ordinance of God for every believer,' affecting all the providences of a day, and closely linked with meditation on the Word. 'You say, "If I pray I'll prosper." That is only half the truth. If you meditate on the Word and pray, you'll prosper.' 'Prayer will be very lame and dry if it does not come from reading the Scriptures.' 'May we be able to spread our Bibles on the Mercy-seat, and read them by the light of the cloud of glory,' he once prayed. He spoke of prayer as 'seed sown on the heart of God;' meditation, as 'letting God speak to us till our heart is throbbing;' and fasting, as 'abstaining from all that interferes with prayer.'

'I do not think,' he said, 'we ever pray the Lord's Prayer with all our heart, without laying up something we shall be thankful for in the future.'

'It is not right for God's people to say when a matter for prayer is put before them, "O, what can *my* prayers do?" What can *your God do*?'

'God likes to see His people shut up to this, that there is no hope but in prayer. Herein lies the Church's power against the world.'

'It is a sign the blessing is not at hand when God's people are not praying much.'

'Hezekiah's prayer got a large answer. When you send in a petition to the Lord leave a wide margin that He may write a great deal on it.'

'Always follow your work with believing prayer' was his counsel to a busy worker. When presiding at a district prayer-meeting, a request for prayer was handed in by a woman whose 'husband had gone amissing.' Dr. Bonar began his prayer thus: 'O Lord, here is a sad case,—a man amissing. Thou wast once amissing Thyself, but Thy parents sought Thee till they found Thee in the Temple. Lord, seek and find this poor man and restore him to his wife and family.' At the close of a missionary meeting he was asked to pray, and in doing so drew the thoughts of those present to the Lord's promise to His Son in the Second Psalm: 'Ask of Me, and I shall give Thee the heathen for thine inheritance,' etc. His solemn closing appeal sent a thrill through the audience: 'Saviour, *ask, and the Father will give Thee.*' After illustrating the truth that God gives us as much as we ask for by the story of Joseph's brethren getting all the

sacks filled that they brought to him, he said in prayer :
' O Lord, Thou art our Joseph. We bring to Thee our
empty sacks. Do Thou fill them all ! '

One Sabbath, when explaining to the children how
when they were weak then they were strong, he referred
to the fact that the finest fruits, such as grapes and
melons, grow upon stalks so weak that if left to themselves they would trail along the ground, never ripen, and
be destroyed. The gardener has to prop them up and
support them firmly that they may grow and come to
perfection. In like manner the Good Gardener has to
tend and support His weak plants, and to graft them
into the True Vine, that they may grow in Him and
bring forth fruit fit for the Master's use. Then he
offered the touching request : ' Lord, pity the weakness
of the plants that bear the fruit of the Spirit.'

His prayer one New Year's Day was memorable to
those who were present :—

' Thou tellest our wanderings, and Thou hast been
writing an account of our lives up till this date. This
year Thou hast begun a new chapter. Lord, may there
be always in it something about Thy glory. " This day
My servant gave a cup of cold water and plucked a
brand from the burning." Perhaps Thou wilt come
Thyself this year, and finish the record by telling that
at this point Thou didst come Thyself with the crown ! '

His thanksgiving-prayers on Communion Sabbaths
will long be remembered, and many of his requests before
and at the Tables.

' The clouds which have arisen from the marshes of
our sins need new bursts of the Sun of righteousness to
melt them away. Shine forth ! shine forth ! '

' As the bread is broken and the wine is poured out,
may we feel that He is scarcely an absent Saviour,
though unseen.'

'As we get into the enjoyment of Thy love may we find that we need scarcely any other heaven either here or hereafter—only more of that love and the continuance of it.'

'Lord, if Thou lookest for us, Thou wilt find us under the apple-tree.'

At the close of the Communion Sabbath in October, 1886, Mr. Inglis of Dundee, who had been assisting in the services, asked prayer for himself and his people. Dr. Bonar took up the request in his closing prayer:—

'Lord Jesus, Thou art the Intercessor. Present his petition to the Father, and add our names to it, for blessing on himself and his elders, on his congregation, on his missionary. And one thing more, Lord Jesus, come quickly Thyself!'

The old-fashioned form of service was always retained in Finnieston: the Action Sermon, the Fencing[1] of the Table, the three Tables following, and then the Closing Address with its message to old and young. The fragrance of these services and the words then spoken, still linger in the hearts of many of God's children.

'At the Table, remember Christ and forget yourself.'

'Jesus is walking to-day among the seven golden candlesticks, and He will stop here, at our Communion Table, to see if any of you want anything from Him.'

'There is nothing between a sinner and the Saviour, but there *is* something between the sinner and the Lord's Table.'

'However weak you are, if you value supremely the atoning blood, come to the Table.'

[1] 'Fencing,' he always explained as declaring by whose authority the Table was spread. The word is used in old Scotch law.

'God's people have a ravenous hunger for a crucified Christ.'

'"Little children" is the name for the family of God in every place and at every time. John learned the name from Christ at the first Communion Table. He only said it once, and John, leaning on His bosom, caught it up and repeated it.'

'At the Lord's Supper (John xiii. to xvi.) the characteristics of six of the disciples are seen. John, the type of a true communicant, realising his own sinfulness and liability to fall, but yet not rising from his place on Christ's bosom. Judas, to outward appearance as near as John, but an unworthy communicant, hardened, often warned, but to no purpose. Peter, ardent and warm-hearted, but one who yielded too much to feeling, forgetting that feelings fail, though faith does not. Thomas, a suspicious, questioning, sad cast of mind, but a real disciple. Jude, a thoughtful, growing Christian. Philip, a slow mind, from want of meditation and reflection, not grasping the truth sufficiently.'

Many years ago, a lady from a neighbouring congregation took shelter from the rain in the porch of Finnieston Church, on a Communion Sabbath, while Dr. Bonar was giving an address from Matt. xxvi. 48: 'That same is He: *hold Him fast.*' She could not hear the address, but over and over again, as she stood in the porch, the words of the text came to her ear like a message from the Lord, 'That same is He: *hold Him fast.*' The first part of the closing address was specially for the children, who always gathered in the front seats of the gallery, and were quiet and interested spectators while the bread and wine were handed to the communicants. Sometimes their thoughts were directed to a Communion time of long ago on the heathery moors, under the open sky, or to Communion Sabbaths not so long before, in the days of the minister's own boyhood, in Lady Glenorchy's Chapel in Edinburgh. When pressing the children to come to Christ, and then, with their parents, to come to the Lord's Table, he told the story of an old gentleman whom he remembered in the Chapel, who did not become a communicant till he was fifty years of age. He did not know the Lord when he first went to speak to the minister, Dr. Jones, about joining the church, and he told him he was not ready to become a communicant. It was not till he had come back six times that he was able to say he knew the Lord, and had a right to come to His Table. In applying the story to the children Dr. Bonar told them he wanted them to be like that good old man, 'not in being so long of coming, but in being sure that you are saved before you come. It is the same bread for the grown people and for the children. I am an older man now than almost any of my congregation, and I find I give out the same food I need for myself.'

The address never concluded without reference to the Lord's Second Coming as the motive for more earnest work, and more earnest prayer.

'Do much, and say little about it, and think not about what brethren say of you. Pray much, and you will be very near the King, for He has a special love to petitions.'

' "Behold, I come quickly." O sinner, are you ready for that long eternity? What if it comes to you some day suddenly? O believer, have you done all you would fain do? Is it no fault of yours if souls are not saved? O elders, are you devising means for winning souls? O deacons, are you like Stephen, of whom I often say he thought in the midst of his deacon's work how to commend his Lord? O people of God, are you remembering that "*quickly*"? Time is short.

Are you praying much? Are you letting your light shine?'

'Christ's nearer coming casts deeper solemnity over every Communion.'

The day's services were always brought to a close by singing three verses of the Ninety-eighth Psalm :—

> 'With harp, with harp, and voice of psalms,
>   Unto JEHOVAH sing :
> With trumpets, cornets, gladly sound
>   Before the Lord the King.
>
> Let seas and all their fulness roar ;
>   The world, and dwellers there ;
> Let floods clap hands, and let the hills
>   Together joy declare
>
> Before the Lord ; because He comes,
>   To judge the earth comes He ;
> He 'll judge the world with righteousness,
>   His folk with equity.'

This custom, begun in Collace, was continued in Finnieston, and wherever or whenever that psalm is sung it will always stir the heart of Dr. Bonar's old hearers, bringing back hallowed recollections of 'days of heaven upon earth.'

' I beseech you to keep Christ, for I did what I could to put you within grips of Him. I told you Christ's testament and latter-will plainly, and I kept nothing back that my Lord gave me. I gave Christ to you with good-will.'—*Samuel Rutherford.*

CHAPTER XII

A Basket of Fragments

THERE was no part of a minister's work which he did not try to render useful both to himself and to others. A marriage, a baptism, a funeral, were all opportunities for good. At Collace, he heard of a woman awakened by his address at her marriage ceremony.[1] He sometimes, on such occasions, referred to Proverbs xii. 4 : 'A virtuous woman is a crown to her husband,' and paraphrased it thus : 'She makes his house a palace, and himself a king.' 'Remember,' he would say, 'God grudges you nothing if you take it from His hands through Christ.' At other times, he spoke of husband and wife as 'helpmeets,' and compared them to the two sides of an arch, with love as the keystone : 'And see what burdens an arch can bear ! '

The baptismal service was never a mere form, but a time when all the congregation felt that Father, Son, and Holy Ghost were drawing near to bless.

'The sacraments of the New Testament are signs between Heaven and earth. Baptism is a sign from Heaven that God remembers little children, and looks upon them in love, saying, "Suffer little children to come unto Me," etc. The Lord's Supper is a sign from earth to Heaven that we remember our Lord's dying command : 'This do in remembrance of Me "; and keep it till He come.'

[1] See *Diary and Letters*, p. 119.

' I consider the baptism of infants to be, not a confession of our faith, but of God's interest in us. I am in the way of putting it thus : "Remember, parents, to tell your children that on the day of baptism they were presented to the Three Persons, and the water was meant to be a sign and seal that Father, Son, and Holy Spirit offered salvation to them. Ask them, have you accepted the gift offered?'

He called on a young mother in Collace soon after the birth of her first-born son, and, after asking what name she meant to give the baby, he said, ' I never knew the meaning of these words in Psalm ciii.— 'Like as a father pitieth his children,' etc.—till I heard my own little infant cry. How I pitied her, how I wanted to help her, and yet I couldn't!' When the parents brought the child to be baptized a few weeks afterwards, he gave him the name ' William,' though he had not been reminded of it. After the service he said to them, ' Ah, you forgot to write down the baby's name, but there will be no mistake about it on that day when it is written in the Lamb's Book of Life.'

' How solemn it is for you,' he said to another before the baptism of her little one, ' to look on that child and wonder, "will that head ever wear a crown of glory? and will these lips ever sing His praises? and will these eyes ever see the King in His beauty?"'

One Friday evening a stranger from the Highlands came to the manse to ask that his baby might be baptized on the following Sabbath. While talking with him Dr. Bonar found that he was not a communicant, though evidently a converted man. He asked him why he was not, and the man replied that a very peculiar experience was needed to fit any one for going to the Lord's Table. Dr. Bonar tried to show him that an interest in Christ was sufficient, but the man still kept to his point. At last, seeing he was deeply in earnest, he told him he could not baptize his child on the coming Sabbath, but asked him to go home and search the New Testament for the qualifications laid down as necessary for admission to the Lord's Table, and to return in a fortnight and tell him what he had found. The man came back at the time appointed, but with a very different expression on his face. He and his wife had looked through the New Testament, but could find no extraordinary experience mentioned as necessary, so he was ready now to go to the Lord's Table. His after-life testified to his sincerity and faith in Christ.

At a baptism on one occasion, he spoke to the parents about Jesus as being the only holy child ever born on our earth. The mother reminded him of this when her baby was taken away soon after, and added, ' My little one is just as spotless now.'

His love for the children showed itself in the interest with which he followed them year by year. Each had a place in his prayers, and they fully returned his affection. They would linger in the church as he went from the pulpit to the vestry, in the hope of having his hand laid on their head, and hearing him call them by their name. One little child called him 'the minister with the laughing face.' It was not uncommon in Collace to see groups of children round him as he rode about from place to place on his pony. One of the touching sights on the day on which he was buried, was that of the children round the grave, with their sad and wistful faces. Some time after his death, a little child was heard praying, ' O God, bless Mr. M'Intyre, and send back Dr. Bonar, for we 're wearying to see him ! ' He spoke with unhesitating certainty of the conversion of children.

' We ask Thee, Lord, to raise up a generation of

believing children. We do not ask Thee for a generation of believers, but of believing children. " Is anything
too hard for the Lord ? " Faith is a gift, and a gift that
a child can take.'

' A young hand may be placed on the head of the
scapegoat as well as an old hand.'

' God's heart is so quick and so tender that He can
hear the hosanna of a little child.'

' " Out of the mouth of babes and sucklings Thou hast
perfected praise "—Thou hast filled up the choir of
heaven.'

' Christ would have wanted one of the marks of
Incarnate God if the story of His blessing the little
children had not been narrated, for " Behold, God is
mighty and despiseth not any." '

The Apostle Matthew, he used to say, must have been
very fond of children, for his Gospel is full of references
to them. He thought Paul must have been a famous
preacher to children, for he had so much to tell about.
He had been in perils of waters, in perils of robbers, in
perils in the sea, in shipwrecks, etc. And he did preach
to the children, for he witnessed ' both to small and
great' (Acts xxvi. 22).

Wherever he went, he liked to visit the Sabbath
school, and used to urge other ministers to provide
something specially for the children on Communion
Sabbaths. At Crossford, where he often visited his
friend Mr. Manson, he was not unfrequently the means
of helping and cheering the teachers in their work.
His words are still remembered : ' Be sure and aim at
the conversion of the children. They are never too
young to come to Jesus. I hope you pray for each of
your scholars by name. That has a wonderful effect on
your teaching. Never come to your classes without
first being in prayer.' ' Kindness to those you teach is

part of the teaching,' he used to say. In a country village where he was staying, he was told that the children had a bad habit of running after passing carriages. He took the opportunity at a children's meeting in the evening of asking them to tell him the name of the only man we read of in the Bible who ran after a carriage. The answer was 'Gehazi; and he was not a man to be imitated!'

Not being able to be present one evening at the monthly meeting of his Sabbath-school teachers, he sent the following *Report* to the Superintendent :—

'MEETING OF TEACHERS IN JERUSALEM

(2 Chron. xxx. 22)

MONTH OF ABIB, A.C. 726

'*The Superintendent.*—The King; his name Hezekiah, *i.e.* "Jehovah is my strength."

'*The Teachers.*—Levites who "taught the good knowledge of the Lord. Some of them discouraged; they spoke of their difficulties, those they taught not always caring for their teaching, and many of them very dull in understanding. Some of the teachers spoke of fancying they had not the gift of teaching, and should resign.

'*The Superintendent's Address.*—Hezekiah "spake to the heart" (see margin). Hezekiah "spake to . . . all." Hezekiah reminded them that their theme was "the knowledge of the Lord." It was a royal and hearty word in season. *N.B.*—A note of his address : "My friend Isaiah reminds me that it is this knowledge that is to fill the earth one day, as the waters cover the sea. Go on, then. Tell the "Good Tidings." Tell them to reason with our God, who can make their scarlet sins disappear, and their souls be whiter than the snow, through the "good knowledge" of Him who is to come.

'The meeting was held in the hall on Mount Zion, within sight of the palace. It was a very happy meeting. Our reporter refers to the lively "singing and the great gladness;" and mention is made of the prayers also going up to Jehovah's dwelling-place.'

His interest in the members of his young women's Bible-class was unwearied, and many owe their first religious impressions to his faithful lessons. To them, as to the members of the young men's class, he succeeded in imparting a love for God's Word and for Scripture truth which became characteristic of them.

One Tuesday evening at the class, he referred to 'the bricks of Babylon'—how every brick had on it the king's stamp. 'So,' he said, 'everything we do should have the King's stamp on it.' One of his hearers, not long after, was set to the tedious work of cleaning a feather-bed. Many a time she felt tempted to hurry over it, but 'the bricks of Babylon' kept ringing in her ears, and she had to do it all faithfully. When Dr. Bonar called to see her, she said to him, 'O these bricks of Babylon were a trouble to me!' 'Were they on your dusters and brooms?' he asked. 'No, on a feather-bed!' she replied, to his great amusement. The story was repeated to a servant, who said, 'Well, I hate cleaning the knives, but I can't but do them thoroughly now.'

Nowhere, perhaps, was his personal influence more strongly felt than in his young men's Bible-class, and there was no part of his work which in his later years he gave up more reluctantly. Its first place of meeting was in the little room behind the old church, where for many a year, in spite of discomfort and inconvenience, the young men gathered round the teacher, who was ever bringing to them out of his treasure things new and old. One book of Scripture after another was opened up with unfailing freshness and originality. Not long before his death he was singularly pleased with a letter he received from one who for years had wandered about the world, and had carried with him, through all his vicissitudes, the memory of Sabbath evenings in the Bible-class. 'After seeing so much of the world, and, after passing my fortieth year, there is nothing which has so deeply impressed itself on my life, and engrained itself into my very existence, as the solemn lessons you taught us in your Bible-class.' And when pressed by temptation and the allurements of sin on every side, 'there were silent voices speaking to me from that Bible-class which I dared not disobey.'

When members of the class left town or went abroad, he was never too busy to write to them, and their letters were a source of constant interest and pleasure to him. The young men, on their part, felt the sympathy of a heart that was always young. In his busiest time he has been known to call on a young man in his lodgings at ten o'clock at night, hoping to find him at home then, as he had been unsuccessful before. He would go far out of his way on a Sabbath evening to take a young man with him to the class, walking along with his arm in his, and chatting in a way that put him entirely at his ease. A question as to his spiritual welfare would be accompanied by a kindly touch of his hand on the young man's shoulder. 'That touch remains with me still,' said one, long years after.

Sometimes he had a gathering of the students connected with the church at his house, and these meetings he always greatly enjoyed.

'Last night,' he writes of one such occasion, 'I had at my house a gathering of students connected with the congregation—about thirty. . . . At worship I showed them that Paul went to college at Jerusalem,—was a clever student,—had for his professor Gamaliel, the very best in his line,—imbibed all his views, etc. But the Lord transferred him to another college, when he, at a holiday time, had taken a trip to Damascus, and had offered to be of any use to his idol, Gamaliel.'

At the close of one of these gatherings he prayed

with peculiar solemnity : 'And when we all meet together again, may it be with our bosom filled with sheaves !'

The young men who used - to gather together in Finnieston, are scattered now all over the world. The meeting-time has not yet come, but when it does, it will be true of them : 'these shall come from far ; and, lo, these from the north and from the west ; and these from the land of Sinim.'

CHAPTER XIII

Among His People

To the members of his congregation Dr. Bonar was both friend and father. Not only was he quick to recognise their faces, but their different circumstances touched and interested him, and made him feel his visitation a pleasure and benefit to himself as well as to them. 'He was that ta'en up aboot *me*,' were the words of one of them, as she recalled his thoughtful interest in her in times of need.

How much importance he attached to this part of a pastor's work is shown in a letter written to Dr. Somerville from Collace in the year 1850 :—

'. . . There is a blessing resting on visiting. What else is fitted to make us know the state of our flocks? Were it not for their good but only for our own, is not this department of work most important? It is only thus we can know our people's spiritual state, and I would go on in this work weekly, if not daily, even if not a soul got good from it but myself. I see the sad wounds of my flock—I see their slow growth in grace—I discover how few really are awakened, how few are in earnest, how very few are saved. It is humbling and painful beyond most things. Of course, there is a kind of visiting which is simply useless, if not hurtful, to minister and people, but visiting with this design is truly soul-exercise. It is a luxury oftentimes to find out truth in the Word, and prepare our sermons for the people, so we need this self-denying mixture to temper our preparations. I daresay you admit all this as much as I do, and yet still cry, " O for a way of profitably visiting !" Dear brother, this is the gift of God. Holiness of heart and life is what I find I need more than anything, a heart daily filled and burning with fresh views of divine love. This is what I seldom have in visiting, and yet I see that if I had that, it would make visiting like the gardener going among his plants and watering them as he saw need, while the Sabbath sermons would be the heavy showers.'

His methods of finding out the state of his people's minds were often very ingenious. He and some other ministers were discussing this subject one day. He said, 'I find it a very good plan to ask when I am visiting, "What was your chapter at family worship this morning?" In this way I find out whether they *have* family worship, and if they have paid attention to it!'

He used to tell with great enjoyment of a remark made by some women as they watched him passing their door in the mission district. 'Why does Dr. Bonar walk so fast?' said one of them. 'Why,' said another, 'do you not know the messengers of the gospel must go swiftly?'

One day he called on a good woman, and found her busy at her washing-tub. 'O Doctor,' was her salutation, 'you always find me in a mess.' 'But there's some one helping you,' he replied. 'No,' she said wonderingly. 'Yes,' he said, 'your Elder Brother is with you.' 'From that day to this,' said the good woman, 'I have never begun a day's work without remembering "My Elder Brother is with me."'

One who was attending his communicants' class told him that she was not yet one of God's children, but was very anxious about her soul. She had been brought up carefully, but had been taught more of the Law than of the Gospel, and it was hard for her to believe that salvation could be hers by the simple acceptance of Christ. While talking with her one day, Dr. Bonar drew a hymn-book out of his pocket and read the well-known lines :—

> 'Nothing either great or small—
>   Nothing, sinner, no ;
> Jesus did it, did it all,
>   Long, long ago.'

Then he said to her, ' I think you are trying to put a
bit to Christ's robe of righteousness.' The words rang in
her ears all day, and, just before going to bed, the light
shone into her heart, and she saw the simplicity of the
way of salvation. She said, ' I felt full of shame to
think I had been doing such a thing.' From day to day
she went on feeding on the truth, and learning more and
more of the Word of God from her pastor's lips ; but
she had not openly confessed Christ to those around
her, though she felt she ought to do so. ' One evening
at the prayer-meeting,' she said, ' I got the word I had
been waiting for for six months. Dr. Bonar was speaking
about the "anointing oil," in Exodus xxx. 22-32, as a
type of the Holy Spirit given to believers. " Some of
you," he said, " have had the oil poured over you, but *you
wipe off the drops with your hand*." '

When calling on a member of his congregation one
day, she said to him, ' Do you know how I first came to
know I was saved ? I dreamed that you were talking to
me, and at last, as you rose to go away, you said, " So
you don't want to be indebted to Another ? " I awoke
and saw it all.'

To an aged member of his flock he said, ' You must
keep fast hold of the text which was written for you :
" Even to your old age I am He ; and even to hoar hairs
will I carry you " (Isaiah xlvi. 4). Just as you carried the
children when they were young, so the Lord says He will
carry you now when you are old.' His words dropped
by the wayside were the seeds of life to many. A
Sabbath scholar never forgot the impression made upon
him by the minister putting his hand on his shoulder
one night and saying, ' Matthew, be like Matthew the
publican. He left all, rose up, and followed Jesus.'
Meeting a young friend on the street he asked her
what her name was. She said, ' Christina.' ' Well,' he

said, 'you have Christ in your name. I hope you have Him in your heart.' One November afternoon he called upon a student who had just joined his Bible-class. The sun was shining into the room, and Dr. Bonar remarked upon it and said, 'I am sure it does not hinder you in your studies; and if you have the Sun of righteousness shining in your heart would it not help you?' When visiting one who was ill, he turned to a stranger who was sitting in the room, and asked her if her name was in the Lamb's Book of Life? She said, 'Oh, sir, my name is not in your books.' 'Oh no,' he said, 'not in my books, but is it in the Lamb's Book?' 'I hope so,' she replied, and quoted the verse, 'If we hope for that we see not,' etc. 'Oh, but that is not the meaning of the verse at all,' said Dr. Bonar, 'you must have more than a hope,' and he showed how she might even now know that her name was in the Book of Life. The conversation was blessed to her, and she became a true child of God.

His acts of loving ministry were countless. He would toil up long flights of stairs to take a new remedy to some one in pain, or to find lodgings for one who was friendless and homeless. He would carry a bottle of beef tea in his pocket to a sickly woman, or a picture-book to while away the long hours of a child's illness. A servant who had belonged to the church left for a situation in the south of England, where she remained for fifteen years. During all that time, Dr. Bonar wrote frequently to her, and sent her each of his little books as they were published, 'and,' she said, 'I am only one of many to whom he did the same.' No service was too small for him to do for any of Christ's little ones, and the joy of his service was as remarkable as its ceaseless-ness. 'Love is the *motive* for working,' he used to say, 'joy is the *strength* for working.' His sunny face as he came into a sick-room brought healing with it, and his brightness was infectious. 'Now, remember,' he said to some friends in parting, 'whenever I see you looking sad or downcast, I will ask you when you cut the Book of Psalms out of the Bible!'

One day he called on an invalid and said, 'I have brought you a new medicine.' 'What is it?' she asked, 'Here it is. "A merry heart doeth good like a medicine!"'

If sent for to pray with careless people when dying he seldom or never refused, but he did not consider it a necessity to go. He thought they made it a sort of extreme unction; but to visit God's people in sickness he considered a duty. Ministering to the 'household of faith' was a form of service he constantly pressed upon others, and presented to them in various aspects. 'It is no small matter to help one another,' he would say. 'To keep a believer's lamp bright is one of the highest benefits you can confer on a dark world.' 'God loves His saints so much that He will give a reward to any one who gives one of them a cup of cold water!'

'Paul says that, even for the sake of comforting the saints, he would wish to abide in the flesh.'

After preaching in Dudhope Church, Dundee, one Sabbath, upon John the Baptist in prison, a gentleman came into the vestry and said to him, 'I am going to see a dying elder, I will try to tell him what you have been saying.' 'Ay,' said Dr. Bonar, 'and tell him Christ will come to visit *him*, though He did not go to visit John; that was for our sake.' His friend, Mr. Manson, when laid aside by illness, had spoken of himself as a 'cumberer of the ground.' Dr. Bonar wrote to him :—

'You say it is not wonderful that you are not getting strength, for you are "only a cumberer." Brother, it is cumberers that are spared!'

His sympathy with those in sorrow had been learned by passing through the same sad discipline. When Mrs. Bonar was so unexpectedly taken away from him in October, 1864, he wrote to his brother Horatius :—

'I think that the Lord who used to give me health to work is now saying, "Will you seek to glorify Me by bearing and enduring?"'

To other friends he wrote :—

'Our time is shortening. The Master has been reminding me of this very solemnly, changing the blue sky over my head by the shade of lasting sorrow.

"But yet I know I shall Him praise."'

'We must learn more and more how to *suffer*. "Thy will be done" is one of the heavenly plants that Jesus left the seed of when He was here. We must cultivate it in our garden. And so also there is another, "The Lord thinketh upon me,"—a plant cultivated by King David when he was an exile in the wilds of En-gedi. This plant is the believer's "Forget-me-not."'

An old friend had been talking with him one day, soon after Mrs. Bonar's death, and as they referred to the many friends who had gone before, and specially to his own great loss, Dr. Bonar was for a few moments quite overcome. Then, quickly recovering himself, he said in his bright way, 'But the best is yet to come!' He had been engaged to give an address to the Young Men's Literary Society on an evening just a day or two after Mrs. Bonar's funeral. He could not take the subject he had intended, but he came as he had promised, and gave an address on some things connected with the Holy Land. The inexpressible sadness of his whole appearance, and his marvellous self-control, made a deep impression on all who were present. 'God does not tell us,' he said, 'to *feel* it is for the best, but he does ask us to *believe* it.'

'Master, that disciple is weeping,' would be enough to

draw the Saviour's attention when on earth. And we can all so speak to Him still.'

'I often read at funerals the twenty-first chapter of Revelation, and I do it with this connection in my mind : " There shall be no more sorrow, nor death, nor pain, nor crying," and " I will give of the fountain of the water of life freely." I always feel that the Lord wanted to put these things within sight of one another. If we would draw more of the living water from the wells of salvation, we should have less sorrow. Drink more, believer. What aileth thee, Hagar? The well is just beside thee. Drink, and go on your way.'

Hearing of the sudden death of one of his people he hastened to the house to see the daughter who was left an orphan. He did not say almost anything to her, but gently put his arm round her and laid her head on his shoulder. When the news of his own sudden removal passed from one to another, from many lips broke the sorrowful words, ' I have lost my best earthly friend ! ' and some wept for him as they had never wept for any friend on earth before.

It was often a matter of surprise that strong and vigorous as he was himself, he could sympathise so tenderly with the sick and suffering. His words to them were always full of comfort.

' It is worth while being wounded to have the hands of the Great Physician upon you.'

' If we cannot say like Paul " this light affliction," let us at any rate try to say, " It is but for a moment." '

' Those who sing loudest in the kingdom will be those who on earth had the greatest bodily suffering. We pity them now, but then we shall almost envy them.'

' We have got more from Paul's prison-house than from his visit to the third heavens.'

'A believer is an Æolian harp, and every event of his life is just the passing wind drawing out the music. And God hears it.'

'"In the world ye shall have tribulation," *but draw the closer to Me.*'

There were two thoughts he often left with God's people in sickness. One was that they might do a great work for the Lord by praying much, and that it is really promotion to be, not down in the valley with Joshua, but with Aaron and Hur on the mountain-top. The other thought was that they are *teaching angels* (Eph. iii. 10). Angels learn much by visiting God's people. They know nothing of suffering themselves, but they learn from the patience and joyfulness of suffering believers. When the sick one enters heaven, some of the angels will say, 'Oh, here is my teacher come!'

Many outside of his own congregation sent for him in times of sickness or trouble. One Saturday evening a lady called at the manse and begged him to go to see her son, who was hopelessly ill. As he went into the room the young man closed a ledger that was lying on the table before him, and said, 'There, now, I 've written the last word I 'll ever write in it.' 'And what then?' asked Dr. Bonar. They drew their chairs to the fireside and began to talk together. Little by little the Spirit of God began to work, and the dying man was led to Christ. His joy was quite unusual—so great that his mother was afraid it might be a delusion. One day when Dr. Bonar was with him, he said to him, 'You will be experiencing something of the joy unspeakable.' 'It 's more than that,' said the dying man, 'it is so great. It is joy *unthinkable.*' A young man, whom he visited at another time, was brought to the Saviour on his deathbed, and filled with great peace in believing. He had been careless and worldly until he was taken ill. One day listening to a brass band playing under his window, the tune recalled to him former scenes of gaiety in which he had taken part, and the thought, 'Am I going into eternity with all these sins upon my soul?' forced itself upon him, and was the means of his awakening. As he drew near his end, he one day said to Dr. Bonar, 'Do you think my mind can be growing weak, for I don't care now for any but the common texts, such as "The Son of man is come to seek and to save that which is lost!"' Shortly before his death he said, 'Jesus came so near to me last night, that I almost felt Him breathing.'

Not long before his death Dr. Bonar was asked to visit a family in great affliction. They were not members of his church, but he went at once, and continued his visits till they were no longer needed. Both father and daughter were dying at the same time. The former was full of joy at the prospect of being with Jesus, and could sing of victory in the midst of great bodily weakness. With the daughter it was different. She had peace, but not the confident assurance and joy that her father had. This troubled her not a little, and she told Dr. Bonar how it distressed her. He said, 'Well, Jeanie, you have peace, have you not? You are resting on what the Lord Jesus has done for you? You see your father was much older when he came to the Lord, and he had more to be forgiven. Consequently his joy at so many sins forgiven is greater than yours.' This answer cheered and comforted her, and so much blessing did she get from his continued visits that she longed daily and hourly for them. Six weeks after her father's death she fell asleep in Jesus on a Sabbath morning. Throughout the day before, whenever there was a ring or knock at the door, she said to her mother, ' I hope this is Dr. Bonar now, mother!' Shortly before she passed away she was heard saying, 'Do come now, quickly, Lord Jesus. Oh, please do come!'

A young woman was taken to the hospital, incurably ill. Dr. Bonar went to see her, and before leaving said to her, 'Remember us in prayer.' She had been feeling very sad, and these words were like new life to her. It was not 'we will remember you,' but 'you will remember us'; and she saw there was still work for her to do, though laid on a bed of sickness.

One who suffered much said when he asked her if she were not longing to be at rest, 'No, I am not wearying for death, but I do hope the Lord may come before I die!'

'Think upon the Lord when you can, and He will think upon you when you can't,' he used to say to sick people. In all his visitation, fear in going to cases of sickness was unknown to him. During the smallpox epidemic in Glasgow he visited some patients week after week. When missionary in St. George's, Edinburgh, he visited a man so ill with typhus fever that no one else would go near him. His kindness touched the sick man's heart, and made him willing to receive the truth. This fearlessness characterised him in every point of duty. He was a firm and determined total abstainer, long before total abstinence was much spoken of, and was not afraid to denounce the drinking customs of the country wherever he went, as well as from his own pulpit. When he first went to Collace he gave great offence by refusing to drink the whisky which was always offered to him when visiting, and the young minister was pronounced to be 'awfu' proud.' However, when it was understood that he would take milk or cream instead, it became an invariable custom to give it to him. One old woman, as she gave him a glass of milk, said, 'It's rale nice, sir, it's the sap o' Macbeth's Castle!' Before he had been long in Collace the one public-house in the parish was closed through his efforts, along with Mr Nairne's influence; and it has never been reopened. In Finnieston district more than one poor drunkard was brought out of bondage into the liberty of Christ through his personal instrumentality. An earnest and consistent member of the church dates the beginning of his changed life to one Saturday evening, when Dr. Bonar found him near the door of the Mission-hall, and, drawing his arm within his own, led him upstairs into the Gospel Temperance Meeting. That night the man signed the pledge, and became soon after a believer in the Lord Jesus Christ.

At a meeting of the 'Mizpah Band' in Glasgow, formed chiefly of those who had been reclaimed from drunkenness, Mr. Moody turned to him after several had given their testimony and said, 'Now, Dr. Bonar, give us *your* testimony.' He at once rose and said, 'Mr. Moody, I have no testimony to give, for I was free-born!'

When giving reproof, he was as faithful and fearless in carrying out the Apostle's injunction: 'reprove, rebuke, exhort,' but in a way that seldom gave offence. He used to say, 'A man is never safe in rebuking another if it does not cost him something to have to do it.'

'Look at Christ's gentleness in His dealings with us. We never find a ruffle of irritation on His lips. When He wants to reprove the forwardness of His disciples, He does it by a little child. Was there ever a gentler reproof given to a backslider than that given to Peter: "Simon, son of Jonas, *lovest thou Me?*"'

'It is a test of our progress in sanctification if we are

willing to have our faults pointed out to us, without getting angry. Why should we take offence at being told we are not perfect?'

'God tells us to love reproof. I don't know any one who ever took rebuke better than Eli. "It is the Lord!" When Nathan said to David, "Thou art the man," he did not flare up as Herod did. No. He said "I have sinned," and went away to write the Fifty-first Psalm.'

An old lady in his congregation used always to sit in one particular part of her room, because when she lifted her eyes from her work she could see Dr. Bonar's portrait on the wall. 'His eyes always rebuke me,' she said, 'whether in his picture or in himself. These other ministers whom I used to be with, they just agreed with me in everything I said, but catch Dr. Bonar doing that!'

He was asked to visit an invalid lady whom he did not know, and found her suffering from nervous depression. After he had talked with her he said before leaving, 'Now, you have far too little to do. I am going to give you something to find out for me,' and left her some Bible exercises to work out. She grew quite interested in her new employment, and in a short time was nearly well. A mother told him how for twenty-four years she had prayed and made efforts for her son's conversion, but he was still unsaved. Dr. Bonar said, 'Speak less *to* him and speak more to God *about* him.' The remark repeated to the young man impressed him much, and not long after he was brought to Christ.

He was told of a woman in the mission district who professed to have been converted. After he had been to see her, he said he did not think she was really changed, or her house would have been cleaner. He was quite right, for the woman's profession turned out to be insincere.

A gentleman whom he knew to be very excitable told him that during his illness he had had a vision of angels, and had felt one of them touch him as he lay in bed. Dr. Bonar quietly remarked, 'Have you a cat in the house? Don't you think it may have been the cat?'

Sometimes he took playful ways of reproving or trying to put matters right when he thought it needful. The following letter to his brother-in-law, Mr. William Dickson, will explain itself :—

> '*"Fields of Ephratah,"*
> *Summer-days of* A.D. 1872.

'MR. EDITOR,—I find in my peregrinations, that not a few, both ministers and people, who take a deep interest in the Sabbath school, are annually brought into straits and difficulties at the S.S. Breakfast. They complain that they neither can get a good supply for the body, nor hear comfortably (there being almost no room for sitting), so as to get their spirit refreshed. They suggest that a larger 'Upper Room' should somewhere be found. The Master's Upper Room seems to have been large and airy—at least held comfortably all who came. Excuse me troubling you with this note, but you are understood to be most willing to take any suggestion that may help on the cause, and promote the interests of the young.—Yours in the common faith and hope, A FELLOW-LABOURER.'

He was at one time troubled by some of the people coming in late to church. As he was reading and commenting on the tenth chapter of Acts one afternoon, he came to the verse : 'Now therefore are we all here present before God.' He stopped and said, 'I think that is more than some of us could have said this morning !' Another time he said, 'A great many were late this morning—not like Mary Magdalene, *early* at the sepulchre.'

His candour and straightforwardness sometimes made

him appear unsympathetic, for he never tried to please any one at the expense of truth. 'There are some people who can stand anything but flattery. If no one ever praises you, you are all the better for it!' After the meeting in 1888 to celebrate his ' Jubilee,' an old Collace friend remarked to him that it had been a 'grand meeting.' He replied, 'Yes, but I think there was too much praise of man, and too little to God. I never thought I did more than draw the water and let the flock drink.'

The story with which he closed his address on that same evening was one which he often told in illustration of what humbles a minister, and delivers him from self-satisfaction.

A Grecian painter had executed a remarkable painting of a boy carrying on his head a basket of grapes. So exquisitely were the grapes painted, that when the picture was put up in the Forum for the admiration of the citizens, the birds pecked the grapes, thinking they were real. The friends of the painter were full of congratulations, but he did not seem at all satisfied. When they asked him why, he replied, 'I should have done a great deal more. I should have painted the boy so true to life that the birds would not have dared to come near!'

CHAPTER XIV

Manse Memories

AT the beginning of his ministry Dr. Bonar said in one of his letters: 'This is a time that seems to require prayer more than preaching even, at least so I often feel. And persevering prayerfulness — day by day wrestling and pleading—is harder for the flesh than preaching.'

As years passed the 'main business of every day' to him was prayer, and latterly, when overwhelmed by work,—visits, letters, interruptions, engagements of every kind,—it was his rule to devote two hours every day, before going out, to prayer and meditation on God's Word. When the settlement of his colleague, Mr. M'Intyre, in 1891, had relieved him of some of his former duties, his Sabbath evenings were spent in prayer in his study. A card hung on one side of his mantelpiece on which were printed the words, ' *Dimidium studii qui rite precatur habet*,'—' He who has truly prayed has completed the half of his study.' Early visitors to his study in India Street were familiar with the sight of his figure standing at his desk writing letters, as was his habit always after breakfast. In the afternoon he visited regularly from one o'clock till nearly five, and every evening was filled up with a meeting of some kind. Friday and Saturday were kept as days of preparation for Sabbath, and no visitor was admitted to his study on Saturday unless his errand were of great importance. One who had much intercourse with him in work had occasion to call on a Friday afternoon when he was busy with his preparation for the pulpit. He appeared like one lost to himself in communion with God, and the visitor left, feeling overawed. Like John Bunyan in his dream, he had seen a man 'with his eyes lifted up to Heaven, the best of books in his hand, the law of truth written upon his lips, and the world behind his back.'

His study-hours during the week were constantly interrupted, and it was sometimes difficult to see how preparation for his many meetings and classes was ever accomplished. 'There were many coming and going, and they had no leisure so much as to eat,' was sometimes literally true in his experience. Yet he never went to his own pulpit or to a meeting unprepared, and he spoke often of the necessity of first receiving a blessing ourselves from the subject to be spoken of, before giving out to others.

'Use for yourself first what the Lord teaches you, and if He spare you, use it for others.'

'When you have got a blessing, take time to let it sink into your own heart before you tell it out.'

It was a favourite thought of his that when a blessing is got from the Lord, part of it is to be given away. 'There is "*seed for the sower*," ' he used to say, 'as well as "bread for the eater." ' He spoke of Psalm xxiii. 5 : '" My cup runneth over." He filled it, and then poured in more! Stop! No, let somebody else get a share. He gave me an overflow for the sake of others.'

His splendid constitution, his vigour of body, added to his regular habits and his great calmness of mind, made possible for him what few other men could have attempted. Often he referred with thankfulness to the unbroken sleep he enjoyed at night. In his study he

was at home, and every corner of it spoke of himself,
everything in perfect order—no book or paper ever out
of its place. 'Untidiness,' he used to say, 'is un-
christian.' His Bible always lay on the table, and his
Hebrew Bible and little Greek Testament on a small
table by the fireplace. Till his eyesight began to fail
slightly, he used a very old Bible of his father's which
he valued much. On its blank pages are written shorthand notes of his conversations with his old minister,
Dr. Jones, when he joined the Church in 1830, and
other jottings from sermons of his which had impressed
him. On another page he has written these lines in
shorthand :—

> 'Behold the book whose leaves display
> Jesus the Life, the Truth, the Way ;
> Read it with diligence and care,
> Search it, for thou shalt find Him there.'

In his study hung the text he was so fond of, and
had had printed for himself : '*But Thou remainest.*' A
lady called to see him one day, in great sorrow and
depression of mind. Nothing seemed to bring her any
comfort. All at once, as they talked together, Dr.
Bonar saw her face light up, and she said, 'You don't
need to say anything more. I have got what I need ;'
and she pointed to the words of the text which had
caught her eye : '*But Thou remainest.*' He used to recall often a scene in his study, when a working-man came
one evening to see him in great distress about his soul.
During their conversation the light broke in upon him,
and, striking his hand on his knee, the man exclaimed,
'I never all my life expected to have joy like this !'

One of the treasures of his study was a piece of
Samuel Rutherford's pulpit, which always lay on the
mantelpiece. Another much-prized relic was a panel of
Lady Kenmure's pew in Anwoth Church. His reverence

for everything connected with the saints of former times was well known, and was often a subject of playful raillery on the part of his friends.

When in America, in the summer of 1881, he visited Northampton, out of love for the memory of Jonathan Edwards and David Brainerd, and wrote to his daughter at home :—

'*Northfield*, 23rd *Aug.* 1881.

'My dear Marjory,—I have been taking a quiet walk among shrubs and pines on the slope of a hill, and the little burn gave me opportunity to sit down and work away, making waterfalls, etc., as if in Arran or in Mull.

'On Saturday last, Isabella and I, with Major Whittle, Emma Moody, and a nice old minister from Philadelphia, made out a visit to Northampton, the town of Jonathan Edwards. You know how much I desired to be there, and our visit was most interesting. But we missed you, for there were some views which would have afforded you grand work for your pencil. We sat under, and climbed so far up, the two old elm-trees planted in front of his house by Jonathan Edwards, and I can *sell* you, when I return, a piece of the bark ! You will have to sketch from my rude materials Brainerd's tomb, which we next visited, and some other gravestones, full of interest. The old church, the scene of the great Revivals, was burnt many years ago.'

In his diary he wrote, in a different strain, his reflections and feelings in connection with this visit :—

'I bless the Lord for this day with all its sacred memories, "Is the Spirit of the Lord straitened ?" Is not Jesus Christ the same yesterday, to-day, and for ever ? Father, Thou hast brought me at this time of my life across the sea, to stand at this spot, and there pray and call to mind "the days of the right hand of the Most High." Surely Thou hast in store very much blessing for me and my people and my land ! Come as near, come in the revelation of the same glorious holiness as to Thy servants then.'

And next day, Sabbath, August 21st, he writes :—

'Much stirred up by yesterday's visit to Northampton, and the train of thought and prayer it led to. . . . Lord, give me fully what is meant by "that Christ may dwell in your heart," and by

" Christ liveth in me." I preached on Isa. liii. 2, but did not feel [helped]. I fear that yesterday, having got a full cup, I did not set it down before the Lord on the mercy-seat with thanks and praise, and with the appeal, Eph. iii. 20-21.'

Many a journey he made to spots of historic interest, and he would go any distance to see the grave of a martyr, or the home of a saint of God. In 1860 he made a pilgrimage through Dumfriesshire and Kirkcud-brightshire along with Mr. James Crawford of Edinburgh, and wrote to Mrs. Bonar during their wanderings :—

'*Kirkcudbright, 2nd August* 1860.—Of course we made a pilgrimage to the churchyard and its martyrs' graves, accompanied by a very intelligent policeman who knows some Latin, and helped us to read the tombstones and search for the grave of Marion M'Naught.[1] We did not succeed in finding this grave, but we found the site of her house where Samuel Rutherford used to call. It is just coming down to make way for another, so I brought away a stone of it ! That stone must have sent back the sound of the voices of both Samuel Rutherford and Marion M'Naught, as well as of Blair when his horse stopped at the door, and he found his two friends ready to give him a welcome.'

On this journey he wrote one of his amusing letters to his brother John, dated from Anwoth, and purport-ing to be from Samuel Rutherford :—

'*3rd August* 1860.

'SWEET AND WORTHY BROTHER,—You did well some years ago to visit the scenes of my former labours. Did you not agree with me in calling the swallows that build their nests at Anwoth Church, "blessed birds"? I see two of your friends have this summer come to tread in your steps—one of them is a younger brother of yours, the other writes after his name, Eccl. Scot. Lib. E.C. There was no such church in my day, but I always said that Scotland's sky would clear again. And I dow [2] declare that, if only they will go home more prayerful than they came, this visit to Anwoth will not have been in vain. But, perhaps, dearest and truly-honoured brother, you would like to know a little about

---

[1] One of Rutherford's correspondents, the wife of the Provost of Kirk-cudbright.

[2] Can, am able ; frequently used in Rutherford's *Letters*.

their journey. Let me tell you, therefore, that they came by way of Kirkcudbright. While there they sought out the house of Marion M'Naught. This generation (who are never long content with what their fathers did) are at this moment pulling that dwelling down ; but your two friends have picked out of the crumbling lime a piece of stone (which no doubt they will send to you) which must have echoed back my loud burst of surprise and joy on that memorable night when Robert Blair, my fellow-prisoner and true servant to his master, came from Ireland straight to Marion M'Naught's dwelling. They have been away at her tomb also, which is marked by a flat stone near the spot where two martyrs lie waiting for the Day of Resurrection. I may tell you, besides, that they set out for Dundrennan Abbey, where that idol-loving Queen Mary took refuge for a night. Dear and trusty brother, I was not in the way of going aside to see even broken idols, and, if I mistake not, neither are you. Your friends did far better next day when they visited Borgue and sought out the old house of my friend the Laird of Roberton, Carleton also, and Knockbrex, all men of God, men who would own no hireling for their pastor, and who lodged Christ when others would give Him no roof for His head. They have this afternoon been looking down on Cardoness, and Cally, and Rusco, and Ardwell, as well as walking up my "Walk." If they might only walk in my steps so far as I tried to be Caleb-like ! I persuade myself that it is so far well for this generation that they built a monument to me, inasmuch as it was not to myself (if I dow think and say this), but to the cause which I ever loved and defended. Your brother is reported to be about to preach in Anwoth on the coming Sabbath. This will be all well if only he preach Him who is worthy to be praised, and so worthy to be preached, and if he will cry up that Plant of Renown, in spite of unwilling hearts, that love to hear the news of a passing-away world.

'I should perhaps advise them to visit Wigtown, and to go homeward by Glenkens. O Earlston ! Earlston ! ye stood fast and well in the day of battle.

'But I have written too much. I hold my peace here. Remember my love to your wife, and say that she has the good wishes of one who signs himself,—Your unworthy brother,

S. R.'

He often amused himself by writing in this strain, and he and his brothers exchanged many such letters.

From Haworth, in Yorkshire, he wrote again to his brother John :—

'*Not far from Haworth,*
15th July 1878.

'DEAR AND HONOURED BROTHER,—Some years ago (was it not in 1867 ?) you kindly visited my church and resting-place, though I myself had gone away to the "mountain of myrrh" to spend a few days there with Wesley and Whitefield and John Berridge "till the day break." It seems that a brother of yours has called at Haworth on the same brotherly errand. He heard the clatter of the pattens which the people here use, old and young, and he saw the place in sunshine, when it looks pretty well. He could not fail to notice "The Black Bull" and "The White Lion," public-houses near my church, out of which (when the windows were nearer the ground than now) I often chased drinkers and loungers found there after service began, and you would have smiled to see the haste they made to escape by window or door. Your brother stood on my resting-place ; you know it is marked by no inscription, but the slab that covers my bones is right in front of the Brontés' grand tablet on the wall. . . . The old house where I lived is the old piece of the present parsonage, and your brother reverently walked along the track in the churchyard by which I used to go down from the house that was my abode to the House of God. He went up to my pulpit, too, and how could I help wishing that he may yet see in the pews of his own church as many weeping eyes and bowed-down heads as I often saw all over these seats ! But do you know that they are going to pull down this church and build a new and larger one ? I am almost sorry—though what is a building but a platform erected in order to get the true stones hoisted up into their places ? Your brother (is he quite free from that reverence for holy spots which Stephen, in Acts vii., shows to be no part of worship ?) was overheard asking the schoolmaster if he knew where "the clerk's house" stood, in which I was once prostrated by an overwhelming discovery of divine grace and glory. But that house is long since removed ; it was a mere room near the church for the clerk's use. He was asking, too, for the place where I began to know the Lord—Todmorden ; the people often call it "Tommorden." It is ten or twelve miles from Haworth, as you know.

'But I daresay you are tired with this long epistle, as your brother was when he got back that night to Keighley. So I bid

you heartily farewell, not doubting to meet you some day in
brighter sunshine than Haworth ever knew.—Your brother,
                                        ' WILLIAM GRIMSHAW.'

Another letter of this kind he wrote on the occasion
of his brother's ' Jubilee' at Greenock in 1885 :—

                    ' *Paradise, the Third Heavens.*

' DEAR AND HONOURED BROTHER,—I cannot be present in
body at your jubilee next week, being detained a willing prisoner
in the King's Palace here ; but I send my loving salutations, and
hope you are in good case, albeit ye be sometimes wechted with
your fourscore and two years. I know ye handle the pen of a
ready writer, but, for all that, it may be weel for you to look into ye
buik I send you, to wit, some old sermons of mine, which ye may
preach when ye run dry. It seems you were ordained in 1835.
Now, two hundred years before that (1635) there was a dial[1]
or horologe set up in the garden of my Lady Kenmure by an
ancestor of yours. Ye have seen it, and read on its face, " Joannes
Bonar, fecit."

' Hoping to meet you in Immanuel's Land when the great
jubilee trumpet shall be blown,—Your very loving brother,
                                        ' SAMUEL RUTHERFORD.

' Misspend not your short sandglass, which runneth very fast.'

During the sittings of the General Assembly in 1882,
he spent a day in visiting Ormiston and other places of
interest. He describes it thus to Mr. Manson :—

' You will have been visited, I suppose, by some of my family in
search of primroses and spring flowers. Meanwhile, their father
has been doing duty (1) as a preacher of the Word at Lanark on
Sabbath ; (2) as an ecclesiastic ; (3) as a lover of good men, such
as John Knox and George Wishart, on (if not *in*) whose footsteps
he was treading yesterday. For you must know that, while
the brethren were battering the crumbling walls of the " Estab-
lishment," I did yesterday go on pilgrimage. I set out with
Mr. Glendinning, who knows all that region, to visit some
localities of interest in Midlothian. We saw where Knox and

---

[1] When walking in the grounds of Kenmure Castle one day, Dr. John
Bonar and a friend who was with him had their attention drawn to an old
sun-dial in the garden. After carefully scraping away the moss which had
gathered over it, they read the inscription, ' Joannes Bonar fecit !'

Wishart took their last farewell of each other, and the large (the largest in Scotland) yew-tree under which Wishart preached. This was at Ormiston House. It was very interesting, also, to stand on high ground and look around. Yonder is Saltoun where Fletcher the statesman lived. . . . There, yonder, is Pencaitland, where, in old days, Calderwood was minister. . . . But—I must off to the Assembly.'

'Scotland will never know,' he said, 'till the Great Day, what it owes to its martyrs' prayers, when they lay for days and months hidden in the moors and caves. God put them there on purpose.'

In his friend, the Rev. J. H. Thomson of Hightae, he found a sympathetic and enthusiastic co-worker in the field of covenanting lore, and during fifteen years he kept up a constant correspondence with him on subjects relating to the Reformers and the Martyrs. When editing an edition of the *Scots Worthies* and when preparing both *Letters* and *Sermons of Samuel Rutherford* for the press, Mr. Thomson was his unfailing referee. Sometimes he addresses him as 'My dear Interpreter,' 'My dear Zaphnath-paaneah' (*see* margin, Gen. xli. 45), 'My dear Philo-Rhaetorfortis,' or 'Amice foederatorum.'

'Glean more and more in the fields of Bethlehem,' he writes, 'and, when you please, "let fall of purpose handfuls for me."'

'There is something about Alexander Peden's sermons that takes me more than almost any man of that time. I wish we had more of him.'

'Peace be with you. May the people of Hightae find that their minister comes in for a large share of the answer to the martyrs' prayer.'

At the close of a letter, in reference to the transcription of some sermons of Samuel Rutherford which Mr. Thomson had undertaken, Dr. Bonar says :—

'Should you not preach to your people what you find so

satisfying to your own soul in Samuel Rutherford?—Yours truly, dear Interpreter, who gives out to pilgrims things "rare" if not wonderful.'

At other times he signs himself, ' Yours truly in Him who ever hears the cry, Rev. vi. 10'; ' Yours truly in Him who cares for the dust of Zion more than any of us do.'

'In July 1880,' Mr. Thomson writes, ' Dr. Bonar came to assist at the dispensation of the Lord's Supper at Hightae. It was a visit much to be remembered. He was in full vigour of mind and body, and gave no less than five addresses, perhaps the best being his sermon to the children on Sabbath afternoon. On the Tuesday we started on a long-promised expedition to the Enterkin Pass. The morning was fair, but as we got near Elvanfoot drops of rain gave ominous warning of the showers that afterwards overtook us. At Elvanfoot we got the mail-gig for Leadhills. The driver at once recognised Dr. Bonar, and showed us no little kindness, walking with us across the moor after reaching Leadhills, until we came to the head of the pass, where the ground is about 700 feet above the level of the sea. The road down the pass no longer exists. It has been washed away, and in its place there remains only the loose shingle on the hillside that runs down to the ravine below, in which rushes along the Enterkin Burn. It was not easy to keep one's footing on the loose pebbles, but Dr. Bonar went along with the agility and confidence of a born mountaineer until we came to the foot of the pass, where the prisoners were rescued from the soldiers by their Covenanting friends. Though the rain fell heavily as we came down the pass, his cheerfulness never flagged, and he discussed the possibilities of Defoe's graphic account of the rescue with all the interest of one familiar with the story from his early days. . . . Dr. Bonar spoke much as he wrote. A genial humour ran through his conversation. He loved to express himself quaintly, but it was always as a Christian scholar whose chief study was the Bible, and one of whose leading aims was to tell about its treasures to others. His delight in the Reformers and Covenanters, and especially in Samuel Rutherford, arose very much from the conviction that their chief study and chief aims were like his own. Communion with the saints was, therefore, a leading characteristic of his life. It gave directness to his studies and a charm to his conversation.'

Dr. Bonar liked to trace a family connection with good Colonel Gardiner, and Mrs. Bonar claimed kindred with James Renwick the martyr. The Greyfriars' Churchyard in Edinburgh was a favourite haunt of his, and many a friend did he take to see the martyrs' grave and the stone where the Covenant was signed. He loved his native town, and was always glad when occasion led him back to Edinburgh. In one of his letters he tells of an amusing interview with a cabman soon after coming to Glasgow. When he had paid his fare, the man looked at him with a half-smile, and said, ' Sir, you micht gie me anither saxpence, for we 're baith Edinburgh men !'

The earliest recollection of his childhood was the firing of the Castle guns in 1815 to celebrate the victory of Waterloo. He often went to look at the old house in Paterson's Court, Broughton, where he was born on the 29th of May 1810, and where his early years were spent. His home was a bright and happy one, where family affection and healthy enjoyments went side by side with simple piety. To their early training all the family owed in great part their thorough knowledge of the Bible and of the Shorter Catechism, and the stores of paraphrases and hymns which they held in their memory. Andrew was the youngest boy, and was always quiet and studious. His first literary effort was a ' History of the Rabbits,' which he wrote when he was eleven years old. The gentleness and modesty which became so characteristic of the man were early apparent in the boy. On the day on which he gained the Dux Gold Medal of the High School in 1825 he came home as usual, and said nothing about it till his mother asked at the dinner-table, 'Well, Andrew, and who got the Gold Medal to-day?' when he quietly drew it out of his pocket. The death of his father in

1821 was the first event which left an impression on his mind, and he very often referred to it.

When his son was spending a summer session in Edinburgh, in 1872, he wrote to him :—

'Do you ever look along at the spot where your father and grandfather, uncles, and aunts used to encamp? Only think, it is half a century now since the day when your grandfather was carried to his last resting-place in the Canongate Churchyard from Paterson's Court.'

'You congratulate me on my birthday being at hand. . . . To you and your sisters I send my hearty thanks and my prayer that if you be spared as long as I have been since first I drew breath near where you now are, in one of the rooms of that pillared house in Paterson's Court, you all may have enjoyed as much as I have done of the "glorious Gospel of the blessed God," through which we find communion with God restored.'

After a visit to Edinburgh and to the house in 24 Gayfield Square, which had been his home at another time, he writes to Mrs. Bonar :—

'I saw the room we studied in so long, and *where I remember first of realising a found Saviour.*'

When the Queen came to Edinburgh on one occasion, he took his two youngest daughters with him to see her. As they were walking about, they met his old friend, Mr. Walker of Perth, and Dr. Bonar said to him, 'You see I've brought my children in to see the Queen.' 'Very good,' was Mr. Walker's reply. 'Yes,' said Dr. Bonar, 'we saw her, but we were not changed ; but "when we see *Him* we shall be *like* Him."'

The summer holidays were always spent with his family in the country or by the sea. He was much attached to the East Coast, associated as it was with his early recollections, but many of his summers were spent among the wilder and grander scenery of the West Highlands. One of his letters to Mr. Manson

from Mull, in the summer of 1882, records a visit to
Iona to which he often looked back with great interest:—

' Graignure, 25th August 1880.

'MY DEAR FRIEND,—I returned from Iona last night, having
spent five days in that region. Our Sabbath (the Communion)
was a delightful day ; outwardly all was still, calm, and bright
sunshine, the sea smooth as if it had been of crystal, and as to the
inward work we had the deepest attention and solemnity. While
Mr. Blacklock conducted in Gaelic the forenoon opening services
under the blue sky on the "field of the Druids " (the last of the
Druids are said to be buried there), I took the services in the
church. After the first Table, we who were English-speaking
came out to the open air and gave place to the Gaelic worshippers
who then sat down at the Table. We had with us a sample of " the
Great Multitude from all nations," for there were with us a United
Presbyterian minister (Robertson of Irvine), an Episcopalian minister from Norfolkshire, the Established Church minister of Glen-
urquhart, and an English Presbyterian from Liverpool, while Mr.
Blacklock represented the country, and I the town. As we crossed
and re-crossed the Sound to get to the Manse, those in the boat
kept singing praise.

' By the bye, the wife of an old elder here paid me as great a
compliment as was once paid to you in Rannoch. She said that
my English was well understood by the Gaelic people, for "it was
not grammatical !" [1] Tell me all you discover of Covenanting
times—Carsphairn is redolent with such memories. . . . Janie is
going to supplement my letter, so that I may close, subscribing
my name.

I am A. A. B.
As you at once see ;
Sojourning in Mull,
And trying to cull
Sermons from stones
And Culdee bones !'

Another letter gives a glimpse of his employments in
the Highlands :—

' On Sabbath I was sailing across the Sound of Mull to preach
at Loch Aline. The sea was like the "sea of glass " in the Apoca-

---

[1] The old woman's exact words were, ' We understand you, for you have
no grammar ! '

lypse, so that you see if you had a snatch of "Paradise," I had a glimpse of the "New Earth." . . . We have a good deal of biography with us ; some poetry, a little Latin, and German and French and Hebrew. Very miscellaneous, you may well suppose. All this is an appendix to the Book of Nature, which we came here to study.'

Besides reading and walking, his holiday occupations were varied by occasional hours of hoeing and weeding. Nettles and dandelions were mercilessly attacked, generally by his umbrella for want of a better weapon, and every paper on the pathway had to be cleared away. Some of his friends professed to let their gardens lie waste in expectation of his annual visits. He had a great horror of an untidy manse-garden, and used to remind the owner that 'æsthetics are next to ethics.' When visiting an old friend in Dumfriesshire he wrote home saying he was busy putting the garden in order, and added :—

> 'If you want a field of labour
> You will find it anywhere !'

His favourite poets, Milton and Cowper, were generally his companions in the country. He delighted in sacred poetry, and read and often quoted Montgomery's *Hymns*, the Olney *Hymns*, and Hart's *Hymns*. Though he found it difficult to quote any of these correctly in the pulpit, he could repeat easily and fluently any of Dr. Watts' well-known hymns, which he had learned from his mother in his childhood. Sometimes on a Sabbath evening, when his day's work was over, he would read aloud or have his children read to him, passages from Baxter's *Saints' Rest*, or Rutherford's *Letters*, or Ambrose's *Looking unto Jesus*, or John Bunyan's story of the pilgrims crossing the river. Latin and English classics, etymology, and topography were his recreations. His reading was extremely careful and minute, and he had a knack of picking out whatever in a book was noteworthy, though he seemed to have only read it hurriedly. In taking up a volume out of his library one turns involuntarily to the blank leaf at the end to see what is marked there as specially interesting. His comments are written freely and are sometimes amusing. A book written many years ago by a Moderate minister has this note: 'Moderatism sometimes points out the moral lessons well, but oftener shows how to overlook the true sense.' At the end of his copy of Marshall *on Sanctification*, he has written: 'There is real endowment for holiness wherever justification has taken place, even if little felt. But the best endowment is not only the fact of justification but also the knowledge of that fact.' On a copy of Faber's *Hymns* which he gave to his daughter he wrote: 'On her birthday. With the apostle's caution, 1 John iv. 1.' He added the following note to a volume of sermons which he sent to his son: 'Poison; to be taken in small doses and to be used along with what Christiana got for her boy in the House Beautiful from Mr. Skill, a purge made *ex carne et sanguine Christi.*'

The Hebrew and Greek Testaments were his constant study, and he used to ask young ministers when they came to see him, 'Do you still keep up your Greek and Hebrew?' If they hesitated or said 'no,' he would say, 'Read one verse in Greek and Hebrew every day and you will be surprised how it will help you.' He is remembered in his student days as stirring others up to a proper study of Hebrew, and no other student of his time had an equal talent for languages. He was remarkable for his diligence and improvement of time, and for his indomitable energy. Nothing that he tried to master baffled him except singing, which he was never able to acquire. His great desire was to learn even one tune, that he might be able to help at a meeting or sing by a sick-bed, but he never succeeded.

Naturally shy and reserved, he was the life of any company where he felt at home, and he had the charm of perfect naturalness, and an entire want of self-consciousness. The continual sunshine in which he lived made him attractive to both old and young, and his humour, instead of decreasing, grew more intense as he grew older. One of his friends remarked of his home life that it was a new illustration of the truth that wisdom's ways 'are ways of pleasantness, and all her paths are peace.' His letters to his children are brimming over with fun, intermingled with the most serious and loving words. As birthdays came round he always made reference to them at family worship. 'Bless the one of our number whose birthday this is. May this be a day for heavenly favours and heavenly gifts.' One of his daughters said one morning with a sigh, 'I am a quarter of a century old to-day.' Immediately he rejoined, 'You have reached half your jubilee!' On a card, which he sent as a birthday greeting to his youngest daughter, he wrote :—

> 'Better and wiser every day,
>   Till every hair on your head be gray !'

His family had presented him with a reading-lamp on his birthday, and he expressed his thanks in the following letter to his daughter, then in London :—

. . . 'Hoping to see you very soon, I write to-day merely to acknowledge your gift on my birthday—for I understand all of you joined in it. It was very kind and mindful in you all. I began a poem on the occasion, but the muse deserted me very soon. Here is the fragment, however :

> 'A son and daughters four of mine
>   Resolved together to combine
>   Their father to enlighten—
>   That so there might be nothing found
>   Within his study, all around,
>   To startle or affrighten.'

.　　.　　.　　.　　.　　.　　.

Good-bye,—Your affectionate father,　　　ANDREW A. BONAR.

Many years ago when at Collace he sent to a friend of Mrs. Bonar's in Edinburgh before her wedding, the following

'HEADS OF MARRIAGE SERVICE

To be delivered when Miss W—— becomes Mrs. Y——

I. Your past experience. *N. B.*—The wide field of unmarried life.

II. Your prospects as they appear to cool and impartial and thoughtful friends.

III. Your imaginary discovery of a complete continent of excellences in each other.

IV. Your sober realisation of each other's faults, failures, follies, etc.

V. The question—will you now proceed? Yes or No. Speak audibly and without faltering.'

His postcards were often a source of amusement to his friends. The following one was sent to Dr. Somerville as an apology for not being present at a meeting :—

'20 *India Street, Saturday.*

'Αδελφέ μοῦ ἀγαπητέ,

Necesse est me adire Greenock hodie, quia crastino die οἱ μαθῆται συνάγονται κλάσαι ἄρτον.

Saludad á todos hermanos. La gracia sea con todos vosotros.

ANDREW A BONAR. הָרֹעֶה בִּפְנֵחֲסַתֶּן

From Northfield he wrote in 1881 to his youngest daughter :—

'MY DEAR MARY,—What a country this is! They give us curry and beefsteaks to breakfast, and potatoes and squash and doughnuts! At dinner we often get sokotash, a mixture of Indian corn and beans. A large bird (more than twice the size of our red-robin) comes morning by morning to the field before my window to get worms, and it is the American robin-redbreast. We have pine-trees instead of fir-trees.

'But I'll tell you two or three things I do not quite like, though everybody here is as kind as possible. One is, their roads—not kept in good repair either in town or country. Another is, the people do not bring Bibles with them to the church, nor do they sing the Psalms. And still another—the Sabbath-school children in their churches do not learn a catechism-lesson. They are far behind us in all these things, so that I like our own land after all, and shall be glad to return. I hope to find you wonderfully improved, body, soul, and spirit.—Your affectionate father,

'ANDREW A. BONAR.'

Another letter to his son is a playful criticism of his book, *Letters of Ricardo to Malthus.*

'*Glasgow, 25th November* 1887.

'MY DEAR JAMES,—It seems to me that you have edited the *Letters of Ricardo to Malthus* with great skill, and evidently with great care. I have no doubt that your book will be very interesting to all students of Political Economy, giving the private discussion (so to speak) of the great subject by two such men as Ricardo and Malthus. Cobbett's bitterness (at p. 162, note) in criticising Malthus is the raciest part of the book. . . .

FOR MARY (MRS. BONAR)

' Notice at p. 45, "Mrs. Ricardo, standing by me, has made me express myself in a more than usually bungling manner."

'*Inference.* Never stand near Dr. James when he is writing.

'At p. 54, a certain lady, Mrs. Smith, asks Ricardo to procure for her some letter of Malthus. In reply he says, "Knowing that I had many which would not discredit you, I assented."

'*Query.* If any friend should ask me for such a specimen letter of Dr. James Bonar could I say, "Having many which would not discredit him"? I could send one letter of three sentences, another of two, I believe !

'At p. 240, might not the editor when mentioning "Huish, near Chippenham," have added in a parenthesis ["Chippenham ! where the little church stands in which J. B. and M. M. were united in holy matrimony."]

' One great defect occurs at the very outset. You have not written my name on it. . . . I go to-morrow to open a new church at Scone, where Scotland's kings used to be crowned. I think I must bid the congregation remember the "King of kings," singing

" Bring forth the royal diadem,
And crown *Him* Lord of all ! "

—Your affectionate father,　　　　　　　　　　　　　　A. A. B.

CHAPTER XV

Nearing the Goal

IT was not only to the saints of other days that his affection was drawn out, but his love for the brethren was shown in his deep and lasting attachment to those who enjoyed his closer friendship, and to others whom he knew little, but loved because they loved the Lord. He believed in the communion of saints, and one of his chief regrets at the abolition of the Fast-Days preparatory to the observance of the Lord's Supper, was the loss of the brotherly fellowship which was always enjoyed at these times. Speaking one day of hermits he described them as 'earthworms,' and said, 'a man can't meditate when he is always alone. He needs to have intercourse with others to stir him up to meditation.' 'When are we to meet?' he writes to a friend. 'Sometimes it seems to me to be true of *meetings* what Arnauld said of *rest*: 'We shall *meet* in eternity. O day of glory! O day of our gathering together in Him!' 'Are you not saddened by Spurgeon's illness?' he writes to another friend. 'What can we say but Ezekiel xi. 13, and sing "God lives! bless'd be my Rock!"' The friends of other days, and those whom he regarded as his own children in the faith, were very near his heart. His love for the Jews, begun so early in life, continued unabated to the end. Anything connected with them or their land was to him of peculiar interest. Next to the joyful hope of the King Himself on the throne was the thought of a restored nation worshipping at His feet, and a land to which had been given back 'the beauty of Lebanon and the excellency of Carmel and Sharon.' Nothing was more gladdening to his heart than the news of one and another of the sons of Israel being brought into the fold of Christ. Writing to Dr. J. H. Wilson, regarding the baptism of a Jew which was to take place in the Barclay Church, Edinburgh, he says :—

'We shall try to remember you on Sabbath when you expect to baptize C——. A branch of the "old olive-tree" will be waving in your church in the person of these two sons of Abraham. May you find peculiar blessing on yourself and on your people !'

To another friend he writes :—

'I anticipate great pleasure from meeting with Mr. S. We must get good olive oil from him, he is a berry of the good olive-tree' (Rom. xi. 24).

An amusing interview took place between Mr. Rabbinovitch and himself in a friend's house. Mr. Rabbinovitch rose from his chair to offer it to Dr. Bonar as he came into the room. He tried to prevent him from rising and said, 'No, no, *to the Jew first*!' Mr. Rabbinovitch replied, 'But thou shalt rise up before the face of the old man !'

Often in later years he refers in his letters to those who have passed away from the old circle of friends. 'You notice William Burns must have got over the river, and in at the gate of the Celestial City a month at least before John Milne. Well, he and Milne and Patrick Miller, and Robert M'Cheyne, and James Hamilton, have been talking over the past.'

'Did you notice Dr. Keith's death [1880]? in a good old age—eighty-nine—like the Patriarchs. He has gone on to "New Jerusalem," and soon probably the last of

the four who in 1839 travelled Palestine together, may
make up to him. Oh, it will be glorious to stand within
the gates of ' Jerusalem that cometh down from heaven,'
and to see the King in His beauty in His own land—
Immanuel's Land ! '

' I have been thinking that saints certainly remember
those they left behind, and are certainly looking forward
to the day of "our gathering together in Him " ; but
they do not miss us as we miss them.'

Christians of all denominations were his friends, and
many who differed widely from him in opinion loved
him with a deep affection. He liked to remind believers
of their duty to all saints, and the blessedness of united
prayer and united effort.

' In holiness we must go on together, not alone. You
will not get on by separating yourself to read and pray.
It must be " along with them that call on the Lord."
We are to climb Pisgah together, and from the top see
the stretch of the land. But we are not to go alone.'
' God loves unity, and so He loves a united cry, a petition signed by more than one.' ' Christ liked to come
to the feast when He was going to give blessing. He
liked to come to the upper room when they were all
assembled there.'

He was firm in adherence to his own principles, and
those who did not know him well had no idea of the
determined force of will that lay beneath his gentle
kindliness. Independent in word and action to the last
degree, what others might think or say of him was to
him of no consequence. Occasionally his determination
was almost provoking, and yet, in the end, it had often
to be admitted that he was right ! The nickname of
' Old Obstinate,' which his friend Mr. Patrick Miller of
Newcastle gave to him in early days, stuck to him to
the last. ' " Who sweareth (engageth) to his own hurt

and changeth not," is sometimes a troublesome text to a man's conscience,' he wrote to a friend who in vain had begged him to change his plans. Another time he wrote :—

'I could not be away another Sabbath for a long time. It not only interrupts the begun chain of ordinary lecture, etc., but it disturbs (1) my Young Men's Class ; (2) My visits to the Sabbath-school (which I could not even last Sabbath commence) ; (3) My evening prayer-meeting ; (4) My own equanimity !'

A Presbyterian to the backbone [1] and a loyal Free Churchman, his sympathies, in latter years especially, went out far beyond his own church. He loved the gatherings together of God's people, and in the Conferences at Mildmay, at Perth, in his own city, and in many other places, his presence and his words were an inspiration.

On one occasion, when addressing the Mildmay Conference, he spoke of the Old Testament saints as being not inferior givers to the saints of the New Testament. He referred to Moses being commanded by God during the erection of the Tabernacle to stop the people from giving more, and quaintly threw in the remark, 'I don't find it necessary to do this when I go to the country to preach for a collection at the opening of a new church !' 'There is a chapter,' he said, 'one of the longest in the Bible, that I don't believe any one here has read all through. It is the seventh of Numbers. It tells that one of the princes of Israel wished to give a gift to God, and asked Moses if he might. Moses did not want to answer of his own accord, and so he asked God. God said, "Let him give it. He will like to do it, and you will lay it out on a table"—just as brides do with their wedding gifts to show how their friends love them.

[1] While his son was at Oxford he wrote to him : 'How do you get on with the Thirty-Nine Articles ? They are good and sound—all except that about bishops,' etc.

The prince gave a silver bowl filled with the finest of the wheat, and a golden spoon. The next day another prince came with the same request, and brought the same gift, and all the princes of the twelve tribes did the same. David, at his death, bequeathed to the Lord's service more gold than is contained in the Bank of England,[1] besides what he had given during his lifetime. In the New Testament we read of one Joseph or Joses, surnamed Barnabas, who sold his estate in Cyprus and gave the price of it to the Lord. On one occasion Paul and he were on a missionary tour in Cyprus, and one afternoon Barnabas proposed that they should take a walk together, and said, " If you like to come with me I will show you the estate that I sold and gave to the Lord." So they went together, and when Paul saw it he said, " Barnabas, what a beautiful place this is ! It must have cost you many a pang before you sold it. Do you never grudge having done it ? " " Never," said Barnabas, " the Lord has made all up to me, and more. Men never call me Joses now ; it is always ' Barnabas, the son of consolation.' " '

In giving an address at the Perth Conference upon ' Faith ' he supposed some of the later disciples saying to each other, ' Come, let us go to the apostle John and ask him to tell us about his conversion. He is an old man now, and old men like to give reminiscences of their youth.' So they went to John, and found him at home. When he understood the object of their visit he said, ' Come in and sit down, and I will be delighted to tell you all about it,' and beginning with that night when for the first time he leaned his head on the bosom of his Master, he went on to tell how some of them

[1] Mr. Balfour-Melville, who has kindly supplied these notes, remembers that a banker sitting beside him at the time added up the sum as recorded and found this was correct.

had had their consciences awakened because of sin, and John the Baptist's preaching had deepened that feeling, but did not relieve it, till one day he said, ' Behold the Lamb of God that taketh away the sin of the world.' ' Then,' he said, ' two of us went to Him, and He was so gracious to us, and dealt with us so tenderly, that that night we gave ourselves to Him.' Then he told them of all that he had seen of Jesus till the close of His life, and of all his own experience since ' But,' said he, ' I have continued a sinner to the end, for when I was in Patmos, and was shown the great things that were shortly to come to pass, like a sinner I fell down to worship before the feet of the angel which showed me these things. I forgot he was but a servant,—a fellow-servant,—and that I must worship only God.'

From all parts of the world letters came to him asking for prayer, for counsel, for direction, and his opinion was regarded as final by many in all sections of the Church of God. Of the blessing received through his books he had grateful testimonies from time to time. Not long after the publication of the *Narrative of a Mission of Inquiry to the Jews*, a lady in England wrote telling him that it had been the means of the conversion of an infidel. Two of his smaller books—*The Gospel pointing to the Person of Christ*, a book for inquirers, and the *Brook Besor*, written for invalids—were very greatly blessed. A copy of another of his little books, *What gives Assurance*, was given by a gentleman to one who through serious illness had fallen into depression of mind. When visiting her husband, after the good woman's death, he told him that a great change had come to his wife after reading that book. ' She was just another woman, and she kept the precious little book in the " brods o' her Bible," and only parted once with it to a neighbour on condition that it should be returned.' She passed away in peace, repeating to herself shortly before the end,

> 'Safe in the arms of Jesus,
> Safe on His gentle breast!'

He had a singular gift of letter-writing. His letters were generally very short, but in almost every one—even in those about the most ordinary subjects—there is a word or a thought which makes them valuable. For example, he writes to one and another of his friends:—

'When you come to see us, come to help us by prayer, as well as to drink water out of our well.'

'Come and spend a day or two here. We might perhaps be mutually refreshed. Remember Emmaus.'

'Pray for blessing, for it is like the dew which Gideon prayed for. It falls where it is sought.'

'Be thou in the fear of the Lord all the day long. Keep under the light that beams from Jacob's ladder, and you will always have a Bethel-fear.'

'Dwell in the Tabernacle under the Shadow of the Almighty, and not a drop of wrath shall fall on a hair of your head. Walk, too, in the light of the cloud of glory over the mercy-seat. It is New Jerusalem glory.'

'Let us be like Jacob's sons; go often to Joseph—our Joseph. The corn of the Nile that overflows yearly is the best, and is the likest to the corn of our God, proceeding as it does from His overflowing and everflowing love.'

'Behold the fowls of the air! how merrily they sing, not troubled about next day's food or clothing. Be as they. Sing to your God and Father merrily to-day, and let the morrow take thought for itself.'

'What was the last nugget of gold of Ophir you found in reading the Word? Do you not often say with one of your old friends, the Fathers,

> "Adoro plenitudinem Scripturarum."'

'What of the gold-diggings?' he writes again; 'Any recent discovery in the knowledge of Him who counsels us to buy "gold tried in the fire"? Does not this mean such things as these, viz.

> 'Buy of me your ransom-money.
> 'Buy of me your golden harp.
> 'Buy of me the golden streets of the New Jerusalem.
> 'Buy back Paradise, for "the gold of that land is good."'

'I was greatly refreshed yesterday by two words from the mouth of the Lord in the verse, "For a small moment have I forsaken thee," etc. (Isa. liv. 7). The words are חֶסֶד עוֹלָם "the mercy *of an eternity!*' What is this that is coming to us, brother? *The mercy of a whole eternity!*'

'Notice Zech. ix. 13 : "I have filled the bow with Ephraim." When He uses you, He just makes you an arrow—fills His bow with you.'

'Follow the Shepherd, and remember, if you are following Him you will be sure to get a good mouthful of pasture every now and then. Our Shepherd would not lead us where nothing is to be found.'

'The "fragments" in the baskets, would not they keep for many days?'

One letter closes with the request, 'Sometimes think on us and ask something for us, for we are needy.' And another, 'This week is our Communion. *N.B.*—Remember in prayer a congregation in Glasgow needing rain from heaven.' Inside the envelope of a note addressed to one of his people is written : 'With the prayer, Eph. iii. 14–20, and the request, 1 Thess. v. 25. *N.B.*—Eph. vi. 18.' With a small subscription sent to a friend he wrote :—

'From an old disciple who remembers what the Master's blessing can do (John vi. 11). A barley loaf and a small fish from Scotland.'

'Prayer for saints and for those who "minister the gospel" is the oil which keeps bright all the weapons we use,—sword, shield,' etc.

'Study the fifteen prayers of Paul,' he wrote to one of his people, 'six in First and Second Thessalonians, two in Ephesians, two in Philippians, two in Colossians, two in Romans, one in Hebrews.

'Pray them too, and pray them often, and pray for me also.'

His letters help to explain how he was able to go on giving out to others from day to day so continually. His hand was always on the key of the storehouse of all grace, and his God was ever supplying all his need :—

'As to Saturday I have great, because conscientious, difficulties, because of my own soul which cannot stand three successive weeks of giving out, in Perth, Dundee, Edinburgh, and Kelso. Ah, brother, I am only longing to be so full that out of me shall flow rivers, ποταμοί —whole Niles or Rhines or Jordans—of living water. Happy day ! and "yet a little while." '

'Vessels are not fountains. Vessels need to be filled as well as to give out to others.'

'Here is something to remember, Isa. xxvii. 3 : " I will water it every moment." When Alexander Somerville and I were in the Botanic Gardens we asked the superintendent about that passage. It is spoken of vines, and yet A. S. had in vain inquired in the East about it, for they all said that they did not water their vines. . . . " Well," the man said to me after a little thought, " I 'll tell you what it may be. Notice the little tendrils of the vine. They have generally a drop at the end. This is to be accounted for by the fact that the vine has the power of condensing the vapour in the atmosphere around it, and so it keeps itself supplied with moisture." Is this not very instructive ? God's vines are furnished with the capacity of drawing in moisture from around even when no shower falls (no sermon, no special ordinance), invisible as is the process to human eyes.' [1]

[1] This verse, 'I will water it every moment,' he called 'the Old Testament Eighth of Romans.'

The solemn sense of responsibility which he felt as a minister of the gospel is shown in his copy of Bridges' *Christian Ministry*, which he has marked and annotated till it has become almost a new book, in many ways descriptive of his own ministry. Nothing, however interesting, was allowed to interfere with the one great object of his life. In an address which he gave to the Finnieston Young Men's Literary Association in 1883 he told how some time before he had begun the study of Hebrew synonyms with the intention of perhaps writing a small book on the subject. He had made some progress in it, but stopped because he found it was interfering with his one great work. Even ordinary reading was not allowed to take up much of his time. If told of a very interesting book he would say, 'Lay it aside and I will read it in the holidays.' He watched himself with almost painful carefulness, and stirred others up to the same prayerful vigilance. One of his solemn sayings in regard to ministers was, 'The sins of teachers are the teachers of sins,' and he often quoted a remark about the Old Testament saints, 'Beware of the bad things of good men.'

'Let us stir one another up in the pursuit of holiness—fellowship with God. Samson's strength was only *indicated* by his long hair. It had a secret spring. Our success would not be our strength, nor would our enlarged preaching and diligent visiting; yet these will begin to grow if we have access to the hidden source.'

'I am more than ever convinced that unholiness lies at the root of our little success. "*Holy* men of God spake to the fathers." It must be holy men still that speak with power. The only good thing I feel at present is the Word, and God there.'

'Write soon and tell me anything fitted to stir the

soul in sleepy days. . . . Do you ever feel that when
there are no symptoms of converting work going on
among your people, your own soul gets ungirt for work?
I often find this, and I feel it at present. Even the wise
virgins slumber.'

'Did you ever feel in preaching as if you were a blunt
arrow? I felt so yesterday until about evening, when
the Archer seemed to sharpen the point.'

Though unsparing of his own strength, he was always
considerate of others. 'When your foot swells,' he used
to say, 'the Lord does not want you to travel.'

During his summer holidays in 1890, he wrote to his
Biblewoman, Miss Walker, cautioning her against over-
working herself in his absence :—

'*Aros Cottage, Salen, Isle of Mull.*

'To the DEACONESS WALKER,
who labours much in the Lord, greeting.

'Grace and peace be multiplied to you, day by day. A very old
friend who lived in the land of Midian once gave a most needful and
wise advise to a worker who was doing his best to shorten his
valuable life. The worker's name was Moses, and the friend was
Jethro. The people came to Moses "to inquire of God," and he
was never done listening to them. "They stood by him from
morning to evening." But wise and gracious Jethro saw it, and
said, "*The thing that thou doest is not good*," and showed Moses
how to "*make it easier for himself*": "so shalt thou be able to
endure, and this people shall go to their place in peace," instead
of letting him kill himself on their account! Is not that a good
lesson for your study, that your mind may be perfectly at ease in
taking *a long holiday*?

'The Pastor of the congregation sends this message to the
Deaconess, thanking her for her blessed work in the past, but
hoping that there is to be an hundredfold more to give thanks for
in days coming.

'Meanwhile, pray for all the congregation and all the souls in
the Mission District "without ceasing." And so, with the words

of another old friend whom "the Spirit clothed" (1 Chron. xii. 18), this letter closes : "Peace, peace be unto thee, and peace be to thine helpers ; for thy God helpeth thee." Amen.

' Twenty-third day of the seventh month, 1890.'

' See that your last days are your best days,' were his words to believers, 'not like David, of some of whose descendants it was said in praise, "they walked in the *first* ways of their father David."' He seemed to have a solemn fear in his latter years lest he should "lose the things he had wrought," and not receive a full reward.

' We are not to indulge for a moment the belief : " Oh, I must count on a season of languor in my Christian life." Where did you find that in the Bible ? " Like the palm-tree flourishing," etc. Ask any gardener and he will tell you it is a sad indication of any plant to stop growing.'

' Our root is in Christ, and in the " love that passeth knowledge." We will grow up and flourish if our roots are in such a soil. If spared to old age, our fruit will be abundant. In our younger days a great deal is *blossom*, but as we grow older it is *fruit*. It does not make such an appearance, but it is more enduring.'

To others his earnestness and eager longing for the salvation of souls seemed to increase with his years. It was noticeable at the time of his ' Jubilee' (1888) how he exerted himself in every possible way, as if feeling that his days of work for the Master might soon be over.

' Plenty of work here now, and winter has come, but His yoke is "easy." Did you ever notice Christ says it is χρηστός, as if alluding to Χριστός.'

' It is constant work, but it is " vineyard " work, and work for the Master, who bore the burden and heat of the day.'

' We are alive, and many whom we started with have reached the goal. " In death there is no remembrance

of Thee." Let us give thanks for life and work, even
for care and weariness. " This is the fruit of my labour "
— τοῦτό μοι καρπὸς ἔργου.'

'The night cometh, but thereafter the morning! the
Resurrection-morning, when we shall know the results of
present labour, and when we shall see Him as He is. . .
It is a solemn thing to look back on so many years as I
have had, and to look a little onward and see the Eternal
Shore.'

'Oh, the memories of the past!' he wrote to an old
friend. 'It needs the "Man that is the hiding-place"
to keep them!'

Even when on his holidays, his people and his work
occupied most of his thoughts. 'I am beginning to
think of home and work in Finnieston,' he wrote to a
lady in his congregation from his holiday retreat. 'I
have been long away, but only I can work for you all at
a distance in more ways than one.' From his summer
quarters in Anwoth, he wrote one of his quaint and
beautiful letters to two other members of his flock :—

'HONOURED SISTERS,—I am fain to reply to a question stated to
me by a friend of yours and mine, who is here on a short sojourn.
The question you have put is anent one passage of God's word, to
wit, that in Matt. xviii. 10 where it is written, "Their angels do
always behold the face of your Father." Ye say that a godly Professor of Divinity thinks that this teaches us "that angels, because
of their charge over these little ones, have errands into the presence
of their Father, and so have got a liberty to deal familiarly with
Him (so to speak) which they would not have had but for the sake
of the little ones." This is a blessed truth, I doubt not ; howbeit
there is yet more honey to be found dropping from that wood of
the Tree of Life, if only Jonathan's rod were dipt in the comb a
second time. If we be spared to speak face to face, it will be
pleasanter than to write about it with ink and paper, as the beloved
John said on a like occasion to the "Elect Lady," as ye may read
(2 John 12).

'But will you let me say yet more, for it is good that we as travellers to the same country stir up one another to quicken our pace. I know ye are not taking your Inn for your home, but are minding your inheritance in New Jerusalem. Ye need not marvel if every day some cross, less or more, be your portion. Till ye be in heaven, it will be but foul weather, one shower and then another. But if there were twenty crosses for this year written down for you in God's book of providence, they will soon be past ; ye will soon be at the nineteenth, and then there is but one more, and after that nothing ! for then ye shall lay your head on His bosom, and His own soft hand shall dry your face and wipe away your tears. Is this not true, worthy ladies, that it is a king's life to live upon the love of Christ ? I said this long ago to a worthy friend now in glory, and I think ye will say it was well spoken.

'My old mansion here, from which I used to go forth to my "walk" among the shady trees, has long since been taken down, and even so we also ourselves shall be ere long. But like the Sisters of Bethany, whom Jesus loved, your hearts' desire is to Him who is the Resurrection and the Life, who is coming soon to give us our house which is from heaven, which shall be eternal. He cannot come too soon.

'The minister of Christ who used to preach the word to your souls, and whom ye failed not to encourage many ways, intends to return home from his sojourn in these parts.. In the end of this week he goes back with his household to the place of his ministry on the banks of the Clyde, though not so near your dwelling as formerly. You will not forget him, as he will not forget you. Pray for him, as I once said to Gordon of Garloch here, that in his work he may be "fraughted and full of Christ."

'Yours in His lovely and longed-for Jesus.'

Earthly honour had little attraction for him. The degree of Doctor of Divinity, conferred on him in 1873, gratified him as a token of regard from his own University of Edinburgh. To be asked to occupy the highest position in the Free Church as Moderator of her Assembly was a real cross to him, and made him write to Mr. Manson : 'It is a terrible dilemma I am placed in ; for letters come to me insisting that my responsibility will be something more than ordinary if I refuse —and yet I think, in accepting, the responsibility is no way less. Alas! how far down our Church has come when it asks such as me to take this office!'

His ambition was to 'know Christ,' and this one aim simplified his whole life. His obedience in the smallest details was very striking. It was not so much that he did not do wrong, but that he seemed always to do the things that pleased God. Those who lived with him cannot recall a single unworthy action in his life. Step by step he walked with God, doing everything as in His sight. 'You are not very holy if you are not very kind,' he used to say, and this spirit of love characterised his own actions. 'I have settled all—glad to be able to send out a cluster of grapes to moisten the parched lips of my brother,' he writes when sending some books to Mr. Milne in India. A favour shown to himself he regarded as shown to Christ in one of His members. For some friends who had given him the present of a Bible, he wrote in acknowledgment of their kindness :—

'AN INCIDENT, NEITHER CANONICAL NOR APOCRYPHAL,
BUT TRUE.

'There were two sisters, related spiritually to Martha and Mary of Bethany, " whom Jesus loved," and who loved Jesus.

'Many years after the Master had gone away, and when many were beginning to talk about His coming back soon, these two sisters thought in their hearts that, meanwhile (since the Master was not here), they would like to show kindness to one of His disciples for His sake. They sent therefore sixty-six clusters of choice grapes, bound together in one.

'The disciple wondered, thanked them in his heart, prayed for rich returns of blessing on Martha and Mary, and sent back this request :

'My dear sisters, will you help me to press the grapes into the cup which I shall try to hand to you from week to week, when we meet to taste the New Wine of the Kingdom?' Eph. iii. 14-21.

To another member of his church he wrote a very

characteristic note of thanks for a present received from her :—

'*Decr.* 15*th*, 1885.

'A grateful Pastor, whose great-grandfather had charge of the Sheep in Fetlar and Yell, Shetland Isles, sends thanks to the Sheep who has so kindly presented him with Shetland wool, so soft and warm !

'Great Shepherd of the Sheep, bless this member of Thy flock with a new blessing and a fuller !'

Burdened as he must have been with the care of others, his calmness and freedom from worry were very remarkable, as well as his happy and ever-thankful spirit. 'We should be always wearing the garment of praise, not just waving a palm-branch now and then.'

'Thanksgiving is the very air of heaven.'

'There is one ear that listens to every note of praise from every one of His people. Never say, "*I* need not praise Him. He will not miss *me* out of the choir." "Bless the Lord, O *my* soul."'

'Why should we be afraid to rejoice, when God is not afraid to trust us with joy ?'

'Jacob said, "I shall go down to the grave with sorrow." What a mistake ! He went down singing !'

'"All joy and peace in believing." "*All* joy," complete joy, that will fill every crevice of your vacant heart. "*All* peace," that will not allow room for a single fear.'

'The oil of joy calms down the waves of trouble.'

'God's people,' he said, 'sometimes take fits of sea-sickness in sailing to Immanuel's Land. They give way to hard thoughts of God.' He asked some friends on whom he was calling how they were getting on. They said, 'Not very well ; we are not getting the rich food for our souls we used to get. We were just saying we are getting husks now.' 'Oh, I see,' was his reply.

'You've been having a grumble-meeting! Did you ever notice when we grumble to one another we grow discontented and bitter, and that is grieving to the Holy Spirit? But, when we go and tell the Lord, it has a very different effect. We get tenderness and sympathy.'

Speaking one day of the conversion of the Philippian jailer, he said, 'Oh, brethren, I see it now! They had spread the Gospel over the whole city by their *prayers* and *praises*, and they thought it was to be by their *preaching*!'

'A gloomy believer,' he said, 'is surely an anomaly in Christ's kingdom'; and gloominess was the last thing to be associated with him. An indescribable sweetness and mellowness characterised his old age, and robbed it of all sadness. Left alone, the last of a family of eleven brothers and sisters, his old friends nearly all gone from him, his joy in Christ triumphed over every sorrow.

> 'Garments fresh, and feet unweary,
>   Told how God had brought him through.'

'This season,' he wrote in October 1882, 'has been sending me back to eighteen years ago—a never-to-be-forgotten time (his wife's death). I thought then that life could never again be lightsome, but I find that the more of Christ we enjoy, the more we are able to bear.'

'When we have truly found Christ, we can go through the world alone.'

'If you are a child of God, there is nothing in the world you cannot do without, and have a heaven in the want of it.'

When the last of his brothers was taken away, and he alone was left behind, he stood beside his grave—the only mourner with a smile on his face. As the earth was heaped on the coffin he turned to a friend beside him and said, 'I know that he shall rise again!' More than once, referring to his age he said, 'I don't feel that I am an old man, but I know I must be, for Barzillai was fourscore years old, and the Bible says he was "a *very aged man*!"' His friend Major Whittle asked him one day if he had found it harder to be a Christian as an old man than as a young man. Dr. Bonar turned his sunny face towards him and said, 'Oh, I don't think anything about growing old. I just keep on, doing each day's work by itself, and looking to the Lord for daily grace. I don't feel old. I feel just as young as I ever did.'

His last summer holiday, in 1892, was spent at Braefield, Portpatrick, and the pleasant walks and rambles there will ever be a sunny memory to his friends. He preached in the Free Church during his stay, and took a great interest in the open-air meetings begun on Sabbath afternoons by his son-in-law, Mr. Oatts. On the last Sabbath of August he conducted the meeting himself, and as he was walking home a stranger came up to him and asked if he might speak to him. He said he had been for thirty-seven years in America, and was home for a holiday, had read all his books, but had never expected to see himself. When returning to Glasgow a few days later Dr. Bonar stopped at Stranraer and visited an aged friend, Mrs. Cunningham, at North-west Castle. 'When I met him at the railway station,' writes her son, the Rev. J. G. Cunningham, 'he told me that he must call for his old friend the Rev. George Sherwood, and he carried out his purpose, playfully disregarding the remonstrances of his family against the additional fatigue. I accompanied him, and was struck with the swift pace which he easily maintained. On our way I was accosted by an ostler belonging to one of the hotels, who asked me with respectful interest to tell him the name of the old minister who was with me, "for," said he, "I saw him at the Port, preaching in the open air, and I was glad to hear him." Dr. Bonar shook hands warmly with his grateful hearer, to whom that sermon had given a real and unlooked-for pleasure. The interview between my dear mother and Dr. Bonar was truly affecting. They knew well that it was their last meeting on earth ; and they spoke with calm and grateful hearts of the "goodness and mercy" which had followed them for more than fourscore years of pilgrimage, and of their hope of welcome at no distant date into "the house of the Lord for ever." Within a few months both of the venerable pilgrims met again "in that better country into which no enemy ever entered, and from which no friend ever went away." '

The failure of his strength was very gradual, and not very perceptible except to those around him. His handwriting grew less firm, and his memory began to fail him in little things. One day, not very long before his death, a gentleman met him in Howard Street, and found that he was quite confused as to where he was. He kindly put him on the right way, and as they parted Dr. Bonar thanked him and said, ' I 've just been thinking that I have been like Peter when the angel took him out of prison. Poor man, he did not know where he was ! '

On the 31st of October 1892, writing to a friend about the sudden death of Mr. Inglis of Dundee, he says : ' What a surprise to find himself all at once among those who "do immediately pass into glory." . . . May we be "found of Him in peace," like our brother, when our evening comes.'

The post had sounded his horn at his chamber-door, and from the Celestial City had come the message : ' Thy Master has need of thee, and in a very little time thou must behold His face in brightness.' His last days were spent in the same unceasing ministry for others that had been the joy of his life, and, as he lay on his dying bed, it was to his work that his thoughts were ever turning.

After only two days of illness, he passed away on Friday, the 30th of December 1892.

'When I think of dying,' he once said, 'I think of it something in this way. I fancy myself going home from a meeting some night, and I feel not very well. I get worse, then I become unconscious, and then I know nothing more until I am in the presence of a Throne. There are seats around the Throne, and I am pointed to one which is vacant. I am told that it is for me. Then I see a Hand, and when I look at it I see it is a pierced Hand, and it holds a crown over my head! But, oh! the weight of glory is so great I cannot bear it, and so I lift it off, and cast it at the foot of the Throne, saying, "*Thou* art worthy; for Thou wast slain, and hast redeemed us to God by Thy blood!"'

CHAPTER XVI

Faith and Doctrine

' LORD, never let any one occupy this pulpit who does
not preach Christ and Him crucified,' was Dr. Bonar's
prayer one day in his own church ; and his oft-repeated
desire for himself was that he might never to the day
of his death preach to his people, or be with them in
any of their meetings, without saying something about
what gives peace to the sinner.   Once, after preaching
in St. Peter's, Dundee, upon the text, ' Thine eyes shall
see the King in His beauty,' Mr. M'Cheyne said to
him as they walked home together, ' Brother, I enjoyed
your sermon ; to me it was sweet.   You and I and many,
I trust, in our congregations shall see the King in His
beauty.   But, my brother, you forgot there might be
many listening to you to-night, who, unless they are
changed by the grace of God, shall never see Him in
His beauty.'

Whether as the effect of this kindly reproof or not,
certain it is that Dr. Bonar never afterwards preached
a sermon in which he did not commend Christ to the
unsaved, and rarely, if ever, closed without urging on
his hearers the immediate acceptance of the Saviour.
' A sinner,' he often repeated, ' so long as he is un-
pardoned, has a right to only one thing in the universe
—only one—and that is the blood of the Lord Jesus
Christ.'

The atoning sacrifice of the Son of God formed the

central point of all his preaching. The Cross was 'the
breaking of God's alabaster-box, the fragrance of which
has filled heaven and earth.' This little world was 'the
altar of the universe on which lay the Almighty Sacrifice. The Incarnation was but the scaffolding for the
Atonement. It is the Cross that shows us the love of
God at a white heat. The earliest form of worship
was the lamb slain : Behold Abel's altar ! The latest
form of worship is the Lamb slain who is now on the
throne of the universe.' Round the Cross he gathered
the whole Word of God, and all the dim foreshadow-
ings of type and prophecy met in Him who died on
Calvary. The infinite fulness of this Sacrifice—'a whole
Christ between the humblest sinner and the smallest
drop of God's wrath'—God's only-begotten Son, 'the
half of His own joy given up for a time for us'—was
what he rejoiced to proclaim. To many his preaching
of Jesus Christ as the living personal Saviour was a
revelation and the beginning of a new life. This
Saviour and His atoning work stands between the
coming sinner and every dark and difficult doctrine.
Longings for pardon, for rest, for peace are met by the
simple acceptance of this Saviour, whose blood speaks
peace to the conscience and whose love brings rest to
the heart.[1] So powerful is this sprinkled blood that it
can carry a sinner into the holiest of all to hold communion at the Mercy-seat with a reconciled God and
Father. 'One touch of this cleansing blood seals the
soul for service.' Its voice—like the sound of the waves
on the shore—is ever speaking peace in a believer's ear,
'sometimes loudly, sometimes less clearly, but always
speaking.' 'If a believer can do without the blood he is
a backslider.' 'At the Bush Moses was forbidden to draw

---

[1] He used sometimes to quote, with warm approval, the saying of a
devoted Methodist minister, '*Live in the* Sacrifice ! *Live in the* Sacrifice.'

nigh, but afterwards on the Mount he went up into the very presence of God. What made the difference? At the Bush *there was no sacrifice.*' [1]

Once when asked by Mr. Moody to tell the young ministers gathered at Northfield the secret of a consecrated life, his simple answer was, 'I can only say to my young brethren that for forty years there has not been a day that I have not had access to the Mercy-seat.'

When saying good-bye to some friends in whose house he had been staying, one of them said to him, 'Dr. Bonar, you are like the palm-tree flourishing in the courts of the Lord.' He turned round, and, laying his hand on his friend's shoulder, he said eagerly, 'And if we are planted in the House of the Lord, then you know where our roots will be? *Under the altar.*'

The Person and work of the Lord Jesus Christ occupied him at all times. When holding Him up before any who were seeking salvation, he used to say:

'Salvation is not fleeing to the shadow of the great Rock, but it is fleeing to the Man who is a Hiding-place, and laying our head on His bosom.'

'Many want salvation, but they do not want the Saviour.'

'The work of Christ is the open door for the sinner, but Christ Himself stands behind it waiting to welcome him.'

An invalid lady in the country sent him a message that she had not enough of joy. He sent back the answer, 'Tell Mrs. C. it is not more *joy* she needs, but more of *Christ.*'

A Christian Jew who had brought another to church with him met Dr. Bonar as he came out, and told him

[1] When reading at family worship the narrative of God's rebuke and Israel's repentance in Judges ii. 1-5, he said before closing the book: 'Sorrow can never put away sin, sacrifice alone can do that; so they not only wept at Bochim, but "they sacrificed there unto the Lord."

about the young man's difficulties. 'He won't receive Christ.' 'Ah,' said Dr. Bonar, 'that's because you don't know Him. All who know Him receive Him.'

'Draughts of the water of life are just fresh views of Christ. The promises are streams coming down from Christ's heart.'

'Peace is the mantle dropped by Christ.' 'The invitation, "Come unto Me," is like the waving of the fringe of His robe as He moves along by the shores of the Sea of Galilee.' Christ's life of obedience was 'a walk from Bethlehem to Calvary without a stumble.' His righteousness was 'the robe in which He walked through our world every day, and which, when He had finished His walk,—as Elijah left his mantle to Elisha,—He left for us to wear.' To get a deeper sense of sin is to look at the price paid for our pardon.'

'If ever there was anything that, more terribly than hell itself, showed the sinfulness of sin, it was the Saviour's agony in the Garden.'

'When we count the pieces of the Ransom-money, may we see what a terrible evil sin is.'

'It is not a sight of our sinful heart that humbles us, it is a sight of Jesus Christ: I am undone, *because mine eyes have seen the King.*'

'If deep sorrow and remorse could blot out sin, hell would be a great Calvary.' 'There is nothing Satan fears so much as the blood of Christ.' 'Purity of heart (Psalm xxvi. 6) depends upon the place we are giving in our consciences to the blood of Christ.'

'Power over habits of sin may be gained by confessing sin.' 'He breaks the power of cancelled sin.' We can also say, 'He breaks the power of sin confessed.' 'No man ever honestly confesses before God the sin he has done till that sin is taken away. It is a full pardon that makes a man guileless.'

Of one who dwelt very much upon sin, without, as he thought, dwelling sufficiently on the power of the blood to cleanse, he said, ' I think his gospel is the miry clay.'

' We are called " more than conquerors" not at the end of our course, but while it is going on.'

' You need not be afraid of too much grace. Great grace never makes a man proud. A little grace is very apt to make a man be puffed up.'

' Sin is not simply going against our conscience ; it is going against the law, though conscience keep silence.'

Some one told him that for six months she had not consciously committed any sin. ' And are you not very proud of it ?' said Dr. Bonar. ' Yes,' she replied, ' I am ! '

' Faith grows upon the soil of felt sin.' ' Great faith is simple faith. If you are seeking great faith, remember the simpler it is the greater it will be.'

' There was a defect in the faith of many who came to Christ to be healed. But it was not the strength of their faith Christ looked to, but the reality of it. They got the cure, though the hand that touched Him trembled.'

' " My " is the handle of faith.'

He made frequent use of four lines of a hymn written by his brother :—

> ' Upon a life I did not live,
>   Upon a death I did not die ;
>   Another's life, another's death,
>   I stake my whole eternity.'

' When I write a hymn,' he says in a letter to one of his children, ' I think it will begin

" *Looking always to Jesus.*"

' I am not sure of the way some people sing " There is life for a look." It must be a *steady* look.'

To one seeking full assurance he wrote :—

' Just as the bitten Israelites were healed every time they felt the bite of the fiery serpents, simply by looking to the Brazen Serpent, so we, every time we feel our soul dark, or sad, or unbelieving, are directed to fix our thoughts *at once* on Christ, the Lamb of God and the Priest. "Look unto Me and be saved" (Isa. xlv. 22). "They looked unto Him and were lightened" (Psalm xxxiv. 5). "Therefore I will look to the Lord" (Micah vii. 7). "Run the race looking (not at your own feet, or thinking of your own running but) *unto Jesus*" (Heb. xii. 2). Compare this with God looking on us, and on what we look to. "The bow shall be in the cloud, *and I will look upon it*, and remember the Covenant" (Gen. ix. 16). "When *I see* the blood I will pass over you" (Exod. xii. 13). *We* look on the blood of Atonement, and God looks on *us* well pleased when we are so employed. Do you sometimes sit down and sing to yourself such a hymn as—

> " Walk in the light, so shalt thou know," etc.
> " I heard the voice of Jesus say," ' etc.

' Doubts and fears are not marks of God's children. They are remnants of the old nature—specks upon the eye of faith. You should give them no quarter.'

' If you say it is good to have doubts, you are just saying, "I will not take all that God offers." Faith takes a whole Christ for itself : " My Lord and my God." '

One who had not assurance he described as believing in Christ, but not believing what He says. ' Faith dwells at Jerusalem. Full assurance goes into the palace and sees the King's face.' ' It is the privilege and the duty of believers (looking at the blood) not to have a fear or a doubt. You can't honour God more, you can't please the Holy Spirit more, or Christ more, than by putting unbounded confidence in the blood.'

' Would it have been right,' he asked, ' for the prodigal to sit at the table dropping tears into his cup, saying, " I can't be glad," when the Father said " It is meet that we should make merry and be glad?" '

' John did not rise from the Table because there was a doubt about himself and his steadfastness. He leaned all the harder [ἀνέπεσεν] on his Master's bosom.'

His adherence to the old truths never wavered, nor his simple unquestioning faith in the Word of God as his guide. Some of his last sermons were preached upon subjects in the Epistle of Jude, which many shrink from as unpleasant and unpopular. Sin and its punishment—eternal banishment from God's presence—were part of the 'whole counsel of God' which he must declare. 'To fall into the hands of the living God—to be crushed between the millstones of omnipotence.' 'Jesus spoke these terrible words about hell in the eighteenth of Matthew, with a little child in his arms.' 'No one preached more about hell than Christ did. You remember His thrilling narrative of the rich man and Lazarus; as if He would pursue the sinner with a flaming sword until he entered the city of refuge. But "they will not believe"—although Lazarus was the preacher, and his text, "Not a drop of water to cool the tongue."'

'I think He will weep over the lost as He did over Jerusalem. It will be something to be said for ever in heaven, "Jesus wept as He said, Depart, ye cursed." But then it was absolutely necessary to say it.'

'I think that the shower of fire and brimstone was wet with the tears of God as it fell, for God has "no pleasure in the death of him that dieth."'

A lady whom he was asked to visit during an illness said to him, 'I've been trying for some days with all my might to believe in annihilation; but I can't.' 'I can tell you something better,' said Dr. Bonar. 'If you believe in Christ your *sin* will be annihilated.'

Divine sovereignty was a subject he often referred to in his preaching, but never as an impassable barrier between God and a sinner.

'You will never get light by looking into darkness. Paul does not plunge into the depths and drown himself. He stands on the shore and adores: "O the depths!"' etc. (Romans xi. 33).

'"Strong meat" is not what are called the "deep doctrines" of Scripture. "Strong meat" is really what you had last Sabbath at the Communion-table—"the finest of the wheat."'

'Doctrine and hearing of the Word abound,' he wrote after a visit to the North, 'though the doctrine is not what we in the South reckon to be the very truth, for sovereignty is thrust in at all points as if to overawe the sinner, and make him draw back from touching even the hem of the garment. They say that they do it to empty and humble the sinner. Oh for showers of the Spirit! for, when the Spirit comes, all things take their proper place.'

'Take care,' he used to say, 'that you never mix anything with the "finest of the wheat."' Referring to the doctrine of election he said, 'If God were to reveal your election to you, you would believe in yourself instead of in Christ.' At another time, speaking of the same subject, he made the striking remark, 'We have often found that Satan takes the substantial food, which God has provided for His own children, to poison sinners with.' One of his quaint sayings, in stirring believers up to more watchfulness, was: 'If Satan was dangerous when Paul wrote his epistles, how much more dangerous must he be now, for he has got so much more experience?'

Some one remarked in his hearing that she did not like doctrine; it was not practical. At once he replied, 'Doctrine *is* practical, for it is that that stirs up the heart.'

The work of the Holy Spirit was a special feature of his preaching, and the love of that Spirit as revealed in His written Word. 'Every line in this inspired Bible is wet with the dew of the Spirit's love.'

'"The sword of the Spirit"—the sword which the Spirit uses. The sword is made up of various parts: the long blade, the handle, etc. And so the Scriptures have many parts, but the Gospel is the sharp point by which it pierces the soul.'

The Word of God, from Genesis to Revelation, was the food by which his soul was nourished, and the weapon by which he fought his battles and gained his victories. So readily did a scriptural phrase or a scriptural illustration drop from his lips, that it almost seemed as if he thought in scriptural language. As he was walking home from church one evening, his daughter offered to carry his umbrella for him. He declined to give it to her, and said to a friend who was with them, 'We always like to have something in our hand when we are walking. I have noticed that. I wonder if we shall have the same feeling hereafter, for, do you notice, they carry "palms in their hands"?'

On the morning of the last day of his life, a friend called just as he was having a poultice administered. He looked up brightly, saying, 'I am just like Hezekiah: I am getting on a plaster!'

A meeting of special interest had been held from which one of his daughters had been unavoidably absent. As soon as he returned from it, he said to her, thinking of her disappointment, 'Remember there were two angels absent from the Ascension!'

A friend once referred at a meeting to his originality in finding subjects for sermons and addresses, and said, 'I don't know where Dr. Bonar gets all his texts.' Dr. Bonar lifted his Bible and quietly held it out to him.

His prayer one morning was, 'Make Thy Word a candle to reveal sin, and a leaf from the Tree of Life to heal.' In public reading of the Scriptures, no portion was ever passed over because of its difficulty or obscurity, but every word and phrase were explained with care and minuteness. An exposition of the first eight chapters of 1 Chronicles [1] was given with the preface : ' This is God calling the roll of mankind ; ' and what at first had seemed a record of unmeaning and forgotten names, became a history of men and women, with hopes, and fears, and aspirations like those of a present time.

As he read the fifth chapter of Genesis, with its melancholy refrain,—' and he died, and he died,'—he came to the twenty-fourth verse, ' Enoch walked with God : and was not ; for God took him.' He stopped and said, ' A triumphal arch amid the tombs ! '

Another remark of his on the same subject was : Enoch walked with God, and one day he took a very long walk, for he never came back again ! '

When describing a scriptural incident he sometimes gave full play to his imagination, and, with a graphic touch here and there, brought the whole scene vividly before the eye, as for example, when he described the poor woman of ' the wives of the sons of the prophets ' (2 Kings iv.) following Elisha's instructions, and sending her sons to borrow empty vessels from her neighbours. ' Reuben, you go up the street, and Samuel, you go down the street, and ask all the neighbours for the loan of empty vessels.' ' But what will they say to us, mother ? ' ' They will say nothing, but give you the dishes ! '

Sometimes his quaint use of a scriptural illustration had a happy effect in restoring harmony or carrying a point. A well-known instance of this was his reference to the students in his closing address as Moderator of the Free Church Assembly in 1878. ' We need not be very much surprised,' he said, ' that those young

---

[1] He contributed ' Readings in 1 Chronicles ' to the *Quarterly Journal of Prophecy*, from 1857 to 1861.

"sons of the prophets" are rather prone to question
the positive conclusions of older men. This was the
tendency of the "sons of the prophets" even in the
days of Elisha. There were schools, if not colleges,
at Bethel and at Jericho : and you may remember how
the youthful disciples there, not satisfied in regard to
Elijah's translation, insisted that fifty of the most
gifted of their number should go and search hill and
valley for themselves. Again and again did the prophet
assure them that it would prove only a waste of time
and labour ; and when at length he yielded, and they
went forth with all the confidence of youth, how did it
end? They came back to report that the old prophet
was right after all. No doubt he smiled with mild satisfaction as he reminded them, "Did I not say unto you,
Go not !"'

A friend one day asked him what he thought about
the young man mentioned in Mark xiv. 51. 'I have a
fable about him,' he said. 'He heard the singing in
the Upper Room—the Lord was leading it—He raised
the tune, and then the fishermen joined in it so heartily
that the young man stopped to listen. Then he
watched them as they went out, and followed them over
the brook Kedron, and was lying among the olives to
see what would happen when the band of soldiers came.'[1]

Some friends were talking with him about the fact
that a stranger is very often used for the conversion
of one whose parents and friends have prayed and
watched over him. Dr. Bonar said, 'Now, give me
a scriptural illustration of that.' No one did, so he
said, 'Timothy, "*my own son in the faith.*" The child
of Eunice and Lois ! I daresay Eunice was greatly

---

[1] 'Bonar's fables' were what some of his friends called his speculations
on Bible incidents. Mr. Moody used to say, 'Now, I want to hear some
more fables !'

disappointed that it was not she, after all, that was used. It was an itinerant evangelist !'

Speaking of Eutychus (Acts xx. 9) he said, 'It's not fair of Dr. Watts to make Eutychus a warning to sleepy hearers. He's a warning to beadles to ventilate the church properly !'

As authority for beginning public worship with the singing of a psalm, he quoted Elisha's example in 2 Kings iii., when he asked for a minstrel to play, and the camp was calmed and solemnised.

To a friend he remarked about 1 Cor. xvi. 12 : ' What a comfort that verse is ! People sometimes write so pressingly : " You must come, it is an opportunity of usefulness." Paul says Apollos would not come, and he is not blamed for it.'

' Did you ever notice, in Acts xvi. 6, 7, how the Holy Ghost guides the heralds of salvation to their proper sphere ? On two occasions the Holy Spirit hindered Paul from going to places he wished to visit —Asia and Bithynia. He was (so to speak) candidate for these two places, but the seven churches of Asia were reserved for John's ministry, and Bithynia (1 Pet. i. 1) for Peter's. Paul must go away to Macedonia.'

' Why did Thomas not go to the meeting that night with the other disciples ? I think he said, " What is the use of going ? *The Master* won't be there ! " '

Upon 1 Sam. iii. 4 he remarked, ' I think God spoke in Eli's voice so as not to frighten Samuel.' Peter he described (Matt. xvi. 22) as 'the New Testament Uzzah trying to hold up the Ark.'

His commentary cn Dan. vi. 18, 19, was 'Never put your name to a paper you have not read !'

A favourite fancy of his was, that the star in the East was the old Pillar-cloud.

He used to say that he thought the beggar at

the Beautiful Gate of the Temple had been a careless and unbelieving man, or he might have been healed long before; for we read, in Matt. xxi. 14, 'that on a certain day the blind and the lame came to Christ in the Temple and "He healed them."'

'It is a very striking thing that there is not an instance of any one in the New Testament bringing a gift to Christ when he came to be healed. Yet in the Old Testament we see this was a common custom.'

'Paul had to escape in a basket! the man God wrought such wonderful things by, had to escape in a most commonplace way. I daresay some people would like that Elijah had been fed by eagles rather than by ravens; but that is not God's way. He delivers believers in a common way.'

'Where did the ravens get the flesh they carried to Elijah? I think they picked it off Baal's altars!'

He liked to talk about angels and their work for us, and used to say he had not one guardian angel but hundreds.

'Why did the angel tell Peter in the prison to rise up "quickly"? Because he knew that, if he did not rise at once, he would go to sleep again! Even angels never lose time. They have plenty of work to do for the Lord.'

'Angels will never be kings. They will always be servants.'

'It is a good thing angels were not sent to preach to us. I would go far to hear an angel preach, but I don't think I would get much good from his sermon. I would come away thinking of his beautiful words and his persuasive tongue, but perhaps saying, "It is all very well for that angel to talk about the miry clay, but he does not know how stiff it is! He never was in it."'

'"The tongue of angels" is the only bit of his experience in the Third Heavens that Paul gives us. He seems to have heard angels speak, or perhaps sing. Paul was a man of extraordinary grace to be contented to be so long upon earth after being in the Third Heavens, and not to pine to be back. He heard "unspeakable words" there. I think he must have heard the Saviour's voice speaking to His redeemed ones.'

'Reading the Gospels,' he said, 'is like walking in Galilee. There is nothing I enjoy more.'

He talked of the men and women of the Bible as of his familiar friends, and could not bear a suggestion of the Old Testament saints being on a lower platform than those of later times.

'We shall sit down *with* Abraham, Isaac, and Jacob in the kingdom—not *above* them—for they hoped in God while still in the shadows.'

'Elijah had such fellowship with God that he could say, "The Lord before whom I stand." Gabriel could not say more than that when he came down in afterdays.'

'Did you ever notice that when the Jews said that Stephen blasphemed Moses, the Lord put upon him the same glory that He put upon Moses, and his face shone?'

In reference to the indwelling of the Holy Spirit, he said, 'There was the same well of water in the soul of the Old Testament saint as in the New Testament saint, but the water in that well never rose very high except in a few cases. We may say the well was just half-full in Old Testament times. But when Christ had finished His work, when "Jesus was glorified," then the rivers poured out of the well, because the waters poured in so abundantly. There never were two ways of saving souls. Always by union to Christ through the indwelling of the Spirit.'

'God fed His church on crumbs at first,' he used to say. 'Enoch lived on two crumbs of the bread of life, for all revealed Scripture then was "the seed of the woman," etc., and "Behold, the Lord cometh!" etc. But what a life he led on these two crumbs! And Noah in the Ark with no more. How that man stood out against a whole world! O brethren, how the crumbs of the Bread of Life feed!' 'Caleb lived very much on one promise for forty years.'

When visiting his people he used to ask, 'Do you read regularly through the sixty-six books of the Bible, and not trust to little text-books?' 'Have you got a letter from the King to-day?' was a favourite question, when he wanted to introduce a conversation on that morning's portion of the Scripture.

Some friends who were studying the Book of Ezekiel told him they did not understand it very well. He said, 'I am glad you are reading Ezekiel's book before you meet him. What would he say if you met him in heaven and told him you had never read his book?'[1]

Often he used to say, 'Notice the *little* things in the Bible.' One morning, at the weekly meeting in his study, when the Bible-woman and missionary met with him for prayer, Miss Walker gave as her text for the day, 1 Cor. xv. 58, 'Be ye steadfast, unmoveable,' etc., 'forasmuch as ye know that your labour shall not be in vain in the Lord.' 'Stop!' said Dr. Bonar, 'is it "*shall be*" in your Bible? Look again. "Forasmuch as ye know that your labour *is* not in vain in the Lord."'

He strongly insisted that a text must not be taken

---

[1] He more than once took this way of impressing on others the import-ance of reading the Old Testament, and the impossibility of understanding the New Testament without the Old.

out of its connection to suit our purposes. 'Once,' he said, ' I was visiting a young man dying of consumption, and one day I found both his wife and himself much brighter than before. They said they had got a text which had encouraged them greatly. It was, " I shall not die but live," etc. They had no right to the text, and the young man died soon after.'

The whole Bible was to him bright with the promise of the Lord's Return, and this expectation gave joy and hopefulness to his whole life. Sorrow and bereavement made him think of the glorious time when 'death shall have become resurrection;' pain and suffering reminded him of the 'new heavens and the new earth' yet to come. 'You will soon be a king. Why not think of your kingdom?' he writes to a friend. 'Are you content with the Lord's gracious letter to you when you might rather be wearying for Himself? I know that "this same Jesus" is as precious to you as to any of us, but when will you be a " man of Galilee," gazing up into heaven?' To another friend he writes: 'Are you loving Christ's appearing and His kingdom? If not, He hath somewhat against thee.'

'Many people nowadays,' he said, ' miss out the first part of the verse: "the grace of God which bringeth salvation," and go on to talk of the next part: " denying ungodliness and worldly lusts," etc. You say "that's dreadful!" Yes, but I know some Christians who miss out the last clause altogether: " looking for that blessed hope!"'

'Some Christians make a great mistake. They think that because Christ said it was expedient that He should go away, therefore it is expedient that He should *stay* away! He went away to present His finished work to the Father, but He must come back again.'

'I find the thought of Christ's Coming,' he said, 'very helpful in keeping me awake. Those who are waiting for His appearing will get a special blessing. Perhaps they will get nearer His Person. I sometimes hope it will be so, and that He will beckon me nearer to Him if I am waiting for Him ; just as at a meeting, you often see one beckoned to come up to the platform nearer the speakers.'

At a meeting in Philadelphia in 1881, to bid him farewell, the chairman—the late George Stewart—closed his address by saying that 'the Lord, the Righteous Judge, would give to His dear servant a crown of righteousness at the great day.' He sat down, and, on rising to reply, Dr. Bonar said, '" *And not to me only, but to all them also that love His appearing.*" '

As his ministry drew near its close, he often said to his people, '*I* may not live to see Him return, but I expect some of you listening to me will.' And to a friend he wrote : ' Christ's Coming is nearer and nearer. " When He cometh (we may say in another sense than the woman of Samaria, and yet like her) *He will tell us all things.*" ' His Prophetic Lectures, delivered once a month on Sabbath evenings, from 1879 to 1883, will long be remembered. He had great enjoyment in them himself, and his voice, which even then was often feeble, seemed to regain its power as it proclaimed, through the crowded church, the Coming of the King of Glory. He very seldom spoke of his own death, though his diary shows how often it was in his thoughts.

When referring at his weekly prayer-meeting to the death of Dr. Somerville, who that morning had passed away, he spoke of what is called ' preparation for death,' and of 'dying grace.' 'I doubt,' he said, 'if there is such a thing, more than just the grace we need to live every day. Comparatively few of God's people have triumphant deaths. You are not triumphant when you fall asleep, and that's what death is,—falling asleep. We should be living so that we could be ready any day to go. If you were to go to call on some Christian friend, and the servant were to tell you at the door, " Oh, he's gone ! " Would you feel you almost *envy* him ? Are you living so that the only difference in your life really that death would make—if you were told "an hour later and you will be gone"—would be to make you say, " Well, my fellowship with the Lord will be *closer* then, but I've had fellowship with Him all day." When Elijah was told he was to be taken up, he went on doing his ordinary work, visiting the schools of the prophets. The only difference in his action was, that he wanted Elisha to leave him, that he might spare him the pain of the separation. But he did not spend the day in prayer or in any special *preparation*, as we call it. What we need for death is just what we need every day : the Saviour Himself with us.'

' We have boldness to enter into the holiest by the blood of Jesus. What more do we need in going into His presence ? '

' " The *dead in Christ* shall rise first." A beautiful expression. It always reminds me of a mother with her dead infant lying on her bosom. Christ has His dead lying on His bosom, waiting for the resurrection.'

' The man who sees Christ in life is sure to see Him in the valley of the shadow of death.'

One who had always had a fear of death told him on her dying bed, that she had completely lost it by fixing her thoughts on that passage, ' I have the keys of hell and of death.' She thought, ' If Jesus has the keys of death, then the first face I shall see will be His ! '

'Rest—glory—Christ. I think these three words,' he said, 'tell all that we know of the intermediate state. The Holy Spirit always hastens us on to the resurrection.'

'The intermediate state is Heaven's Upper Room, where the Master is, and where He will say unutterable things.'

'Elijah would get a welcome when he went up, but what work he got, we can't tell. We do not know what work disembodied spirits get to do. Down here we are just at school, and in the lowest class too. But we shall have our grand work afterwards.'

He sometimes used a familiar illustration to describe the intermediate state after death. 'There are the two classes: the ungodly and the godly. A man who has committed a crime is arrested and put in prison. Although judgment has not been passed upon him, he is securely locked up, and deprived of all his liberties. The terrible thought, that he must appear before the Judge and hear His final sentence, is always before him. The state of the godly, on the other hand, may be illustrated thus. A rich friend invites you to dine with him. On the appointed day you go to his house, and are shown into the drawing-room, where the guests are received by the host. The time until all the invited guests have arrived is passed in meeting friends, and in the presence and society of the host. When all have assembled, a bell sounds, and the whole company pass into the dining-hall where the feast is spread. So it will be at the great Supper of the Lamb.'

'Live for the Lord to-day, and look for His Coming to-morrow' was a rule he impressed on others, and carried out in his own life. The love of Christ constrained him to service beyond that of most men, and made that service a delight. Preaching was a necessity of his life. He never grew tired of it, and sometimes, indeed, found it difficult to get as much as he wanted. When one of his elders remonstrated with him for preaching too often during his holidays, he replied :—

> ''Tis joy, not duty,
> To speak His beauty !'

' I long,' he says at another time, ' to speak to the troubled soul about Jesus the Peace-maker, saying to the waves and storm " Be still."' In a letter to the Rev. D. M. M'Intyre, June 19th, 1891, he writes, ' I am not, and never was, a great or popular preacher. I have been only an earnest expounder of God's Word, longing to save sinners and edify the saved.' A friend remembers when a boy, hearing him preach in Regent Square, London, in the year 1850, and the deep impression made on his mind by the sermon—' The joys of the Man of Sorrows ' (Acts ii. 26). A few weeks after he again heard him preach at Rait in Perthshire, and was struck with the fact that his sermon was not less able, and his delivery not less earnest in speaking to the quiet country audience than when addressing the ' great congregation ' in Regent Square. If he spent a Sabbath in the country without preaching, he felt more tired at the close of the day than if he had preached three times. At Collace, Mrs. Bonar refers to his having preached nine times in one week ; and he himself writes in refusing an invitation to preach in Perth :—

' I see you thought you would bait your hook well to catch me by offering a triple service.'

' I go to Glasgow to Alexander Somerville on Monday, and to James Hamilton, London, immediately after, so you see I have some elements of the wandering Jew in my constitution. O that I were as wandering Paul and Barnabas ! They were Christ's true "knights - errant," *i.e.* servants (*knechte*), who went forth whithersoever He would.'

On one occasion he went to Blairgowrie to assist the Rev. Malcolm White at his Communion services. He arrived at six o'clock on Saturday evening, and hurriedly took some refreshment, so as to get to the top of Hatton Hill before dusk. From there he saw the beautiful view over the strath, but his chief object was to visit the birthplace of Donald Cargill, the martyr. Though it was late before he and Mr. White reached home, he showed little sign of weariness, and asked what his work was to be next day. When told, he said, 'I would not have left home had I known you had so little for me to do!' and a children's service had to be added to what most men would have considered quite sufficient work for one day.

In July 1890 he closes a letter to his son with these words : 'Why am I spared so long in health is a question I often ask. One thing I know—it must be that I may preach and commend Christ and Him crucified wherever and whenever it is in my power.'

In great loving-kindness God spared him the bitterness of being laid aside from his beloved work. Though feeble, voice and hand were still busy in the Master's service, when, at that Master's bidding, he left his work below for the ministry of the Upper Sanctuary, where still ' His servants serve Him.'

APPENDIX

The following extract from Bonar's Introduction
to his revised edition of Nettleton's Life (1854)
is a fitting appendix to the concluding chapter
on his *Faith and Doctrine*.

In a Preface to the Second edition (1860), Bonar, in
the light of the great revival of 1859, adds this
comment:

' Ireland, Wales, and Scotland, have been, during
the past year, the theatre of the Spirit's mighty
works, in a way not inferior to what was witnessed
in the time of Nettleton. And let us not fail to
note that the very same Calvinism which was
wielded so effectually by Dr. Nettleton in his day,
amid the scenes of revival wherein he was used
as an instrument, has been used in our day, and
in our land, by the Great Head of the Church,
who is " exalted a Prince and a Saviour, to give
repentance unto Israel and remission of sins."
Who can say that Calvinistic doctrine has
clogged the wheels of the chariot, when he casts
his eye over the churches in Ireland, Wales, and
Scotland, where these have been the truths
believed and proclaimed, while the Holy Spirit
has come down in power and majesty?'

Andrew Bonar's Introduction to
' Nettleton and his Labours '

THERE is a natural aversion to *authority*, even the *authority of God*, in the heart of man. And hence it has been that, both then and now, there have been zealous men who have loudly protested against those doctrines of grace usually called *Calvinistic doctrines*, pretending that the souls of men are by these doctrines lulled into sleep as far as regards their responsibility. Now, though such an abuse of these scriptural truths has often been manifested where men have grown lukewarm, yet the very opposite influence is that which they ought to exert; and whoever reads Dr. Nettleton's history, will see with what tremendous force they may be employed to awaken the conscience.

Vinet has remarked, that that very delicate psychology which goes prying into all the motives of the soul, surprising all its secrets, extorting from it confessions, ferreting into its obscure corners, giving to the soul the consciousness of all its evil, is, after all, dangerous to the soul. The knowledge of one's self is then turned into a study,—a matter of curiosity. The sorrows of repentance are unwittingly transformed into the pleasures of self-love; nay, the reproaches of conscience become the pleasures of the intellect; and so we do not enter into, but rather go out of ourselves.—(Vinet's *Homiletics*.) Such treatment of the human heart becomes mere philosophy. But not dissimilar in its result, because really carrying on an analogous process, is the method pursued by some in regard to the special doctrines of grace,—the Calvinistic doctrines. They have so preached and prelected

on them, so argued and defended them, that, in their
hands, these truths have become little better than dry
theses; and the preachers of those truths have dropt
the tone of solemn, tender, conscience-rousing Boanerges, and become merely able defenders of favourite
themes. In admirable contrast with such treatment
of doctrine, Dr. Nettleton's preaching, avoiding this
error altogether, set these high truths before his
hearers, on all occasions, in a most thoroughly practical form. They saw in them the God of majesty,
glory, grace, dealing with rebels, and were bowed
down before Him.

We said, that when men dislike these truths there
is at the root a dislike of authority,—*God's authority*.
Men forget, or willingly are ignorant, that the *will
of God* is 'the Rule of rules, the Law of laws, the Justice
of all justice, the Equity of all equity, the Right of
all right'—(Calvin.) They think and speak *as if
God had no reasons* for what He does, because *we do
not know* His reasons; they will not be content to
travel humbly onward until the day of Christ, when
'the mystery of God shall be finished'; they insist
on everything being explained to them clearly now,
that they may perceive why God acts thus. But why
should not we wait till the time for such explanations
arrive ? Why should we run the risk of losing our
footing, and being drowned in those great deeps, while
we insist on fathoming them ere we will believe that
they are God's unfathomable depths?

It is worthy of notice, that it is *John*,—he who so
fully opens up to view the love of God,—John who so
expatiates on every proof of divine love, John who
seems to feel the beating of the heart of God-man more
than any other,—he it is whose pen is so constantly
guided by the Holy Ghost to refer to the doctrines
of sovereign grace. It is he who records the words:
'I know whom I have chosen,' and, 'I have chosen
you,' in xiii. 18; xv. 16; and it is he who speaks so

often of those whom '*the Father hath given*' to Christ;
—and is not all this *Election?*[1] It is he who records
the words of Jesus: 'I lay down my life *for the sheep;*'
—the method of salvation, '*one* for *all*'—and is not
this *particular Redemption?*[2] It is he who tells how
Jesus said: 'No man cometh unto me, except the
Father, who hath sent me, *draw him;*' and 'except it
be given him of the Father,'—who relates the conversation, John iii. 5; and who tells that a believer
in Christ is born not by natural descent, not by his
own fleshly will, not by the persuasive power of any
other man's reasoning, '*but of God;*'—and is not
this *Special Grace;*[3] It is he who records, more
than once, such declarations of Jesus as these: '*Every
man* that hath heard and *learned of the Father, cometh
unto me*'—'all that the Father giveth me *shall* come to
me;'—and is not this *Irresistible Grace?* There is no
free will here.[4] It is he who has so fully given our
Lord's words about His sheep: 'None shall pluck them
out of my hand; they shall never perish; none shall
pluck them out of my Father's hand,'—'Of those
whom thou hast given me, I have lost none,'[5]—and
then, xiv. 16: 'The Comforter shall abide with you
for ever;'—and is not this the doctrine of the *Perseverance
of the Saints?*[6] We might add, it is he who, without
attempting to reconcile the two truths, states so
broadly God's 'blinding the eyes, and hardening the
hearts' (xii. 40) of the Jews; and yet their own sin
being their ruin—'they believed not,' (xii. 43,) 'For
they loved the praise of men more than the praise of
God.'

Whitefield, and Edwards, and Nettleton, never
found themselves, nor those they addressed, hindered
by these great truths; they were helped by them, not
hindered. No wonder; for do not each of these doc-

[1] John x. 11; vi. 37, 39; xvii. 2, 6, 9, 11, 12. [2] John vi. 44, 65.
[3] John i. 13. [4] John vi. 45; vi. 37. [5] John x. 28, 29; xviii. 9.
[6] John xiv, 16.

trines at once turn our eye on *God himself*, and cause
us to hear His voice saying: 'Come now, *let us reason together*, saith the Lord?'

They lead us to the fullest and freest *Gospel*. If
they teach that men naturally hate God, nay, that
'*they hate Him without a cause*,' (John xv. 25), they
also teach, that as truly as man is so thoroughly base
and unholy that he can hate God, even God in Christ,
('Me and my Father,' John xv. 24), although there
is not one reason in God that gives occasion to this
hatred, yet, on the other hand, God is so gloriously
gracious, that he can love man '*without a cause*.' He
can, out of merest grace, without there being one single
quality in man to call it forth, freely love the sinner, and
freely provide justification. If the man hated 'with-
out a cause,' ($\delta\omega\varrho\varepsilon\alpha\nu$), the Lord justifies 'without a
cause' in us ($\delta\omega\varrho\varepsilon\alpha\nu$), (Rom. iii. 25.)* The warrant to
the sinner goes forth in these terms: 'Whosoever will,
let him come and take of the water of life freely,'
($\delta\omega\varrho\varepsilon\alpha\nu$), without waiting till there is in him one excel-
lence that might seem likely to induce God to give it
(Rev. xxii. 17). You sinned *gratuitously*, you may be
saved *gratuitously*. And if it seem a strange preface to a
free Gospel-call, in the eyes of some, to tell sinful men
that it remains with God to leave their eyes closed,
or to open them on the things announced and prof-
fered to their acceptance, still it is the very method
pursued by our Lord in Matt. xi. 25, 28: 'I thank
thee, O Father, Lord of heaven and earth, *that thou
hast hid these things from the wise and prudent, and
hast revealed them unto babes.*' '*Come unto me, all*

* One of the unfair and unfounded insinuations of Arminian
writers is, that Calvinists say, 'God has no reasons for what
He does.' We say, that He has no reason drawn from
anything in us. He *has* most wise and satisfactory reasons;
only these are not grounded on anything good *in us*; even as
the sinner has his reasons for hating God, but not because of
anything *in God* fitted to produce or justify that hatred.

ye that labour and are heavy laden!' It is His method,
too, in John vi. 37, and in iii. 5, 15. And no wonder
after all! For, see, it declares that this Gospel-call, this
invitation of rich, boundless love, need never fall on
any man's ear in vain, however depraved, hardened,
desperately wicked he may be, since the same God
of holy love who sends it has the power to turn that
heart in the very moment the invitation comes to it.
Love is *so unlimited* that it can sweep away the very
unwillingness of the sinner to whom it addresses its
message of grace! Is not this glad tidings?—free
unlimited love, a flood that is not turned aside into
another channel by meeting the rock in its way, but
that rises behind it till its waters pour over it in a
cataract!

Nor let us fail to notice, that all the doctrines of
grace are beams from the glorious *person of Christ*.
There we may see them in their centre: (1) The
person of God-man is a proclamation of *election*—
the *principle* of election—inasmuch as it is an everlasting monument of His having passed by angels, and
come, in mere grace, to the help of *man*. (2) The
person of God-man is a proclamation of *particular
redemption*, and all the completeness of atonement
involved therein; for who is He but the one man who
dies for the people, for *'all the children of God,'* (John
xi. 52),—the second Adam, who tastes death for every
man of His family, His many sons, (Heb. ii. 9). Again,
(3) The person of Christ is a proclamation of the
doctrine of *special grace*; for from that fountain cometh
the regenerating Spirit to man; so that if you see the
stream of 'repentance' in any one, you trace it up to
its source in 'the Prince and Saviour exalted to *give
repentance*,' (Acts v. 31), and 'quickening whom He
will,' (John v. 21). Then, (4) The person of Christ
proclaims *irresistible grace*, inasmuch as it is after the
pattern of his resurrection from the dead that every
believing one was raised from the grave of sin (Eph. i.

20), ' according to the *energy of the might of God's power, wrought in Christ,* when raised from the dead;' and inasmuch as we can never fail to connect with His person such remembrances, as that He on earth called men and they came,—whether it were a Lazarus out of his grave, or a Matthew out of his tomb of corruption. (5) The person of Christ proclaims the *perseverance of the saints*; for we never can forget His own representation of himself as *bearing home* the sheep on His own shoulders, and causing new joy in heaven by its safe arrival.

And let us add on this subject, that *the person of Christ* (associated, of course, with what He wrought) being to us the centre and core of all the doctrines of grace, we have a brief and satisfactory answer therein to those who allege that they cannot disentangle the sinner's free access to the offered salvation from the difficulties that beset some of these doctrines. We point, in this case, to the centre doctrine of all,—*the person of Christ*,—' the great mystery of godliness,' and tell that this, at least, is clear, and plain, and indisputable,—viz., that God *commands you to go to Him.* Go, then, and He will be to you what the woman of Syrophenicia found Him to be (when she could not unravel the apparent frown contained in His words),— a bottomless fountain of grace; and every child of Adam is warranted at once to approach to this and use it. Deal with *himself* here, if other truths perplex you; and solve all questions as to whether or not *you* were specially intended when this fountain was opened for sinners, by drinking of it; or, in other words, by willingly receiving Christ himself, and putting your soul at His disposal.

We must assert one other truth in connexion with these doctrines of grace. Most assuredly they are fitted to lead a man and a minister of Christ (witness Dr. Nettleton) to be zealous of good works, and zealous for souls,—bent upon God's glory, and bent upon the salvation of men. As to the latter, which specially some call in question, how plain is it that, believing what we do, we can despair of no man so long as he lives, and so long as there is the Spirit of grace to convert men. Besides, we know that our Lord desires us, and expects us to travail as in birth for the souls of men, apart from what success we may have. This is *His will*; and to know this aright makes ministers anxious, earnest, holy, prayerful, intensely covetous of souls. There may be nothing present to excite; still the same high duty, and the same ever-remaining hope of the Holy Spirit's working, furnish sufficient motives to produce steady and fervent effort. And thus (with holy Bradford, who, in prison, before going to the stake, defended these doctrines of grace) they can yearn over men, and expostulate with them: 'I pray you, I desire you, I crave it at your hands with all my very heart; I ask of you with hand, pen, tongue, and mind, in Christ, for Christ, through Christ, for the sake of His name, blood, mercy, power, truth, my most entirely beloved, that you admit no doubt of God's mercies towards you!' Yes; *we work*, and pray, and travail for souls, *because God worketh* to will and to do of His good pleasure; and holds over our head the crown of glory, which shepherds who have the Shepherd's heart receive at the day when the chief Shepherd shall appear.

COLLACE, *April* 1854.